Hugh Prince

Critical Human Geography

'Critical Human Geography' is an international series which provides a critical examination and extension of the concepts and consequences of work in human geography and the allied social sciences and humanities. The volumes are written by scholars currently engaged in substantive research, so that, wherever possible, the discussions are empirically grounded as well as theoretically informed. Existing studies and the traditions from which they derive are carefully described and located in their historically specific context, but the series at the same time introduces and explores new ideas and insights from the human sciences as a whole. The series is thus not intended as a collection of synthetic reviews, but rather as a cluster of considered arguments which are accessible enough to engage geographers at all levels in the development of geography. The series therefore reflects the continuing methodological and philosophical diversity of the subject, and its books are united only by their common commitment to the prosecution of a genuinely human geography.

Department of Geography   MARK BILLINGE
University of Cambridge   DEREK GREGORY
England   RON MARTIN

Critical Human Geography

The Arena of Capital

Michael Dunford and Diane Perrons

First published 1983 by
THE MACMILLAN PRESS LTD
London and Basingstoke
Companies and representatives throughout the world

ISBN 0 333 28262 0 (hard cover)
ISBN 0 333 28263 9 (paper cover)

Typeset in Great Britain by
STYLESET LIMITED
Salisbury · Wiltshire

Printed in Hong Kong

To Lotte

ACKNOWLEDGEMENTS

The author and publishers wish to thank the following who have kindly given permission for the use of copyright material:

Associated Book Publishers for a table from *Prospects of the Industrial Areas of Great Britain* by M. P. Fogarty, published by Methuen & Co. Ltd. The Association of American Geographers for extracts from *Perspectives on the Nature of Geography* by Hartshorne. B. T. Batsford Ltd for tables from *The Inter-War Economy 1919–1939* by D. H. Aldcroft, and *The Growth of British Industry* by A. E. Musson. Cambridge University Press for maps from *A New Historical Geography of England Before 1600* by Darby. *Capital and Class* for diagrams from an article by Ben Fine in *Bulletin of the CSE*, vol. 4, no. 3. The Controller of Her Majesty's Stationery Office for data from *Report of the Royal Commission on the Distribution of the Industrial Population, Survey of Industrial Development and Report on the Location of Industry*. Croom Helm Ltd for tables from *Patterns of European Urbanisation Since 1500* edited by H. Schmal. Institut National de la Statistique et des Etudes Economiques for an extract from *Economie et Statistique*, no. 97. The Institute of British Geographers for extracts from 'The British Hosiery Industry at the Middle of the Nineteenth Century: an Historical Study in Economic Geography', *Transactions and Papers*, no. 32 by D. Smith. Lawrence & Wishart Ltd for an extract from *Capital*, vol. III, by Karl Marx. McGraw-Hill Book Company (UK) Ltd for a figure adapted from *An Introduction to Modern Economics* by Robinson and Eatwell. New Left Books and Monthly Review Press for extracts from *Marxism and Hegel* and *From Rousseau to Lenin* by L. Colletti. Oxford University Press for a table from the article 'Studies in Mobility of Labour: Analysis for Great Britain' by Makower, Marschak and Robinson, in *Oxford Economic Papers*, no. 2, May 1939, and for data from *Peaceful Conquest: the Industrialisation of Europe, 1760–1970* by S. Pollard. Presses de la Fondation Nationale des Sciences Politiques for tables from *Crise du Féodalisme* by Guy Bois. Routledge & Kegan Paul Ltd for an extract from *Political Economy and Capitalism*, 2nd edn, by M. Dobb. Sage Publications Inc. for a table from the article 'Cyclical Rhythms and Secular Trends of the Capitalist World-Economy: Some Premises, Hypotheses, and Questions, produced by the Research Working Group on Cyclical Rhythms and Secular Trends, published in *Review*, vol. 2, no. 4 (Spring 1979). Copyright © 1979 The Fernard Braudel Center for the Study of Economics, Historical Systems and Civilizations, State University of New York. The Times Newspapers Ltd for an extract from the article 'For Britain See Wales' by R. Williams published in *The Times Higher Education Supplement*, 15 May 1981. The Union for Radical Political Economics for a table from *Review of Radical Economics*, vol. II, no. 4, Spring 1979.

Contents

Part I   Historical Materialism and Geography

Part II   The Geography of the Transition from
          Feudalism to Capitalism

Introduction: Modes of Production and Spatial
Development 86

Preface and Acknowledgements

We started to work on the ideas and arguments which are now presented in this book in 1976, at a time when an interest in Marxism and the way in which Marxist concepts could be used to analyse a variety of scientific and political questions was growing in Britain. As the years have passed, the nature and content or our work, and of the book itself, have changed almost continually, and sometimes quite radically, as a consequence not only of our own intellectual development, but also of debates and arguments within Marxism and within geography.

An earlier version of Part I was presented at the Anglo–French Symposium on Science and Ideology in Geography held at Emmanuel College, Cambridge, in April 1979, while the arguments set out in Chapter 12 were first developed in a paper written with Mike Geddes which was published in 1981 in the *International Journal of Urban and Regional Research*. In developing our ideas we have also benefited greatly from participation in the activities of the Conference of Socialist Economists, which has provided a forum in which many of the theories and concepts which lie behind this study were communicated and discussed.

But in the present text, debates about theory and differing interpretations of events are not discussed in any detail: without reviewing or criticising perspectives with which we are not in full agreement, we often adopt particular positions; and without commenting on debates and controversies which have occurred, we frequently seek to integrate arguments which are sometimes seen as standing in opposition to one another. The reason for our not referring explicitly to debates that have played an important role in forming our ideas lies, however, not in any wish to devalue them, but simply in our desire to avoid too many deviations from our main goal, which is to present an analytical reconstruction of the process of uneven development and of the evolution of the geography of contemporary Britian.

In pursuing this goal we have been helped by many people. Our debts to writers who are in most cases personally unknown to us, but on whose work we have drawn, are acknowledged in the notes and references at the end of the book. We would, however, like to take this opportunity to thank Sue Adams, Fran Cook, Alison Mudd, Brian Short, James Thompson, Helen Warner, Mike Geddes and Bob Radford, all but the last two of whom work, or worked, in one capacity or another, at the University of Sussex, and who have helped us either by typing and almost endlessly retyping the manuscript, or by commenting carefully and very helpfully on draft chapters or on the presentation of material. Our thanks are also due to Susan Rowland, not only for drawing or reproducing the diagrams included in the text but also for her assistance with questions as to how the information concerned could be represented most effectively, while Derek Gregory gave us considerable encouragement and support in addition to his comments on an earlier draft which were of great help in revising the manuscript for publication.

We would also like to thank Keith Povey for his help with copy-editing and proof-reading, Fred Dunford for help with indexing, and Steven Kennedy and everyone at Macmillan for the speed and efficiency with which the book was produced.

Brighton, Sussex MICHAEL DUNFORD and DIANE PERRONS
December 1982

List of Tables

List of Figures

Part I

Historical Materialism
and Geography

Introduction: Towards a Materialist Conception of Geography

In writing this book our primary aim was to present an account of some of the major changes in the structure of the space-economy which have accompanied the development of capitalism. The discussion is focused mainly on Britain and the history of some of the regional contrasts, which are such a striking feature of its contemporary geography, are traced. Its object of study is therefore in some ways similar to that of studies concerned with historical geography or with the historical origins of the economic geography of present-day Britain.[1] But in terms of perspective it differs radically from much of this writing in that the framework for analysis is built upon the materialist conception of history originally elaborated by Marx and Engels, and upon the work of historians and economists concerned with the development and functioning of capitalism as a social and economic system.[2]

More specifically we seek to set out an historical account of the process of uneven development indicating the connections between forms of spatial differentiation and forms of organisation of production, distribution, consumption, and circulation, and between territorial inequalities and phases of economic and social development. In Part II we focus upon the geography of the transition to capitalism, looking at the development of agriculture, at town—country relations, and at changes in the location of industry with particular reference to the development of proto-industry. In the third part we outline the way in which the structure of the space-economy was transformed with the development and extended reproduction of industrial capitalism. The basis of this account lies in the identification of a sequence of regimes of accumulation characterised by the relative importance of different phases in the development of the material and social process of production designated as manufacture, machino-facture, and scientific management and Fordism, and of different modes of consumption.[3]

A corollary central to the ideas developed in this part of the book is the view that an understanding of the labour process is the linchpin of any satisfactory attempt to incorporate a non-naturalistic conception of geographical conditions and of spatial differentiation into analyses of the overall process of social reproduction. The arguments advanced in Parts II and III are, in other words, associated with a specific conception of the nature of geographical enquiry and of its relation to other fields of study.

Throughout its history geography has been dominated by perspectives that can be described as being materialist, and yet it has either been relatively unaffected by the development of Marxism, or has been developed quite consciously as a competing materialist theory of society, especially by some of the German founders of modern geography. In the nineteenth century it was left to a few anarchist writers such as Kropotkin and Reclus to present a critique of established positions,[4] while in the first half of the present century few writers, even if they were politically on the left, sought to break with orthodox ideas. As a result, the development of the arguments in this book presupposes a critique of some of the conventional modes of geographical analysis and the development of a number of specifically Marxist concepts, while the mode of analysis that we shall advocate – and indeed the work of some historians who are at present paying more attention to the role of geography in history – leads to a redefinition of geography itself and of some of its key concepts. It is to this task that Part I is devoted.

In the past, one of the most striking characteristics of geographical writing has been an almost continuous pre-occupation with issues pertaining to the status of geography. These dicussions have conventionally raised two related sets of questions. One set has been connected with the social and educational role of geographical knowledge, and has elicited contributions both from those who wish to see an increase in the influence of geographers in major areas of decision-making and the educational system, and from those who are critical of the historical connections between geography and the military, commercial, and planning strategies pursued by dominant groups and of the ideological role of geographical teaching. This body of writing has raised important questions about the practical role of geographical knowledge and about the relation between the development of geographical thought and the historical process of social development. But these issues are underlain by a set of more fundamental questions about the scientific status of geographical research. This second set of questions has given rise to a more extensive body of literature concerned with the object, method, and concepts of geography, and, indeed, of social research in general.

Studies raising these issues within geography differ from comparable work in many other social sciences in that they have tended to focus on problems connected with the definition of the object of geographical analysis and with the differentiation of geography from neighbouring fields of study. These problems face all institutionally recognised disciplines, but they seem to have been felt much more acutely within geography and have periodically been a central focus of geographical writing. One of the reasons for this fact lies in the acceptance by geographers of a subdivision of knowledge which cuts across subjects such as geography and history, but it must be remembered that this particular intellectual division of labour also creates problems for disciplines concerned with vertical segments of an essentially interdependent reality. It will be contended here, however, that these problems stem not from any special difficulty in identifying an object of geographical analysis, but rather from the lack of methodological awareness and theoretical development within geography and from its isolation from the other social sciences. These weaknesses have frequently been the direct result of some of the unsatisfactory ways in which geographers have sought to establish the distinctiveness of their field of study, since some of the most widely accepted definitions of geography have resulted in its domination by empiricist and naturalistic ideologies which have been incapable of furnishing adequate accounts of the phenomena studied by its practitioners. This situation has in turn given rise to questions about the scientific value of geographical analysis and to the apportionment of its object between neighbouring fields of study. Some of these attempts to define geography will be outlined and criticised. But one of our main aims in the first part of this book is to show that geography does in fact have an object of analysis which enables it to be recognised as a relatively autonomous field of study, and that the real problems confronting it relate instead to the kinds of method and to the concepts that have been used in geographical research.

It was in relation to problems concerning the methodological and theoretical status of the discipline that the quantitative revolution constituted such an important step forward. One of its main contributions was to demonstrate, in the face of much opposition, the relevance of theory within geography, and at the same time it ensured that geography in Anglo-Saxon countries would play a more important role in the examination of spatial planning problems. The advantages of this research tradition were counterbalanced, however, by new difficulties caused by the curious way in which the object of geographical analysis was redefined and distinguished from those of neighbouring fields of study, and by the limitations associated with the method and concepts employed and elaborated during the quantitative revolution. The types of theory used to explain geographical phenomena, and the preoccupation with abstract spaces, isolated geographical thought from real processes and the real world, and, apart from a treatment of some technical planning issues, led to an inability to cope adequately with the problems experienced by those living in specific localities. These weaknesses eventually led to a retreat from theory, particularly when ecological and regional and urban problems were more strongly brought to the fore with the slackening of economic growth and the deepening of an economic and political crisis in the early 1970s.

New methodological and theoretical progress in geography now depends upon the elaboration of the basic tenets of historical materialism to analyse geographical issues. Most work in geography has been based upon empiricist epistemologies. Some of the problems with this view of knowledge will be outlined, and an alternative method associated with historical materialism, which overcomes these inadequacies and provides a more satisfactory basis for explaining geographical phenomena, will be elaborated. Some of the concepts used by geographers, particularly those of nature and space, will also be shown to be inadequate. Once these and other concepts elaborated more recently have been shown to be unsatisfactory, alternative interpretations of nature and space based upon the main ideas of historical materialism will be developed. These new concepts are not only more satisfactory than those employed in much of the geographical literature to date, but they also have the advantage of uniting the question of the relations between the natural and the human world with that of the structure of geographical space. But the development of these ideas presupposes a preliminary clarification of some questions relating to the object of geographical study.

1 The Object of Geographical Analysis

1.1 Introduction

Many of the problems faced by contemporary geography stem from the lack of a precise definition of its object and from arbitrary distinctions between geography and neighbouring fields of study. This situation may seem strange to many people since the discipline is a very old one with roots in Classical Antiquity.[1] On the other hand, the foundations of modern geography are usually assumed to lie in the more recent past in the processes of discovery and exploration of the world and in the development of cartography between 1400 and 1900. The period of exploration actually continued through the nineteenth century, but in the years up to 1900 the main continental outlines were established with reasonable accuracy, while the need for accurate records of geographical information for commercial and military reasons led to the development of a method of recording locations, to the evolution of map projections, and to the mastery of the associated tasks of compiling and revising maps. When these processes had been largely completed, modern geography began, starting with the work of two important early-nineteenth century German scholars, von Humboldt and Ritter.

The development of modern geography was accompanied, however, by the development of a number of other sciences concerned with aspects of the natural and human world which are also limited to the surface of the earth, including geology, history, and the various social sciences. It was the development of these disciplines that seemed to narrow the scope of geographical research, posed serious problems for geographers seeking to define the object of their discipline and its position within a new intellectual division of labour, and led to the subdivision of geography into many subdisciplines which subsequently acquired different degrees of autonomy and sometimes established links with other sciences.

The main attempts to resolve these problems can be outlined by discussing four views about the nature of geographical enquiry. They are the views:

1. that geography studies the relationship between 'man' and nature or between the human and natural world;
2. that geography is distinguished by its chorological point of view;
3. that geography studies the spatial arrangement of phenomena rather than the phenomena themselves; and
4. that geography is the study of 'naively given sections of reality' such as landscapes or regions.

These positions are not mutually exclusive. Indeed several of them often co-exist within the work of individual geographers. Many regional studies are, for example, essentially concerned with the complex interpenetration of human beings and nature within specific regional contexts. But in spite of the ways in which they overlap in practice, these four views are associated with the use of different criteria to establish the distinctiveness of modern geography, and so they can be distinguished from one another, and can be examined separately.

More important, the problems posed by the emergence of new sciences were reinforced by the elaboration of inadequate concepts and by the adoption of unsatisfactory methodological positions by geographers. Included under this heading were weaknesses connected with unsatisfactory accounts of the relations between the natural and human world and of the process of human social development, with the use of empiricist methodologies, with the view that the spatial and temporal properties of objects are separable and rather secondary characteristics, and with the view that the spatial and temporal sciences cannot be generalising sciences because they are concerned with unique phenomena. The last two positions have their origins in the widespread acceptance by many geographers of distinctions between spatial, temporal, and systematic sciences whose roots lie in the way in which geographers have interpreted the concepts of absolute space advanced by Newton and Kant on the one hand and the Kantian theory of knowledge on the other.

Newton believed in 'a space composed of points and a time composed of instants which existed independently of the bodies and events that occupied them'.[2] In his system there was, in fact, an absolute and infinite space that existed as a distinct physical and empirical entity and was independent of any object and of human experience. Space could therefore be viewed as an absolute and boundless receptacle in which material objects may be situated and of which any given part may or may not be filled with matter. This conception of space enabled many geographers to argue that geography studies those effects produced by the implantation of an object studied by the systematic sciences in a spatial framework.

But the acceptance of a concept of absolute space, and of a special status for disciplines concerned with the spatial arrangement of phenomena, stems more from the way in which some geographers have interpreted the work of Kant, who actually studied and taught geography, and who has had a profound influence on modern geographical thought. Until about 1768 Kant held a relative view of space, according to which space depended on there being objects that are spatially related and could be reduced to the spatial relations between these objects. But he then switched to an absolute view, because he came to the conclusion that it was necessary to use some non-relational concepts and to define conventional points of reference.

The view expressed by Kant must however be distinguished from Newton's. It was held by Kant that space, like time, is empirically real, but transcendentally ideal. By this he meant that space is limited to possible sense experience, and that it cannot be applied to transcendental objects, that is to objects that transcend possible sense experience, and are non-sensible and un-experiencable, but which nevertheless play an important role in his philosophy. He also argued that space and time are *a priori* forms of the intuition. By this he meant that our concepts of space and time are not empirical notions derived from our experience of the world, but necessary presuppositions of any experience. In his view they structure and organise an individual's experience, for they contribute certain necessary features of it, and they stem from the human faculty of sensibility which projects spatiality and temporality on to the world. In other words, no observations would make sense and be meaningful unless concepts of space and of time, which were not abstracted from immediate sense experience, were presupposed as being known prior to experiencing objects, and unless spatial and temporal properties were capable of being projected on to the world.

Kant's views about space and time formed part of his theory of knowledge. In the seventeenth century the main alternative to empiricist theories of knowledge was rationalism. One of the main characteristics of rationalism was its identification of knowledge with what an individual human being can know with absolute certainty about the world in which he or she lives. The concern with certainty led the rationalists to draw the standards by which all knowledge is to be judged from logic and mathematics instead of from observation and experiment. In their view the validity of human knowledge depends upon its conformity with the deductive standards of proof already established in logic and mathematics, and stems from the capacity of individual human beings to apply innately known and universally valid rational principles.

The major achievement of Kant was a synthesis and reconciliation of elements of rationalism and empiricism into a single theory of knowledge, whose aim was to justify the scientific theory of Newton which, in Kant's view, provided certain and universally valid knowledge. Kant maintained that any instance of human knowledge of the world is the result or joint product of intuition or sensibility (that is, of an individual's perception or immediate awareness of an object) and of thought or the understanding that supplies the *a priori* concepts or categories which are applied to what is given in intuition. In short, it stems from the faculty of sensibility, which contributes the content of our knowledge, and the faculty of understanding, which contributes the form of the phenomenon.

This claim puts Kant in opposition to rationalism, but it also amounts to a rejection of the classical empiricist understanding of thought. The empiricists generally maintained that thoughts and ideas are not a second, independent source of human knowledge, but must themselves be derived from experience or sense impressions, if they are to be meaningful. In other words, all of our knowledge was thought to be derived from sense data, understood phenomenalistically as impressions, which are quite separate from material things, and our most general concepts were believed to be obtained only by abstraction from that which is given in sense experience.

Although he disagreed with the phenomenalist interpretation given to sense data by the empiricists, Kant accepted that our knowledge may begin with the receipt of sense impressions. But, since it is not possible to draw inferences from some instances to all instances, propositions resting solely on sense data cannot be universally valid and necessarily true. Similarly the notion of causality as a mere constant conjunction between observed events is incapable of providing an adequate account of causal necessity. In Kant's view some of our knowledge possesses a degree of certainty and universality which empiricism cannot explain. As a result, he maintained that some sciences contain judgements that are synthetic, that is whose predicate is not contained in the concept of the subject and, therefore, tells us something new about the subject, and *a priori*, that is universally valid and necessarily true. He then sought to show how such judgements can be justified by showing that they followed from certain necessary presuppositions of any sense experience and knowledge, that is from concepts of space and time, which were thought to be necessary general conditions for any intuition of an experiencable object, and from the Kantian categories of the understanding, of which an *a priori* concept of causality is one instance, whose application in accordance with certain synthetic *a priori* principles was thought to be presupposed by any synthetic empirical judgement of science. By proving to his satisfaction the validity of these arguments, Kant was led to the conclusion that human knowledge cannot stem exclusively from experience. In short he was led to the view mentioned above, according to which human knowledge must in fact have two independent sources. The first is intuition, which depends in part upon the characteristics of the external or internal mental object, and in part upon our subjective perceptual apparatus which contributes certain necessary features of our experience such as spatiality and temporality, and which gives rise to appearances or sensible objects. The second is the understanding, which supplies the categories or pure concepts of the understanding whose application enables us to interpret the empirical objects given in intuition.[3]

Geographers have drawn several conclusions from these ideas. They include the view that knowledge about the spatial and temporal arrangement of phenomena is quite distinct from knowledge about their true nature and about the natural and social laws governing them, and the view that the spatial and temporal properties of objects are separable and rather secondary attributes. These views have serious consequences for geographical research. In particular, acceptance of the first of these two statements has led many geographers to argue that the study of the spatial and temporal arrangement of phenomena is undertaken not by science but by special kinds of subjects, such as geography and natural and social history, whost task is to produce ordinary empirical descriptions of phenomena at different places and different times, whereas the scientific study of these objects is undertaken by true sciences whose task is to produce eternal and universally valid knowledge through the application of the *a priori* concepts of the understanding to our initial experiences.[4] Although it is questionable whether Kant accepted the implied distinction between two mental processes taking place in two stages, he nevertheless argued in the introduction to his *Physische Geographie* that geography is a propaedeutic or introduction to true scientific knowledge: 'the name geography . . . designates a description of nature, and at that of the whole earth', and geography shows 'the place in which every object on the earth is really to be found'.[5] We do not plan to discuss the validity of our interpretation of Kant or, indeed, of the inferences drawn by geographers from concepts of absolute space and from the Kantian theory of knowledge, but, in the next section, we shall seek to argue against the ascription of this status to geography, and to criticise the conclusions outlined above and their consequences for geographical research.

1.2 Geography as the study of the relationship between 'man' and nature

It has frequently been argued that geography is not distinguished by its possession of a distinctive object, but that it is a science that studies the relationship between 'man' and nature or between the natural and human world.

The study of the relationships between human beings and nature has been a recurrent theme in the history of Western thought, reaching its high-point in the eighteenth century with the publication of Montesquieu's *De l'Esprit des Lois*, and it has been regarded by many geographers as the central focus of their discipline, particularly since the time of von Humboldt and Ritter. In practice there were some important differences between the two founders of modern geography, but Wrigley has suggested that their classical conception of the subject possessed three important common characteristics.[6]

(1) They criticised the writings of earlier geographers on the grounds that they were largely descriptive and ill-organised, presenting geographical information in a haphazard and unsystematic fashion, and they both advocated the careful assembly of detailed and accurate factual material and its subsumption under a number of laws expressing relationships of cause and effect.

(2) They believed that in the final analysis there are no methodological differences between the social and natural sciences, and that both are concerned with the construction of general laws.

(3) Both of them usually agreed that a major purpose of geographical study is to investigate the ways in which the physical environment affects the functioning and development of societies.

The last of these characteristics played a particularly important role in Ritter's teleological viewpoint. He believed that there is a necessary direction in the process of social development, and that this direction is the product of predetermined human responses to natural conditions that had themselves been designed in accordance with a divine plan aimed at meeting human needs.

In part under the impact of the rapid progress that occurred in the natural and biological sciences in the second half of the nineteenth century, geography developed as a subject concerned with the morphology and historical development of natural or non-human phenomena, and as a social science that studied the conditioning of human beings by natural and also by biological conditions.

One of the main influences on geographical writing was the rapid progress that occurred in the biological sciences after the publication of *The Origin of Species* in 1859. Darwin's theory of evolution and species formation demonstrated the historicity of nature and was associated with the rejection of finalist conceptions of the relationship between living beings and their environment. This theory was designed to account for the succession of forms of plant and animal life on the earth, and was centred on the theory of natural selection. It depended upon the production of a continuous supply of genetically unique individuals through the transmission and modification of hereditary characteristics, and upon the operation on these individuals of selection pressures in the form of selective morality and fertility rates which allowed the preservation of favourable inherited individual variations and the rejection of unfavourable ones, and an ecological theory of the source of selection pressures with the survival in the struggle for the appropriation of nature of those variants best fitted to the changing inorganic and organic environmental conditions. It turns out that no necessary direction of development is implied by Darwin's theory. Although every change has a determinate material cause, natural selection acts through the complex interaction of the processes of variation and environmental change which have no necessary direction. The order we observe in the living world is not, therefore, the product of a divine plan. In other words it is not predetermined by a 'plan of nature' and predetermined responses to nature's plan. Instead it is the product of a historical process.[7] As a result, his views are quite incompatible with the teleological viewpoint of many geographical writers.

These ideas also contributed to the foundation of the

historical sciences of nature. Within geography the concept of evolution led to a concern with historical development and to generalisations about the history of geographical forms, but not to a concern with the processes underlying this historical movement.[8]

In the nineteenth century and the early twentieth there were two other ways in which Darwinian ideas influenced geographical research.[9] On the one hand, the emphasis upon the intimate connection between plant and animal species and their habitat gave an impetus to the use of organic analogies to express the idea of the interrelatedness of things and the complex interconnection of objects found in the same area, and also to a concern with the relationship between the environment and the distribution and activities of human beings. On the other hand, the idea of a struggle for existence and the theory of natural selection were taken from natural history and proposed as eternal natural laws regulating the historical process of social development. The theory of natural selection is, however, specific to the biological sciences and cannot be applied to explain the development of human societies. The class struggle in societies takes place on the terrain created by determinate social relations of production, and is quite different from the struggle for existence in the plant and animal world, which is conditioned by a natural setting providing certain means of subsistence that cannot be increased by the efforts of the plants and animals themselves.[10]

The conception of human geography as a subject that studies the influence of the natural environment on human beings and on human activities has been referred to as geographical materialism by Wittfogel, and it culminated in the development of environmental determinism in the late nineteenth and early twentieth centuries, particularly in the USA with the elaboration of Ratzel's ideas by Semple and with the work of Huntington and Griffith Taylor. According to this type of theory, human beings, their characteristics, and their activities are largely determined by so-called geographical conditions, that is by the surrounding climate, soils, and other natural conditions, while these conditions are conceived as causes that are not themselves the effects of human activity.

Since the determinists often believed that different peoples in identical environments would normally do different things, this argument was frequently qualified by granting a limited role to biological determinations. This concession to biologism was in marked contrast with the earlier position of von Humboldt who vigorously maintained a theory of the unity of the human race, treating the whole of humanity as one race without consideration of religion, nationality, or colour, and opposing theories emphasising the importance of racial differences.[11] Geographical materialism, together with other forms of bourgeois determinism, was accordingly based upon a conception of human social and cultural development that stressed the continued operation of predetermined biological and environmental conditions.

Starting with Ratzel's contribution to political geography and with his organic interpretation of nation states, which emphasised both the mystical notion of the indivisibility of a people and its land and the idea that states, like organisms, are engaged in competitive struggles for territory, geographical materialism also laid the foundations for the geopolitical writing of Kjellen and Haushofer.[12] The links between these theories and the expansionist policies of Nazi Germany eventually led to their abandonment, and indeed to the temporary abandonment of political geography as a field of study.

The environmentalist theme also came to be criticised both on conceptual and substantive grounds and because of the development of new ideas about the methodology of the social sciences. But this conception of geography has nevertheless continued to exercise considerable influence over the subsequent development of geographical thought. Debates as to whether natural conditions could be conceived as providing a range of possibilities among which human beings are able to choose according to their particular needs or as giving rise to a probable human response are rooted in this conception of geography, while the view that geography is human ecology and is concerned with the mutual relations between human beings and the natural environment also stems from the classical tradition. With the exception of those studies that focus on the effects of human activity on the historical and cultural landscape and on local ecological systems, monographs in landscape and regional geography have often been based on a division of their objects into natural and human elements with some kind of primacy being accorded to natural conditions. This procedure and the preoccupations of classical geography are also reflected in the organisation of traditional regional texts, which usually begin with natural conditions such as geology, climate, soils, and vegetation, and then proceed to study population, settlement, and economic and social activities.

The main objection to this definition of geography is that it has almost invariably been associated with inadequate or false concepts of the relation between human beings and nature. This type of objection has been expressed by many geographers, including Hartshorne. He believed that this definition presupposed the splitting into exclusively human and environmental or non-human parts, of things that in reality are complex and indivisible products of human and natural elements, and that it introduced an unwarranted dualism into geography by dividing these elements between the natural and human branches of the subject. Physical geography is then conceived as a historical science of nature that studies the natural laws governing the atmosphere, biosphere, hydrosphere, and geosphere, while human geography seeks to connect these natural phenomena with human beings at a distance by means of strange forces, influences, controls, and causes.[13]

Not all geographical discussions of this relationship are based on the concept of a simple separation between natural and human phenomena. In the case of Vidal de la Blache, regions were considered to be distinctive units whose character or personality resulted from an intimate connection between human beings and nature that had developed over many centuries. In this case the conception of the relationship between human beings and nature included both the action and effect of human beings on nature and the adjustment of human individuals to the local environment, and it entailed an examination of the material culture of each region as a record, in the form of useful objects produced by human labour, of the actual historical relationships between human beings and nature. Vidal de la Blache also thought that the integration of means of livelihood, social organisation, and

place, gave rise to distinctive *genres de vie*.[14] These concepts
provide a much more satisfactory basis for studying the
relationship between human beings and nature, even though,
in spite of their debt to Durkheim, they generally paid too
little attention to social structures and could not easily be
adapted to cope with the impact of industrialisation, but for
our present purposes it is sufficient to note that this concern
with the intimacy of the connection between human beings
and the land is best linked with a regional view of geography.

A different kind of objection was made by Dickenson in a
paper urging the acceptance of landscape geography, when he
claimed that 'a science cannot be defined on the basis of particular causal relationships' but 'must have a definite body of
material for investigation'.[15] While one may object by arguing
that the interpenetration of the human and natural world
does provide a body of material or a class of data for study,
it is nevertheless true that it does not provide an adequate
criterion for distinguishing geography from a number of other
sciences. A case in point is anthropology, which conceives
the human individual as a natural being, and studies societies
in which the relation between human individuals and nature
and between culture and nature is central to an understanding
of the functioning and development of society, while the
connection between nature on the one hand and human
activity and mental processes on the other are important
themes in biological and psychological research.

1.3 Geography as a chorological 'science'

The view expressed by Hartshorne himself was that geography
cannot seek its place among the sciences on the basis of any
particular category of phenomena that it studies, and that it
is distinguished instead by its viewpoint or method. He claimed
that this view was shared by Hettner, by Richthofen, who
was able to draw on statements made by von Humboldt and
Ritter, and by Kant. His main argument was that 'each of the
systematic sciences has its own class of objects to study',
whereas geography has none.[16] Since it does not possess its
own set of particular phenomena, geography is barred from

membership of the so-called systematic sciences, although its exclusion does not mean that it is unique or exceptional among the sciences, because much the same is true of history.[17]

Hartshorne argued that knowledge is a unit which is arbitrarily divided into a number of fields or disciplines. These disciplines belong to three classes of science, each of which extends over the whole field of knowledge:

1. the systematic sciences, which concentrate on particular categories of phenomena: the botanist studies plants, the zoologist animals, the various social sciences, such as sociology, economics, and political science, concentrate on particular aspects of social life, etc.;
2. the chronological sciences, which concentrate on the variations of phenomena and their interconnections through time, and require 'scientific description' to analyse the interrelations of diverse phenomena in any period and causal relations of development through time; and
3. the chorological sciences, which arise from the causal relationships existing in the complex of heterogeneous phenomena at one place and the causal connections among phenomena at different places.

In the view of Hartshorne geography is a chorological science. But what is the nature of this particular chorological science? Hartshorne insists that the essential characteristics of geography should be determined by its past development. In his own account of the development of the discipline in *The Nature of Geography* he argued that geography is the study of 'areal differentiation'. In *Perspective on the Nature of Geography* he pointed out that this phrase was introduced by Sauer in 1925 in *The Morphology of Landscape* in paraphrasing Hettner's concept of geography.[18] According to Hartshorne the concept itself stems from Richtofen's synthesis of the views of von Humboldt and Ritter and has been most fully expounded in Hettner's writing:

The goal of the chorological point of view is to know the character of regions and places through comprehension of the existence together and interrelations among the different realms of reality and their varied manifestations, and to comprehend the earth surface as a whole in its actual arrangement in continents, large and small regions, and places.[19]

Hartshorne argued that the statements of Vidal de la Blache are similar in meaning, especially in the form in which Cholley restated them in his *Guide to the Student of Geography*:

> The object of geography is to know the earth, in its total character not in terms of individual categories of phenom-ena, physical, biological and human arranged in a series, but rather in terms of the combinations produced among them, because it is these combinations which create the different physical and human aspects which the surface of the earth reveals to us. It is an astonishing variety of aspects which the surface of the earth reveals to us: oceans, contin-ents, and overlying them, all the diversity of vegetational landscapes, of systems of culture, forms of settlement and the organisation of area (*'espace'*) by the human groups.[20]

In other words, the concept encompasses the appearance of the landscape, the way in which human beings live, and the way in which they organise the space at their disposal, and it focuses upon the differences in certain things from place to place and the differences in combinations of phenomena in each place. This discussion of the concept of areal differentia-tion then led him to reformulate his original definition of geography and to argue that 'geography is concerned to provide accurate, orderly and rational description and inter-pretation of the variable character of the earth surface'.[21]

Having defined geography, Hartshorne pointed out that the variable character of the earth surface is composed of complex and varying integrations of heterogeneous phenom-ena interrelated in a variety of ways both at every place and among places on the surface of the earth. The enormous com-plexity of these integrations makes it necessary to study 'interrelations in limited segments of integration over large areas', that is, topical or systematic geography, but to under-stand the character of each part of the surface of the earth it is also necessary to study 'more complex integrations in small units of area', that is, regional geography. He believed that any truly geographical study involves the use of both approaches. He also accepted that geography must seek to classify and interpret phenomena that have been described, but he maintained that the interpretation of the variable character of the earth surface could only partially be based on law-like statements and that geography could not be a fully fledged nomothetic science:

> as in any science, we seek to secure that approach to certainty and universality of knowledge that is made possible by the constructing of generic concepts and laws of interrelations among factors. But the manifold variety of different and incommensurable factors involved in many features of our object of study, the complex world of the earth surface, permits interpretation only of part of our findings by that desired method. A great part of what cannot be explained by this method is nonetheless essential to an understanding and interpretation of areal variations from place to place. Hence, we are forced to measure and, as best we can, interpret an unusually large number of unique cases.[22]

In short, he believed that geography is a chorological science determined 'by its method of study rather than by the kinds of thing studied, and that among the space sciences it is concerned to study the earth surface, differentiated from place to place by interrelated elements significant to man'.[23]

This conclusion that geography is distinguished by its method of study rather than by its possession of a distinct object is associated with the distinction made by Hartshorne between the systematic, chronological, and chorological sciences. We have already suggested that this subdivision of the sciences is questionable. In Hartshorne's case it is connected with the views that the objects studied by the systematic sciences are naive entities that are immediately distinguished by any common-sense subdivision of the natural and social world, and that the objects studied by the systematic sciences are not unique. Any acquaintance with these sciences would indicate that neither of these propositions is true. As Blaut has pointed out, when Hartshorne stated that 'we must construct our own objects by intellectual activity' he was only advising geographers to do what every systematic science was and is doing, and he even identified a real object for geographical study and a number of subject-matter concepts or theoretical objects that can be used to define the object of geographical enquiry: namely the complex world of the earth surface, areal differentiation, and areal integration.[24] In the second place, the objects studied by the systematic sciences are unique, and so their ability to develop theory cannot be dependent upon the existence of identical cases for consideration. It follows that Hartshorne has not established a case for the methodological distinctiveness of geography or what Schaefer has called 'exceptionalism', and that he has not proved that it is impossible for geographers to construct and use theory. His views were in any case based on a narrow conception of theory, since he believed that theories are composed of generic principles derived from observed spatial associations between phenomena, and that their role was merely to assist studies of the functional integration of phenomena in areas. Once it is acknowledged that geographical theories can involve a specification of causal mechanisms and causal processes, the development of theory can be seen to be an even more realistic option.[25]

1.4 Geography as the study of the spatial arrangement of phenomena

One of the important steps in the development of the locational tradition in geography occurred in 1953 with the posthumous publication of an article by Schaefer, in which he argued that 'to explain the phenomena one has described means always to recognize them as instance of laws' and that 'geography has to be conceived as the science concerned with the formulation of the laws governing the spatial distribution of certain features on the surface of the earth'.[26] This paper was largely an attack on what Schaefer called 'exceptionalism', that is the view that geography as a chorological science must employ a distinctive idiographic method and that this method gives geography its status as a separate branch of knowledge. As has already been suggested, the chorological sciences cannot be thought to be methodologically distinct simply because they are concerned with unique phenomena, and so it is true that geography is not exceptional in the sense proposed by Hartshorne. It is therefore necessary to agree with Schaefer's conclusion, but it must be emphasised that this does not imply or require acceptance of his positivist methodological position.

Having begun by opposing methodological exceptionalism in geography, Schaefer proceeded to make a different exceptionalist claim for it. Like many writers in the locational tradition he maintained that geography is limited to the study of the spatial arrangement of phenomena in an area, in contrast to the phenomena themselves, and suggested that its task was to construct morphological laws rather than process laws, with the latter being produced by the systematic social sciences. These arguments amount to an exceptionalist claim because they involve the attribution of a separate and special nature to the object of geographical analysis. As in the case of methodological exceptionalism, this conception of geography is based upon a distinction between chorological, chronological, and systematic sciences. The difference is that in the locational tradition this distinction is connected with the view that it is possible to separate the spatial and non-spatial characteristics of empirical objects and real-world processes, and to study them in isolation from one another without altering or affecting the excluded properties of the object or process in question.

An acceptance of this thesis lies behind several procedures that occur not only in locational analysis but also in related subjects such as urban economics.[27] One of these is for an object to be studied initially by systematic sciences that are thought to be able to abstract from its spatial and temporal characteristics and to treat them as inconsequential. Once this task has been accomplished, the object can be reinserted in its spatial setting, and the separate effects produced by space can be identified and analysed by the chorological sciences, which in their turn are thought to be able to neglect, treat as inconsequential, or consider as exogenously given the non-spatial characteristics of mental, social, and natural phenomena. The alternative procedure is for the spatial aspects of an object, or for regularities in its spatial distribution, to be isolated from the outset and studied without regard to its other characteristics by the chorological sciences. Both of these procedures can be observed in locational analysis. The latter has sought both to detect and isolate patterns and regularities concealed in the complex spatial forms observed in the real world, and to construct abstract models for the study of spatial forms, patterns of regional specialisation, and relations between different places or regions. These two steps are thought to be mutually dependent, in the sense that models are either presented as hypotheses to be checked against empirical evidence or as theories that can be used to interpret observed statistical regularities, while, on the other hand, empirical studies are intended to contribute to the process of theory generation by distinguishing regularities that are not immediately apparent, due to their superimposition upon one another in reality and to their modification by random disturbances. By virtue of their restriction to the spatial characteristics of phenomena these types of analysis can at best, however, only provide a partial explanation of any real situation. Indeed they can even be extremely misleading when the type of abstraction involved is ignored, and when it is presumed that spatial variables alone can account for any spatial form, let alone for changes in spatial structures. In view of the fact that the characteristics of areas stem in part from the non-spatial properties of objects existing in them, locational studies employing this type of abstraction are precluded from giving a full account of geographical phenomena. Many geographers would accept this statement. It was pointed out by Hartshorne, for example, that the interpretation of the relation between phenomena requires an understanding of the diverse phenomena whose interrelations extend over space, and that 'these phenomena . . . form part of the character of each area'. The same point was also made by Hettner who warned geographers against 'the neglect of differences in the content of areas'.[28] The same general argument applies to all other disciplines characterised by this mode of abstraction because none of them will be able to provide an adequate explanation of any real object.

The problems posed by the attribution of a special status to the object of geographical enquiry are reinforced by the use of ahistorical, fixed, and eternal conceptions of the main elements of mental, social, and natural space. If geography is to be a subject able to explain the spatial arrangement of phenomena, at least four resulting weaknesses of locational analysis will need to be overcome:

(1) The spatial setting is frequently assumed to be given and not produced, and is often interpreted naturalistically. In the case of theories of regional trade and specialisation, for example, considerable emphasis is placed on the existence of different regional resource endowments, but these endowments are often thought to be natural, and their genesis is seldom explained. These differential endowments subsequently combine with restrictions upon mobility and costs of movement between regions to produce new regional structures. The consequent modification of resource endowments is occasionally acknowledged, but such modifications are considered to be of secondary importance compared with the initial endowment in any account of regional specialisation and trade, despite the existence of widespread evidence showing how the conditions for economic growth are themselves in many cases the consequences of previous economic activity.[29] Similarly, theories of industrial location pay insufficient attention to the fact that the spatial setting, that is the disposition of labour, raw and semi-finished material inputs, markets, and transport routes, has been historically determined, and that the prevailing locational conditions continue to be modified with and by the implantation of a new enterprise in an area and by its effects on local labour and product markets, etc.

(2) Certain processes are usually examined in an abstract and relatively undifferentiated spatial context, and the resulting spatial forms are treated as general models of observable spatial patterns. In developing analytical principles it is obviously necessary to make a number of simplifying assumptions about the structure of the spatial framework to make the argument manageable, but to explain real concrete events the procedure should then be to examine the operation of these processes in real spatial contexts and not to use idealised landscapes as models for the real world.

(3) The authors of locational studies frequently abstract from the non-spatial aspects of the objects and processes studied. In particular, much location theory is concerned with the production of spatial structures through the location of an object in a simplified spatial setting in accordance with certain abstract locational principles. Accordingly, industrial and agricultural enterprises are located at points that minimise the costs of transport incurred in purchasing inputs and selling outputs, or commercial enterprises are located so as to maximise sales in a spatial market. In each case the nature of the object and the non-spatial aspects of the process are treated as being unimportant or exogenously given. Yet the locational requirements and the locational structure of these enterprises depend upon the nature of the enterprise and its activities, and change with changes in the operations of production, circulation, and distribution in which they are engaged, while the spatial context in which these enterprises are established has an effect not only upon their location but also upon their nature and their non-spatial characteristics. The consequence of believing that the spatial arrangement of phenomena is a separable object of study and is what is studied by locational analysis is, therefore, that it is impossible for locational analysis on its own to provide an adequate explanation of spatial structures and, particularly, of their evolution.

(4) Natural and ahistorical categories are often used to express the relations and processes accounting for the production of spatial forms, and the resulting spatial structures are themselves often considered to be natural ones. It is, for example, very common to find locational models that analyse economic processes by distinguishing certain general conditions characterising all forms of production, even though these general conditions are nothing more than 'abstract moments with which no real historical stage of production can be grasped'.[30] Subsequently these abstract and eternal elements are identified with the form they assume in capitalist societies (for example, human labour is equated with wage-labour, and produced means of production with capital), and the conditions of capitalist production are considered to be the eternal conditions of all production and not transitory and historically determined ones. This procedure is exemplified both by

locational models built on the basis of neoclassical economic theories,[31] and by the research traditions stemming from the work of the Chicago School of urban ecologists. One of the main elements of the Chicago School's approach to the study of urbanisation was an account of urban spatial structure in terms of ecological processes of competition, dominance, invasion, and succession that were characteristic of what its members called the biotic level of a social system and that resulted in the appearance of natural social areas. Having been derived initially by analogy with plant ecology, these biotic processes were subsequently explained by reference to formal economic laws, and were eventually represented in much more sophisticated neo-classical models of residential location and urban spatial structure. The second main theme in the work of the Chicago School was the view that culture is produced by nature or by the ecological framework. This thesis found expression in the claim that urbanism as a way of life was produced by the city, that is by large, dense, and heterogeneous settlements, and it led to a large number of empirical studies linking different ways of life and various social problems with particular urban spatial contexts such as slums or suburbs.[32] These two arguments can be represented by a simple diagram:

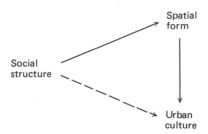

Since social processes are treated naturalistically, the spatial structure is treated as an objective, natural or quasi-natural framework which conditions human activity and to which human beings must adjust. The set of relationships between these elements is, in fact, much more complex than those portrayed in this diagram, but the main point is that these models are unable to provide an adequate account of the specific social processes determining the characteristics and development of spatial structures in particular social and historical contexts and, as a result, misrepresent the impact of spatial structures on human activities.[33]

These problems connected with the conceptualisation of social or spatial processes, and these weaknesses, stem in part from the failure of locational analysis to recognise that the spatial and temporal aspects and the true nature of things simply cannot be separated.[34] The physical and human world must be comprehended as a complex of continuously changing elements and processes. It is composed of objects and structures that are produced by certain activities or processes, which persist through a certain period of time and sometimes are subsequently reproduced, undergoing in both cases continuous modification, and which eventually are qualitatively altered, pass away, or are destroyed. All of these elements and processes have their own times and their own rates of change, which depend upon their specific characteristics and their articulation with other objects and processes making up the structure of the whole, and they acquire certain attributes by virtue of their co-existence and interpenetration with these other elements and processes. Their temporalities and rates of change can often be perceived and measured, as in the case, for example, of the processes of production, circulation, distribution and consumption, and of the useful objects created, exchanged, and consumed, or the processes of constitution and development of cultural formations and cultural objects. The complex intersection of these objects and activities and their rates of change constitute the real historical process, and provide an indispensable basis for the construction of meaningful periodisations.[35] All of these objects and processes also occupy segments of space, or rather of space—time, with some of them entailing movement from one part of space through a sequence of positions to another, and they all have the property of extension or scale which, like temporality, depends upon their articulation with the other objects and processes comprising the whole. At any moment they occupy a place or position in relation to other objects and processes situated in this space, and this relative position leads to their acquisition of additional relational properties. The way in which objects acquire relational properties of this kind is illustrated, for example, by the way in which the qualities of a property development can be affected and its profitability augmented by the juxtaposition of offices, luxury shops, and luxury housing.[36] The extensiveness of these objects and processes and the extensiveness of their effects provide the basis for the construction of appropriate regional-isations and the determination of appropriate scales for their analysis.

The implication of this argument is not only that all material and immaterial objects and events have spatial and temporal dimensions, but also that these dimensions cannot be separ-ated from their other properties because they are essential conditions for the existence of any object or event and because they affect, qualify, or modify many of their properties, with the result that the separate aspects of an object studied by disciplines distinguished in this way cannot be recombined additively. It therefore follows that an adequate conception of any object or event must be based upon a unified theoretical framework, and that it is no more possible for the systematic sciences to abstract from the spatial and temporal aspects of phenomena than it is for the chorological sciences to abstract from the phenomena that form the content of an area.

In an earlier section we criticised methodological exception-alism, and we argued that geography is not methodologically distinct, because it is possible to identify types of spatial forms and types of causal processes and, hence, to construct theory. In this section we have argued that geography cannot be distinguished by the special nature of its object, and by its concern with the spatial arrangement of phenomena rather than with the phenomena themselves, because the structure of space can only be understood by exploring the relations between spatial structures and specific natural and social pro-cesses. In short, geography cannot have a special nature as a chorological science.

1.5 Geography as the study of landscapes and regions

The study of the variable character of the earth surface and of regions was a central theme in Hartshorne's conception of geography, but we have distinguished landscape and regional geography as it developed in the inter-war period because it was associated with an attempt to identify those phenomena that constitute objects that geography alone could claim to study. In landscape geography, landscapes were considered to be material objects that appear to ordinary sense experience, and, because of the double meaning of the German word '*Landschaften*', limited areas or regions. As a result, it was sometimes argued that regions are real objects.

In this research tradition the task of the geographer was thought to be one of examining all that is visible on the surface of the earth, and of investigating the characteristic associations of phenomena observed in the landscape. One of the representatives of this point of view was Sauer, who argued that 'area' or 'landscape' is an object of geographical study 'because it is a naively given, important section of reality', and that this object enables geography to be distinguished from the other sciences.[37] The term 'naively given' seems to mean something that is immediately or directly given to ordinary sense experience, but this notion would then be based upon the empiricist misconception according to which the mind passively reflects the external world. Moreover, to the extent that the subject-matter of any science departs from common-sense objects, this criterion will be unable to provide a basis for a complete classification of the sciences. Sciences can be distinguished on the basis of their real objects, that is the aspects of concrete reality they study, or on the basis of their theoretical objects, that is the concepts developed to account for these real objects. In the early phases of their development some sciences can be thought of as studying naively given objects, in the sense that they employ naive concepts of objects that are immediately identifiable and distinguished in ordinary sense experience, as in the case of early classifications of plants and animals, but the development of a science is associated with the development of new concepts, and with the departure of their subject matter from common-sense objects.

The study of landscapes, by being interpreted in an extremely narrow way, has also tended to restrict the scope of geographical enquiry to those objects and characteristic associations between phenomena that can be observed in the landscape at any moment in time. In fact, various types of landscape geography can be identified, but most of them share a preoccupation with the visible landscape, which is well illustrated by Brunhes's statement that geography studies what can be observed when the earth is surveyed from a balloon.[38] One problem with this view is that what can be observed is only a frozen image of things that are continually changing, while what is most strongly emphasised are elements that are more slowly changing, motionless, and hence more permanent. Apart from any illusions caused by this type of image of the landscape, many of the processes and human activities that take place in it, and that create and shape it, cannot be observed and studied when the domain of enquiry is restricted to one or even to a sequence of such images of the material landscape. The result is that these processes and activities are often excluded from consideration, and that the formation and development of the landscape and the activities of its inhabitants remain unexplained.[39]

1.6 Conclusion

It would be naive to think that it is only geography that has faced problems in defining its object of analysis and in clarifying its relation with other disciplines. In fact serious difficulties are confronted in any attempt to establish a definition of what constitutes a discipline and to draw up criteria that can be used to differentiate one subject from another. As a result there are many disagreements about where the limits of the various disciplines can sensibly be presumed to lie, about the nature of the connections between them, and, indeed, about the capacity of the existing array of disciplines to adequately treat the various aspects of natural and social reality.

It has already been suggested that it is possible to distinguish a discipline as a relatively autonomous field of study on the basis of its possession of a distinctive object. In the last section we also pointed out that landscape geography involved the identification of subject-matter concepts which allow the recognition of geography as an ordinary systematic science rather than a separate chorological one. It follows that geography need not be thought to be different in kind from the other sciences, and that the task of geographers wishing to define their field of study is to identify subject-matter concepts. Once this has been realised, it is relatively easy to identify several suitable concepts, including the views that geography studies landscapes and regions, areal integration and areal differentiation, or spatial forms and spatial structures. The problems with each of these definitions of what geographers study is that they are often associated with the use of inadequate concepts. In the field of regional geography, for example, many fascinating studies have been produced, but the regional approach to geography has often been associated with the use of naturalistic ideologies and with a lack of concern with the wider historical processes which produce and break down the unity and coherence of specific regions. The concept of areal integration also poses problems, because it is imbued with the idea that spatial forms are simply complex articulations of phenomena which can be interpreted by means of generalisations about associations between phenomena rather than through the analysis of specific processes, while spatial expressions seldom involve the use of precisely defined concepts,[40] and spatial analysis frequently rests on the idea that the spatial distribution of phenomena is a separable object of study.

Provided that some of these conceptual difficulties can be overcome, it does however seem reasonable to conclude, at least provisionally, that geography is distinguished from the other sciences not by its method of analysis, nor by the special nature of its object, nor by the fact that it studies a particular relationship, that is the relationship between human beings and nature, but by the fact that it studies a particular real object, that is materially determined spaces or landscapes, and that its task is to develop those concepts necessary for an understanding of this object of analysis.

2 The Question of Method

In the course of our discussion we have noticed how some traditions in geographical research have argued that geography is a law-finding science in the same sense as the natural sciences, while others have suggested that geography does not conform with this model of science. We have also commented critically on some concepts of nature and of space found in the geographical literature. In fact there has been a tendency for geography to oscillate between methodological positions and between conceptions of its subject-matter that can be broadly classified as being either materialist in the traditional sense or idealist. In opposition to these one-sided theories we wish to argue that historical materialism provides a basis for resolving some of the methodological and conceptual problems faced by geographers. To do this, we shall try to spell out the implications of the processes of material and ideal causality, both of which are incorporated in Marx's conception of human practice but which are normally developed one-sidedly in traditional materialist or idealist theories, for the formulation of a more adequate method of analysis.

We shall begin by outlining some competing methodological positions held in the social sciences, emphasising the connections between geography on the one hand and classical empiricism and Popper's falsificationism on the other.[1] Some of the problems with these views of knowledge will be outlined, and an alternative materialist conception of knowledge, which overcomes these inadequacies and provides a more satisfactory basis for explaining geographical phenomena, will be elaborated. In addition we shall try to indicate some of the implications of a materialist epistemology for the process of abstraction, and at the end of the chapter we shall comment briefly on the relation between theory and practice.

The competing views about the ways in which geography can be distinguished from neighbouring sciences, which were identified in the last chapter, were in many cases associated with different views about the extent to which it is possible to formulate and use law-like statements in geography. Writers belonging to the classical and locational traditions usually argued that there is no essential difference between the methodology of the natural and social sciences, that geography is an ordinary generalising or nomothetic science, and that it should therefore employ a methodology abstractly modelled on that of the natural sciences, or, more precisely, on an empiricist conception of their methodology. The main competing view about the methodology of geography is the one expounded by Hartshorne. He did not disagree in principle about the characteristics of the methodology of the natural and social sciences, but he maintained that geography possesses its own distinctive idiographic method, and that in describing and interpreting individual cases it can make only limited use of scientific laws.

The differences between these two groups of writers are, therefore, ones of degree rather than of kind. What is almost more striking than the differences between them is the fact that they share the same views about the methodology of the natural and social sciences, and that this shared position puts them both in opposition to the other main methodological current in the social sciences. The main competing viewpoint is the one associated with the claim that the social sciences are hermeneutic or interpretative sciences which are distinguished from the natural sciences by the use of the method of *Verstehen*. The aim of this procedure is to enable the social scientist to place him or herself in the position of his or her human subject and to see the subject's actions from the subject's own point of view. A method of this kind clearly has an important role to play in areas concerned with human action and human behaviour.

In the past, almost all geographical writing has been based on an empiricist conception of the relation between thought and its object. In empiricist epistemologies it is maintained that all knowledge is derived from sense experience, and the elements of our knowledge are believed to belong to the realm of possible experiences, impressions, and appearances depicted in the human mind. Scientific knowledge is recognised as involving not only observation but also the construction of theories and laws enabling us to explain and to predict phenomena that have been, or will be, observed. But empiricist theories of knowledge usually involve the claim that these theories and laws must be derived or inferred from theory-independent observational premises, while theoretical concepts and statements are often thought to be reducible in meaning to empirical ones.

Within geography this type of position is reflected in the widely held view that geographical research should begin with observation and the collection of naively given facts, data, and evidence, and that it should then proceed to construct generalisations by means of induction, that is, make general statements on the basis of the discrimination of empirical regularities or repeated conjunctions between observed events.

In the early twentieth century a more radical version of empiricism was developed by the logical positivists of the Vienna Circle in which a theory of knowledge was combined with a theory of meaning. The central doctrine of logical positivism was the verification principle of meaning, according to which a statement can only be valid and meaningful if it is either analytic or empirically verifiable. Any other type of statement was held not merely to be unscientific but to be nonsensical. It was this version of empiricism by which geography was most profoundly affected at the time of the quantitative revolution.

Now one of the central problems of classical empiricism and of inductivism lay in the fact, to which we referred in our discussion of Kant's theory of knowledge, that the inference from observational premises to theoretical conclusions cannot rely purely on analysis or tautological principles and cannot be justified by reference to experience. Inferences from particular instances to unrestrictedly universal statements involve the use of the method of induction. But, as Hume had shown, a movement from statements about some instances to statements about all instances, or from statements about events that have been observed to statements about events that have yet to be observed, cannot be justified, and so the method of induction has no rational foundation, at least in the sense that it is incapable of being inferred either from other principles of logic or from experience. It is only by assuming that the course of nature will not change, even though such an assumption cannot be justified, at least within the framework of an empiricist epistemology, that science can proceed.

The problem of induction was taken up by Popper in his writing on the philosophy of science, including *The Logic of Scientific Discovery*, *Conjectures and Refutations*, and *Objective Knowledge*.[2] Popper agreed with Hume's view about induction, but he attempted to sidestep the problem by arguing that science neither uses nor needs induction. His critique of inductivism was based on the view that it confuses questions about the origin of scientific knowledge with questions about its justification. He drew a sharp distinction between these two issues, and maintained that the question for the methodology of science is not the genetic one about how a theory originated but one about how a theory that has been formulated stands up to empirical testing. In his view, theories are constructed not by inductive procedures but by bold flights of the imagination and by speculative thinking, whereas their scientificity depends on the possibility of testing them by means of observation and experiment. He argued that in science theory always precedes observation, and that a scientist always approaches reality with a theory or question that determines what observations will be made. But he also claimed that scientific theories, unlike non-scientific ones, can be tested by deducing observational consequences from them in conjunction with certain specified initial conditions, and by comparing these consequences with the outcome of observation and experiment. Although individual observations that are compatible with a theory cannot be used to verify it, since observations only relate to particular instances whereas theories relate to all instances, a basic observation statement that denies or falsifies an observational consequence of a theory can, in Popper's opinion, be used to refute, reject, or eliminate it. One counter-instance would in practice not be sufficient to justify the abandonment of a theory, but Popper believed that theories should not be retained by the successive introduction of *ad hoc* hypotheses designed to accomodate counter-instances, and, moreover, that the search for counter-instances gives rise to the formulation of theories with a higher informative content and a greater degree of corroboration. A scientific procedure that aims to reject or eliminate theories also has the advantages of relying only on deductive logic to derive the observational consequences of theories and observation and experiment to test them. It was on the basis of this argument that Popper concluded that science can be perfectly rational, but it means that no theory, however long or widely it has been accepted, can ever be more than a hypothesis or conjecture.

These views about the methodology of natural science and its rationality were subsequently criticised, particularly by Kuhn and Feyerabend. It was pointed out against Popper that theories cannot be conclusively falsified any more than they can be conclusively verified, because observation statements are interpretations in the light of theories and are not theoretically neutral, with the result that it is not necessarily possible to decide whether to reject the theory, the observation statement, or both, when a negative instance is observed. It was also argued that the history of science plays an important role in explaining its logic and methodology and in explaining the development of changing conceptions of scientific rationality.

The facts that logic and observation are not alone an adequate basis for the rejection of existing theories, and cannot be used for theory choice when new theories involve radical conceptual innovation, have given rise to several competing conceptions of scientific activity. Kuhn presented an account of the sociology and history of science based on the recognition of phases of normal scientific activity, in which a shared body of theories and models is extended and applied to particular problems, and of phases of revolutionary scientific activity, when anomalies between existing theories and observation induce scientists to switch to a new paradigm not solely on the basis of logic and observation but also on socio-psychological grounds.[3]

Building on Kuhn's account, Feyerabend developed a more radical thesis. He insisted that scientists have not adhered to a given set of methodological rules and procedures laid down by scientific methodologists, and that adherence to a rational method would have prevented some of the most important scientific discoveries from being made and incorporated into modern science. He suggested that scientific activity should proceed in a context characterised by the coexistence of a prolific generation of new theories on the one hand and an application of the seemingly contradictory principle of tenacity on the other. In other words scientists should be able to hold on to existing theories even in the light of evidence as to their inadequacy, but at the same time a wide range of different theories should always be found in any scientific community. As a result he opposed the formulation of methodological rules, arguing instead that 'anything goes' is the only principle that does not inhibit scientific progress.[4]

So far we have focused on Popper's method of constructing and testing theories. But in providing an account of explanation, Popper used the same covering-law model that had been developed to analyse testing and prediction. To explain an event E entails, in his view, deducing the statement that E occurs, occurred, or will occur from a covering law or laws in conjunction with a set of initial conditions.

As a result of his belief in the unity of science Popper extended his views on the logic and methodology of the natural sciences to the social sciences, arguing that they too must use the hypothetico-deductive method of inventing hypotheses and testing them empirically by deducing their observational consequences, and must use the covering-law model of explanation. This type of method was widely invoked by geographers during the quantitative revolution, when they argued, for example, that locational theories generated predictions about observed spatial distributions that could be tested empirically, but Popper would in all probability have questioned the applicability and value of this procedure in geography, because geography, like history, would have been conceived by him as being a particularising science.

Popper wished to use his falsification principle as a demarcation criterion for distinguishing science from non-science. One of his main targets was Marxism. He believed that Marxism is unscientific because it employs *ad hoc* hypotheses to protect its main propositions from evidence that is incompatible with them, but he also opposed it on the grounds that it is historicist and that it attempts to construct laws of historical development and to make historical predictions. In *The Poverty of Historicism* he proceeded to argue that history is a particularising science interested in unique sequences or constellations of events rather than in laws and generalisations, and that in providing causal explanations of these events it employs laws that are so general that they do not need to be stated.[5] This distinction between the theoretical and historical sciences, and between an interest in universal laws and particular events, is reminiscent of the one proposed by Hartshorne between the systematic and temporal sciences.

One of the problems with Popper's more general criticism of historicism is that it is based upon a specific and narrow conception of laws as correlations or constant conjunctions between classes of elementary and repeatable events. In fact a covering law is itself a constant conjunction between events whose deductive consequences are capable of being tested empirically. In this way the problem of induction was thought to be circumvented by locating causal necessity in the deductive structure of the inference from the law and the initial conditions to the event to be explained.

Marx believed, on the other hand, that it is possible to formulate laws explaining underlying historical forces, laws expressing tendencies, and laws of social mechanisms in societies in which human beings create their destiny in unmastered natural and social conditions, and that specific events are only comprehensible if they are understood as being constituted by general laws regulating the functioning of society at specific stages of its development.[6] It must however be emphasised that these laws do not entail specific outcomes or specific sequences of events, let alone suggest that any society will pass through a specific sequence of stages or follow a single predefined historical path. The laws proposed by Marx are analogous to those used in the historical sciences of nature such as the Darwinian theory of evolution. In both cases the actual course of events cannot be known in advance, and in the social world they depend upon the interaction between a complex variety of subjective and objective factors and forces.

Within the Marxist tradition itself, however, a variety of methodological and theoretical viewpoints have been expressed.[7] In the account developed below we shall draw in particular upon the work of Colletti.

In a materialist epistemology, the aim of theory is the continuous development and elaboration of concepts that correspond as closely as possible both to the representation in thought of some real object or concrete historical process and to what actually goes on in reality, while its development is based upon analytical and experimental procedures that can be used to investigate and change the concrete world. The starting-point for such a project is the view that 'there can be no thought unless there is something previously given to be thought'. In other words, 'the objectivity of reality, i.e. the condition for there being a content to knowledge, is a condition for the existence of thought'.[8]

Given this acknowledgement of the real existence, independently of the knowing subject, of an external world composed of real individuals, their mental and physical activities, and the material conditions of their existence, it is necessary to develop a method that will enable us to acquire knowledge of it. As Colletti has pointed out, this method must be based upon the recognition that there is a dialectical relation between thought and reality in which 'reality and thought appear alternately as limiting condition and as that which has limiting conditions placed upon it'. On the one hand, empirical reality or the concrete world is that which is objective, and hence external to and independent of thinking subjectivity, and 'thought in relation to it is something on which limiting conditions are placed'. On the other hand, we can only arrive at a recognition and knowledge of external reality through thought, that is through a process in which reality is reproduced by thought, assumes a mental form in our minds, and emerges as a product of thinking and comprehending.[9]

Colletti uses a whole series of oppositions to refer to these two processes. These oppositions include real process and logical process, *ratio essendi* and *ratio cognoscendi*, and determination of the abstract by the concrete and the concrete by the abstract. He points out that 'the first one is an instance of efficient or material causality, where it is the empirical or sense data which condition and thought which is conditioned', whereas the second one is an instance of the inverse process, referred to as final or ideal causality, where the notion instead of appearing as a result of the elaboration of perception and representation into concepts is an *a priori* condition for the acquisition of knowledge about reality.[10]

The identification of these two causal processes leads to a methodology that recognises the role of theory in the construction of our knowledge, that is, the contribution of the thinking mind to what we call knowledge. Theory precedes the observation of facts, since 'facts come to mean something only as ascertained and organized in the frame of a theory', and since 'we need to pose questions before responses can be obtained'.[11] But the ideas employed by science are not *a priori* categories that are independent of experience, that is hypostates or ideal essences, but hypotheses. The latter can be elaborated and compared with observational data and the actual course of events, and they can be modified or replaced by new concepts and theories that correspond more closely with reality. Unlike *a priori* categories the concepts used in science are specific and changeable ones.[12]

These scientific categories must in turn be formulated by a process of analysis or abstraction that proceeds from the concrete and real subject, for example a historically determinate society and its conditions, but this process is often underemphasised or misconceived in many theoretical social sciences. A misunderstanding of this process has resulted in particular in an uncritical use of indeterminate abstractions or *a priori* categories in the social sciences, and it lies at the root of the central problems with those theories used by geographers during the quantitative revolution and with neoclassical conceptions of the economy on which much location theory is based.

The general problem was highlighted by Marx in his repeated critique of Hegelian philosophy. Marx argued that the Hegelian method is the source of certain types of mystification because of its inversion of the relationship between subject and predicate.[13] By this he meant that a general concept that ought to be a predicate of some real object is made instead into an independent entity existing in its own right, whereas the real subject, the real empirical world, becomes an objectification or embodiment of this abstract idea, that is, an external, phenomenal form of the idea or a predicate of its own hypostatised predicate. This critique of the Hegelian dialectic provides the key to understanding Marx's critique of the Hegelian conception of the modern representative state and his critique of the actual separation of the state representing the general interest from society as well as its basis in private property, [14] and it also underlies his critique of the method of the bourgeois economists and of modern commodity production whose inverted and alienated form is reflected in their theories.

In a discussion of their method rather than of the way in which their theories reflect the structure of capitalist economies, Marx argued that the bourgeois economists treat real historical relations as the objectification of hypostatised abstractions. In his view they 'substitute for the specific institutions and processes of the modern economy generic or universal categories that are supposed to be valid for all times and places', and then, in a subsequent step, they interpret the former as the realisation of these abstract and eternal ideas. For example, wage-labour observed in specific, historically concrete situations is identified with labour in general, that is with labour as the universal condition for the metabolic interaction between a human being and nature, while capital is conceived as an instrument of production and stored-up labour ignoring the specific qualities that make the means of production into capital in specific types of society.[15]

As Colletti has pointed out, this critique was reconstructed by Dobb in his *Political Economy and Capitalism* and in *Theories of Value and Distribution* when he distinguished between two types of abstraction.[16] Determinate or specific abstractions are constructed by excluding certain features

present in any actual situation, either because they are the more variable or because they are quantitatively of lesser importance in determining the course of events. To omit them from consideration makes the resulting calculation no more than an imperfect approximation to reality, but nevertheless makes it a very much more reliable guide than if the major factors had been omitted and only the minor influences taken into account.

Indeterminate or generic abstractions, on the other hand, are based 'not on any evidence of fact as to what features in a situation are essential and what are inessential, but simply on the formal procedure of combining the properties common to a heterogeneous assortment of situations and building abstraction out of analogy'. Generalisations must obviously distinguish something that is common to the phenomena to which they refer, but the problem with this second procedure is that 'in all such abstract systems there exists the danger of hypostatising one's concepts' and 'of regarding the postulated relations as the determining ones in any actual situation' and as the essence of contemporary economies. To illustrate this argument Dobb referred critically to the way in which economists attempt

> to arrive at generalisations which will hold for any type of exchange economy and which will necessarily prevail in any situation in which there are scarce resources with alternative uses, by abstracting phenomena of exchange from the productive relations and the property and class institutions of which they are the expression.

The problem is that 'once this abstraction has been made it is given an independent existence', and it is assumed to represent the essence of reality instead of one contingent facet of it.[17]

Many of the limitations of the dominant tradition in economic thought, and of locational models based on neoclassical conceptions of the economy, stem from the use of this type of abstraction. Aglietta has indicated two main failings of mainstream economic theory:

> firstly, its inability to analyse the economic process in terms of the time lived by its subjects, i.e. to give an historical account of economic facts; and secondly, its inability to express the social content of economic relations, and

consequently to interpret the forces and conflicts at work in the economic process.

In his view these problems originate in the postulation of economic subjects displaying *a priori* types of specified rationality that are alleged to be characteristic of human nature, and in the subsequent definition of economic relations as 'modes of co-ordination of the predetermined and un-alterable behaviour of these subjects' which in their turn lead towards an equilibrium state.

In Aglietta's view the problems that result from the use of this method can be overcome by posing different theoretical questions founded on the method advocated by Marx and related to an alternative theory of social regulation. Beginning with a conception of a social system as a hierarchy of con-stitutive relationships, Aglietta focuses instead on the regula-tion of systems that are able to reproduce their characteristic structures in new forms, that is on those processes that enable what exists to go on existing, and on the forces that lead to qualitative changes in their structure and mode of functioning.

The differences between these two conceptions of the economic process lie in part in different methods. The approach advocated by Aglietta is based on the view that the progression of thought does not simply consist of hypothetico-deductive phases in which the conclusions already implicitly contained in an axiomatic system based on indeterminate abstractions are elaborated. He proposes instead a procedure stemming from the method elaborated by Marx, and based on the co-existence of a process of moving from the concrete to the abstract and one of moving from the abstract to the concrete. He therefore maintains that the movement of thought entails both an analytical process in which determinate abstractions are constructed, and an experimental procedure in which the hierarchy of concepts, from which it is possible to develop a theory of regulation, are set out and developed by the incorporation of more concrete content into them.[18]

The implications of this two-fold process, of moving from the concrete to the abstract and the abstract to the concrete, for the method of political economy, and indeed of geo-graphical analysis, were illustrated by Marx in the *Introduction* to the *Grundrisse der Kritik der politischen Ökonomie*. In this text he pointed out that the population of a given country is the basis and subject of the entire social act of production, and that this population, together with its distribution among classes, between town and country, between the different branches of production, and so on, is the real premiss of scientific studies of its economic and political structure. But the population cannot be the starting-point for the presentation and exposition of a scientific analysis of the country. The reason for this is that this premiss would have no meaning if we did not know the classes of which the population is composed, the elements on which these classes depend, such as wage-labour and capital, and the categories on which the latter are based, such as exchange, the division of labour, and so on. A scientific treatise must therefore begin its exposition with the most comprehensive mental generalisations, and proceed through increasingly specific particularities included within and depending upon the more general categories, rather than with the population which is none the less the premiss of the whole procedure.

The implication of this method is that the material world can only be made intelligible by first of all being analysed to produce a succession of increasingly simple and general determinations. These categories are abstract and one-sided relations of a concrete and living whole that is already given: that is, one aspect or analytic feature abstracted from the concrete and real object. And they are the outcome of the elaboration of perception and representation into concepts: that is, of an analytical process of formation of knowledge moving from empirical reality to its most general and abstract elements. But, once this process has been completed, it is necessary to proceed in the opposite direction, beginning with what are in this case abstract, mental generalisations or ideas and moving towards the more specific, less general characteristics of the object in question. This method of advancing from the abstract to the concrete is an experimental procedure in which concrete reality, which cannot be reduced to the concept, appears in thought as a synthesis or concentration of many determinations and relations, and it is the way in which the thinking and comprehending mind appropriates the concrete and reproduces it as a concrete that has assumed a mental form.[19]

The scientific analysis in *Capital* accordingly begins with commodities, and the value form of the labour product when it is produced for exchange 'as the most abstract but also the most highly generalised form taken by that product in the bourgeois system of production', and then proceeds through the more specific forms of money and capital. This procedure nevertheless avoids *a priori* constructions because the category 'besides having its meaning as a generality or idea and therefore as a logical prius is here grasped in relation to the particular object from which it was abstracted'.[20]

As well as being an account of the logical prerequisites for capitalist production, the logical process outlined in *Capital* is also a rational reconstruction of its historical prerequisites, but Marx emphasised that these categories presuppose the currently existing substratum from which they have been abstracted, and pointed out that once the foundations of capitalist production have been laid the conditions for the rise of capital become consequences of its existence.[21] This process of moving from the abstract to the concrete should not therefore be confused with the process by which the concrete comes into being. As long as the mind's conduct is merely contemplative or theoretical, the real subject remains outside the human mind, leading an independent existence.

But human thought does not merely play a contemplative role and is not simply concerned with the interpretation of the world. One of the central roles of human thought and of finalism or ideal causality is in directing practical human action and changing the world in accordance with human needs. The reality studied by thought is therefore partly constituted by human activity, while human thinking is concerned in part with the study of its own effects on the world. It follows that the co-existence of causality and finalism in scientific research has implications not only for empiricist views about the methodology of science and the process of abstraction, but also for related views about the objectivity of science and about its detachment from its subject-matter and from the social and political system in which it is developed.

Empiricists generally believe that scientific statements are descriptive and objective, and they draw a sharp distinction between judgements of fact and value, and between the determination of means and ends in practical situations. Hume and Ayer both argued, for example, that science is detached in the sense that it leaves the object studied unchanged as a result of scientific activity, and that scientific statements are neutral descriptions of the facts as they are observed.[22] Value judgements or aesthetic and moral judgements, on the other hand, were conceived as expressing subjective attitudes, emotions, and feelings towards the subject of the statement. They argued that the latter are unlike scientific statements in that they are incapable of being inferred from the facts and of being either true or false. The resulting view that science is a dispassionate study of the facts, and that value judgements are incapable of being scientific, is associated with a practical distinction between means and ends that is made not only in the natural but also in the social-policy sciences. According to this distinction, studies of the technical means for securing specified goals and of the implications of alternative policies are thought to fall within the domain of the applied natural and social sciences, whereas the practical activity of making recommendations and choosing among alternative courses of action is thought to be a value-laden and non-scientific activity.

It has already been pointed out that scientific knowledge cannot be acquired independently of evaluative statements and that factual statements are projections of our preconceived ideas onto the world. It follows that there is a relation from value to fact. However, the values embodied in scientific hypotheses and questions are usually believed by empiricists to be eliminated by the outcome of the process of observation and experiment. On this view the objective statements of science still have no implications for human action, and there is no relation from fact to value. Values cannot therefore be inferred from facts and cannot be based on and shown to be appropriate by scientific findings.

The connection between facts and values and means and ends is more complex than this type of position allows. What this account of the methodology of science tends to overlook is the role of human practice in assessing the truth or otherwise of our thinking about the world, and the way in which the scientificity of statements about the world depends upon their ability to help us to change it in accordance with specified ends. Scientific findings are in fact both hypothetical and normative, in the sense that they are evaluated via experimental and industrial activities that seek to demonstrate their truth in practice. But this fact is not recognised by those epistemologies that overlook the criterion of practice.

In the second of the *Theses on Feuerbach* Marx pointed out that:

> The question of whether objective truth can be attributed to human thinking is not a question of theory but is a practical question. [An individual] must prove the truth, i.e. the this-worldliness of his [or her] thinking in practice. This dispute over the reality or non-reality of thinking which is isolated from practice is a purely scholastic question.[23]

Value judgements and a practical engagement in the situation being studied are inevitably present in scientific research. But value judgements are present 'as judgements whose ultimate significance depends on the degree to which they stand up to historical–practical verification or experiment, and hence on their capacity to be converted ultimately into factual judgements'. This connection between value judgements and factual judgements 'is precisely the link between science and politics, between knowledge and the transformation of the world, that Marx accomplished in the historical–moral field', while this co-presence within Marx's work of science and ideology represents, continues Colletti, 'its most profound originality and its strongest element'.[24]

It has been argued so far that geography possesses an object of analysis that enables it to be distinguished as a relatively autonomous field of study. Some of its problems stem not from the lack of an object but from the complexity

of its object and the inapplicability of empiricist epistemologies, and of the dominant conception of laws as constant
conjunctions between events, to its subject-matter. But,
once an alternative conception of laws as laws of social
mechanisms is adopted, these difficulties can be overcome.

What we now want to do is to look at two central concepts distinguished in discussing the object of geographical
analysis. They are the concepts of nature and space. Both
of them must be reconceptualised along materialist lines by
building on the notions of material and ideal causality
introduced above.

3 The Concept of Nature

The question of the relation between human beings and nature has been one of the central themes in geographical thought. Geographical writing on this issue has, however, tended to underemphasise the role of social determinations, and to have been dominated by naturalistic ideologies, that is by theoretical frameworks concerned explicitly or implicitly with the conditioning of human individuals by nature and with the determination of geographical forms by natural conditions. These theories tend to focus upon two processes:

(1) The first is a conditioning of human thought and human activity by an individual's own physical and biological structure; that is a conditioning by his or her own nature as a natural human being. The identification of this relationship is frequently associated with an immediate reduction of human social and cultural forms to the underlying biological characteristics of the human animal, or even with a reduction of a human being to what he or she has in common with other animals.

(2) The second is a conditioning human thought and activity by external nature; that is, a conditioning by the natural or geographical environment. In this case the human individual is considered to respond in some direct but usually unspecified way to his or her environment, sometimes in a manner influenced by his or her biological characteristics.

These theories tend, therefore, to stress the primary significance of predetermined biological and environmental conditions, and to designate these conditions as the base on which human social and cultural structures are subsequently established and by which they are conditioned.

Both of the processes outlined above are based on misleading conceptions of the relation between the human and natural world. The first process simply reduces human and social conditions to biological conditions and fails to recognise the specificity of the human individual as a natural being, and the radically new contribution with respect to the animal world made by the appearance of human labour and the social relations of production in human societies. As a result, this view is associated with an unhistorical and naturalistic conception of human beings and human society, and, by uncritically projecting contemporary conditions backwards and forwards, it leads to the interpretation of certain broad historical and social forms such as private property and class division as being inherent in humanity. The second process posits an unmediated relation between human beings and external nature, or one operating through biological processes of competition, selection, and adaptation. The effect of nature on human beings is, however, always mediated through society and varies therefore with the form of social organisation, while what is called the natural environment is increasingly shaped by human activity, which has changed it in accordance with its natural laws. Since the natural context is increasingly the product of human activity, many problems that are frequently attributed uniquely to nature, such as the occurrence of natural hazards like floods, and their impact on human beings, depend in fact upon the way in which human societies have altered nature and upon the extent to which measures of prevention and control have been implemented.[1]

Now the physical and biological framework provides certain very general conditions within which the process of human social reproduction takes place. But, in the absence of human intervention, changes in environmental conditions and in the genetic constitution of human beings take place at a much slower tempo than changes in economic, political, and cultural arrangements, and so they cannot conspicuously differentiate the phases of human history or explain the changing forms of human spatial organisation.[2] A satisfactory theory must be based instead on the primacy of economic and social structures, and must designate this level, conceived as including the relevant natural and biological conditions, as the basis of the changing modes of human appropriation of nature, of human social and cultural development, and of the evolution of their territorial structures.

In outlining their own conception of history, Marx and

Engels attributed an important place to physical and biological circumstances, but they did not interpret these
conditions naturalistically. As they pointed out in *The
German Ideology*, the premises of their materialist conception
of history are 'real individuals, their activity and the material
conditions of their life, both those which they find already
existing and those produced by their activity'. The existence
of living human individuals and their material context are, in
fact, the first premises of human history, and the first facts
to be established are the physical organisation of these individuals and the geological, oro-hydrological, climatic, and
other natural conditions in which they find themselves. 'All
historical writing must set out from these natural bases and
their modification in the course of history through the
action of [human beings].'[3] What are called geographical
and biological conditions therefore play a role in the materialist
conception of history, and 'much recent Marxist writing has
probably gone too far in ignoring the role of natural milieux
in history',[4] especially in the case of early history, because
'the original conditions of production cannot themselves
originally be produced and are not the results of production'.[5]

The term 'nature' is used by Marx to describe those aspects
of reality that are both independent of human beings and
mediated or capable of being mediated with them, although
human beings are also conceived as being part of nature.[6] As
the material or matter with which human beings are faced,
nature is in itself already formed, and it is subject to physical,
chemical, and biological laws discovered by the natural sciences
in constant co-operation with material production.[7] This
connection between natural science and human production
was emphasised as early as 1844 in *The Economic and Philosophical Manuscripts*, when 'Marx had already discovered
that the productive activity of [human beings] is the basis
of their history and at the same time the indispensable
substratum of the history of nature, hence too of the natural
sciences, which from the dawn of history have developed step
by step with human productive activity'.[8] It is not possible
for a human being to defy the laws of external nature or to
escape the limitations imposed by his or her own physical
and biological structure, but it is possible for an individual

as a conscious and thinking being to acquire knowledge about them and to use this knowledge to satisfy his or her needs and aims.

For Marx a human individual is both a natural being and a thinking being, that is a generic natural being,[9] with a set of needs and conscious objectives which require satisfaction. These needs include: 'natural needs, such as food, clothing, fuel and housing', which 'vary according to the climatic and other physical peculiarities of his [or her] country', but the number and extent of his or her so-called necessary requirements, as also the manner in which they are satisfied, are themselves products of history, and depend therefore to a great extent on the level of civilisation attained by a country; and acquired needs, which are produced by human beings in the course of their productive activity and change in the course of human history.[10]

The production of human needs plays a central role in the materialist conception of history. In *The German Ideology* Marx and Engels point to three simultaneous moments of human social activity. The first historical act and the fundamental condition of all subsequent history is the production of the means of subsistence necessary to meet what Marx called natural human needs and to sustain and reproduce human life. The second point they make is that the satisfaction of this need and the act of satisfying it, which depend both on the physical organisation of human beings and on the material conditions of production, lead in turn to the creation of new needs. In the third place, individuals who are daily reproducing their own life also begin to propagate the human race through the act of human sexual reproduction, and the resulting increase in the human population plays a major role in expanding human needs.[11]

The relation between a human being and his or her needs on the one hand, and nature subject to natural laws on the other, is established in and through the labour process or human productive activity in which '[an individual], through his [or her] own actions, mediates, regulates and controls the metabolism between him [or herself] and nature',[12] while the starting-point for the elaboration of a satisfactory conception of the relation between the human and natural world and between social and natural processes is an analysis of the 'appropriation of nature on the part of an individual within and through a specific form of society', and hence an understanding of 'socially determined individual production' or 'production at a definite stage of social development'.[13]

In this chapter our main aim is to develop this argument in two stages, by examining production initially as a relation between an individual and nature and identifying those abstract elements common to all real historical stages of production, and by only subsequently introducing social determinations and the concept of the social relations of production.

As Colletti has pointed out, the key to understanding individual production lies in an acknowledgement of the co-existence and interpenetration of two simultaneous processes, namely a material process and a teleological process, while

> the simultaneity of these two processes, each of which is the inversion of the other, but which together form the *umwälzende* or *revolutionäre Praxis* referred to in the *Theses on Feuerbach*, is the secret of and key to historical materialism in its double aspect of causation, or materialism, and finality, or history.

In traditional materialism human beings are seen as products of their environment, but it is forgotten, according to Marx, that human beings in turn change their circumstances. It is not therefore enough to consider practical—material circumstances as the cause, and human beings as their effect. The opposite process must also be taken into account. Human beings are an effect of objective material causes, but they are 'also the cause of this cause', and 'the latter is also the effect of its own effect'. In order to explain this argument, Colletti continues by pointing out that, as a product of objective material causation, a human being is also and simultaneously the beginning of a new causal process, opposite to the first, in which the point of departure is no longer the natural environment but a concept, idea, or mental project of the human agent. This second process, whose prius is an idea, and in which, therefore, the cause is not an object but a concept, the object being the goal or point of arrival, is the so-called final causality, the finalism or teleological process as opposed to the efficient causality or material causality in the case of the first process. 'An end', according to Kant, 'is the object of a concept in so far as this concept is regarded as the cause of the object, the real ground of its possibility, and the causality of a concept in respect of its object is finality.' In other words, finalism inverts the sequence of efficient causality. In the latter case the cause precedes and determines the effect, while in the former case the effect is an end, an intentional goal, and therefore it determines the efficient cause, which in turn simply becomes a means to accomplish it.[14]

These two processes are central to Marx's conception of human productive activity or human praxis, while human labour provides the essential link between human beings and external nature, since it includes:

1. the action and effect of a human being upon nature, because the product of labour is the objectification or externalisation of the labourer's subjective ideas, the realisation of the idea or project with which the labourer set about his or her task, and the result of a process in which nature has been adapted and made to conform with the labourer's needs and aims; and
2. nature's action and effect on human beings, since in the labour process an individual adapts him or herself to nature by recognising and taking account of the specific nature of the materials employed and by changing the form of matter in accordance with its natural laws.[15]

Production is the objectification of human ideas. But the idea, or ideal motive, and the plans and designs according to which nature is transformed to meet human needs and aims, both determine the object and are determined by it, in the sense that nature can only be modified in accordance with its natural laws and by recognising the specificity of the materials used in the labour process. But, since the external world which conditions human beings has increasingly been shaped and altered by human activity, human beings are increasingly conditioned not simply by natural conditions and processes but by what they have made of nature.

The labour process is the process in which '[an individual], through his [or her] own actions, mediates, regulates and controls the metabolism between him [or herself] and nature'.[16] In its simple and abstract elements, common to all forms of society the labour process is composed of three elements: (1) purposeful activity, i.e. work itself or the use of labour power, by which Marx meant the capacity to work; (2) the object on which that work is performed; and (3) the instruments of that work. In the course of this activity the instruments of labour are used to effect an intended alteration on the object of labour in accordance with the relevant natural laws. The purpose of this activity is to produce use values that serve to satisfy specific human needs either as means of subsistence or means of production. The term 'means of production' is used to cover both the object and the instruments of labour. The object of labour includes natural materials provided directly by nature, 'which labour merely separates from their immediate connection with their environment', for example in mining, hunting, fishing, and forestry in so far as timber is felled in virgin forests, etc., and raw materials which are products of previous labour.[17] 'An instrument of labour is a thing, or a complex of things, which the worker interposes between him [or herself] and the object of his [or her] labour and which serves as a conductor, directing his [or her] activity on to that object. He [or she] makes use of the mechanical, physical and chemical properties of some substances in order to set them to work on other substances as instruments of his [or her] power, and in accordance with his [or her] purposes.'[18] In a narrow sense these instruments include natural materials and specially prepared tools 'through which the impact of labour on its object is mediated, and which therefore, in one way or another, serve as conductors of his [or her] activity'. In a wider sense we may include 'all the objective conditions necessary for carrying on the labour process' but which do not enter directly into it including 'the earth itself', which is 'a universal instrument of this kind, for it provides the worker with the ground beneath his [or her] feet and a "field of employment" for his [or her] own particular process. Instruments of this kind, which have already been mediated through past labour, include workshops, canals, roads, etc.'[19] What Marx called labour-power, or the capacity for labour, is 'the aggregate of those mental and physical capabilities existing in the physical form, the living personality, of a human being, capabilities which he [or she] sets in motion whenever he [or she] produces a use-value of any kind'.[20] Human labour, when it is combined with the necessary means of production, 'is itself only the manifestation of a force of nature, human labour power'.[21] Labour is, therefore, a process in which a human being 'confronts the materials of nature as a force of nature'.[22]

In the case of the abstract labour process, we find that both the subject and object of labour are ultimately determined by nature. On the objective side, human labour is dependent upon means of production furnished by nature without human intervention. Moreover, 'when [an individual] engages in production he [or she] can only proceed as nature does itself, i.e. he [or she] can only change the form of the materials', while 'even in this work of modification he [or she] is constantly helped by natural forces',[23] which include the active human subject. On the subjective side there are also natural constraints that limit historical change. The labour process is ultimately bound to the physiology of human beings, and labour's purposes are limited objectively by the material at their disposal and its laws, as well as subjectively by the structure of the drives and needs of human beings. Marx goes on to suggest that external natural conditions make possible and limit the productivity of labour and the associated multiplication of human needs, but he also emphasises that the productivity of labour 'is a gift, not of nature, but of history embracing thousands of centuries', and that with the passage of time the relevant natural conditions change and the natural limits recede.[24]

However, the ultimate determination of the subject and object of labour by nature provides a basis for rational action. In the labour process a human being acts upon external nature and changes it by altering the forms of matter in accordance with its natural laws. This 'active side' is neglected by traditional materialism. But once it has been created, the world of use-values, composed of human labour and natural material, confronts human beings as something objective existing independently of them, just as the material of nature itself confronted them before they had acted upon it.[25] Under pre-industrial conditions the objective natural moment is dominant, while in industrial society the moment of subjective intervention asserts itself in increasing measure over the material provided by nature. The more primitive a human being is, the more he or she is subject to natural limitations; the more advanced he or she is, the more human creativity dominates nature. Human beings are increasingly conditioned not by nature, but by what they have made of themselves.[26]

The relation between a human being and nature therefore involves a mutual interpenetration of an individual and nature within the natural whole. Marx described this relation with the term 'metabolism', indicating a process of circulation or exchange of material,[27] and he argued that the labour process is 'the universal condition for the metabolic interaction [*Stoffwechsel*] between [an individual] and nature',[28] where human labour includes both the action and effect of a human being on nature, that is, finalism or ideal causality, and nature's action and effect on a human individual and his or her activities, that is, efficient causality or material causality.[29]

The argument has so far been based on a conception of the human individual as a physical and natural being, whereas a human being is a social and historical subject, whose most essential characteristic is his or her involvement in social relations of production. It has also focused on production as a materially and teleologically determined process between a human individual and his or her natural setting rather than as a social process.

In *The German Ideology*, Marx and Engels pointed out how the production of means of subsistence and the reproduction of the human species lead to an expansion of human needs, an extension of the division of labour, and an increase in social intercourse paralleling the increased co-operation and interdependence of the agents participating in production. The development of the productive forces and the extension of the division of labour led successively to the separation of industrial and commercial from agricultural labour and of the town from the country; to the separation of industrial from commercial labour; and to the division of tasks between individuals co-operating in definite kinds of labour, with the relative position of these individual groups being determined by the way in which work was organised in these different spheres of economic activity. In their view, the various stages in the development of the division of labour correspond to different forms of property; that is, the existing stage in the division of labour determines also the relations of individuals to one another and their rights with respect to the material, instrument, and product of labour. From the earliest moments of human history the production of the means of human existence and the procreation of the species appear both as a natural relation and as a social relation

in the sense that it denotes the co-operation of several individuals, no matter under what conditions, in what manner, and to what end. It follows from this that a certain mode of production, or industrial stage, is always combined with a certain mode of co-operation, or social stage ... Thus it is quite obvious from the start that there exists a materialist connection of [human beings] with one another, which is determined by their needs and their mode of production.[30]

The interdependence of human beings is, in fact, the second implication of the two processes outlined above and the second central tenet of historical materialism. With the development of the division of labour, a human individual engaging in productive activity not only produces and reproduces his or her relationship with nature, but he or she also produces and reproduces his or her relationship with other human beings. In addition, the acceptance of Marx's definition of human nature as a series of functional relationships between a human being and nature, and between a human individual and other persons, means that human beings also produce themselves in the process of production, and that by acting on external nature and changing it they also simultaneously change their own nature, by altering their relationships to other persons and to nature, and by developing their own potentialities.[31] The reason for this is that

1. an individual's relationship to nature is at the same time his or her relationship to other persons, because the natural object is actually the objectification of human ideas, because production is intersubjective communication, and because, in the words of Marx, 'the sensuous world . . . is . . . the product of industry and the state of society', while
2. an individual's relationship to other persons implies his or her relationship to nature, because in order to relate to other persons he or she must relate to the natural object itself.[32]

It follows that 'for Marx, there can be no production, that is relationships of [human beings] to nature, outside or apart from social relationships, that is relationships to other [individuals] ; and there can be no relationships between [human beings] that are not a function of relationships of [human beings] to nature, in production'.[33]

Having originally been grasped with the concept of social intercourse introduced in *The German Ideology*, these relationships were finally expressed by the concept of the social relations of production, which Marx defined in the following way in *Wage-Labour and Capital:*

In the process of production, human beings act not only upon nature but also upon one another. They produce only by working together in a specified manner and by reciprocally exchanging their activities. In order to produce, they enter into definite connections and relations with one another, and only within these social connections and relations does their action upon nature, does production take place.[34]

In consequence, human production is always the 'appropriation of nature on the part of an individual within and through the mediation of a specific form of society'.[35] An analysis of the actual historical relation between human beings and nature, and an analysis of the spatial dimension of the process of social reproduction, must therefore start out from an analysis of the actual historical development of the productive forces and of the social relations of production. The starting point is, in other words, the material mode of production, or the material content of society, and the social form in which it is organised. The material mode of production is composed of human beings with their historically acquired capabilities as agents of production, such as skill, strength and knowledge on the one hand, and of the conditions and means of production on the other hand. The social form or the social relations of production in which these material elements are embedded gives these material elements new relational social properties, which are shaped by, but which also have an impact upon, the process of material development.[36] An acceptance of these ideas does not mean that natural laws and natural determinations are ignored. They have to be reckoned with in every form of society, but the particular structure of each society 'determines the form in which [human beings] are subjected to these laws, their mode of operation, their field of application, and the degree to which they can be understood and made socially useful'.[37] But it does mean that geographical theories that focus upon natural determinations and overlook the role of social determinations are completely inadequate and misleading as accounts of their objects of analysis.

The differences between these two approaches can be illustrated by outlining the differences between Malthusian and Marxist theories about the relation between population and resources. Malthus argued that surplus population and poverty were natural conditions stemming from the tendency for population growth to outstrip the available means of subsistence. Marx, on the other hand, sought to show how surplus population arose from determinate economic and political structures, from the effects of capital accumulation and the changing composition of capital on the demand for labour, and from the forms of integration of different social systems into a combined world system.

Malthus was an important representative of the landed interests in early-nineteenth-century Britain. He developed a theory of differential rent based on the law of diminishing returns, which attempted to show that rent is based on the quality of the land, and he sought to defend the Corn Laws, which ensured that landlords received high rents. He also developed a theory of effective demand, which was designed to show the possibility of a general over-production of commodities and the essential role of rent spent unproductively on consumption and personal services in maintaining aggregate demand.

His principle of population claimed that population growth would always tend to outstrip the available means of subsistence because, in the absence of checks on population growth, population would tend to increase geometrically whereas food supply would only increase arithmetically or, according to a second formulation of his thesis, because food supply would increase more slowly than population because of the law of diminishing returns. This principle led to the conclusions that poverty is a natural condition, resulting from the operation of an eternal law of nature, that misery is a necessary means of checking growing numbers and preserving a balance between population and resources, and that it is futile to attempt to ameliorate the conditons of the poorer classes. Widespread poverty was accordingly attributed to natural laws rather than to the organisation of society.

Both of Malthus's main propositions proved to be false. The rate of natural increase of the population has fallen, while improvements in agricultural productivity have increased food production. One of the main problems with this argument concerns the law of diminishing returns, which provided the theoretical foundation for the view that food production cannot increase as fast as population. This law is based on the claim that if all but one of a group of the 'factors of production', that is land, labour and capital, are held constant, the addition to it of equal additional amounts of the remaining factor or factors will result, after a certain point, in diminishing or increasingly small increments in total output, and it was applied initially to show that the application of equal additional amounts of capital and labour to a fixed amount of land would eventually lead to diminishing returns or to a falling marginal product. But this law only applies in situations in which the production technique remains unchanged (Figure 3.1). It therefore omits the question of the development of science and its impact on methods of produc-

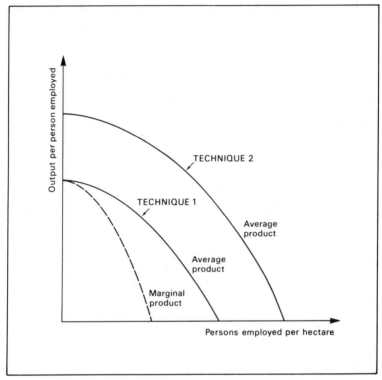

FIGURE 3.1 *Technical progress and agricultural productivity*

tion. This observation also entails an amendment of the Ricardian theory of land rent, because differential rent does not require diminishing returns but only presupposes different degrees of fertility on different plots of land or differences in the results from the application of successive amounts of capital and labour to the same piece of land.[38]

Marx observed that there is a tendency for bourgeois economists to represent capitalist relations of production as eternal categories and to fail to recognise the historical specificity of economic laws. Marx and Engels levelled these criticisms against the Malthusian principle of population. They argued that an abstract law of population only exists for plant and animal communities, and only then in so far as human beings have not interfered with them,[39] and they claimed that every type of human society has its own law of population. In the first volume of *Capital*, Marx argued that a surplus population is a relative phenomenon, and he showed how a relative surplus population can emerge under the capitalist mode of production as a result of the effect on the demand for labour of changes in the rate of capital accumulation and in the composition of capital. Accumulation with a constant composition of capital, that is a constant ratio of constant to variable capital, will normally lead to a shortage of labour, to increased wages, and to a reduction in the rate of surplus-value. The fall in the rate of surplus-value would then lead to a slower pace of accumulation and to a reduction in the demand for labour. The reproduction of a reserve of unemployed and under-employed workers would lead to a fall in wages, the restoration of the rate of surplus-value, and a relaunching of the accumulation process. Marx then proceeded to show how the increase in the demand for labour can be contained, and how the reconstitution of a surplus population and the reproduction of a reserve army are facilitated by changes in the technical composition of capital which reduce the relative importance of its variable constituent. [40]

One of the most striking applications of the population principle occurred in response to the 'famine' in Ireland in the period 1845—9, when the British government accepted a Malthusian interpretation of the origins of the problem, and rigidly adhered to what it thought to be the principles of political economy, providing virtually no assistance to the starving population. Yet, even though the population of the country fell from approximately 8.2 million persons in 1841 to 6.5 million in 1851, as a result of sharp increases in the mortality and emigration rates, a surplus population continued to exist, and as Marx pointed out, even greater losses would be required if the destiny of Ireland was to be the 'sheep walk and cattle pasture of England'. In fact net emigration continued, and the total population of Ireland continued to decline until the 1950s.

In contrast to other writers of the day, who attributed the problem solely to an imbalance between the quantity of resources available in the country and the size of its population, a point which can in any case be refuted empirically simply by noting that the quantities of food exported from the country during this period and the stocks of imported food which the government refused to release for fear of upsetting the market would have been more than sufficient to meet the needs of the entire Irish population, Marx pointed out that it was necessary to pay attention to the changes in the structure of production which lay behind the appearance of a surplus population.[41]

Malthusian theories have recently been revived. The contemporary neo-Malthusians argue that the limits now stem from the deterioration of the environment, disequilibria in natural systems, and the depletion of finite reserves of natural resources such as fossil fuels and minerals, all of which are attributed to population growth, and they believe that further technical and scientific progress in agriculture aimed at increasing food supplies will lead to additional environmental problems. These assertions lead them to demand controls on population growth, since it and not determinate economic and political structures is thought to be the unique cause of these problems.

Contemporary neo-Malthusians form part of a wider ecological movement, in which they can be distinguished by their emphasis on population growth as the central problem. The concept of ecology was originally introduced in 1868 by the German biologist, Haeckel, as the name for a subdiscipline of zoology. Having distinguished the functioning of a biological organism from its relationship with the outside world, he proposed that the word 'ecology' be used to designate the study of the relationship between animal species and their inorganic and organic environment, with the main focus being on the relation of animals with other animals and plants living in mutual association with them. The modern discipline is much wider and more complex than the one envisaged by Haeckel. It is concerned with the mutual relations of dependence between a community of plants and animals and its habitat, and it focuses on the establishment of balance or equilibrium in mature ecosystems.

The extension of general ecological research to include

human beings within its domain has resulted in the founding of a new discipline called human ecology. This discipline draws on the categories and methods of the natural and social sciences to study the relationship between human beings and ecological systems, and 'its central hypothesis is that industrial societies through the processes of industrialisation and population growth are producing ecological contradictions which must lead in the foreseeable future to their collapse'.[42]

Ecology is a natural science even when it includes within its domain the results of human activity. Human beings are natural beings, but ecological thinking does not provide an account of the reasons for human intervention, and any attempt to discuss these within this framework involves the transmutation of ecology from a science into a reactionary ideology. The connection between the natural world and ecological systems and the activities of human beings is social, and its explication requires an elaborated social theory or at least some basic assumptions about the historical process of social development.[43] The issues raised by human ecology can therefore only be studied by developing an analysis of the determinate economic and political structures and the specific social mechanisms which lie behind the appearance of surplus population, and which are leading to the destruction of nature and of balanced natural communities.

It is not unmediated natural and biological conditions but rather determinate material and social modes of production that determine the forms of appropriation of nature that have appeared in the course of human history. By recognising that so-called natural conditions are socially produced and that the effect of geographical conditions on human beings is socially mediated, and by claiming that determinate economic and social structures, that is the structures and relations of production, and not natural conditions are the basis of human society and culture and of their territorial structures, the framework of analysis advocated here will lead to a different interpretation of many problems traditionally studied in the geographical literature.

The argument outlined above also has implications for the concept of space. The conception of nature as a complex of natural and social conditions of production, and as in part a product of human intervention and human activity, plays a central role in understanding the structure of geographical space and, therefore, leads us towards a reinterpretation of another central concept in geographical thought. This reconceptualisation also has the advantage of uniting the question of relations between the natural and human world with that of the structure of geographical space. The aim of the next chapter is, therefore, to show that the spatial structure of society can be studied by analysing the mutual interdependence of (1) different social and material processes of production, and (2) the natural and socially mediated conditions of production in which they occur.

4 The Concept of Space

Space has been construed by geographers both as a natural space governed by natural laws, which is studied by the historical sciences of nature including physical geography, and also as a natural and social space studied by human geography. In the 1960s and 1970s the study of spatial forms and spatial structures, understood as including the spatial organisation of objects and persons, patterns of regional specialisation, and the functional connections between activities in different areas, along with the complementary elaboration of methods for the analysis of spatial systems, were perhaps the central themes of geographical research.[1]

In an account of the ways in which space has been analysed, Castells has argued that there has been a tendency for space to be considered either as a natural or quasi-natural framework which conditions human beings, or as something entirely fashioned by human thought and human action. He objected to both of these groups of theories on the general grounds that nature and culture are, as we have pointed out, indissolubly united in a dialectical process of historical development.[2]

Each of these types of theory provides a partial but significant insight into an understanding of spatial structures. In naive materialist theories emphasis is placed on the material and social conditions necessary for, and within which proceeds, the production and reproduction of the material means of human existence and of human life itself, but they tend to be analysed naturalistically.

In the case of idealist theories, on the other hand, there is a tendency to focus uniquely upon the ideal element that is contained in every material and social relationship between human beings and the world surrounding them. It is recognised in some cases that the ideal element is not simply a passive *post facto* representation in thought of this relation with external geographical conditions, but is in fact an active component of it. Yet the relationship between human beings and the conditions confronting them cannot be reduced to this ideal component even though it cannot exist without it.[3]

According to Godelier, these ideal realities include the scientific and technical knowledge used by human beings in acting on the natural and social world surrounding them, in controlling the processes occurring in it, and in transforming it into material and social means of human existence or what he has called intellectual means of production, such as taxonomies of climates, soils, plants, and animals, and rules for the production of tools and implements. They also include those concepts and rules necessary for the emergence and reproduction of the social relations within which production takes place. One example is the notion of kinship in hunting and gathering societies, such as those of the Australian aborigines. In these societies relations of kinship function as relations of production, since they govern the territory over which hunting and gathering can proceed, organise the composition of the groups engaging in these activities, and determine the division of the product.[4] But the relations of kinship themselves cannot emerge and be reproduced from generation to generation without there being socially defined concepts and rules of filiation, alliance and residence on which a notion of kinship and non-kinship depends.

In our view the act of placing an analysis of the labour processes forming part of the overall process of social reproduction at the centre of a study of the reciprocal relations between human social activities and their spatial setting enables the material and ideal sides of human existence to be integrated into a single conception of geographical space and of the process of spatial development. On the one hand each labour process is conditioned by geographical circumstances and by its spatial setting, as the proponents of naive materialist theories suggest. But on the other hand it is through this process that the relation between human activity and its external conditions is regulated and shaped, and it is as a result of its mediation that these external conditions are increasingly a product of previous human activity and of humanly mediated natural processes. It follows that geographical space is in fact both the context within which the overall process of social reproduction unfolds, and the product both of the natural and social processes involved in those activities that form part of the social division of labour and of humanly modified natural processes by which it is reproduced and transformed. A second implication is that the aim of human geography can be defined as the analysis of space as the context for and an expression of the natural and social processes involved in the process of social reproduction, and as the study of the use and production of space by historically determinate societies. In the rest of this chapter our aim is to indicate how an analysis of these activities and of their material and social context can be developed in a way that will enable us to begin to elaborate a theoretical framework for the study of space and of its transformation. We shall begin by indicating the ways in which space acts as a context or framework for human activity. And in a second step we shall go on to discuss the ways in which it is modified by human action and by the processes of human social reproduction.

Space as a socially mediated context for human activity

In general we shall use the expression 'geographical space' to refer to a delimited part of the earth at its surface. The word will accordingly denote an extension of land or water and the air space above it, together with its material and social content and the spatial disposition of the objects and beings found within it. In other words, geographical space is a portion of nature and of the natural resources found both on and in the ground, in the water, and on the seabed, although a natural reality only becomes a resource when it can be used directly or indirectly to meet human needs, and when human beings have the technical means of separating it from the rest of nature and making it serve their ends. A natural reality consequently becomes a resource at a definite moment in history and for a definite period of time, at the end of which it is either exhausted or abandoned.[5] But geographical space also and increasingly includes the material and social conditions of production created by human activity in conjunction with natural processes and the human beings living and working in the area concerned. In short the expression will be used mainly to refer to the elements contained in an area and to the disposition of its content.

As they have been defined above, territorial or spatial structures are the naturally and socially given basis of human existence. In other words, they are the natural and social context or framework within which natural processes and the process of social reproduction take place, and by which these processes are conditioned in the sense that they are modified by the conditions in which they occur or are adjusted in order that they can be inscribed in a specific spatial context. The term 'spatial structure' accordingly denotes the set of material and social conditions that are necessary for, are used in, and shape, the material and social processes of production forming part both of the social division of labour and of the processes of production, distribution, circulation, and consumption. On this account, spatial structures give rise to significant and inseparable relational and non-relational properties, and can in fact influence the overall trajectory of the society concerned.

It is possible to distinguish two interdependent aspects of geographical space as a societal framework.[6] In the first place, space is a use-value in the sense that it is a necessary material condition for the processes of production, distribution, circulation, and consumption comprising the process of social reproduction. Many of the facts about the geography of a society are in this case facts about its productive capabilities. This material environment includes:

1. Space or land as an objective condition necessary for any labour process, in the sense that it is required as a simple support for the means of production, distribution, circulation, and consumption, and that it serves 'as a foundation, as a place and space providing a basis of operations' whose shape and location have implications for the character and effectiveness of the activities taking place upon it.[7]
2. Space or land as a segment of nature or more usually of humanly modified nature that acts as a means of production,

circulation, or consumption, as in the case of resource deposits, waterfalls, navigable rivers, agricultural land, and buildings. It may act, for example, as an object or instrument of labour entering into direct, individual production processes. Alternatively it may provide certain general but necessary use-values or infrastructures not introduced into the direct production process, such as physical conditions of exchange, means of communication and transport, and collective means of production like irrigation facilities. In the absence of general conditions of this kind production could not take place or could not take place as effectively. In most cases the use-values concerned are necessary for other related labour processes on which the success of a number of specific processes of production collectively depends.

3. Space or locality as a zone inhabited by a certain number of human beings living at a certain relative density with specific, historically acquired productive capabilities and human needs.

4. Space as a site with certain advantages and disadvantages for certain kinds of activities by virtue of its location relative to other means of production and reproduction of a social formation, such as supplies of available labour and means of production and transport. The possibility of combining and of facilitating interaction between different objects and processes by integrating them geographically gives rise to certain useful effects which are sometimes referred to as the useful effects of agglomeration or external economies.[8]

In other words, geographical space is composed of the specific material conditions necessary for the labour processes forming part of the social division of labour, and useful objects necessary for the reproduction of human life, while its content and configuration as a use-value constrain and limit the processes of material production, distribution, circulation, and consumption and its own reorganisation.

As well as being a use-value that is used in and shapes individual labour processes, geographical space is also, and in the second place, subject to a system of property rights, that is to the conventional or legal expression of the relations of production. Areas of land and the useful objects they contain are always subject to a set of abstract rules of property or possession regulating the ownership and the alienation and transmission of land and its material and social resources, and determining access to them and their control and use in concrete processes of appropriation. These rules are usually embodied in normative principles backed by processes of legitimation, and by various types of repression or sanction prescribing certain forms of conduct and forbidding others, and they are organised into heirarchical systems. Access to natural and humanly created resources and their appropriation always take place within and through specific sets of property rights and relations of production. These rights determine the form of access to the social and material conditions existing in geographical space and organise and influence the specific form of the labour process. They also give rise to certain forms of distribution of the product produced in the social process of reproduction, and they define the broad inequalities between the members of a society and, in the case of class-based societies, its major class divisions.[9]

Space as a product of human social activity

These spatial and territorial structures are, however, continually reproduced, modified, or transformed by the processes taking place in this naturally and socially given spatial framework. The existing and new human activities forming part of the social division of labour take place in and use this historically produced spatial framework, and they lead in their turn to the reproduction and modification of the inherited spatial structure and to the creation of a new spatial framework that will form the basis for subsequent human productive and non-productive activity. Industrial activities, for example, make use of the existing pattern of spatial differentiation inherited from the past, by locating and developing in those places where the material and social conditions required for their specific production processes are such as to provide the best opportunities for achieving the ends dictated by their form of organisation and the social system to which they belong. The location of industrial activities is dependent on socially mediated natural and socially produced conditions of production and reproduction and on general relations of interdependence within production, that is, on an industrial space developed and transformed by previous industrial and human activity. It follows that spatial and territorial structures are also the outcome, product, or result of specific natural and social processes. These processes include those through which use-values, which are to function as means of production in subsequent cycles of production or as means of consumption for the agents engaged in production, are produced, and through which the social relations of production and the social position of the agents of production in relation to one another are reproduced. In other words, spatial structures are produced and reproduced through the action and effect of human beings and human activities, through the operation of humanly mediated natural processes, and through the functioning of objective laws of social reproduction on and in an inherited spatial framework.

A more systematic analysis of the way in which spatial structures are produced and reproduced can be developed by building on the conception of the process of social reproduction outlined by Marx in the *Grundrisse*. In this study he pointed out that the historical process of social reproduction is composed of four interdependent moments: production, distribution, circulation, and consumption.[10]

Production is the predominant moment, and is defined as the process of appropriation of nature in accordance with human needs. It includes the totality of the individual labour processes forming part of the social division of labour in which use-values necessary for productive consumption or for the reproduction of the agents of production are created or transformed, and it entails a distribution of the agents and of the instruments of production among different kinds of economic, political, and cultural activity and between different localities.

Distribution is the second moment, and determines the way in which, and the extent to which, agents participating in production in a specific way share in the products resulting from their own activities and from those of the other agents with whom they co-operate in production. It is in the form of ground rent, for example, that landed property shares in the total social product, but this type of distribution presupposes the existence of large-scale landed property as an agent of production. In a similar way the products of economic activity destined for auto-consumption and of wage-labour performed by the members of a household in many types of society are distributed in a manner that is structured by, and that serves to reproduce, gender divisions and the relations of domination on which they are based.[11]

The third moment mediates between production and production-determined distribution on the one side, and consumption on the other. Circulation is, accordingly, the process in which products are transferred from those who own them at the moment when they have been produced to those who intend to consume them, and in which an individual acquires the products into which he or she wishes to convert the portion of the total product that he or she has been assigned in the process of distribution. The activity of transporting use-values to the place at which they are to be consumed is an extension of production into this sphere of circulation.

In consumption, the objects created in production are consumed either productively as objects of labour in new labour processes belonging to the next cycle of production, or personally, to secure the reproduction of the agents of production or those who have shared in the total product.

As a whole, this process, composed of four interdependent, material and ideal moments, reproduces the material basis of society and its individual members, but it also and simultaneously produces and reproduces the relations of production in which they exist and the social classes of which class-based societies are composed.

In the course of human history the structure of the space-economy, by which we mean the complex of economic and social objects and activities found in a specific area and its spatial arrangement, is increasingly a product of a spatial and functional differentiation of the process of social reproduction which itself unfolds on an increasingly wide scale.[12] But at any moment in time its structure can be conceived as a physical and functional system which is reproduced in the course of the processes of economic and social reproduction centred in the locality. It is composed of four interdependent elements:

1. Production, or the spatial expression of the means of production and of the general conditions of production; that is, the distribution and characteristics of those activities involved in the production of use-values and the geographical location of the various lines of agricultural and industrial production.
2. Consumption, or the spatial distribution of the agents participating in the processes of production, distribution, consumption, and circulation, and of the individual and collective means of consumption necessary for their reproduction; that is, the spatial expression and characteristics of those activities relating to the reproduction of the agents of production and to the individual and social appropriation of the products of human activity.
3. Distribution, or the spatial expression of the flows of claims on the social product between agents participating in different ways in production and circulation or controlling resources necessary for these activities; that is, the spatial expression and characteristics of the claims deriving from the system of property rights and from the social relations of production.
4. Circulation, or the spatial distribution of the means of material and social circulation and the geography of the exchanges within and between the activities of production and consumption; that is, the spatial expression and characteristics of the means of communication and transport, of the activities of commercial and financial institutions, and of the functional connections within production, within consumption, and between production and consumption.

In some ways the concept of a spatial system outlined above resembles the one developed by Castells.[13] It must be emphasised that in actuality it differs radically from it, in that it is underlain by a conception of human praxis and human agency that is quite different from the one advanced by Althusser on which Castells drew.[14] In addition, it must be stressed that what we have called the spatial organisation of these elements of the overall process of social reproduction depends upon a complex set of interdependencies between them, and, in particular, can only be understood as an inseparable part of processes that are simultaneously economic, political, and ideological. The spatial dimension of the elements we have identified cannot, in other words, be separated from the other qualities they possess or from the social and historical processes to which they belong.

It is possible to extend and develop this conception of a spatial system in a number of ways. One is by differentiating the activities of production, distribution, circulation, and consumption according to the relations of production by which they are structured. It is to this task that we shall turn in the next chapter.

5 Modes of Production and the Structure of the Space-Economy

By placing human social activity and human labour at the centre of geographical analysis and by using a more social and historical conception of the economy, geographical theory can be reconstructed by drawing on the classical tradition in political economy. In the seventeenth and eighteenth centuries the spatial dimension actually played a central role in economic analysis,[1] while early-nineteenth-century economists like Ricardo and Marx situated geographical issues in a wider social and economic context.[2] But, from their time, locational analysis developed as a separate and largely independent branch of study, while economic theory tended to conceive most economic processes as taking place on the head of a pin. A renewed interest in this earlier tradition means, therefore, that a link can be established with a mode of analysis of economic and social processes that has paid more attention to, and is more appropriate for, the study of geographical questions.

It does not follow that geography is a part of political economy. It will continue to be distinguished from economics and from neighbouring fields of study by its specific object of analysis, that is the spatial forms of human appropriation of nature and of human social organisation, by the formulation of theory to account for this object, and by the construction of theoretically informed studies of concrete processes of spatial development. Geographical space is both historical and social and

is completely inscribed in nature, but geography is neither history, nor economics, nor a natural science. *Geography is the study of spatial forms and structures produced historically and specified by modes of production.* This definition does not lay any claim to open a new field of scientific activity or to resolve the conceptual and the methodological problems of geography. It is an element in the debate.[3]

One of the first attempts to use the concept of a mode of production in geography was by Harvey when he was trying to develop an account of what he called urbanism in *Social Justice and the City*, but at that time he came to the conclusion that it was not adequate as an analytical tool for the study of the relationship between society and urbanism and adopted instead ideas about modes of social, political and economic integration.[4] In this book one of our main aims is to show that concepts developed by Marx can in fact be used to study geographical phenomena. In order to do this it is necessary to explain in a little more detail what Marx meant by mode of production.

It has already been pointed out that at each stage of human history individual human beings start out from a historically created relation of human beings to nature and from the reciprocal relations of individuals to one another which each generation inherits from its predecessors. These inherited circumstances are modified by the new generation, but they also prescribe the conditions of its existence. The material and intellectual conditions of action on nature and of production of the material base of society, or what Marx called the productive forces, have a determining effect on the organisation of society and its transformation, although they do not give rise to necessary forms of social evolution. Societies do however have similarities with others, and form types with similar forms of functioning and specific and limited possibilities of development. The framework outlined above for the study of the reciprocal relations between the natural and human world, and of the production and use of space by historically determinate societies, can therefore be developed by outlining some of these broad characteristics of, and changes in, the structure of the mode of production and the functioning of the process of social reproduction.

Marx used the term 'mode of production' to designate both the labour process, system of production, or technical process of production, and the social form of production, or historical form of the social process of production. We shall generally use it to refer to a combination of a specific material manner of working, that is, a specific active relation of human beings to nature and specific method of using the productive forces to produce use-values, and a specific social way of producing, that is, production taking place within the context of a specific set of social relations between individuals.

In *The German Ideology* Marx and Engels distinguished four forms of property corresponding to various stages in the development of the social division of labour: tribal property, the ancient communal and state property of antiquity, feudal property, and modern bourgeois property.[5] Marx's own analysis of pre-capitalist modes of production was, however, largely concerned not with the mode of functioning of previous societies but with the establishment of the conditions necessary for capitalist development. In his account in the *Grundrisse* of the development of the relation of human beings to the conditions of production he focused on the historical process by which labour is separated from the objective conditions of production, that is from the land and soil, from the necessaries of human existence, and from the instruments of production, and comes to face them as alien property. He outlined, in other words, the dissolution of the relations in which the worker appears as a proprietor of the land and soil, as in the case of communal landed property and petty land ownership, the dissolution of the relations in which the worker appears as a proprietor of the instruments of production, as in the case of craft-based work and the guild system, the dissolution of the relation in which the means of consumption are possessed by the worker before production, and the dissolution of the relations in which the workers themselves belong directly among the objective conditions of production, as in the case of slave or servile labour.[6]

The starting-point of this historical process was the naturally arisen, tribal community which was based on the communal appropriation and use of the land and the objective conditions necessary for the reproduction of the individual and the community. In the view of Marx communities of this kind were characterised by a 'natural unity' of labour with its material presuppositions mediated only by membership of the community. These early communities were originally engaged largely in hunting and gathering, fishing, and cattle-raising, and only subsequently and to a limited extent did they establish forms of settled agriculture. In addition they were characterised by an elementary division of labour confined to an extension of the division of labour existing in the family or the kinship group. Marx distinguished four broad types of primitive community, or rather four alternative paths out of the primitive communal system, namely the Asiatic, Slavonic, Ancient Classical and Germanic communes. The major distinction between them lay in the predominance of different forms of property in the means of production and reproduction. In each of these types of community the process of production and the increase in population, aimed at reproducing the individual proprietor and his or her family, at reproducing their relation to the commune, and at reproducing the commune as a whole, were at the same time new production, which gradually modified and suspended the objective and subjective conditions on which it was based rather than reproduced them, and led to the decline of the communal system.

The second and third forms of property distinguished in *The German Ideology* were further developments of the property relations resting on the clan system. Ancient communal and state property proceeded 'from the union of several tribes into a city by agreement or by conquest', and was accompanied by the continuing existence of slavery, which had developed with the disintegration of the communal system. Communal property that included the property of the citizens in the city slaves was the main form of property, but private property emerged alongside it. By now, the division of labour was more elaborate. Industrial and commercial labour had already been separated from agricultural labour and was the basis of the distinction and opposition between town and country, while opposition between states representing urban and rural interests and between industry and maritime commerce within the town emerged with the development of this system.[7]

Whereas classical antiquity started out from the city and its small territory, and its history was the history of cities

founded on landed property and agriculture, the Middle Ages
started out from an extensive and sparsely populated countryside, and its history proceeded through the contradiction
between town and country.[8] Feudal property assumed the
form of a hierarchical structure of land-ownership in the
countryside, giving a feudal nobility power over a subjected
producing class, composed in this case not of slaves but of
servile peasants. In the towns that developed in this period
property assumed two forms. One was individual ownership
of one's own labour and of small capitals, composed almost
solely of the necessary tools of a craft. The other was the
corporate property of the guilds of master craft workers and
merchants that in time was to confront, as an alien form of
property, the journeymen and apprentices and the casual
labourers who escaped into the towns from the surrounding
countryside. The division of labour was relatively underdeveloped, both in the countryside where it was rendered difficult
by the strip system alongside which rural industry developed,
and in the towns where there was no division of labour within
the guilds and little between them. But, where a division of
labour between production and trade developed, when it had
not survived from antiquity, it resulted in the formation of a
special class of merchants.[9]

The evolution of feudalism subsequently led in most cases
to a transition from feudalism to capitalism, and to the establishment of the bourgeois form of property. But it must be
emphasised that these forms of property were not conceived
by Marx as the economic bases of systems of production that
succeeded one another chronologically, and were not presented as an account of the actual course of human history.
They were presented instead as forms of property that could
be differentiated from one another by virtue of the fact that
they were based in most cases on ownership by the immediate
producer of different combinations of the objective conditions
of production, and that they constituted the economic foundation of different types of community. At one pole the
immediate producer owned or possessed the land, the instrument, and his or her own capacity to work. In other types of
community one or more of these elements was owned or
possessed by other persons. At the same time the different

forms of property were identified as analytical stages in the process by which the labourer was separated from, and ceased to be included among, the different objective conditions of production. In fact, what Marx was presenting was a logical history. The actual course of events was infinitely more complex, and it, together with the changing relations between town and country and changes in the pattern of spatial development with which it was associated, can only be understood by developing more concrete historical accounts and analyses of the internal dynamics and actual evolution of different types of society. In the next part of the book it is to this task that we shall turn.

Part II

The Geography of the Transition from Feudalism to Capitalism

Introduction: Modes of Production and Spatial Development

In the first part of this book we introduced the concepts of efficient and ideal causality, and we used them to develop an abstract account of (a) the role of human activity in shaping and forming the world in which human beings live and in creating and modifying the structure of the space-economy, (b) the manner in which human activity is itself conditioned by social and by socially mediated natural and technical conditions, and in which such conditions function as means and instruments for achieving human aims and projects, and (c) the way in which the conditions with which human beings are confronted are increasingly the result of previous human activity. In our view, a satisfactory conception of process in human geography must lie in a recognition of the centrality and interdependence of the processes associated respectively with the concepts of efficient and ideal causality and of the dialectical consequences of their interaction. In other words, it lies in an acceptance by geographers of arguments constituting the linchpin of Marx's materialist conception of history.

At the end of the last chapter four forms of property corresponding to various stages in the development of the forces of production were distinguished: tribal property, ancient communal and state property, feudal property, and modern bourgeois property. In this part of the book we intend to focus on the last two forms of property and the corresponding stages in the development of the social division of labour, and our aim is to indicate some of the broad connections between them and the process of spatial development. More specifically we shall try to show how some of the main changes in the structure of the social and economic system, and in the process of social reproduction in Britain and in some other parts of Western Europe in the years since the establishment of a developed feudal mode of production in England in the eleventh century, have been associated with a continuous modification of, and adjustment to, existing forms of spatial differentiation and, in the longer term, with markedly new forms of use of geographical space. In examining the spatial dimension of the process of social reproduction, attention will be focused in particular upon the changing geographical concentration of economic activity, changing relations between town and country, and the changing pattern of regional specialisation.

It is necessary, however, to qualify and clarify our intentions in a number of ways. In the first place it has to be recognised that a task of this kind, involving generalisations about the course of history, could not be properly accomplished even in many lifetimes of research. Our aim is, in fact, a more modest one of developing and applying the ideas introduced in the first section with a view to presenting some general hypotheses about the development of the space-economy in Britain and in Western Europe. Conclusions can only be drawn on the basis of detailed historical research. In other words, they presuppose a careful analysis of primary source material and of a much wider range of secondary material than we have been able to consider, on the one hand, and a much fuller specification of the causal processes connecting the structure of space and society, on the other. But historical research must itself involve the use of theoretical hypotheses, and must be directed towards the global comprehension of social systems and of their forms of development.[1] Otherwise, one risks sliding into the empiricism that is so characteristic of much of the traditional work in economic history and in historical geography. It is in this way that we would seek to justify the project we have set ourselves.

In the second place, emphasis is placed upon general mechanisms of development which lay behind long waves in the development of the economy and society of West-European countries, and an attempt is made to show how they were conditioned by and gave rise to specific types of geographical structure and specific forms of spatial development. A corollary of a concern with long phases of development is that particular attention is paid to turning-points at which the tempo and direction of development changed both quantitatively and qualitatively. Of course, processes of historical and geographical change are continuous, and important elements of continuity can be identified in the historical geography of Europe because of inertia, and because of the way in which structures inherited from the past are reproduced or modified in ways that preserve some of their main characteristics. In abstracting from elements of continuity we do not wish to deny their significance.

At the same time, the emphasis upon general determinations means that we tend not to be concerned with the complexity of historical and geographical events, and to abstract from much of the variety that can be identified both in the experience of those living in different regions and in the way in which general processes work out in particular localities.[2] In our view, it is by showing how hypothesised mechanisms of the kind we discuss were qualified and modified, and how they were supplemented by other processes, that the complexity of the actual course of human history can be reproduced.

In addition, the everyday actions of the common people and indeed of the dominant classes, which shaped and in some ways determined the course of history, tend to be underemphasised, while the specific ways in which the class struggles, of which processes of development and change were composed, were fought out are not documented in any detail. At the same time, the impact of class struggles aimed at transforming the relations of production, which were invariably present but which varied in intensity, is not given particular emphasis, largely because relatively more weight is attributed to structural necessity in determining the context and limits within which development proceeded, and in shaping the most general characteristics of the long-run evolution of space and society in an epoch that belongs to what Marx called 'the realm of necessity'.

For all of these reasons the studies that follow in this and in subsequent chapters must be viewed simply as preliminary accounts of some of the most general characteristics of the process of spatial development in Britain, and in some other parts of Western Europe, and of their connection with the overall functioning of society. In this part of the book we shall begin by examining the geography of the transition to capitalism, paying particular attention to (a) the genesis and structure of the feudal mode of production and of its characteristic spatial structure, and the transition from a feudal mode of agricultural production to a system of capitalist farming; (b) the development of medieval towns as centres of trade and industry, the characteristics of guild-based industrial production and of merchant capital, and the evolution of the urban system in pre-industrial Europe; and (c) the development and characteristic spatial structures of domestic industry, the putting-out system, and early factory-based industrial production, and the connections between these forms of industrial organisation and changing relations between town and country and changing patterns of regional specialisation. But, in examining these processes, we hope that we shall also be able to indicate the nature of the mechanisms leading to the establishment of a developed capitalist mode of production in England, and to present a brief account of the geographical framework within which the early phases of capitalist accumulation unfolded.

6 The Restructuring of Agricultural Space in the Transition from Feudalism to Capitalism

6.1 The genesis and structure of the feudal system

The development of feudalism in Western Europe was a complex and a spatially and temporally uneven process, but, broadly speaking, feudal societies emerged between the sixth and tenth centuries after the collapse of the Roman Empire and during or after the barbarian conquests. They were formed in most cases from a synthesis of elements released by the disintegrating slave-based mode of production, on which the Roman Empire had been constructed, and elements supplied by the communal modes of production of the invading Germanic tribes, as they had been modified by Roman pressure and by the form of martial organisation adopted by the army during the actual conquest.[1]

This synthesis resulted in a variegated typology of social formations. The core region of European feudalism was composed of Northern France and zones contiguous with it, in which there was a balanced synthesis of Roman and Germanic elements. In these areas feudalism assumed its classic and most developed form, while the resulting feudal societies had a profound impact upon outlying zones such as England where, in the years following the Norman Conquest, a centralised feudal structure was superimposed upon the feudal system which had been developing within Saxon society. In areas to the south of this core region, including Provence, Spain and Italy, 'the dissolution and recombination of barbarian and ancient modes of production occurred under the dominant legacy of Antiquity'. In Italy the urban civilisation of late Antiquity broke down to a lesser extent than it did in other parts of Europe, and 'municipal political organisation . . . flourished from the 10th century onwards . . . , while Roman legal conceptions . . . qualified feudal landed norms from the start'. In contrast, to the north and east of the core region, 'in Germany, Scandinavia, and England, where Roman rule had either never reached or had taken only shallow root, there was conversely a slow transition towards feudalism under the indigenous dominance of the barbarian heritage'.[2]

Within these major regions the spread of feudalism was topographically uneven. In mountainous zones manorial organisation was limited, and marginal but independent peasant communities continued to exist, while non-feudal societies with non-feudal agrarian systems persisted on the fringes of western civilisation throughout the Middle Ages in the Celtic uplands of Britain, in the islands of the extreme west, and in some Celtic enclaves on the European mainland itself. (Some of the places and areas referred to in the text are indicated on Figures 6.1 and 6.2.)

The economic systems of feudal societies were predominantly non-commercialised natural economies, that is non-market economies, were based on a low level of development of the material forces of production, and were characterised by the fact that consumption was the main object of economic activity. The output of feudal societies was almost wholly agricultural, and, while there were important regional contrasts between, for example, the agricultural systems found in different natural contexts, some 80 to 90 per cent of the population would on average be engaged in mixed arable and pastoral farming. An enormous proportion of this output was normally absorbed by self-sufficient communities and did not enter the market circuit.

The basic enterprise of feudal production was the feudal estate.[3] These landed estates were owned by lay or ecclesiastical lords. Initially and classically they were delegated grants of land vested with certain legal and political rights, and were given by a lord to a vassal in return for the vassal's doing homage and swearing an oath of fealty to the lord. The lords concerned would normally in their turn be the vassals of higher lords from whom they held delegated grants of land. In other words, a feudal system would at least initially be

FIGURE 6.1 *Towns and cities referred to in the text*

associated with the existence of a chain of dependent tenures and of a corresponding hierarchy of territorial lords composed, at the bottom, of local notables and, at the top, of great magnates owning immense stretches of land.[4]

Each estate normally consisted of several separate manorial units, while the land of the manor was usually divided into a demesne, which was directly cultivated for the lord, and

FIGURE 6.2   *Areas referred to in the text*

small- or medium-sized peasant plots, held by peasants who in the majority of cases were unfree in the sense that they were servile or dependent.[5] The peasants possessed but did not normally own the holdings they worked, but the relationship between lords and peasants was not characteristically a contractual one. In practice, a small number of producers who were not serfs were found in most medieval communities, often in the ranks of the landless labourers and smallholders. The members of this group were characterised by the fact that they had to render to the lord only those services with which their holdings, if they held land, were burdened, and by the fact that they were allowed freedom of movement and freedom to alienate their property. However, the majority of peasants were dependent. This second group included both those who were descended from slaves and were legally unfree in the eyes of public law, and those customary tenants who were not servile by birth, but whose subordination to their lords and control by the customary law of the estate were hardly distinguishable from those characteristic of peasants with hereditary servile status. The existence and enforcement of serfdom served to keep the peasants concerned on their holdings and guaranteed the payment of rent and the performance of services. But, even though they were required at some times and places to carry them out, the peasants who belonged to this group were characterised not by the performance of compulsory labour services but by the fact that legal regulations restricted their freedom of movement, freedom to marry and found a family, freedom to buy and sell goods and to dispose of their own capacity to work, and freedom to leave property to their heirs.[6]

This open institutionalisation of practical limitations on peasant freedom formed the basis on which feudal lords were able to extract a surplus from the peasantry. In other words, surplus appropriation was dependent upon certain politico-legal relations of compulsion. The surplus was appropriated in the form of labour services performed on the lord's demesne, and of rents in kind or, once the amount of money in circulation had increased, in money, and in the form of various taxes, legal payments, and seigneurial dues, including payments for the use of essential services monopolised by the lord, such as milling, baking, and grape-pressing. In addition to rent payments and to the seigneurial dues and levies which are sometimes referred to as *banalités*, peasants holding land were also subject to tithe payments and royal taxes.

The actual structure of the feudal estate varied quite sharply both at any moment in time and in the course of the evolution of feudal systems. The ratio of demesne to peasant arable tended to fluctuate by a large amount between different manors, estates, and regions, with demesne arable accounting for anything between 13 and 45 per cent of the total arable acreage, while the average and actual sizes of peasant holdings tended to vary even more sharply.[7] Some peasants possessed holdings that were large enough to fully occupy and support them and their families, and owned one or even two ploughs and plough teams, while a fluctuating group of smallholders, whose plots were cultivated with simple implements and were too small for the adequate subsistence of a family, would have to supplement its output by working on the lords' or richer peasants' lands. In addition, medieval rural communities contained craft workers with smallholdings of their own, and a minority of landless wage-labourers. The latter included workers permanently employed on the demesne, and a small group of temporary workers living on the edge of the commons.

Banaji has distinguished two extreme types of estate organisation. At one end of the spectrum were estates on which demesne cultivation with the aid of slave, servile, or hired labour predominated, and on which peasant holdings were subsistence plots and amounted to little more than a sector of simple reproduction. At the other extreme were those on which the demesne was unimportant, on which peasant holdings had the character of a sector of small-scale peasant production and were capable of generating a more or less substantial surplus over and above the immediate consumption requirements of a peasant family, and on which 'feudal incomes consisted mainly of monetary payments based on tithes and seigneurial rights'.[8] The second type of estate organisation came to predominate in much of Western Europe,[9] whereas the first one characterised the feudal system which was reimposed on the peasantry in Poland by Polish nobles with the increase in grain prices in the late fifteenth century, and which persisted until the eighteenth century, that is the so-called second serfdom.[10]

The characteristics of the rural landscape in different parts of medieval Europe depended, among other things, upon the type of equipment used in agriculture, the system of cultivation, and the density of population in the area concerned, but the broad structure of the mode of agricultural production was correlated with a distinctive form of spatial organisation (Figure 6.3). In the West, most peasant holdings were composed of a house and allotment situated in long-established hamlets or villages, strip tenancies dispersed more or less equally among the open fields which were devoted to arable crops and which surrounded the village enclosures, rights to share in the collective exploitation of common pasture and meadow land, and rights to use the broad uncultivated belt

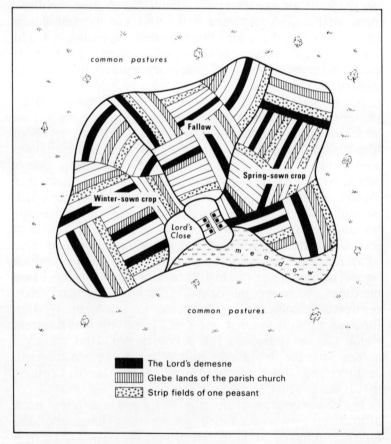

FIGURE 6.3   *A diagrammatic representation of a medieval village and of an open and common field system with a three-field cropping pattern*

beyond the village arable. The demesne was the land attached to the manor and possessed by the master. It was normally composed of an enclosure amounting to a small hamlet, extensive stretches of arable land, which in some cases would be concentrated in large parcels and in others would be dispersed in small plots over different parts of the lands of the village, meadow land, vineyards, and huge tracts of waste.[11]

In hilly pastoral areas, in newly colonised waste and wood land, and in the spaces between old-established settlements, instances of dispersed settlement were to be found, but by the tenth and eleventh centuries the landscape in the densely populated lowland areas of Europe, devoted mainly to cereal production and characterised by strong manorial organisation, was dominated by village communities. These villages were inhabited by peasants belonging to one or, more usually, to several different manors, were surrounded by open-field systems, and functioned as units within which collective forms of appropriation of resources were organised. In most cases villages of this kind would be separated from one another by extensive areas of wood land.

6.2 The functioning of the feudal mode of production

So far we have outlined the genesis of feudal societies in Western Europe and the structure of the feudal mode of production. What we now want to do is to examine the laws of development of feudal systems and the processes underlying the transition from a feudal to a capitalist mode of agricultural production. Three types of model have been used to explain these processes:

1. a demographic or population model based on Malthusian principles, in which population growth, the use of marginal land, and diminishing returns provoked a sequence of demographic crises and of booms and slumps in much of rural Europe;
2. a trade or commercial model associated with writers like Pirenne and Sweezy,[12] in which the dissolution of feudal societies is related to the external pull of urban markets and long-distance trade; and

3. a model emphasising processes of class formation and focusing upon the way in which class struggles led to changes in class relations and, in particular, to the separation of the direct producers from the means of production.

On their own none of these models provides an adequate account of the laws of functioning and development of the feudal mode of production, or of the transition from feudalism to capitalism in Western Europe, with the second model in particular paying scant attention to what happened in the countryside where many of the decisive changes occurred. However, by drawing upon the work of Banaji, Bois, Hilton, and Kula, it is possible to develop a more systematic account of the laws of development of feudal systems, and to show how the functioning and development of interconnected but unequally developed feudal societies led to the early establishment of a capitalist mode of agricultural production in England.[13] In constructing such a model and in outlining the process of transition to capitalism, we wish, in particular, to oppose demographic or Malthusian interpretations of medieval and early modern history, while at the same time recognising the significance of the secular fluctuations in population, output, prices, and wages, which tend to be emphasised only by writers belonging to this tradition. We shall do this by focusing more closely on material processes, and by integrating long-run trends in the level of economic activity into an overall conception of the socio-economic mechanisms characteristic of feudal systems and of petty-commodity production. Indeed only by understanding how systems of this kind function can one begin to develop an adequate account of the relations of class strength, of the class struggles, and of the transformations in class relations highlighted by analyses falling into the third group.

The feudal mode of production was an economy of consumption in the sense that the lords' consumption constituted the most important determinant of expansion in the feudal economy.[14]

[The] consumption requirements of the nobility and the perpetual need to adjust the level of income to rates of consumption were the most powerful determinants in drawing both lord and peasant into production for the market: the lord directly through the consolidation of a demesne economy, the peasant indirectly through the expanding weight of monetary payments.[15]

Because of the expansion of their consumption needs and the increasing cost of military and government activities the lords' demands for revenue tended to increase throughout the feudal period. However, the structure of the feudal systems in the medieval West was such that the rate of seigneurial levy, that is the levy imposed on each peasant, had a tendency to fall in the long run. In the view of Bois this tendency stemmed from a contradiction between small-scale peasant production and large-scale seigneurial property and, in particular, from a balance of power which was relatively favourable to peasant producers whose work was not closely supervised, and who belonged, in many cases, to strong village communities. But it was also a consequence of the low level of development of the forces of production and the slow improvement in agricultural techniques on the one hand, and of institutionalised relationships of surplus extraction which inhibited investment in new productivity-increasing methods of production on the other hand.[16]

In the conditions prevailing at that time, an increase in the volume of the seigneurial levy and in the rate of economic growth could for the most part only be obtained extensively, that is by bringing new land into cultivation and increasing the size of the peasant population, or by restricting access to forest and common lands, which had until then been freely exploited by peasant families, and depressing the standards of living of the peasantry. Seigneurial pressure accordingly led to phases of economic and demographic expansion. But the resulting processes of expansion were eventually associated with declining levels of labour productivity as cultivation was extended onto marginal land, and as reductions in livestock holdings made it more difficult to maintain existing soil fertility levels. At the same time, falling levels of labour productivity led to increases in agricultural prices, and were associated with a fall in the relative prices of industrial goods.

These price movements gave further encouragement to the use of marginal land. The results of these processes of economic and demographic growth, of the fragmentation of holdings, and of increasing food prices included an impoverishment of some sections of the peasantry and falling real wages. But one of the most striking consequences of the falling levels of labour productivity and of the subdivision of holdings which accompanied population growth was a fall in the rate of levy. The main reasons for this can be outlined with the help of Figure 6.4. By using the same method of production and bringing new land with successively lower levels of labour productivity into cultivation, and by farming it at the same level of intensity, 01_1 or $0'1'_1$, as existing land, the levy per person employed, or the amount appropriated by the lord, that is the net output per person employed less an amount required to enable the person concerned to reproduce himself or herself, declined. In other words, in the technical and social conditions prevailing in medieval Europe, the size of the levy could be expected to increase at first, but at a decreasing rate, because a fall in the rate of levy would initially be offset by the effect of increases in the size of the population and of the cultivated area. But, as expansion continued, it would tend to reach a ceiling and eventually to decline.

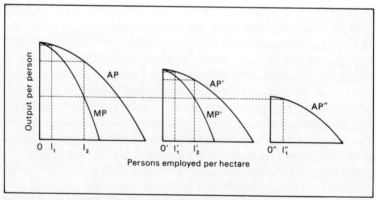

FIGURE 6.4   *Soil fertility and agricultural productivity*

Source: based on J. Robinson and J. Eatwell, *An Introduction to Modern Economics* (New York: McGraw-Hill, 1973)

Once the volume of the levy began to fall, the process of growth itself came to an end. In such circumstances the initial reaction of the seigneurial class was to increase pressures on the peasantry in order to secure a higher proportion of total output, even if it entailed depressing the share obtained by the common masses below the subsistence minimum. But very quickly the ending of the phase of expansion would give way to a protracted recession, characterised by the opposite tendencies to the preceding phase of growth (Figure 6.5).[17]

Bois has argued that mechanisms of this kind lay behind the secular phases of expansion that occurred in Western

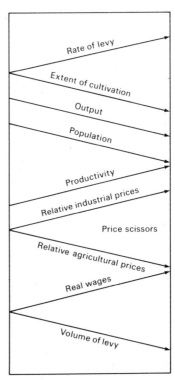

FIGURE 6.5   *The dynamics of a feudal system*

Source: G. Bois, *Crise du Féodalisme* (Paris: Presses de la Fondation des Sciences Politiques, 1976) pp. 357 and 359.

Europe in the twelfth and thirteenth centuries and between the sixteenth and eighteenth centuries, and that these waves of growth created conditions that were increasingly conducive to the development of agrarian capitalism. Increasing absolute and relative agricultural prices and falling real wages encouraged an increase in the size of agricultural enterprises, the concentration of the means of production in fewer hands, and a more widespread use of wage-labourers, on the one hand, and resulted in the complementary expropriation and separation from the means of production of some peasant families on the other hand. Any process of accumulation of this kind was, however, severely restricted by the structure of the feudal system. In particular it was limited by the low level of development of the forces of production and the absence of significant economies of scale, by the high levels of surplus appropriation in feudal societies, and by the defensive strength of village communities. However, in successive phases of expansion, these limits were gradually pushed back, particularly in England.[18]

6.3 The expansion and crisis of the feudal system

Considerable agricultural and demographic growth occurred in Western Europe between the eleventh and early fourteenth century, with the growth process reaching its high point in the late twelfth and in the thirteenth century. In addition, from the second part of the eleventh century onwards, this wave of expansion was accompanied by a slow growth of commercial activity.

Between the ninth and twelfth century improvements in the equipment and harnesses used in ploughing and improved ploughing techniques contributed to an increase in average wheat yields, expressed as ratios of output to seed, from about 2.5:1 to at least 4:1.[19] Waste land was reclaimed and used for arable farming. Initially this extension of the arable acreage occurred through the enlargement of established villages and village territories, but subsequently, and especially between 1150 and 1200, it resulted from the establishment of new hamlets and villages on formerly uncultivated waste land with the encouragement of the leading lords. In the thirteenth century a more active trade in meat, wool, and leather developed. When this occurred, the process of expansion tended to assume the form of the establishment, in the spaces between the villages, of dispersed rural dwellings and permanently enclosed plots devoted to pastoral activities.[20]

After 1250, grain expansion halted, and in the last years of the thirteenth century the limits of cultivation began to recede. On the other hand, the expanding trade in forest and pastoral products raised the value of uncultivated land, encouraged direct seigneurial exploitation of forest resources and the development of a pastoral economy dominated by them, and increased seigneurial pressure on common lands. However, the peasants responded by forming vigorous defensive communities, by intensifying production on village territories, and by struggling to retain as much as possible of the product of their holdings and to gain as much access as possible to common woods, pastures, and fisheries. In the situation depicted in Figure 6.4 the intensity of farming would normally be raised by increasing the amount of work per hectare from l_1 and l_1' to l_2 and l_2', at which points the marginal product on infra-marginal land would be equal to the marginal product on marginal land, but if access to marginal land were to be restricted, the intensity of cultivation might well be increased beyond this point as long as the increment in output accruing to the peasantry was greater than zero. In practice, in the years from 1250 onwards, a phase of internal conquest occurred, in which the length of the fallow period was shortened, crop rotations were improved and communally regulated, and the types of system classified as three-field systems were widely adopted.[21] However, these steps did not counteract the effects of the overall decline in labour productivity and the decline in lordly incomes which initiated the fourteenth-century crisis.

The albeit small improvements in farming techniques and the extension of the arable acreage referred to above were correlated with a major increase in population, particularly in the twelfth and thirteenth centuries. The question of the size of medieval populations is a subject of considerable controversy. Domesday England was much less densely populated than France. Its population has been variously estimated as standing between 1.1 and over 2 million persons in 1086, and as having reached a maximum of 7 million by 1300 (and a minimum of 3.75 million in 1346). The main concentrations of the Domesday population were in the predominantly arable regions in the east and south-east of the country, with the highest densities in East Anglia and Kent, and with densities declining as one moved westwards and northwards (Figure 6.6), while subsequent population growth was most marked in the old-established areas of settlement, and especially in Lincolnshire.[22] The growth in population that occurred in the twelfth and thirteenth centuries was not independent of other changes taking place in the feudal societies of Europe. Output depended to a large extent upon the area cultivated and hence upon the availability of workers and draught animals, while the sub-division of holdings and the opening of new land increased the availability of feudal tenures and often improved the terms on which they were offered, leading in turn to earlier marriage and a higher birth-rate. Variation in the age of marriage was probably the most important deter-minant of population growth and the mechanism by means of which the supply of labour was increased, but the small improvements that occurred in the methods of production also played a part by increasing the supply of food and lower-ing the mortality rate, although a lower mortality rate would also have limited the rate of demographic growth by leading to a reduction in the availability of new tenures for young peasants. But with the subsequent slackening of expansion, falling wages and employment, meagre grain harvests, and rising grain prices contributed to a renewed increase in mortal-ity rates. On this occasion changes in the rate of mortality were of more importance, playing a major role in the reversal of the process of demographic expansion that occurred in the fourteenth century.

The process of expansion was also associated with some important changes in the forms of surplus appropriation and in the social structure of rural England. In particular, in the twelfth century, the expansion of commerce and an increasing circulation of money led at first to the commutation of labour services into money payments, and to the leasing-out of

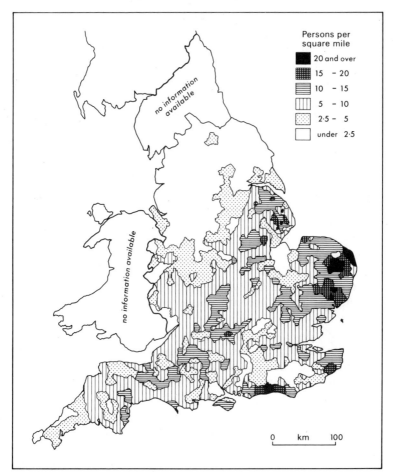

FIGURE 6.6   *The Domesday population of England*

Source: based on H. C. Darby, 'Domesday England', in H. C. Darby (ed.), *A New Historical Geography of England before 1600* (Cambridge: Cambridge University Press, 1976) p. 46.

demesne lands to tenants or the cultivation of such land with the help of hired labourers, whose availability was increased by the growth of population and the penetration of money dealings into the formerly closed circuit of peasant production, while, on the European mainland, feudal incomes were increasingly based not upon rents but upon the profitable exercise of seigneurial jurisdiction. By contrast, in the years between 1180 and the middle of the thirteenth century, in order to increase their cash incomes in a period of rising agricultural prices, landlords in England tended to get involved once again in production for the market, and resumed active cultivation of demesne lands, especially in arable farming areas in the south and south-east of the country in which demesne production had originally been more extensive. In order to obtain an adequate supply of labour, landowners who chose this course of action tried to reimpose labour services. The previous existence of labour services was used as a test for villein status, and villein tenure was established as servile, while continental tests for serfdom, such as merchet and heriot, were added to the list of seigneurial exactions. In this way the lords and the law-courts succeeded in imposing serfdom on customary tenants and in increasing the lords' revenues from them. As a result, the situation of the customary tenant in England was most affected by servile status at the end of the thirteenth and beginning of the fourteenth century.[23]

In addition, technical progress, which reduced the amount of land necessary for the subsistence of a family, and population growth, contributed to a fragmentation and disintegration of peasant holdings, while the mechanisms of growth encouraged a process of social differentiation within the peasantry. The effects of the first of these processes were clearly reflected in a decline in the average size of family holdings. The fragmentation of peasant holdings was accompanied by a depression of the living and working conditions and a marginalisation of the majority of peasants, whose holdings were inadequate in size, who were more severely affected by seigneurial exaction, and who, particularly on the eve of the fourteenth century, became enmeshed in a web of debt. On the other hand, a group of relatively prosperous peasants was also formed, in this case from the minority who succeeded in acquiring larger holdings. As a result, the fall in the average size of peasant holdings was accompanied by the appearance of marked differences in the sizes of peasant plots, and by an increase in the number of smallholders and landless labourers.

In time, this phase of expansion came to an end. By the

early decades of the fourteenth century the cash incomes of many estate-owners were stationary or declining, due to a crisis of demesne profits, difficulties in sustaining rent levels, or both. The fall in the volume of the seigneurial levy was followed by a more general economic and demographic crisis after which the stagnation in seigneurial incomes became much more severe, and by a period of feudal crisis lasting through much of the fourteenth and fifteenth centuries.[24]

The level of activity in agriculture, trade and industry declined. In addition, shortages of food and a succession of epidemics and pestilences led to a sharp increase in the mortality rate, particularly in the towns, which had grown rapidly in the early fourteenth century, and to a pronounced fall in population. It has been estimated by some historians that the population of England started to fall in the 1320s and that it was perhaps beginning to recover at the end of the 1340s. But with the arrival of the Black Death, at first on the European mainland and subsequently in England in 1348, the population of England was reduced perhaps by as much as one-half. The bubonic plague returned in the early 1360s and again in the mid-1370s. As a result, demographic recovery was delayed.[25] The demographic events of the fourteenth century were accompanied by a retreat of arable husbandry from the more marginal land, an expansion of pastoral farming, whose relative profitability had increased, and a conversion of land from arable to pastoral uses. In England, in the fourteenth and fifteenth centuries, some peasant dwellings and gardens, some fields, and even whole villages were abandoned, as agricultural activity was concentrated on more productive soils and as abandoned land was either put down to meadow or overwhelmed and allowed to lapse into waste and wood land.[26] But the most striking changes in the landscape occurred between 1450 and 1520, as we shall show in more detail after discussing the changes in class relations in English farming, and when we come to discuss the economic and material dimension of the events that occurred in the centuries of recession and of renewed expansion that followed the feudal crisis. In this period the expansion of sheep-rearing and of wool production was associated with a pronounced change in the use of land from arable to pasture farming, with the enclosure of many open fields, with the eviction of numerous tenants, and with the desertion of whole villages. Over 2,000 villages located mainly in the eastern part of England have been abandoned at one time or another. A high proportion of them were probably deserted during this phase of feudal crisis.[27]

Between the first plague and the 1370s, as a result of increased seigneurial pressure on tenants and labourers, the rents obtained by English lords were maintained, and wages were depressed. In these years laws designed both to keep down wages and to limit the mobility of labour were enforced as fully as possible, and the restrictive laws of servile villeinage were imposed on the peasantry. But the attempts made by landlords individually and collectively to maintain their hold over their tenants and labourers failed. The appearance of a surplus of land and of a general shortage of labour, along with the resistance of peasant communities and peasant flight, undermined the efforts of the landlords, and contributed to an eventual increase in the mobility of labour and to a material improvement in real wages and in the legal status of the peasantry.

In these new economic and social conditions direct cultivation of demesne lands ceased to be profitable. As a result, numerous demesnes were wholly or partially let out on noncustomary leases in the late fourteenth and in the fifteenth century. At the same time a large amount of land cultivated by peasants was withdrawn from the area of custom and turned into leasehold, while customary tenure itself was converted into copyhold by the act of issuing customary tenants with a copy of the entry in the court roll recording the tenant's admission to the holding. As a result customary tenure was found once more without the taint of servility, for copyhold was regarded as a way of holding land which involved a purely contractual relationship and carried no implications for the legal and social status of the tenant.[28] Consequently, by the end of the fifteenth century, serfdom had practically ended in England. By the end of the sixteenth century it was virtually extinct, not in the sense that labour services on demesne lands had been commuted into money rent, for this was not the distinguishing characteristic of serfdom, but in the sense that the conditions of customary tenure approached those of free tenure.[29]

In the years of feudal crisis extremely large agricultural enterprises were badly affected. On the other hand, substantial holdings both for arable and livestock farming were acquired by more prosperous peasants as well as by manorial officials and priests. In addition, the restructuring of agricultural production led to a consolidation and an increase in the average size of the arable holdings of the middle peasantry, and to a considerable reduction in the proportion of smallholders. Initially these changes in the structure of agriculture ushered in a period of untrammeled petty-commodity production.[30]

6.4 The diverging trajectories of French and English agriculture

A new phase of economic expansion began after 1440, but proceeded slowly and in only a few regions until the beginning of the next century. It lasted until about 1600 in Mediterranean countries and until 1660 in parts of North-West Europe. In the view of Bois, the growth process was accompanied, from 1510 or 1520 onwards, by a concentration of land and movable capital in the hands of the more prosperous members of rural society, by an increasing recruitment of wage-labourers, and by the impoverishment and proletarianisation of small peasants. In other words, the mechanisms of growth in this phase of European expansion were leading, in the West, in the direction of a system of capitalist farming.

In the sixteenth century agricultural prices increased, and customary rents soon lay far below those that would have prevailed on the open market. In addition, the new inflationary conditions reduced the real incomes of many landowners. The landlords responded by restricting peasants' rights to forest and waste land and exploiting the resources involved for their own benefit, and by raising rents on holdings on which they had fallen to a low level. Where peasant property rights were not well established, the actions of the landlords resulted in the expulsion of many tenants, and in the incorporation of peasant holdings into the lords' own farms, or in the formation of larger units which could be leased to capitalist tenant farmers. At the same time, urban interests were attracted by the fact that market rents were in excess of the remaining seigneurial dues, and proceeded to enter the land market on a larger scale and to purchase common land. In doing so, they gave an additional impetus to the dispossession of the direct producers and to the process of proletarianisation.[31]

The actual outcome of these processes in any country or region was strongly conditioned by the balance of class forces prevailing in the countryside. In other words, it depended upon inequalities in the world of feudal production.

At the end of the thirteenth century feudalism was most advanced in Northern France. 'By the density of its population, the volume of its agricultural production, and its place in international exchanges, it influenced the whole of Western Europe in the way that any dominant economy does.'[32] At the same time, demesne cultivation had declined, and small-scale peasant farming had been strongly established. In addition, the fall in seigneurial levies was more pronounced in the kingdom of France than in other European countries, and, as a result, the feudal crisis was more severe. But, by the middle of the fifteenth century, the crisis had led to a restructuring of the feudal system in France, and to a consolidation of the position of the middling peasants as proprietors. On the one hand, the addition to direct seigneurial levies of a centralised levy organised by the royal administration, and the development of monarchical or princely institutions, which guaranteed both the functioning of fiscal mechanisms and the maintenance of the seigneurial regime, enabled the lords to find some salvation in the state, while, on the other hand, the establishment of the peasants as proprietors, and the strengthening of the ties of the French peasantry with the land, made them more effective in resisting expropriation than their English counterparts. One consequence of these changes in the structure of the feudal system was that French lords were less inclined to explore new economic avenues. The mechanisms of growth still worked to slowly undermine small peasant property. Peasant holdings were sub-divided, taxation was increased, real wages for supplementary occupations fell, and many peasants were forced deeply into debt and were obliged ultimately to sell out. But this process of social differentiation was limited by the strength of village communities, and by the fact that the absolutist state generally supported heritability and fixed-fines for customary tenures, as a result of which French peasants were less easily separated from the land.

In England, on the other hand, the effects of the crisis were less severe, in part because of the relative backwardness of the English economy, and in part because the English nobility was able to resolve some of its problems temporarily at the expense of its French counterpart in the Hundred Years' War. In addition, the nobility responded to the continuing crisis of seigneurial incomes, indicated by the events of the Wars of the Roses, by exploring new economic solutions, and was relatively successful in doing so, since the rights of the English peasantry were not sufficiently well-established for it to retain control of the land in the face of seigneurial pressure. As a result, by the end of the seventeenth century, no more than 20 to 25 per cent of the cultivated land was held by owner-occupiers, and 70 to 75 per cent was in the hands of landlords who leased it out to capitalist tenant farmers, whereas, in France, some 45 to 50 per cent of the cultivated land was still in peasant possession.[33]

The reorganisation of French feudalism and the consolidation of the position of the French peasantry not only help to account for the differing trajectories of French and English society in the subsequent phase of agricultural expansion, but they also lie at the root of differences in their agrarian structures which are found in the twentieth century.[34] By virtue of having to a large extent led the way in the formation of European feudalism, and of having been the first to come up against a ceiling of growth, the replacement of feudal structures by ones capable of more rapid development was impeded in France, and the leading role in subsequent phases of economic development passed to producers in other regions.[35]

6.5 The development of a capitalist mode of agricultural production in England

At the time when the feudal crisis of the fourteenth and early fifteenth century was coming to an end, the land in rural

England was predominantly owned by large landlords and by the gentry. The incomes of these sections of the population increasingly came to depend upon land rent, while the collective strength of the landlords and gentry had been increased by their control of the sessions of the peace, which had replaced the manorial court as the focus of local power.[36]

Some land was owned and worked by a group of freeholders, but the manorial lands were generally held by copyholders and tenants-at-will, and by leaseholders composed in most cases of commercial farmers to whom some demesne lands had been let out at market rents on a leasehold basis. The strengths of peasant producers depended upon the size of their holdings, their conditions of tenure, the opportunities for exploiting their holdings, the degree of access to common lands, and the availability of alternative sources of income, but it had generally been diminished by the decline in the cohesive force of the village community. In fact, even though the rights of the English peasantry were too well-established to permit the reimposition of servile villeinage, they were not sufficiently well-established to enable the peasantry to retain control of the land in the face of increasing seigneurial pressure in a new phase of economic expansion.[37]

The pattern of land-ownership and land-holding was associated with a particular geography of agricultural production. In the sixteenth century the country could be divided into two broad agricultural zones: an area of open pasture, used mainly for cattle- and sheep-raising, in the upland zones in the North and West, and in the Gaelic and Celtic areas of Britain and Ireland; and an area of mixed farming in the South and East, with an emphasis upon cereal-growing in the clay vales and on light soils, and upon pasture farming in wood and fen land districts. Most arable farming districts were characterised by nucleated villages surrounded by common fields (Figure 6.3). But, outside of the Midland zone stretching from Dorset to the North Riding of Yorkshire, much of England was already enclosed, either because small, hedged fields had been constructed as and when waste and wood land were originally taken in for cultivation, or because of the early disappearance of the open fields. Most pastoral areas were accordingly characterised by enclosed landscapes and by more dispersed types of settlement.

It was by setting out from and modifying this situation that economic and political processes operating over the next three centuries resulted in the slow establishment of capitalist farming as the predominant mode of agricultural production in England. Between 1650 and 1750, in particular, squeezing pressures were placed on smaller freeholders and on the lesser gentry, both of whom found themselves unable to cope with falling prices and rising taxes, and, although wealth acquired in external trade and in internal economic activity was used to purchase landed estates and to build country houses, land-ownership came to be concentrated in the hands of a small number of large land-owning families. By the end of the seventeenth century large landowners controlled between 70 and 75 per cent of the cultivated land, and by 1790 the great landlords and gentry owned between 80 and 85 per cent of it.[38]

So, from 1500 onwards, the independent peasantry was slowly eliminated as a significant element of the social struc-ture of rural England, and the latter came to be characterised by the existence, at one end of rural society, of a class of capitalist tenant farmers, renting large farms from a market-oriented landlord class, and operating them with the help of wage-labourers, and, at the other end, of a substantial class of landless labourers, formed as a result of the separation of the peasant class from its means of production and consumption on the one hand, and as a result of the effects of population growth on the other.[39] In outlining the way in which the process of social differentiation occurred, it is helpful to divide the period up into at least two parts.

In the sixteenth and early seventeenth century a class of yeoman farmers, composed of freeholders and secure copy-holders, formed some 20 to 25 per cent of the land-holding population. Until about 1650 this group prospered, and some of its members rose to the ranks of the gentry (Figure 6.7). By contrast, less prosperous sections of the peasantry were placed under pressure as landlords succeeded in increasing annual rents and entry fines, in enlarging and consolidating holdings to form large and compact units which could be let to capitalist tenants on a leasehold basis, and in evicting some groups and depriving them of their customary rights.

But in the years between 1650 and 1750 the peasantry as

114

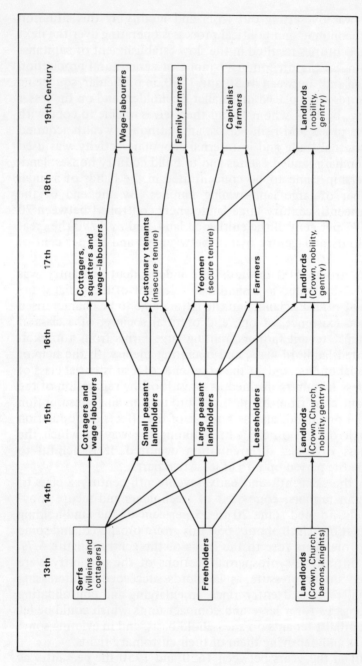

FIGURE 6.7 *Social classes and social mobility in English agriculture from the thirteenth to the nineteenth century*

Source: W. Lazonick, 'Karl Marx and Enclosures in England', *Review of Radical Political Economics*, vol. 6, no. 2 (Summer 1974) 1–32, p. 7.

a whole was confronted by much more serious difficulties, and by the end of the eighteenth century small owner-occupiers only accounted for the ownership of some 11 to 14 per cent of the cultivated land.[40] In years that were ones of agricultural depression in Europe, continuing technical change and a changing pattern of regional specialisation in English agriculture increased competitive pressures on small farmers, and, in conjunction with a switch towards pasture farming, forced a sharper differentiation and process of proletarianisation within the peasantry. More prosperous peasants managed to retain or enlarge their holdings, hired workers, and joined the ranks of the capitalist tenant farmers, or less frequently became commercially-oriented owner-occupiers. On the other hand, after the defeat of the radical movement, whose aims had been to gain economic and political independence for copyholders, to prevent land subject to common rights of use from being enclosed, and to protect small individuals, and after the legal and political changes consequent upon the English Revolution, less prosperous peasants who had formed a significant component of the base of the Levellers found themselves without the security of tenure for which they had pressed. In addition they had been weakened by the decline of the village community. In the new economic circumstances this section of the peasantry was increasingly engaged in production for the market, and many of its members were forced out by their inability to compete with more prosperous improving farmers.[41] At the same time, cottagers and squatters continued to be separated from their holdings and to lose their rights to use the commons, to be proletarianised, and to become increasingly dependent upon wage-labour and rural industry for their living. The process of proletarianisation, along with the dissolution of the monasteries and the reduction in the size of feudal households in the first half of the sixteenth century, played a major role in the original formation of a class of landless labourers. But once a proletariat had been created it continued to increase in size, not only because of continuing proletarianisation, but also because of a growth in the size of the peasant population beyond the level necessary for simple reproduction, and in particular because of increases in the size of already proletarianised families. By 1750 it had

become the largest social group in the countryside.[42] At the
end of the eighteenth century, and even in 1851, the small
farm continued to be an important element of the rural landscape. It was, however, more important in Scotland and Wales
than in England, and, in England itself, it was more important
in the west and the north west than in parts of the midland
and eastern counties. But the most striking feature of English
farming at this time was the existence of large farms using
hired labourers and working almost wholly for the market.[43]

The development of a system of capitalist farming also
entailed and to some extent presupposed the development of
new methods of agricultural production, which could not be
fully developed within the preceding form of agrarian organisation. In addition, the changes that occurred in the material
and social dimensions of agricultural production led to marked
changes in the pattern of regional specialisation and in the
appearance of the rural landscape. In the rest of this section
we shall try to provide a brief account of the main phases of
economic and agrarian development, and of the steps leading
to the enclosure of the remaining open fields and common
lands and to the creation of a network of individually tenanted
farms in enclosed rural landscapes.

In the years following the feudal crisis the rural economy
participated in a phase of growth that can be divided into
two stages. Between 1450 and 1520 wool prices and those of
animal products increased more rapidly than cereal prices,
with wool prices being strongly influenced by the expanding
demand for cloth. In areas suitable for pastoral activities,
increasing prices and the rising profitability of producing
wool and animal products led the landed classes to try to
extend sheep-rearing and pastoral farming, with their low
labour requirements, and to lay their hands on the open fields
and common lands, to enclose them (that is, to consolidate
the land into compact holdings and hedge it), and to put them
down to pasture in order to raise animals. In some cases the
decision by landlords to enclose and to convert land from
arable to pastoral uses resulted in a sharp reduction in the
local demand for labour, and in the depopulation of whole
villages. As a result, enclosure was strongly opposed, particularly in the densely populated clay-land areas in the midland

counties, and government legislation restricting depopulating enclosures was introduced. In conjunction with the subsequent increase in grain prices these measures helped to curtail enclosures of this kind.[44]

Between 1520 and 1650 the prices of grain increased in relation to wool prices, while the prices of animal products moved ahead of those of wool. The area under cultivation was extended, with relatively more land being devoted to cereal production, and some wood, fen, and moor land was taken in for cultivation. In the years stretching from the last quarter of the sixteenth century until the outbreak of the Civil War a new wave of enclosures occurred. In this period land was usually enclosed as a result of an agreement between a group of landowners to enclose a whole manor or parish, often after lesser freeholders had been bought out, and to re-allocate the land in the form of private holdings. As a result, common rights to graze animals on the fallow arable fields and on the former common pastures and to exploit the commons and waste lands surrounding the village were extinguished. The enclosure and consolidation of land played an important role in the introduction of improved methods of arable farming. On the one hand the engrossing, consolidating, and enclosing of land by landowners resulted in the creation of larger and more compact farms. These farms would then be operated either by independent farmers or by capitalist tenants with adequate resources to invest in new methods of production, and who had security of tenure or leases which enabled them to retain a reasonable proportion of the return on any investment they undertook. It was individuals of this kind who made sizeable investments in farm facilities, and who played a major role in introducing new and improved farming practices, which were less practicable on small, unenclosed peasant plots.[45]

The so-called 'long' sixteenth century, which extended from about 1450 to 1640, eventually came to an end, and gave way, in much of Europe, to a crisis in the seventeenth century. The prices of agricultural goods, and in particular of grain, began to fall, the relative prices of industrial products increased, real wages rose, and the rate of population growth slackened. However, the improvements in labour productivity and in yields that had been achieved in English agriculture since 1450 partially exempted England from some of the effects of the more general crisis.[46] Indeed, instead of leading to a reduction in the level of agricultural activity, as they did in much of Europe, the new economic conditions acted, in conjunction with new legislation obtained by the commercially oriented landlords who controlled parliament, in such a way as to accelerate the reorganisation of agricultural production in England. In the face of falling prices and rising costs, tenant farmers in particular sought to make profits by becoming more specialised and by introducing cost-reducing methods of production. Improving farmers continued to introduce the method of convertible husbandry or ley farming, in which the land is used alternatively for a grass ley and for tillage, extended the device of floating water meadows, especially in the south and west of the country, and introduced new fallow crops and grasses, manuring, and stock-breeding. Specialised market-gardening and fruit-growing were developed, particularly in order to supply the London market, and new, improved crop rotations, which made it possible for yields to be increased and for more livestock to be kept, were used extensively on light soils, as occurred in Norfolk and in the Cotswolds. In the densely settled clay vales more land was put down to pasture for specialised dairying or animal-fattening, and the fall in the demand for labour that accompanied this reduction in arable farming gave an extra impetus to the expansion of rural industry in these parts of the country.

The resulting improvements in agricultural productivity allowed some 40 per cent of the English population to be moved out of agricultural employment by the end of the seventeenth century. Indeed, productivity growth was associated with an expansion of output which not only enabled the needs of a growing domestic market to be met, but also, until about 1750, gave rise to a surplus that could be exported, while the export of surplus food was encouraged by the introduction of new corn-laws and of bounties on grain exports in the latter half of the sixteenth century.

Some of the technical improvements introduced in the late sixteenth and in the seventeenth and eighteenth centuries could be and were used in the open fields. But in the seventeenth century many propagandists advocated enclosure as a step towards better farming, and government opposition to it ended, giving way to the passing of pro-enclosure acts. The legislation inaugurated a new wave of enclosures. By 1700 no more than one-half, and probably much less, of the agricultural land in England had not yet been enclosed, and about one-half of the arable acreage remained in open fields. In the eighteenth century a substantial amount of land was enclosed by agreement, but the process of enclosure was completed largely with the help of private Acts of Parliament and the General Enclosure Acts. Some enclosure acts were passed after temporary increases in grain prices, particularly in the late 1720s and in the early 1740s, but most of them were concentrated in the period between 1750 and the early nineteenth century, when there was a more sustained increase in prices, with almost one-half of them being passed during the Napoleonic Wars. The method of parliamentary enclosure tended to be used in unenclosed areas in which enclosure was most strongly opposed and could not be achieved by other means. It was used to enclose about 6 million acres of land, mainly in the midland counties and in central England, or some one-quarter of the agricultural land in the country. About one-third of this area was common pasture or waste land. The rest was made up of formerly cultivated open fields.

As a result of this and of previous waves of enclosure the formerly common but uncultivated land was turned into private property, and the remaining cottagers and smallholders were deprived of their rights to share in the exploitation of the commons and waste lands, which had played an essential role, as a source of fuel and of small animals and birds, in the reproduction of marginalised sections of the rural population. In addition, the open fields were enclosed, and redistributed as compact blocks of land with farmsteads on the holdings. But, even though this led to a more dispersed pattern of rural settlement, the nucleated villages which had formerly been surrounded by open fields remained intact. One reason for this was that the ownership of land and the holding of farms were simultaneously concentrated into fewer hands. A second related reason was the expansion of population and the increase in industrial employment that occurred in the villages, particularly in the Midlands, at the time of enclosure.[47]

6.6 The agricultural and industrial revolutions

The transition from a feudal to a capitalist mode of production presupposes a previous process of accumulation.[48] It is composed of two groups of processes. The first results in an accumulation of wealth in a monetary form, the concentration of this money wealth in the hands of a relatively small number of people, and the appearance of the means of production as alienable goods which can be bought and sold by those possessing money wealth. The accumulation of money wealth itself can occur as a result of a process of feudal accumulation or the expanded reproduction of early agricultural and industrial enterprises. Alternatively it can stem from the realisation of wealth in the sphere of circulation, in the form of interest on loans advanced at high rates of interest, and of profits on funds advanced in commerce, speculative ventures, and colonial trade.

The second set of processes which are closely related to the first are those involved in the separation of a class of labourers from the means of production and consumption, and the appearance of the means of production and consumption as commodities, and as the private property of others to whom members of the class of labourers must sell their capacity to work, that is their labour-power, in order to exist.

So far we have outlined the working of these two processes in the transition from a feudal to a capitalist mode of agricultural production. In addition, we have referred briefly to some of the material changes in English agriculture and to some of the changes in the rural landscape associated with enclosure and with the revolution in farming techniques which occurred in the period extending from the middle of the sixteenth century to the end of the nineteenth. What we now want to do is to explain briefly the role played by these material changes in English agriculture and by the changing social relations of production in the countryside in laying the foundations for capitalist industrial growth. The processes occurring in commerce and in industry will be outlined in subsequent sections.

The development of a capitalist agricultural system played a major role in creating a class of landless labourers separated from the means of production, and obliged, by their lack of property, to sell their labour-power to capitalist farmers or industrialists willing to employ them. Once it had been created, a variety of mechanisms could lead to an increase in the size of this section of the population. In England its size was increased dramatically after 1750 by population growth. One reason for this was a reduction in the mortality rate. A second reason was earlier marriage and an increase in family size, both of which can be attributed to new social conditions and to an expansion of employment.

Whereas young peasant couples, for example, would normally delay marriage until land was passed on to them, and have relatively few children, individuals working in rural industry would marry when they were still young and would have relatively large numbers of children, since a man, woman, and children were often necessary for the creation of a viable production unit.[49] The family lifecycle was itself associated with a secondary source of poverty, since 'with the birth of children, the parents become poor, with their maturation, they become rich, and with their marriage, they fell back into misery'.[50] But in areas in which rural industry developed, a lack of material possessions and conditions of intense poverty were conducive to high rates of population growth.

Until some date between 1820 and 1850, the changes that had occurred in the relations of agricultural production were accompanied both by an increase in the size of the population and by an increase in the number of agricultural labourers in most rural parishes. The increase in agricultural employment can be explained in part by an increase in the demand for labour which occurred in spite of productivity growth because of an expansion in output, an increase in the area devoted to tillage, and the cultivation of formerly uncultivated commons and waste lands.[51]

Of course a balance did not normally exist between the amount of labour available in any particular rural district and the capacity of agricultural and non-agricultural activities to absorb it. In the counties in the east of the country, for example, shortages of labour in some areas and, in particular, shortages of labour for irregular work on large farms in closed parishes, in which settlement was discouraged to avoid the possibility of higher poor-rates, led to the introduction of the gang system, under which predominantly female and child labour was recruited in over-populated open villages to work wherever extra labour was required.[52]

So, by the time the industrial revolution began, a rural proletariat, which had been largely separated from its means of production and reproduction, had already been formed, and was being reproduced on an extended scale by the development of a system of capitalist farming and the growth of domestic industry. Subsequently, from the early nineteenth century onwards, the rate of population growth in rural areas fell below the national average and well below that of industrial and mining regions. A growing number of rural labourers in search of employment and higher wages were pulled into the industrial sector, and moved out of the countryside and into rapidly expanding urban centres as urban industrialisation got under way.[53]

In the second place, by increasing the productivity of labour and the level of output in the agricultural sector, the long agricultural revolution made it possible for a large proportion of the population to leave agriculture and to move into industrial occupations, and ensured that sufficient food was grown to maintain an expanding urban population and that food prices did not increase too rapidly. As a result the modernisation of farming helped to keep down wages and prices, and improved the competitiveness of industrial products, and it helped to overcome the constraints that had traditionally been placed upon sustained industrial development by the inelasticity of agricultural production.

In addition, the expanded reproduction of a class of wage-labourers, and of a class of capitalist entrepreneurs owning the means of production, widened the domestic market for agricultural and industrial goods. It did this in two ways. On the one hand, what had formerly been means of subsistence produced and consumed by a peasantry were now purchased out of wages advanced in the form of variable capital; and raw materials, semi-finished goods, and items of equipment were increasingly exchanged on the open market against constant capital. On the other hand, continuing improvements in the productivity of the agricultural sector, and declining subsistence wage-costs, increased the proportion of the total income of the country's population which could be used for non-food purchases, and fuelled the steady growth of industry.[54]

So, in at least three ways, the transformation of English agriculture helped to create the preconditions for an industrial revolution, and sustained and reinforced the process of industrial expansion, once it was under way.

7 Town and Country in the Transition from Feudalism to Capitalism

7.1 Feudalism and the rise of towns in medieval Europe

By the tenth century small but flourishing towns and strong urban hierarchies existed in many parts of Europe, while in Italy and in some other Mediterranean countries the municipal urban life that had emerged under Roman rule continued to survive. But in much of Europe the countryside had nevertheless become a largely autonomous sphere embracing the whole of social production.[1] Some of the members of every rural household would be capable of making simple industrial products, and some peasants would usually spend part of the time working in supplementary, non-agricultural occupations such as cloth-making. In addition, most rural communities would include specialist artisans, attached to seigneurial households or demesne economies, and village craft workers, especially smiths, who would normally possess smallholdings of their own, but whose surplus labour would be appropriated by the lord in the form of horseshoes, of repairs to ploughshares, or of other products or types of work.[2]

Yet, alongside the 'inflexibility, inertia, and slow motion', characteristic of an economy based upon nearly autarchic peasant households living in village communities, a market-oriented economy and an expanding capitalist system centred on commercial and banking capital slowly developed, and in subsequent centuries it was to become one of the most striking features of pre-industrial Europe.[3]

Initially the growth and differentiation of the aristocracy, the appearance of a small peasant elite, the increase in seigneurial incomes that occurred as the new income generated by agricultural expansion was concentrated in the hands of the dominant classes, and the growing needs of the nobility, led to a slow growth of trade and to a slow increase in the circulation of money. In the fourteenth and fifteenth centuries, in order to meet the nobility's changing and more sophisticated consumption requirements, seigneurial incomes were increasingly realised in the form of cash. The realisation of income in money form gave a further impetus to the exchange of commodities, and, by obliging peasants to sell part of their produce on the market in order to pay money rents and taxes, increased monetary transactions in the rural economy. As a result, the phase of feudal expansion was associated with a growing exchange of industrial and agricultural products, and with the development of long-distance trade in luxury commodities which entered into the consumption of the landed aristocracy and of other sections of the dominant class. The items that were traded internationally included spices, fruits, and silks from the Eastern Mediterranean, expensive luxury cloths produced in the Low Countries and in Central Italy, furs from Eastern Europe, and wines from the Mediterranean, Bordeaux, the Rhineland, Burgundy, and the Paris Basin.

One of the consequences of this growing exchange of commodities was an extension of the social division of labour. Increasing numbers of specialised merchants appeared in newly expanding urban centres, while specialised craft workers and their families ceased to produce solely for the feudal households to which they had been attached, or were separated from the rural contexts in which they had lived, and became apparently autonomous industrial households, living increasingly in urban areas, and making goods for local, regional, and export markets. At the same time, the appearance of an urban population specialising in non-agricultural pursuits stimulated the demand for agricultural products, for the latter were required both as industrial raw materials and, when urban food production became inadequate, as means of subsistance for expanding town populations.[4]

In other words, the functioning of the feudal system was itself associated with a revival and expansion of commerce and industry, with an increase in the size of medieval populations, and with the production and commercialisation of an agricultural surplus to feed that part of the population no longer fully and directly dependent on the primary agricultural sector, and it accordingly led to the re-establishment and growth of towns as commercial, industrial, and political centres, and, in the two centuries preceding the fourteenth-century crisis, to an overall acceleration in the process of urban expansion. Yet, while towns were in some ways dependent upon and conditioned by the rural society in which they developed, in other ways urban development was dependent upon exemption from some of the restrictions characteristic of rural feudalism. In other words, towns were both internal and external to the feudal system. In this section we shall outline the principal ways in which medieval towns were dependent upon rural feudalism. In the next we shall set out some of the connections between urban growth and the development of urban-based craft industry and of merchant and banking capital, and we shall indicate the ways in which towns, if they were to expand, required a limited degree of freedom and independence within the feudal mode of production. It must be emphasised, however, that the word 'limited' is an important one, for the communal independence and political autonomy gained by or conceded to towns in Italy, in Flanders, and subsequently in the Rhineland were, in our view, more of a product than a precondition for the high levels of development of craft industry and of commercial and banking capital in these regions.

In medieval Europe urban growth was most pronounced in Northern Italy, in other regions bordering on the Mediterranean, and in the area between the Loire and the Rhine. By the early fourteenth century the populations of Paris, Venice, Florence, and Genoa approached the 100,000 mark, while London probably had 50,000 inhabitants,[5] and in Italy and Flanders, which were the most highly urbanised parts of Europe, up to 30 per cent of the population lived in towns.

In Italy the major towns were expanding mainly as centres of Mediterranean trade from the tenth century onwards, and they were flourishing as entrepots and as commercial centres well in advance of other cities in Europe. At first, the most important towns were situated in the south of the country, but before long, urban centres in the south had been overtaken by those in the north. By 1100 or so, new urban elites that had emerged in the northern half of the peninsula had set in motion a systematic process of conquering the surrounding countryside and of eliminating what remained of rural feudalism, and urban communes were beginning to dominate the whole of Northern Italy. This process continued until the territories of the towns bordered upon one another, and until the whole of the northern part of the country had become a mosaic of city states composed both of a town and of a surrounding territorial *contado*, from which each city state was able to raise taxes, troops, and grain, and in which it was able to lay the foundations on which it could base its attempts to increase its prosperity *vis-à-vis* its rivals. In contrast with the rest of Europe, 'the most advanced regions of Italy thus became a chequer-board of competing city states, in which the intervening countryside . . .was annexed to the towns: no rural feudal pyramid ever arose'. The reason for this was that the development of a network of city states was associated with radical changes in rural social relations. In particular, new forms of semi-commercialised dependence were imposed upon the peasantry by urban elites, and, by the thirteenth century, the *mezzadria*, or contractual share-cropping system, was common over much of Northern and Central Italy. At the same time, the economic base of the towns themselves was widened by the development from the twelfth century or even earlier of major manufacturing industries.[6]

The second major pole of European commerce was in Flanders. In this part of Europe it was also in the tenth century that cities were established, but the rapid expansion of the Flemish cities in the next two centuries and their thirteenth-century prosperity were based predominantly upon their role as the foremost centres of woollen-cloth production in Europe.

In the thirteenth century the economic centre of gravity of Europe was established half-way between the two main poles of European commerce in the fairs of Champagne and Brie, which occurred around the towns of Troyes, Provins, Bar-sur-Aube, and Lagny near Paris, and where woollen cloth and linen from the north were exchanged for the pepper, spices, and currency of the Italian merchants and money-lenders.[7] But at the end of the century the centre of gravity was moved to Italy.

In England, towns were established and developed as administrative, commercial, and industrial centres, although agricultural pursuits were also followed by urban inhabitants. They were developed on the sites of ancient Roman settlements, around the site of a palace, castle, or monastery, or around existing rural settlements. At the same time, small market towns, fairs, and markets multiplied in the countryside. In 1086 the largest settlement in England was London, with barely 10,000 inhabitants. It was followed by Norwich and York, with 5,000 inhabitants each. In addition there were 111 small boroughs. By 1300 London had 50,000 inhabitants, Bristol had 17,000, and York had 8,000. In addition 480 boroughs and many small market towns existed.[8]

The medieval towns found in England at the end of the thirteenth and the beginning of the fourteenth century have been divided by Hilton into several different groups. On the one hand a range of large urban centres, arising from 'the combined operations of the feudal ruling class, the state . . . and merchant capital' but which also contained peasant markets, included capital cities, great ports, centres of international trade, cathedral towns, provincial capitals, and regional centres. Most county boroughs fell under the last heading.

In addition he distinguished a group of small market towns with between 500 and 1,000 inhabitants, which formed a part of large feudal estates, but which were sharply differentiated functionally from village market centres and from the surrounding countryside. Hilton defined towns belonging to this group as places arising from 'the simple commodity production of the peasants' economy'. They were

> towns where the surplus from peasant family household production was converted into cash . . . partly, of course, so that peasants could buy salt and manufactured goods which could not be obtained in the village, but mainly so

that they could obtain cash for the payment of rent, jurisdictional fines, and tax. Such towns . . . were dominated by the produce market, and by a fairly narrow range of manufacturing crafts in wood, leather, iron, and woollen textiles.

Between two-thirds and three-quarters of English medieval towns were of this type, and this group contained more than one-half of the total urban population.

Towards the end of the Middle Ages a second type of small town appeared with the development of industrial villages in East Anglia, in the Midlands, and in some other parts of the country. In most cases the towns falling under this heading had formerly been agricultural settlements, and in every case they were situated away from regulated urban areas. Usually they were centres of the textile industry, but villages also developed industrially as centres of a variety of metal-using crafts.[9]

So far we have argued that medieval towns depended upon the prevailing social system, in the sense that urban expansion was largely based upon the growing purchasing power of social groups whose incomes were derived directly or indirectly from peasant farming. But it was also the case that the majority of medieval towns were, at least originally, either promoted or protected by lay or ecclesiastical lords. In addition many of them included ecclesiastical or other types of feudal enclave. In fact, feudal lords had an interest in encouraging urban development. On the one hand, urbanisation was a means of ensuring that the needs of the local feudal establishment were met on relatively favourable terms. On the other hand, the promotion of urban development was an important source of additional revenue for the feudal ruling class, for it enabled it to concentrate trade and industry under its aegis, to control them, to tax artisans and traders, and to levy imposts on the processes of trade.

In the third place, medieval towns were dependent upon the surrounding countryside, in the sense that the reproduction and expansion of urban areas was dependent upon the extraction of supplies of labour, food, and raw materials

from rural districts. The historical limits to urban development continued, in other words, to be set by the productivity
of the agrarian economy.

So, for at least three reasons, medieval towns must be considered as products of the form of feudal evolution in Western
Europe, and, apart from the fact that they sometimes shared
part of the same site and some of the same buildings with
present-day settlements, medieval towns were in no sense
linear ancestors of the capitalist towns and cities that succeeded them, or the products of a specifically urban process.[10]

7.2　The roles of guild-based industry and merchant capital in the development of medieval towns

The establishment and growth of feudal towns was dependent
in a more immediate sense upon the success of the urban-based
craft industries and commercial activities upon which the
urban economy was based. Urban craft production was a
form of petty-commodity production, in which family-based
enterprises were organised into a guild system. At least initially production was carried on by small producers, who
owned or rented the premises they used, who owned the
necessary instruments of production, who made outlays on
raw materials and semi-finished goods and purchased consumption goods in advance of production, and who disposed
of the products of their labour, although family-based units
of production of this kind would normally also include one
or two journeymen and apprentices. The activities involved in
distribution were likewise carried on by small family-based
enterprises.

Since enterprises of this kind were characterised by possession by the immediate producer of the instrument of
production, and since the instrument only appeared as an
instrument of individual labour, this type of industrial organisation corresponded to a very low level of development of
the material forces of production. It was also associated with
a relatively limited division of labour between urban-based
craft industries, and scarcely any division of labour within
them. In addition, despite the fact that enterprises of this

kind rested essentially upon the creation of exchange-values, the main aim of production was the subsistence and reproduction of the agents of production as craft workers, so that the production of use-values rather than the accumulation of wealth predominated.[11]

Urban artisans were in turn organised into guilds. Craft guilds came into prominence in larger towns in Europe in the twelfth and thirteenth centuries, and in England in the thirteenth century. In essence the craft guilds were unions of the producers in each craft, which evolved in most cases out of or alongside all-embracing guild organisations. The aim of any guild was to monopolise a particular branch of economic activity, and to protect the interests of the guild's existing members, by controlling relevant areas of trade and the practice of the craft. In practice most guilds sought to control the provision of raw materials and the sale of finished goods. They also tried to prevent the emergence of competition by excluding other groups of people and other areas from the town's monopoly, by restricting entry into the trade or craft, by preventing the entry of competing goods, and by eliminating production in nearby small towns and villages, if necessary by destroying workshops and equipment. In addition most guilds tried to preserve a rough equality between its members by means of controls on recruitment, levels of employment, hours worked, conditions of work, methods of production, output, prices, and the quality of goods.

With the subsequent extension of the market for the commodities produced by artisans, craft workers became increasingly dependent upon merchants. Merchants interposed themselves between artisans on the one hand, and the individuals who supplied them with raw materials and who purchased the finished products on the other hand. They supplied craft workers with working capital and credit, disposed of the finished goods, and sought to use their ability to commission work from the direct producers to adjust output to market conditions and to lower the prices at which they bought goods from them. As a result they stimulated a limited process of economic differentiation between artisan households.

At the same time, many of the masters sought to strengthen their position as employers and to subordinate the journeymen and apprentices with whom they worked. In many workshops journeymen tended to become exploited labourers working for wages, while apprentices ceased to be simple trainees, and were often exploited by being paid no wages or very low ones in the period between the end of their training and the formal end of their apprenticeships.[12]

However, guild-based craft industries did not constitute the real basis of urban accumulation in the Middle Ages. It lay instead in the autonomous development of merchant capital. Similarly, urban elites were not usually composed of urban craft workers. Instead they had a tendency to be composed, according to the size of the centre, of small, middling, or great merchant capitalists.

Merchant capital operates in the sphere of circulation, and its autonomous development is proportional to the extent to which capital is external to the production process, and is not applied in an innovative manner to agricultural or industrial production. It interposes itself as a middleperson 'between extremes which it does not control, and between premises which it does not create',[13] and its expansion depends upon the existence and exploitation of differences between the production or buying-prices and the selling-prices of commodities in separated markets or separated spheres of production, that is upon the possibility of buying cheap and selling dear in international, regional, and local markets.

The circuit of merchant capital can be represented by $M-C-M'$. A merchant capitalist advances a sum of money, M, in exchange for a specific commodity, C, and, in a second stage, sells the commodity, C, for an amount of money, M', which exceeds the sum originally advanced by $M'-M$. The argument needs to be elaborated by considering the role of transport and storage costs. But it should be clear how the profits of merchant capital in its pure form depend upon the exploitation and preservation of differences in buying- and selling-prices. It follows that the operations of merchant capital are quite different from the activity of levying imposts on trade and on the processes of trade, by means of which feudal lords gained from the expansion of commerce.[14]

In medieval Europe merchant capitalists acted as middlepersons in long- and middle-distance trade in luxury goods and in the products of artisans which commanded a wide market, and in the provision at various marketing levels of a wide range of goods to the population in general. Some of them organised the provision of raw materials to urban craft workers and to manufacturers living in the countryside, and organised the sale of the finished products, but without intervening in production itself, and without altering the characteristics of the process of production. In addition, merchants also advanced loan or interest-bearing capital, that is capital whose circuit is represented by $M-M'$. Usually money was lent at usurious rates of interest to the landed aristocracy and to the state, both of whom needed increasingly large amounts of cash to spend on military exploits and largesse, and to tide them over the gap between expenditures and the receipt of the income with which they could pay for them.[15] But they also lent money or materials to craft workers and rural producers, exploiting shortages of credit in town and country.

However, merchant capital was not able to escape the limitations associated with its externality *vis-à-vis* production. In most parts of Europe, when opportunities for interposing itself in the circulation of the products of industry were limited, and until new productivity-increasing methods of production were beginning to be introduced mainly by a new class of industrial entrepreneurs, urban capital was invested in land, state bonds, and tax farming. As a result merchant capital was fused with landed property, the urban elite was transformed into a landed or rentier aristocracy, and the towns were 'refeudalised'.[16]

Now in the last section we pointed out that medieval towns were at least initially and, in many cases, continuously dependent upon the feudal social context in which they developed, and that they continued to be conditioned strongly by the surrounding rural economy. An implication of these features of medieval urbanisation is that feudal towns cannot be construed as 'non-feudal islands in the feudal seas'.[17] But in this section we have pointed out that the development of an urban area also depended upon the success of the industrial and trading activities on which the town's inhabitants relied. As a result, urban growth presupposed, although it was not guaranteed by, exemption from some characteristically feudal restrictions upon human freedom, the acquisition of rights to set up systems of local government and to engage in and control industrial and trading activities, and the development of organisations that were suited to the task of regulating urban economic activity.

The success of urban-based merchants and trading craft workers depended in part both upon the expansion of trade, and upon improvements in the terms of trade, that is in the ratio of buying- and selling-prices. It follows that both of these sections of the population had an interest in, and depended upon, the introduction and enforcement of measures enabling them to control the markets on which they bought goods and the points at which they were sold, on the one hand, and to deny control of them to others on the other hand, to open up new markets, to overcome obstacles to the trading activities in which they engaged, and to regulate the activities of foreign merchants.[18] So, in the Mediterranean, 'the urban economy was based on monopoly of key commodities, defended by embargoes, alliances, war, and piracy: war, diplomacy, and trade were synonymous'.[19] In England, in the fifteenth century, the major wool-exporters succeeded in establishing a staple at Calais (that is, they secured the introduction and implementation of a policy that ensured that wool was only exported through Calais, and that kept foreign merchants out of England and forced them to acquire English wool from English exporters), while the export of cloth was monopolised by the Company of Merchant Adventurers, which was formed from organisations that had originally provided trading facilities in foreign countries for English merchants.[20] By such means merchants were able to maintain or even increase price differences between separated markets, and to increase the volume of trade that they controlled.

An ability to regulate and control commercial activity was not the only or even the most fundamental precondition of commercial success. In order simply to be able to engage in commerce and industry urban inhabitants had to be released from various feudal restrictions. In England the burgesses of a town acquired a restricted and conditional freedom to practice a trade or craft and to act in a corporate capacity. The privileges enjoyed by the burgesses were normally defined and assembled in a charter of liberties granted to them by a leading feudal lord in return for a heavy lump sum and the payment of an annual rent. In general the privileges included: freedom from feudal restrictions on personal status, property, movement, and contract; the right to establish communal, corporate organisations to protect the town and to provide trading facilities; and the right to acquire a corporate monopoly over the local market by means of which the urban elite could control and improve the volume and the terms of trade on which urban growth depended. In most cases the local monopoly was administered, and trading facilities were provided, not by the town government, but by the guild merchant, an association of individuals living in the town, who had trading interests, and who submitted to mutual taxation. As a result, towns 'became distinctive economic and social units just when and because certain places were set apart and defended by laws and privileges making them market and production centres and denying some or all such rights to the countryside around'.[21]

The acquisition and maintenance of privileges of this kind by the members of established urban communities, and the monopolisation of trade, both depended upon strong political and military backing. But urban exclusivism was in its turn a precondition for the development of merchant capital and urban production. In other words, the expansion of medieval towns presupposed the acquistion by the town's inhabitants of a limited degree of freedom and independence within the feudal mode of production, and it depended upon the ability of its inhabitants to exclude the countryside from the town's monopoly of trade and from the guild monopoly of craft production. As a result each town was able 'to exploit the country economically by means of its monopoly prices, system of taxation, guild organisation, direct commercial fraudulence, and usury'.[22]

As towns grew in size and in wealth, some of them sought almost complete political independence. But, unlike the city states in Northern Italy, the English towns were never able to extend the autonomy they enjoyed to complete independence, due to the earlier rebirth of the territorial state, the strength of the monarchy, and the more limited level of commercial activity.

7.3 The development of guild organisations and of the urban system

In the era of commercial and industrial expansion in the thirteenth century, municipal government tended to fall into the hands of patrician oligarchies which included a strong representation of merchant interests, and in England many guild merchants acted as the governing bodies of their towns. At the same time, the members of these ruling groups sought to strengthen their own position by restricting entry to all save important merchants, by raising the prices of the goods they sold, by subordinating craft workers by lowering the prices they paid for industrial products and by beginning to put work out in the countryside, and by intensifying fiscal exploitation of less prosperous sections of the urban population.

Subsequently, at least in Northern Europe, the initial, all-embracing merchant guild usually gave way to more specialised guilds. On the one hand new mercantile guilds were formed by commercial elements monopolising a sphere of the wholesale trade. On the other hand specialised craft guilds representing the less privileged artisans were established. The newly formed craft guilds sought to resist the pretensions of the long-established patrician classes, to break the commercial grip of the merchants, to organise production in a way that was more advantageous to leading craft workers, and to obtain a greater voice in urban government. In many parts of Europe the craft element actually rebelled against the urban patriciates, and in some cases craft workers subsequently acquired a role in town government.

With the slackening of economic growth in the late Middle Ages guilds succeeded in monopolising and regulating all branches of production and distribution, managed to exercise a strong influence over urban government and urban policy, and succeeded in imposing systems of intense monopolistic regulation on all urban-based economic activity. However, the strengthening of guild controls only spurred on merchants who were already progressively diverting industrial production towards unregulated settlements and into the countryside. Some long-established industrial towns successfully switched to the production of luxury goods, but many urban industries declined. In the case of the cloth industry, for example, old centres of production in Flanders and in North-East France, including, eventually, Ypres, Ghent, and the commercial city of Bruges, stagnated, although the industries of towns in Brabant, Hainault, and Champagne which produced less expensive, lower-quality cloth did good business, and in the fifteenth century the woollen-cloth industry in Holland, and in particular in Leiden, got under way. But, in general, towns tended to be abandoned as centres of major industrial activity and grew more slowly until the eve of the nineteenth-century industrial revolution.

In the aftermath of the feudal crisis, the urban population and urban system of early-fourteenth-century Europe were broadly reconstructed. But in the years between 1500 and 1750 few towns were founded, many grew more slowly than in the phase of feudal expansion, or even contracted in size, and towns ceased to be in the van of industrial progress with many smaller ones becoming market and production centres for limited regions. The pattern of urban development in pre-industrial Europe has nevertheless itself been differentiated by de Vries into three broad types, coinciding respectively with part of the so-called long sixteenth century which extended from 1450 to 1640, with the age of the rural proletariat which extended from the early seventeenth century to 1750, and with the years of the new urbanisation which occurred after 1750.[23]

In about the middle of the fifteenth century economic growth began to get under way again, to the benefit of the cities whose inhabitants were helped by the fact that industrial prices were rising while agricultural prices were stagnant or dropping. The ensuing wave of growth lasted throughout the sixteenth century and continued into the early seventeenth century, when it finally gave way, at first in the south and eventually in most parts of Europe, to a new recession.

By 1500, of several thousand settlements in Europe

acknowledged as urban places, 156 were inhabited by 10,000 or more people, while the populations of Paris and Naples were around the 150,000 mark, and Venice and Milan each contained more than 100,000 people. 28 per cent of these cities, and 3 of the 4 with over 100,000 inhabitants, were in Italy. In England the population of London stood between 40,000 and 60,000 persons, while Norwich, Bristol, Exeter and Newcastle had more than 10,000 and York and Salisbury more than 7,000 inhabitants each. In Europe as a whole the situation was very similar to the one that had prevailed in the early fourteenth century, when a somewhat larger urban population supported about 125 cities of 10,000 or more inhabitants, and 4 of about 100,000.[24]

In the years between 1450 and 1640 the number of cities with 10,000 or more inhabitants increased to well over the 200 mark, small cities in general exhibited some growth, but large ones grew most of all, as is indicated in Figure 7.1 and in Figure 7.2 in which the rank–size relationship moves upwards, indicating growth in the size of existing cities and, in particular, of the largest ones, and is extended slightly downwards and to the right, indicating growth of the urban system as a result of the addition of a few new centres (Table 7.1).

In the Mediterranean, all categories of town shared in the general increase in population that occurred in what we have called the long sixteenth century, but elsewhere in Europe the growth process was associated with a marked acceleration in the growth of large cities, and a relative or even, in some cases, an absolute decrease in the populations of many small towns. The viability of towns whose political and economic independence was diminished by new centralised monarchies and of cathedral towns in newly protestant lands was undermined, while the potential of commercial centres like Genoa, Augsburg, and Antwerp and of administrative centres like Madrid, London, and Paris was increased.[25] The population of London, which as early as the fifteenth century had assumed the position of economic and political centre of the country, increased very rapidly over the next two centuries. By the end of the seventeenth century it was in excess of 400,000 persons. The population of Paris, which by this time was not only the political centre of France, but was also

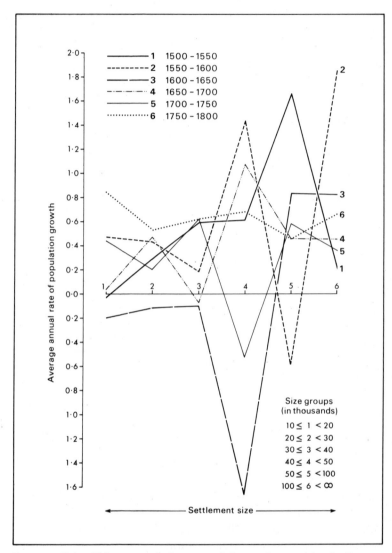

FIGURE 7.1   *Urban population growth by settlement size in Europe from the sixteenth to the nineteenth century*

Source: based on data in J. de Vries, 'Patterns of Urbanisation in Pre-Industrial Europe, 1500–1800', in H. Schmal (ed.), *Patterns of European Urbanisation since 1500* (London: Croom Helm, 1981) 79–109, p. 87.

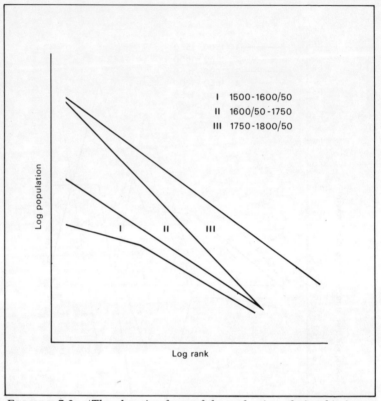

FIGURE 7.2   'The changing form of the rank–size relationship in pre-modern Europe (the graph of the equation: log population of town $i = \alpha - \beta$ log rank of town i)*

Source: de Vries, 'Patterns of Urbanisation in Pre-Industrial Europe, 1500–1800', p. 97.

beginning to assume the role, that had been played for some time by Lyon, of economic capital of the national territory, was about the same as that of London, yet France had twice as many inhabitants as Great Britain.

In the seventeenth century a series of setbacks and a slowing-down or reversal of sixteenth-century demographic growth reduced the number of cities with 10,000 or more inhabitants, and lowered the speed of the process of urbanisation. In the years between 1600 or 1650 and 1750 the population of urban areas continued to increase, as did the proportion of the population of Europe living in cities, but the size distribu-

TABLE 7.1   *The number of cities in Europe by size category,*
1500—1800

Size category	1500	1550	1600	1650	1700	1750	1800
10,000 and less than 20,000	99	100	125	109	116	137	205
20,000 and less than 30,000	28	31	39	38	46	50	66
30,000 and less than 40,000	12	16	18	16	16	22	30
40,000 and less than 50,000	6	8	16	7	12	9	13
50,000 and less than 100,000	7	14	11	16	20	17	32
100,000 or more	4	3	8	10	11	12	17
Total	156	172	217	196	221	257	363
Less than 10,000*	222	206	161	182	157	121	15
Total	378	378	378	378	378	378	378

* The number of cities with more than 10,000 inhabitants at some stage in the
years 1500—1800 but with less than 10,000 at the date in question.

Source: de Vries, 'Patterns of Urbanisation in Pre-Industrial Europe, 1500—
1800', p. 86.

tion of European cities was radically altered. Additions to the
stock of cities inherited from the Middle Ages were extremely
rare. The vast majority of cities did not grow significantly,
stagnated, or contracted. In fact, cities with less than 40,000
but more than 5,000 inhabitants experienced a net loss of
population (Table 7.2). Centres of provincial administration

TABLE 7.2   *The size of Europe's urban population, 1500—*
1800 (in thousands)

Size category	1500	1550	1600	1650	1700	1750	1800
10,000 and less than 20,000	1307	1290	1627	1469	1492	1856	2825
20,000 and less than 30,000	631	730	903	852	1076	1192	1554
30,000 and less than 40,000	399	536	589	559	540	737	1003
40,000 and less than 50,000	249	338	690	297	508	392	551
50,000 and less than 100,000	415	946	708	1068	1345	1793	2254
100,000 or more	450	500	1270	1914	2390	2859	3977
Total	3451	4340	5787	6159	7351	8829	12164

Source: de Vries, 'Patterns of Urbanisation in Pre-Industrial Europe, 1500—1800',
p. 87.

suffered at least a relative loss of standing, and many lost their political autonomy at the hand of absolutist regimes. Seats of ecclesiastical administration declined. Inland trading centres were disadvantaged in comparison with coastal ones. With the transfer of production to the countryside, the expansion of industrial towns was checked by growing rural competition. In fact, most of the towns that declined markedly in this period had been important centres of industrial activity: Toledo, Augsburg, Brescia, Segovia, and Leiden. On the other hand, in the midst of this general slackening of the process of urban development, the urban growth that did occur was heavily concentrated on a small number of very large cities and on a few cities that became very big. The settlements belonging to this small group of very large towns achieved striking rates of economic and demographic growth as political, commercial, and financial institutions and new functions were concentrated in them. In fact, 80 per cent of the increase in the population of cities with over 5,000 inhabitants was attributable to 48 cities that by 1750 had at least 40,000 inhabitants. With the exception of the predominantly industrial city of Lyon, all the cities that came to be very large in this period, and that dominated the urbanisation of the era, fell under the heading of capital city, or port, or both, as did many of the smaller towns that grew at a very fast rate. In England, the population of London increased more slowly between 1650 and 1750 than it had done in the preceding century, but reached 675,000 persons. In addition, many large towns in the provinces grew rapidly. The towns whose growth was most striking were Liverpool, Manchester, Birmingham, Newcastle, and Plymouth, which, with Norwich and Bristol, almost all had populations well in excess of 20,000 inhabitants by 1750. The inclusion of several industrial towns in the ranks of the rapidly growing cities differentiated England sharply from most other parts of Europe.[26]

In addition, a great deal of redistribution of the urban population between regions occurred. The relative position of cities in three broad zones in Europe, which had been fairly stable between 1300 and 1600, and which was to change relatively little in the century after 1750, was drastically altered. In the Mediterranean the urban population declined, and the entire net growth in the population living in cities was concentrated in the north of Europe and, in particular, in the north and west (Table 7.3). However, some cities in the Mediterranean region which acted as outposts of the Atlantic and North-West European trade grew rapidly, while in the north some cities lost large amounts of population.[27]

TABLE 7.3 *The distribution of the total urban population of Europe by region, 1500–1800 (in percentages)*

Region	1500	1550	1600	1650	1700	1750	1800
North & West	16	16	17	26	29	28	32
Central	32	30	30	32	32	33	31
Mediterranean	50	52	52	40	36	36	33
East	02	02	02	03	03	04	04
Total	100	100	100	100	100	100	100

Source: de Vries, 'Patterns of Urbanisation in Pre-Industrial Europe, 1500–1800', p. 87.

In 1750 or so, a new wave of urbanisation began to get under way, but the structure and characteristics of the urban system and the determinants of urban growth were fundamentally altered. The growth of large cities slowed down, at least in comparison with small ones, and large increases were recorded in the number and in the size of small towns, at first in England and eventually in Central and Southern Europe. As a result, the rank–size relationship was extended to the right and moved upwards at the lower end of the distribution (Figure 7.2). By 1800 the number of cities with 10,000 or more inhabitants reached 363, and each subsequent decade brought major gains, while some 200 were added to the category with 5,000 and less than 10,000 inhabitants. This pattern of urban growth can be distinguished from the renewed concentration of the urban population in large cities by which it was followed. The reasons for it lie in part in the more even impact of demographic growth, and in a process of industrialisation which was beginning to transform villages and small towns into important centres of urban manufacturing and urban factory production. In addition, an increase in marketed farm production was expanding the employment base of regional marketing and administrative centres, and an increase in agricultural incomes was leading to a growth of the retailing and service sectors in small country towns.[28]

So far we have presented a brief account of the pattern of urbanisation in early modern Europe. In the next two sections we shall focus upon the growth of capital cities and the development of new international trading systems as a means of identifying and discussing some of the most important dimensions and determinants of the urban growth that occurred in this period.

7.4 The growth of capital cities

One of the reasons for the striking growth of a very small number of large agglomerations in the early modern era lay in the spectacular expansion of capital cities in the centralised absolutist regimes that were established in sixteenth-century Europe, and in the constitutional states by which they were replaced, in the case of England, in the middle of the seventeenth century, and in the case of France, at the end of the eighteenth century. In these cities the growth of the administration, the military, and the legal apparatus led to a major increase in employment.

In the West the absolute monarchies emerged in a period characterised by the dissolution of serfdom. In the view of Anderson they were in fact new forms of feudal political domination, constructed as part of a process of feudal regroupment against the peasantry, in which politico-legal relations of compulsion were displaced upwards to the summit of the state. But, at the same time, the structure of the emerging absolutist regimes was also strongly conditioned by the spread of commodity production and exchange and by the rise of an urban bourgeoisie.[29]

So, supported only by the growth of government employment in Hapsburg Spain, the earliest great power of modern Europe, the population of Madrid increased from several thousand persons in 1561, when it was chosen by the Haps-burg monarch as the capital of its vast empire, to 65,000 by 1600, and to 17,000 by 1630. The explosive growth of Paris from some 150,000 inhabitants and of London from some 60,000 in the middle of the sixteenth century, to about 400,000 inhabitants each by 1650, can be attributed in part to their administrative and social roles as capital cities of absolutist states. However, both of these cities had more varied economic structures than Madrid. In particular, it has been estimated that in 1700 some 25 per cent of London's population was directly dependent upon employment in trades connected with the port. But even in the decentralised Dutch Republic the decision to make The Hague into an administrative centre resulted in its expansion from an over-grown village to the third largest city by the middle of the 18th century, while, under British rule, Dublin was raised from a town with 18,000 inhabitants in 1650 to one with 130,000 in 1750.[30]

The capital cities of absolutist states were usually inhabited by the monarchy and by those connected with it, by individuals with positions in state bureaucracies, by sections of the nobility and gentry, and by many of the individuals living on incomes from government bonds, and so they tended to have a social structure that encouraged the proliferation of services and of luxury trades. Of course, cities of this kind were not devoid of industrial activity. But, in contrast to medieval towns whose industrial output was exported to rural and foreign markets, the artisans of capital cities sold most of their output on markets within their own cities. In turn, the con-centration of government and rentier revenue in the capital and the attendant multiplication of services, along with the attraction of wages in all seasons, drew large sections of the proletarianised surplus population into these great cities. Indeed, since the crude death-rates in large cities were usually substantially higher than the crude birth-rates, the populations of large towns were unable to reproduce themselves by natural population growth, and could only be increased as a result of a large and continuous influx of largely rural immigrants.

In 1650, London had 400,000 inhabitants and contained some 7 per cent of the national population, whereas, in 1750, it had 675,000 inhabitants or about 11 per cent of the population of the whole country. Wrigley has estimated that the increase in London's population by 275,000 persons between 1650 and 1750 would have required an average net inward movement of about 8,000 persons per year. In other words, in this period, the survivors to early adulthood of at least one-half of the annual natural increase in the total population of provincial England would have had to have moved to London for the city to have grown as fast as it did.[31]

The large cities of early modern Europe depended upon more than a large inflow of people from the rest of the national territory. In addition, the system of distribution and transport was reorganised to facilitate the movement of resources from the surrounding countryside to each city, and the rural hinterland of each capital was transformed to supply it with food and fuel. In England the territorial state and the national market were themselves, in the words of Braudel, 'the result of the ebb and flow of merchandise to and from London, an enormous, demanding central nervous system which caused everything to move to its rhythm'. But, as in the case of other large cities of this epoch, the growth of London was 'an example of deep-seated disequilibrium, asymmetrical growth, and irrational and unproductive investment on a nation-wide scale', which in turn were all products of the institutions of the time.[32]

Of course, as we indicated above, London was not merely a capital city. In the century following the fall of English absolutism its growth continued to stem in part from 'the centralisation of political power . . . within an aristocratic political order'. But it also stemmed from 'the replacement of feudalism by an agrarian aristocracy and then an agrarian bourgeoisie, with all its effects in modernisation of the land', and from 'the immense development of mercantile trade'. 'It was a capital centre of trades and of distribution: of skilled craft workers in metals and in print; of clothing and furniture and fashion; of all the work connected with shipping and the market'; while, in the eighteenth century, a significant characteristic of its development was the expansion of financial concerns, and of the tasks of managing and directing much of the activity of other people in other parts of the country.[33]

7.5 The shifting commercial centre of the European world-economy

A second reason for the changing pattern of urbanisation and the disproportionate growth of large towns lay in the development of a new international trading system centred successively upon Italy, the focal points of the Portugese and Spanish empires, Holland, and England (Table 7.4), and in changes in the organisation of trade and commerce that made it possible for them to be controlled from a small number of cities or city states.

In the Middle Ages a Mediterranean trading system, centred upon the North Italian city states and linking Western Europe with the East, had been established, as had a network centred on the Low Countries and the Hanseatic towns which linked North-West Europe with the Baltic, and which came to incorporate Poland and other parts of Eastern Europe from which grain and forest products could be imported.

In the thirteenth century the centre of gravity was established, as we have already pointed out, in the fairs of Champagne and Brie. But, at the end of the century, the fairs of Champagne declined, in part because of the establishment of improved maritime and overland links between Italy and Flanders, and because Italian cloth-manufacturers were no longer content to dye the ecru woollens imported from the north and began to weave their own, giving momentum to the *arte della lana* in Florence. In addition the more powerful Italian economy had greater success in weathering the fourteenth-century economic crisis and the tragedy of the Black Death. As a result, Italy became the undisputed centre of European economic life. Italian primacy was originally divided between four powerful city states and their moneyed elites: Venice, Milan, Florence, and Genoa. But, after Genoa's defeat in the War of Chioggia in 1382, Venice commenced a long but not always tranquil reign as the centre of the European economy and the main link with the Levant, and with the Far East and its sought-after products.[34]

In the so-called Age of Discovery the European world-economy was expanded by the annexation of the Atlantic, and of its islands and coastlines, and finally by the conquest

TABLE 7.4 *The changing centre of the European world-economy*

Dominant centre	Hapsburg Empire	Netherlands (United Provinces)	England	USA
Ascending	1450 –	1575 – 1590	1785 – 1815	1897 – 1913
Achieving dominance		1590 – 1620	1815 – 1850	1913 – 1945
Maturity	– 1559	1620 – 1650	1850 – 1873	1945 – 1967
Decline	1559 – 1573	1650 – 1672	1873 – 1897	1967 –

Source: Research Working Group on Cyclical Rhythms and Secular Trends, 'Cyclical Rhythms and Secular Trends of the Capitalist World-Economy: Some Premises, Hypotheses, and Questions', *Review*, vol. II, no. 4 (Spring 1979) 483–500, p. 499.

of the interior of the American continent. In addition, its links with the autonomous world-economies of India, Insulinde, and China were multiplied. At the same time, the centre of gravity in Europe shifted from the south to the north, at first to Antwerp, and then to Amsterdam, and not to Lisbon or Seville, the centres of the Portuguese and Spanish empires.[35] The new phase of overseas expansion occurred between 1415 and 1550, and was initiated when the Portuguese, with the backing of Genoese capital, began to move into the Atlantic Islands, Africa, India, East Asia, and Brazil. Portuguese expansion started in the midst of the feudal crisis, and was stimulated by the absence of an alternative solution to the fall in seigneurial incomes, by encouragement from the state, and by the opportunities it afforded to merchant capital, as well as by a search for agricultural products and bullion. The exploits of the Portuguese were followed by Spanish colonisation of the Americas. As in the Portuguese case, Spanish commercial enterprise was backed by Genoese capital.[36]

The upward swing in economic activity that occurred after 1450 led initially to renewed prosperity in the Low Countries, Southern Germany, Northern Italy, and, as a result of the discoveries, in Spain. Lisbon became the largest port in Europe and entered the ranks of the large cities, as did Seville, which acted as a centre for the rapidly expanding transatlantic bullion trade, over which it enjoyed a state monopoly. At the beginning of the sixteenth century Antwerp supplanted Venice. Antwerp was functioning as an outpost of the Spanish state, as were Genoa and the merchant-banking centres in Southern Germany. It acted as the principal link between the Baltic and Mediterranean trades and the transcontinental trade via Southern Germany, was made into the main centre of the Atlantic trades of Portugal and Spain, and became the supreme money market in Europe.

But, in the years between 1550 and 1560, for political reasons related to the wars carried on by the Spanish State in the Netherlands, the position as dominant city in Europe passed to Genoa, and the Italian municipal economies which had attained a previous peak of prosperity in 1350 experienced a temporary economic renaissance. In contrast to what had happened earlier, the wealth of Genoa was based not

upon trade with the Levant, but upon trade with the New
World, upon trade with Seville, and upon its task of redistri-
buting via the fairs of Piacenza the huge quantities of silver
that were arriving from America, and that had been moving
along the Atlantic route from Spain to Flanders until they
began to be diverted towards Genoa from 1568.[37]

The economic revival of Italy did not last long. In the years
between 1590 and 1610 the economic centre of the European
world-economy moved to Amsterdam, where it was to remain
for nearly two centuries. So, over a century after Columbus's
voyage in 1492, Genoa, Italy, and the Mediterranean declined.
Italian decline can be attributed in part to growing competition from Dutch and English carriers and merchants in the
Mediterranean. Indeed, 'after 1570 the Mediterranean world
was harassed, bullied, and pillaged by northern ships and
merchants, and these northern merchants made their initial
fortune by seizing wealth around the Mediterranean'.[38] In
other words, the decline of Italy lay not so much in a switch
of trade from the Mediterranean to the Atlantic, in which
Genoese capital was involved, as in the seizing by the Dutch
in particular of the opportunities provided by the new world-
economy, that is, in a human achievement.[39] In Italy, on the
other hand, urban-based industries, which had failed to move
beyond municipal and guild exclusivism and the production
of high-quality goods for an increasingly narrow market, and
whose competitiveness had been reduced by rising costs and
wages, declined, while rural industries were developed less
successfully than in England and in France.[40] At the same
time, urban capital was invested in land and in rentier forms
of wealth, often leaving the national circuit, usually in the
form of loans to foreign governments.

The establishment of the Northern Netherlands and of
Amsterdam — which was already acting as the main grain
market and the main port through which Baltic produce was
being shipped to Western Europe — as the commercial and
financial centre of Europe also lay in part in the decline of
Spain and the successful revolt of the Low Countries against
Philip II. In addition, it can be explained by the exploitation
of some cost-reducing measures in commerce and in some
sectors of agriculture and industry, and by the acquisition

by the Dutch of a quasi-monopoly over northern merchandise on the one hand, and over all the Far Eastern sources of fine spices, such as cinnamon and cloves, on the other hand.[41]

Braudel follows Wallerstein in arguing that every world-economy is divided into distinct and specialised geographical zones, which are functionally interdependent and complementary, but which enjoy increasingly fewer advantages as one moves out from the dominant pole. In 1650, for example,

> the centre was Holland and Amsterdam. The intermediate or secondary zones were the rest of Europe: the Baltic and North Sea states, England, the Rhine and Elbe regions of Germany, France, Portugal, Spain, and Italy north of Rome. The peripheral regions were Scotland, Ireland, and Scandinavia to the north; plus the whole of Europe east of a line running from Hamburg to Venice, Italy south of Rome, and Europeanised America. Much of the New World was a world based on slavery, and the outer reaches of Europe were a second serfdom zone.[42]

After well over a century of prosperity the hold of the Dutch over foreign trade was reduced by the growing economic strength of England and, to a more limited extent, of France. In 1651 the first Navigation Act, which reserved English trade for English vessels and merchants, and which helped England to protect its national market and burgeoning industries more successfully than any other European country, was introduced. Uncharacteristically it was not opposed by the Dutch, who still dominated European commerce, perhaps because Dutch vessels had frequently to put into English ports because of the prevailing-wind pattern.[43] Subsequently, between 1780 and 1815, and after the prosecution of three successful maritime trade-wars against the Dutch, the English rose to commercial and to economic and political leadership of Europe, in what came to be the second phase of English imperialism, and set about a conquest of the globe and the establishment of a formal empire which gave a new dimension to what had mainly been a trade involving the purchase of merchandise and the sale of textiles.[44]

The internationalisation of the circuit of commodity capital and the expansion of international trade in the seventeenth and eighteenth centuries, along with the associated increase in shipping and shipbuilding, were associated with a process of rapid growth of large ports along the Atlantic seaboard. The towns of Lisbon, Seville, and Antwerp, on which Iberian trade had been concentrated in the sixteenth century, did not share in this growth and declined in size. Mediterranean and Baltic ports were also excluded. But, from Hamburg in the north to Cadiz in the south, large ports on the Atlantic coast generally prospered as entrepots, as processing and re-exporting centres for colonial produce, and as provisioning centres for the expanding fleets of maritime nations. Often, as in the case of London, Bristol, Liverpool, and Cork, the populations of port towns increased by 200 or 250 per cent between 1600 and 1750. In addition, because of the strategic role of the navy in mercantilist policies, naval stations supporting whole towns were established by the end of the seventeenth century, as at Portsmouth, Plymouth, Brest, and Toulon.[45]

As in the case of other European countries, English commerce was dominated by monopolistic-regulated companies, that is by groups of merchants and ship-owners exercising a privilege of a royal monopoly of trade with a certain foreign region. A monopolisation of trade was sanctioned for a variety of reasons. One was that it was a means of improving the terms of trade for English merchants. A second was that it facilitated the raising of funds for speculative ventures. A third was that companies of this kind were a convenient source of revenue for the monarchy. But this policy also made it possible for trade to be concentrated upon a small number of ports, and for the expansion of potentially competing ones to be restricted. One example of the importance of such regulations is provided by the city of Bristol, whose golden age is said to have begun in 1698. It was in this year that the triangular slave trade ceased to be a monopoly of the London Royal Africa Company. As a result merchants based in Bristol could play a more active part in this trade, and, at the same time, the participation of the port in direct trade with the West Indies, the American mainland, Ireland and Europe, and in the triangular trade with Newfoundland and south-west Europe increased. Its golden age lasted until 1776, when the outbreak of the war following the American Declaration of Independence, and the growth of rival activities in other ports, such as Liverpool and London, brought it to an end. The impact of these events was reinforced by the rapid expansion of industry and of related port activities in more distant parts of the country. The acceleration of industrial development after 1750, and its concentration in urban areas located in most cases on or near coalfields, radically altered the urban hierarchy and the ranking of sea ports, and played an important role in reducing Bristol from the second largest city and port in 1700 to the fifth city and eighth port in 1800.[46] But at this point in the story we must break off. We shall return to the question of the relationship between industrial and urban development in Britain in the years after 1750 later in the book. At this stage in the argument we still have to trace the history of some of the processes that laid the foundations of, and created the preconditions for, the extended reproduction of industrial capital.

7.6 Merchant capital and the transition to capitalism

The accumulation of mercantile wealth, and the establishment in the seventeenth and eighteenth centuries of a new colonial system dominated by England, but which also involved the French, Dutch, and in the eighteenth century the Portuguese, had a significance extending beyond its connection with the rapid growth of port cities like London, Amsterdam, Hamburg, Bordeaux, and Lisbon. The action of merchant capital and the exploitation of the world by more prosperous countries were, in the terminology of debates about the transition to capitalism, 'external' elements. In an earlier section we indicated that such elements were in fact both external and internal. But, in conjunction with 'internal' changes in the social relations of production and the transformation from below of agriculture and industry, they also played a significant role in laying the foundations for the subsequent phase of industrial expansion.

Commodity production and capital based upon circulation both contributed to the dissolution of existing relations of production, while the accumulation of merchant capital led to a concentration of money wealth into the hands of a relatively small mercantile class. But 'what new mode of production will replace the old does not depend on commerce but on the character of the old mode of production',[47] and whether the money accumulated by merchants was invested in rentier forms of wealth and led to a reinforcement of traditional relations of dependence, or was advanced in modern industry, depended to a large extent upon the context in which it was accumulated, and upon the inducement to invest in manufacturing industry.

As long as capital remained external to production, and as long as profit depended solely upon the exploitation of differences in buying- and selling-prices in separated markets, as they did in the case of merchant capital in its pure form, capital was unable to develop an adequate productive base for sustained accumulation. Indeed, by evening out differences in costs and prices between different spatial zones or moments in time, the autonomous functioning of merchant capital tended to undermine the foundations upon which its continued accumulation depended. In many cases the economic and political arrangements that had allowed the fullest autonomy to merchant capital in the feudal mode of production became fetters on the subsequent development of capitalism. In such circumstances the locus of progress was displaced, and urban capital was often invested: in land, which conferred social distinction; in usurious forms of rent and tax farming, which commercialised feudal obligations, seigneurial revenues, and ecclesiastical tithes, and which often reinforced rather than weakened feudal obligations on the peasantry; or in urban real-estate or commodity speculation. Alternatively, excess capital was invested in land that could be farmed in a modern way and that provided a substantial source of income, or in the industrial sector, in which, almost invariably, little interest was taken in the organisation of production. What happened in any particular case depended upon what was happening in the sphere of production independently and, in some cases, in spite of the actions of merchant capitalists. In Italy, the decline of the once-prosperous city states stemmed in part from the objective limitations of merchant capital and, as we mentioned above, from its inability to move beyond guild and municipal exclusivism and the production of high-quality goods for an increasingly narrow market, while the once-dominant economies of Spain and Holland were similarly pulled down by the weakness of their productive bases and the inability of merchant capital on its own to expand them adequately. Only in England were opportunities found on any significant scale for profitably investing the fruits of speculation and colonial trading in the production process, and in the introduction of cost-reducing methods of production.[48]

The crucial differences between these examples lay in the development of new and more productive techniques of production, the creation of an adequate market, and the emergence from the ranks of the producers of a new class willing and able to invest in the production process. Once capitalist agricultural and industrial enterprises had begun to develop, opposition to the system of state-regulated exploitation through trade and to the pursuit of monopolistic practices by chartered companies increased. The aim of these companies was to establish monopoly prices, to improve the terms of trade for its members, to guarantee commercial profits, and to maintain a favourable trade balance for the national economy. In contrast, members of the emerging bourgeois classes made profits by introducing cost-reducing methods of production and by increasing labour productivity. Since they were able to undercut high-cost producers, they were more interested in policies capable of increasing the level of export demand for their products and the overall volume of trade than in measures aimed at improving the terms of trade. In addition they supported the removal of policies and regulations that acted as impediments to free trade and untrammeled competition.[49] So, as soon as modern capitalist interests secured a degree of political hegemony, and as long as competing capitalist industries were not present in other countries, the mercantilist phase of economic development, whose foundation was unequal exchange on the basis of unequal values, came to an end, and was replaced by a policy of free trade. This type of policy has tended to be imposed on the rest of the world by dominant and economically powerful countries. In this period the country concerned was England. To the extent that it succeeded in imposing free-trade policies on other countries, production was subordinated to prices determined competitively on the world market, and merchant capital was subordinated to industrial capital, with commercial profits becoming the mere income of capital advanced in the sphere of circulation.[50]

What this means is that the transition to investment in industry depended not upon the autonomous functioning of merchant capital, but upon the transformation of industry itself and of its context, and upon the appearance with this transformation of inducements to invest in production. In other words, it was dependent upon the development of new cost-reducing methods of production, upon the availability of abundant supplies of proletarianised workers, raw materials, and industrial equipment, upon the existence of expanding markets for the products of industry, and upon the breakdown of the regime of urban guild regulation and of the hegemony of large trading corporations. In short it depended upon the development of new techniques of production and the dissolution of previous modes of production.

This process of transition also had important implications for the pattern of urban growth. Industries organised under the putting-out system were developed in the countryside away from centres subject to guild and urban community controls, as was manufacturing, which constituted the first historical form of capitalist control over production. In a second stage the development of machinofacture and of the factory system was a predominantly urban phenomenon, but one which revolutionised the existing hierarchy of towns by occurring in areas outside of the limits of control of old corporate towns. With the development of machinofacture, capital seized hold of the process of production itself, dynamically reshaping every branch òf production both technically and organisationally, and revolutionising the technical and social divisions of labour. In conjunction with the revolutions in agriculture and in transport, machinofacture opened the way to the reduction of agriculture to one among many branches of industrial production, to the transformation of the countryside into a sphere of agricultural production, to an accelerated process of urbanisation based on the concentration of modern industry with its own internal dynamic in large cities, and to a radical and continuous reconstruction of the town—country division.[51]

8 Industry in the Transition to Capitalism

8.1 The transition from the guild to the domestic and to the putting-out system

Between the tenth and twelfth centuries the growing exchange of commodities and the extension of the social division of labour that occurred within the framework of the feudal system led, as we mentioned in an earlier section, to a new division between town and country. In particular, industrial activities that had until then been carried on in the countryside were more likely to be pursued by specialised craft workers producing for a wider market, and were increasingly located in new or expanding urban centres, as were commercial functions. The domestic system in which independent artisans used their own raw materials and tools and worked in their own homes continued to exist in rural areas, but most industrial activities became predominantly urban pursuits organised by urban-based guilds. The only important exceptions were a few trades such as quarrying, mining, and the smelting and refining of metals which were necessarily pursued in rural areas. The smelting and forging of iron, for example, required large amounts of charcoal, and so, in England, iron production was concentrated in woodland districts in areas like the Weald and the Forest of Dean, which also possessed, on the one hand, iron-stone deposits and, on the other hand, fast-flowing streams which were required from the fifteenth century onwards to operate bellows and forge-hammers used in the process of production.

But, towards the end of the Middle Ages, a gradual movement of industry from the towns back into the countryside was set in motion, and the guild system slowly disintegrated.

In some cases the development of rural industry was stimulated by the increased use of water-powered machines, which were particularly important in the fulling of cloth, that is in the beating of woven cloth so as to thicken and felt it. But it can be attributed largely to the action of merchant capitalists and of merchant entrepreneurs, who had started to transform rural crafts and to give an impetus to the development and expansion of specialised, export-oriented, domestic industries in predominantly rural districts. In this case the principal attraction of rural areas lay in rural labour-supply conditions.

In the late medieval and early modern periods merchant capitalists were switching to or were adopting a strategy of buying and, often after some additional processing by urban-based artisans, of reselling on regional and extra-regional markets products made by rural craft workers mainly with the help of the existing skills and techniques of rural production. Alternatively a greater emphasis was placed upon a putting-out of certain types of work to family units working in their own homes, rather than upon a strategy of merely buying the products of the petty-commodity producers of the rural domestic system. Instead of simply producing industrial products as use-values for themselves and for feudal lords, rural households, who were less than fully employed and whose agricultural work barely provided enough to support a family and to pay the dues with which it was burdened, were drawn into the production of industrial goods as exchange-values for sale on distant markets. In the case of the merchant capitalists involved, the decision to act in this way was often taken in order to benefit from the relative cheapness of raw materials, to lower fiscal exactions, to undercut urban monopolies, to circumvent the inelasticity of supply of the urban economy, and to avoid guild restrictions on the use of labour and on the quality of the product. But the main reason for encouraging the development of rural industry, and for diverting a significant part of production into the countryside, lay in the fact that it enabled them to reduce the costs of commodity production by buying from or by employing workers who were not already fully employed and whose incomes from industrial work could be depressed below those of their urban counterparts. The main reason why the industrial earnings of rural households were low was that they were frequently supplemented by incomes or subsistence goods acquired as a result of participation in agricultural work on their own holdings and on nearby commercial farms. A second was that there was often intense competition for work in the countryside. It was for all of these reasons that what has recently been called proto-industry, by which is meant a type of pre-industrial industry, whose development constituted a first phase of industrialisation which preceded and prepared the ground for the rise of modern industry, slowly appeared in many predominantly rural regions in Britain and Ireland and on the European mainland.[1]

In the view of Mendels, what was emerging was a type of industry whose final output was destined for non-local markets, which involved not only urban artisans but also, and in particular, rural and often peasant households, and which was associated with a symbiosis between craft industry, commercial agriculture in which extra workers were required at certain critical moments in the year owing to the seasonality of agricultural work, and peasant farming. The development of proto-industry depended in part upon the existence of normally urban-based merchants, and of supplies of raw and auxiliary materials and means of transport, and upon the development of supra-regional markets. But it also depended upon the existence of certain types of agrarian system and specific processes of agrarian development. In particular, it presupposed the existence of peasant households that did not obtain enough output and income from their holdings due to the infertility of the soil or the insufficiency of the land they held, and that were willing to combine craft activity with farming. As a result the workers employed in the industrial sector were not fully dependent upon industry for their means of livelihood and for the wherewithal to pay the dues to which they were subject, at least until the system reached its extreme and ultimate form in which entire families and large sections of the population in rural districts were almost exclusively engaged in one kind of industrial work. At the same time, processes of social differentiation and demographic growth led to the extended reproduction of a large smallholding and semi-landless substratum, as well as of a layer of day labourers, farmhands and servants who lived on the estates of the feudal lords or the farms of the peasants by whom they were employed. The operation of these processes meant that an increasing number of families found themselves cultivating pieces of land whose inadequate size and quality made it necessary for them to seek supplementary sources of income in the industrial sector. In many cases, petty-commodity producers adopted more intensive methods of cultivation and new crops in order to increase the output of the plots of land they held. But eventually they were often forced to neglect agriculture in favour of rural industry. In these circumstances the ownership or possession of land continued to be important, however, at least as a means of securing credit. A variety of other processes had similar effects. At the time of the seventeenth-century crisis a number of grain-producing areas in England were turned over to stock-raising, in the face of competition from other areas of cereal production and owing to the unsuitability of their soils for new methods of cultivation including the system of convertible husbandry. In these stock-raising regions there was often a striking expansion of proto-industry.

In a similar way, members of peasant households took up seasonal jobs in commercial farming which, in its turn, generated surpluses of relatively inexpensive food for consumption in proto-industrial zones and in the towns. As in the case of industry, commercial farming benefited from the existence of a local pool of workers who could be recruited in peak seasons and who were able to maintain themselves by working at other times in subsistence farming and, in this case, in cottage industry. As a result the workers concerned depended neither on relatively high wage payments nor on Poor Law support, which would have cost the landlords dearly. In short the development of proto-industry was associated with, and in important ways depended upon, an articulation and synchronisation of agriculture and industry, usually at the level of a nodal region.[2]

The development of proto-industry was closely bound up with forms of subsistence farming. In many cases it developed in pastoral-farming and stock-raising areas. One of the reasons for this lay in the relative weakness of the manorial system.

In areas of nucleated villages and open-field farming, seigneurial control and community cohesion were strong, and impeded
the expansion of proto-industry, but in areas of individual
farms and enclosed fields, constraints of this kind were absent.
A second reason was the availability of part-time workers, at
least in the months in which seasonal jobs in adjacent commercial farming districts were not to be found. But, as industry expanded in rural areas, the supply of labour was increased
by a variety of other processes, of which some of the most
important were endogenous.

On the one hand, the development of an industrial, alongside an agricultural, base for household economies, and the
proletarianisation of rural dwellers working in industry, often
led to earlier marriage, a decline in celibacy, more frequent
child-bearing, an increasing labour supply, and an increasingly
large rural proletariat, while reductions in the size of peasant
holdings, falling agricultural prices, and social differentiation
in the ranks of the peasantry, meant that the peasant population was often increasingly unable to find enough work on its
own tiny plots, that increasing numbers of peasants were being
forced to seek out supplementary or in some cases alternative
sources of income, and that new markets were being created
for the products of commercial farms. On the other hand, the
loss of common rights, the conversion of land from arable to
pasture farming, and, depending on the precise effects on the
demand for labour and on demographic trends, the consolidation and modernisation of farms, stimulated out-migration
from areas that were or had formerly been devoted to corn-
growing, while the availability of employment and land, and
the absence of communal regulations placing restrictions on
settlement, attracted many migrants to pastoral areas. In other
words the demographic mechanisms which had secured a
rough balance between the size of a family and its farm and,
at the level of a community, between the size of the population and the resources of the region radically altered.
More specifically the controls on fertility and curbs on immigration which were as important as high rates of mortality
in restraining population growth were no longer applied. As a
result the number of families and of villages often increased
sharply as traditional means of livelihood were augmented

by industrial earnings which were not directly related to farm size, and as new garden plots were provided on land that had previously been unused or closed off.[3]

The development of proto-industry occurred on an extensive scale in the textile, leather, and small metal trades in particular, and after being set in motion in England, the southern Low Countries, and southern Germany in the late medieval period, it accelerated in the late sixteenth and in the seventeenth century and, particularly on the European mainland, often survived into the nineteenth or even into the twentieth century. According to Kriedte, the factors lying behind the decisive wave of development at the end of the sixteenth and in the seventeenth century did not differ from those that had operated since the end of the thirteenth century:

> the long waves of the agrarian cycle and the trend periods of population growth connected to these waves by a feedback system; the increasing underemployment in the countryside resulting from population growth; the crisis of agricultural incomes in the 17th and early 18th century which led to a differentiation in production. To this should be added a slight increase in domestic demand resulting from the recovery of real wages . . . as well as a greatly expanding international demand, not least of all in colonial markets whose demand for industrial products was rapidly gaining in importance from the 17th century onwards.[4]

In most of the towns, craft workers struggled to keep guild organisations intact. In some long-established industrial centres in which craft workers successfully switched to the production of luxury goods, guild-based craft industry survived for a while, and in many smaller towns urban industry continued to exist. But in industries whose products were destined for regional and distant as opposed to local markets, merchants generally succeeded in interposing themselves between urban and rural artisans and their materials and markets. It was often in the towns that the final stages of production, requiring the highest levels of skill and contributing a significant proportion of the value-added contained in the finished product, were accomplished by artisans who were either dispersed throughout the urban area or concentrated in workshops equipped with small amounts of fixed capital. In addition, the merchant capitalists who co-ordinated or organised and controlled the whole system were usually based in the towns. As a result, towns played a central role in the edifice of proto-industry.[5] But the expansion of output and the increase in employment with which the proto-industrial development of the late middle ages and of the sixteenth and seventeenth centuries was associated, occurred predominantly in rural districts. It is this fact that provides a partial explanation of the failure of many towns to grow significantly after the fourteenth century.

By the eighteenth century a large proportion of craft activity was carried on in small villages and in rural areas. It was organised in a wide variety of ways, with the specific form of organisation differing between regions, over the course of history, and between and within branches of production. Yet it is possible to make some general statements, for in most cases proto-industry was organised either as a *Kaufsystem*, as a *Verlagsystem*, or as a system lying somewhere between these polar forms.[6] In a *Kaufsystem* independent artisans used raw materials that they had produced or purchased themselves and owned the equipment they used, and they sold the finished products to merchants in a public market place for cash with which they could buy consumption goods and raw materials and could replace worn-out equipment, while the merchants advanced money to buy commodities which could be subsequently exchanged for a larger sum of money. The petty-commodity producers of a *Kaufsystem* were formally independent but were often exploited through trade, and in many cases a system of this kind gave way to a *Verlagsystem*, as and when merchant capitalists succeeded in interposing themselves between craft workers and their materials and outlets, and in monopolising input as well as output markets. In a *Verlagsystem* some or all of the raw materials, semi-finished goods, tools, and credit required to carry out the production process were supplied to virtually wage-dependent workers, with at most very tenuous ties with the land, by merchant entrepreneurs or by some of the more prosperous producers, often through agents and middlepersons whose position and authority varied markedly. The domestic producers were in many cases utterly dependent on the merchants who supplied them with the inputs they needed, and who commissioned work from them, paid them a kind of piece-rate for the work performed and for the reproduction of the elements they had contributed to production, and disposed of the finished product. It was common for the merchant entrepreneurs to retain control of the more capital-intensive finishing processes which, like warehousing, were frequently located in urban settlements, while the regions in which a *Verlagsystem* existed were usually more specialised than areas in which a *Kaufsystem* was present, in the sense that domestic workers in the first type of region tended to produce a part of a commodity, instead of a whole commodity, as was characteristically the case in regions of the second kind.

Of the studies that consider the ways in which these models correspond with the forms of industrial organisation that existed in practice, one that is particularly interesting is an account by Hudson of the wool textile industry in the West Riding of Yorkshire.[7] In it she points out that in the middle of the eighteenth and in the early nineteenth century both of the broad types of system referred to above existed in the West Riding. In the upland areas in the west of the region the worsted industry, which developed quickly from the middle of the eighteenth century onwards, was organised on a putting-out basis. The land in the west was of low quality and was mainly used for pastoral farming. The overwhelming majority of it was held in the form of freehold, and, since enclosure for sheep-rearing had occurred in the late sixteenth and early seventeenth century, manorial control had been weak for some time, partible inheritance had been practised, and processes of social polarisation had been operating, leading to the appearance, at one pole, of a group of sizeable freeholders and leaseholders and, at the other pole, of a class of cottagers and landless labourers.

The low and declining average size of peasant holdings, the inability of the land to support anything other than livestock-grazing and the cultivation of a few oats, the relatively low labour requirements of the system of agricultural production, and a tradition of peasant skills in the production of woollen cloth for household and local needs, all played a part in making this area into a zone of proto-industrial development as early as the fourteenth century. Of course, the development of rural industry was an additional stimulus to the practice of partible inheritance, and led to an increase in the number of households and in the number of people who were less than fully employed by work in the agricultural sector.

By the early eighteenth century the wool textile industry in this area was dominated by small but independent family units, which usually produced a kersey a week to supplement income from the land, although some households devoted themselves to the production of yarn or to the weaving of cloth. But as the years passed the independence and viability of small household units of this kind were increasingly threatened by the subdivision of holdings, by their heavy dependence upon foreign markets on which fluctuations in demand were marked, and by the rise of larger textile freeholders and leaseholders who were capable of accumulating capital, and who began to develop putting-out systems.

It was this agrarian and industrial history that prepared the ground for the development of the worsted industry in the eighteenth century. In the 1750s, in particular, the drying-up of the market for kerseys led to a big shift into worsted production. The worsted branch required more capital than the woollen branch, and the typical worsted concern was larger, and emerged when merchant capitalists, who took no direct part in production itself, and a small number of master weavers, started to develop extensive putting-out systems. In this sector the merchant capitalists who dominated the industry put most of the work out to a large army of cottagers who by this time possessed little or no land, with each household and even whole sub-regions specialising in a particular stage in the production process, instead of carrying out all the phases in the production of a finished commodity.

In the more fertile lowland area in the east, more land was used for dairying and for arable farming, the proportion of copyhold land was much greater, manorial controls were of more significance, and enclosure occurred later. In this area, seasonal variations in the demand for labour in agriculture were more marked, and the appearance of a sizeable class of cottagers and landless labourers was retarded. The size of individual holdings was on average larger, and most units were more self-sufficient in foodstuffs. A rural cloth industry was fairly widespread, but it differed from the industry in the west in a number of ways. In the first place its output included a high proportion of broadcloths and of fine woollen cloths. Second, it was dominated by a fairly large number of relatively independent clothiers who employed several journeymen and apprentices along with members of their families, who combined agricultural production with industrial work, and who were able to use securely held, enclosed and consolidated farms as mortgageable assets as and when they needed credit. Moreover, barriers to entry existed and rules regarding standards were applied. And finally the overall degree of dependence upon exports was less.

In the eighteenth century, even with the expansion of commercial opportunities, the traditional artisan structure continued to be a more competitive way of producing cheap woollen goods. As a result, the woollen branch, which was concentrated west of a line running north—south through Leeds and Wakefield and east of the worsted zone, continued to be dominated by a large number of master manufacturers, who owned their own premises and tools, who bought wool from dealers, who worked it up into undressed cloth with the help of the members of their own families and of a few journeymen and apprentices, and who carried it to the market or to public cloth-halls where it was sold to merchants. But, from the middle of the eighteenth century, many clotheirs began to by-pass the cloth-halls and either to deal directly with merchants on a commission basis or to carry out their own marketing, and by the end of the century some large clothiers were emerging.

On the other hand, in both branches of the wool textile industry, the more capital-intensive processes involved in the dyeing, dressing, and finishing of cloth were centralised from an early date in small specialised workshops and carried out by closely supervised wage-labourers. By the eighteenth

century the vast majority of these concerns were run by
master manufacturers employing skilled craft workers on
traditional terms, and functioned on a commission basis.

8.2 The 'two paths' of the transition from the feudal to the capitalist mode of production

In the last section we outlined some of the main changes that
occurred in the organisation of industry in pre-industrial
Europe, and we pointed to some of the ways in which they
were associated with broad changes in the division between
town and country. In this one we shall refer briefly to some
of the connections between the development of proto-industry
and the emergence of what Marx called manufacturing in
which wage-dependent workers were formally subsumed
under capital; and we shall indicate how it prepared the ground
for the factory system, at least in the textile sector, even
though it was not the only way of establishing the relevant
preconditions, and even though some regions of proto-industry
were not transformed into areas of factory production, but
were deindustrialised, usually under the impact of competition
from more developed regions. The processes of economic
change in industry along with those in agriculture and commerce were also processes of social change, and were closely
bound up with struggles over the trajectory of the process of
social reproduction and with significant changes in the structure of the political system and in state policy. As a result,
we shall also pay some attention to the competing interests
and roles of some of the different social groups involved in
the transition from medieval, guild-based industry to the
manufacturing stage of the capitalist mode of production,
and we shall refer to the part played by England's seventeenth-
century bourgeois revolution in creating the economic and
political conditions in which the process of industrialisation
could proceed.

Following Marx, both Dobb and Takahashi identified two
principal ways in which the transition to manufacturing
occurred.[8] What Marx called 'the really revolutionary path'
was the one that was followed when some independent craft

workers operating in the rural domestic system, some small and medium merchant manufacturers in the putting-out system, and some masters in town crafts, became both merchants and capitalists. At the same time, merchant capital and commercial gain, instead of being the dominant type of capital and the principal form of surplus appropriation, were subordinated to industrial capital and industrial profit. Way one can be characterised as a process of transition in which some independent producers succeeded in slowly accumulating capital, began to purchase raw materials and labour-power on the product and labour markets respectively, started to introduce cost-reducing methods of production, and began to sell their output to the commercial world in general rather than to individual merchants. In other words, when some petty-commodity producers began to organise production on a capitalist basis free from the handicraft restrictions of the guilds and free from control by individual merchants, the first way was being followed, and once 'the capitalist mode of production had asserted itself and the producer himself [or herself] had become a merchant', the sphere of circulation ceased to be the sphere in which the general rate of profit initially took shape, and commercial profit was 'reduced to that aliquot part of total surplus value falling to the share of merchant capital as an aliquot part of the total capital engaged in the social process of reproduction'.[9]

The second path was the one that was followed when some members of the existing mercantile class started to act as capitalist entrepreneurs, by exercising a form of merchant control and direction of the process of industrial production, and by establishing direct sway over it, partly 'to exploit the latter more effectively', and partly 'to transform it in the interests of greater profit and the service of wider markets'.[10] But the relationship of merchant capital to production was essentially an external one, in which its activities were confined to the advancing of materials and credit to individual producers and to the selling of the finished product. As a result, the control of production by merchant capital served historically as a stepping-stone in the transition to large-scale industry, but, in so far as the production process itself was not controlled and modified, it was associated with a tendency to preserve and retain the old methods of production based upon handicraft techniques as its precondition, and in the end it often stood in the way of the overthrow and transformation of the old mode of production. It was in this type of situation that the second path was being followed. But not all merchant capitalists acted in this way. A significant number of them did switch, and focused on the organisation and modernisation of production instead of upon marketing. But in this case they were no longer advancing merchant capital.

In the view of Takahashi the two ways outlined by Marx are historical characterisations of distinct phases in the origins of capitalism,[11] although, as Dobb has pointed out, the two lines of development are far from clearly drawn in practice, differ widely between sectors and regions, and in any case are not wholly distinct.[12] Indeed Marx himself proceeded with his argument by pointing to a three-fold historical transition in which an earlier phase was added to the two paths. In the first place merchants set up industries, as in the case of medieval craft industries, producing luxury goods from materials and sometimes with the help of workers which they had imported from abroad. In some cases, they also brought workers with the relevant skills from foreign production centres. Second, merchants turned small masters into middle-persons and bought directly from individual producers, leaving them nominally independent, and leaving the mode of production unchanged. Third, industrialists became merchants and produced directly and on a large scale for the wholesale market.[13]

The recent writing on proto-industry would suggest that the actual sequence of events was much more complex than most of these formulations seem to imply. But lying behind the identification of two paths, and indeed behind some of the other categories Marx used in discussing the transition to capitalism, are some important analytical distinctions. In this case, what he was highlighting was the distinction between merchant and industrial capital and the change in the relationships between commercial gain and the modernisation of production itself which accompanied capitalist industrialisation. It is therefore a distinction that helps us to understand and to explain concrete historical changes in the organisation of industry, but it does not say anything very specific about the exact empirical form that they assumed.

As Marx has indicated, with the technical transformation of production and the development of the factory system, the relationship between commerce and industry was radically altered:

> Originally commerce was the precondition for the trans-formation of the crafts, the rural domestic industries, and feudal agriculture, into capitalist enterprises. It develops the product into a commodity, partly by creating a market for it, and partly by introducing new commodity equivalents and supplying production with new raw and auxiliary materials, thereby opening new branches of production based from the first upon commerce both as concerns production for the home and world-market, and as concerns conditions of production originating in the world-market. As soon as manufacture gains sufficient strength, and particularly large-scale industry, it creates in its turn a market for itself, by capturing it through its commodities. At this point commerce becomes the servant of industrial production.[14]

A change in and inversion of the relationship between commerce and industry, and between commercial and industrial gain, was both a logical and a historical corollary of the transition to capitalist manufacturing. In the view of Marx it was likely to be a result of the actions of a newly rising class and not of a change in the behaviour of existing mercantile elites, even though the wealth accumulated by merchants can and did play an important role in financing the expansion of industrial capital, at least as soon as they could no longer profit in the old way and capitalist industrialisation was under way, and even though some members of the merchant class may have played an important role in the switch to mechanised factory production at certain times and in certain places. At the time when the transition was occurring it was quite common for the members of these two broad groups to have radically different interests and to come into open conflict with one another. As a result, it seems as if the subordination of commercial to industrial gain was most likely to have occurred via the first way and that it could not have occurred via way two by itself.

Any general statements about the history of proto-industrialisation and about the transition to forms of centralised production must be treated with extreme caution. Yet some type of outline is necessary. It has been pointed out by Marx that what is now called proto-industry emerged when the rural secondary occupations were drawn into the production not of use-values for auto and local consumption but of exchange-values for the general market.[15] As inputs into the process of production were advanced in the form of capital, as manufacturing workshops were erected either by merchants or by petty producers in order to carry out starting and finishing processes, and as domestic workshops were enlarged and operated increasingly with the help of wage-labourers, what had formerly been rural secondary occupations were seized and organized on a manufacturing basis. In the course of time, some types of domestic activity were slowly replaced by work in the centralised workshops of an entrepreneur where, in some cases, work continued to be organised on a manufacturing basis, and where, in others, new, more complex, and more expensive machinery was installed and productivity-increasing methods of large-scale production were introduced. At the same time, the economic functions of the family and household were correspondingly reduced to consumption and the reproduction of labour-power. The process of centralisation of production into workshops was initiated in a wide variety of ways. In some cases it was set in motion as and when a merchant or putter-out added some workshops to his or her counting-house and stockrooms and, as a consequence, started to supervise directly some of the productive labour involved in manufacturing the commodities they sold. Alternatively a few of the petty producers succeeded in enlarging their workshops and in employing a considerable number of wage-labourers. In this way they managed to break through the limitations associated with the family work unit, and in the end they normally managed to give up productive work altogether, and concentrated on the supervision of the work of those they employed, and on marketing. Otherwise, central-

ised workshops were established by individuals who rose
from the ranks of the heterogeneous group of agents and
middlepersons operating in the putting-out system, or even
by individuals who had accumulated wealth outside of the
sector in question.[16]

In an account developed by Schlumbohm a number of
different phases and types of relations of production are
identified: the feudal organisation of industrial commodity
production; the *Kaufsystem*, in which petty-commodity
production interacted with merchant capital; the *Verlagsystem*, in which the sphere of production was being penetrated
by capital; and the development of centralised manufacturing
workshops. He then argues that the stages in the development
of the relations of production that he has identified

> do not constitute a sequence in the sense that they neces-
> sarily had to follow each other. In the course of the histori-
> cal development of an enterprise or of a region or industry
> stagnation or even retrogression could occur, e.g. develop-
> ment might be arrested at the stage of the *Kaufsystem* or
> at a low stage of the putting out system. On the other
> hand a stage could be omitted, e.g. development might
> proceed directly from the *Kaufsystem* to a type of central-
> ised manufacture or from some form of putting out system
> to the mechanised factory. Nonetheless the trend in proto-
> industrialisation, though slow and irregular, is clearly
> recognisable: capital increasingly penetrated into the sphere
> of production, and relatively independent petty producers,
> who owned the means of production they used, were
> transformed into dependent wage labourers. This trend
> could manifest itself in two forms: either the relations of
> production in an older proto-industrial region or industry
> changed, or new industries and regions which were more
> capitalistically organised grew in importance.[17]

A second general point that needs to be kept in mind is
that changes in industrial organisation cannot be treated
independently of changes in the material side of the production process and in the forces of production. The development
and expansion of the domestic system did not simply result

in an extended reproduction of the material and social conditions on which it was based. As a result of the struggles between the producers and those who dominated the system, and of the material progress by which its development was accompanied, on the one hand, and of changes in the general economic environment on the other, it was associated with the appearance of new conditions. In many branches of production these changes could not be reconciled with the preservation of the family economy or of craft skills and craft status for the workers, and so, via the struggles that the resulting tensions unleashed, the domestic system was slowly transformed, and gave way to new types of industrial organisation and to new methods of production that enabled the rate of profit to be increased, or at least to be kept at its existing level. As a result, some of the constraints on the development of the forces of production were lifted.

In what ways did the actions of merchant capitalists create the preconditions for modern industry? It is well known that in branches of production such as mining, metal-smelting, brass-making, the production of battery goods, glass-making, and paper-making, which required large amounts of fixed capital, forms of centralised production were common in the early modern period. Industries of this kind employed large numbers of workers on a wage basis, were protected by absolute monarchs, partly in order that they could obtain revenue from them and partly to reduce to acceptable levels the risks of undertaking essential industrial activities, and were usually set up by aristocratic patentees and merchants, as in the case of the chartered monopolies of Stuart England. But of more significance was the development of rural domestic industry, and the setting up by merchant entrepreneurs of putting-out systems in which urban and, in particular, rural craft workers, who normally owned the instruments of production, were subordinated to mercantile interests.

The movement of sections of merchant capital towards an increasingly intimate control over production was occurring on an extensive scale in England in the textile, leather, and small metal trades in the second half of the sixteenth and in the seventeenth century. As they gained control of production and succeeded in subordinating the mass of the craft workers, merchant entrepreneurs acted in ways that played an important part in breaking down the guild system and in undermining urban petty-commodity production. In the past, the craft guilds had sought to restrict entry and to create conditions of excess supply in input markets and excess demand in output markets, with a view to maintaining a differential between the price paid for materials used by the direct producers and the price they received for the finished product, and in order to secure reasonable conditions of employment and standards of living for those engaged in the craft. By contrast, the aim of newly dominant mercantile elements was to create conditions of surplus in both of these markets, in which they, of course, were purchasers. In order to do this they attempted to concentrate the purchase of raw materials and the sale of finished goods exclusively in their own hands, to increase the degree of dependence of craft workers on individual merchants, and to prevent them from achieving the status of independent capitalists. Of particular importance was the way in which they sought to cheapen supply and to reduce production prices by pressing strongly for changes in guild regulations or by circumventing them.

One of the clearest examples of the subordination of craft workers by a mercantile element is afforded by the history of the twelve great Livery Companies of London.[18] By the early decades of the sixteenth century, those that had originally been handicraft organisations or included a handicraft element had come to be dominated by trading minorities which used the companies' monopoly positions for their own ends. Attempts were made to increase the number of apprentices without regard to considerations as to whether or not all of them would subsequently be able to achieve the status of master, to employ unqualified workers, and to extend production into the suburbs and into the surrounding countryside. But as a result of these actions, the mercantile element often came into conflict not only with urban craft workers, but also with merchants in provincial towns who were not themselves merchant employers of craft workers living in unregulated areas, and who were therefore unable to compete with the products of the rural industries financed by rich London merchants.

On the other hand, by the early seventeenth century, mechanisms of social differentiation had led to the appearance in England of a significant number of commodity producers who had often been under the control of merchant capitalists but who were beginning to rise to independence and to achieve the status of merchant employers or capitalist entrepreneurs. But in this type of case similar attempts were made to ignore guild regulations.[19]

The costs of commodity production were reduced not only by encouraging the spread of rural domestic industry with its low labour costs and by breaking up the guild system, but also by introducing directly or indirectly significant changes in the sphere of production. In many cases the aim of reducing the prices at which they bought goods led merchant capitalists to organise more developed forms of co-operation, and to extend the division of labour within and between domestic units, even though production itself remained under the immediate control of the direct producer, and continued to be based for the most part on the existing techniques of craft production. The concentration of substantial numbers of simultaneously employed workers under the control of a single capitalist with more resources to invest than the producers themselves commanded, accordingly enabled greater levels of output and productivity to be achieved, without major changes in the techniques of production, but through a more effective use of the workers' time, through a subdivision of production into different stages and tasks, or through a closer co-ordination of successive stages in the process of production, and through an extension of the social division of labour. As a result, the family and household ceased to be 'a production unit in the sense that the work process required the co-operation of all its members and all earned an indivisible income through their common labour; instead each family member could earn an individual wage by separate labour'. In such circumstances the family and household was turned into the site at which production occurred, and continued to be a unit only with respect to the processes of consumption and reproduction.[20] At the same time, the independence of outworkers was reduced, since the value of an individual household's output could only be realised within the sphere of activity of a specific merchant. As a result, the capitalist merchant entrepreneur who organised the various stages of production was usually also in a better position to exercise some control over the quality of the product, although in the end the search for more adequate methods of quality control tended to work in favour of the manufacturing workshop and against a geographically dispersed putting-out system.

In some cases merchants set up workshops. In the cloth industry, for example, a minority of merchants established workshops for spinning and weaving, often alongside existing domestic workers, and, in some cases, attempts were made to modernise some of the processes of production, especially those involved in finishing-operations which, as we have indicated, were already being carried out on a factory basis, by using a number of new and improved techniques and instruments and by reorganising the process of production. But on the whole the techniques of production were not improved much before the eighteenth century, especially in the domestic system, where instruments were constrained in size, complexity, and motive-power source by the fact that they were to be installed in the homes of the producers. It was more a matter of applying existing techniques more widely, although the more detailed division of labour that was established in the rural domestic system played an important part in preparing the ground for mechanisation.[21]

In the literature on proto-industrialisation, an emphasis is also placed on the connections between industrial growth and the development of a commercial agricultural sector, which was subsequently to be capable of expanding production without a sharp increase in the prices of agricultural products, and of supplying a burgeoning industrial population with food. In addition, it is pointed out that it helped to generate new needs for agricultural and industrial products, which had formerly been unfelt, unsatisfied, or satisfied in other ways, and led to the emergence of a network of local, regional, national, and international markets, on whose growth its development and the subsequent development of large-scale industry depended.[22]

The process of proto-industrial growth also acted as a spur to demographic growth and to a process of social differentia-

tion within the ranks of the producers, which eventually
transformed a large number of relatively independent producers into wage-dependent labourers. With the development of
the rural domestic system the family became a site for the
construction of new social relations, especially as the importance of women's and children's work increased: old forms of
gender differentiation were broken down, old attitudes to
work and leisure were disrupted, and established consumption
patterns and horizons were transformed.[23] The new system
of industrial organisation was also associated with the appearance of an increasingly large stratum of individuals who were
in part peasants and in part wage-labourers, and who worked
partly in the agricultural and partly in the industrial sector
according to the daily and annual cycle of work. But as the
years passed many of the producers lost their independence,
were restricted to one line of industrial activity, and were
reduced to the status of wage-earners who had to work simply
to pay off advances from merchant entrepreneurs.[24] In other
words, proto-industrialisation contributed to the appearance
and extended reproduction of capitalist relations of production.

The speed and extent of the process of proletarianisation
was conditioned by the ability of petty-commodity producers
to buy the equipment they used, and to finance themselves
in the interval between the purchase or receipt of the materials
necessary for production and the sale of the finished product.
As a result, it was dependent in part upon the economic status
of the immediate producers and, in particular, upon the
ownership or possession of sufficiently large and fertile pieces
of land and the existence of alternative sources of income
which alone would enable them to survive without falling
into debt, without having to mortgage what property they
owned, and without eventually forfeiting it. But it also depended upon the success of the producers in their individual
and collective attempts to preserve what independence they
had, and to resist the introduction of new instruments of
production, which were too large and expensive for them to
buy, and whose use would entail a permanent and irreversible
increase in their dependence on putting-out capitalists, or
which could only be used in the central production facility of

an entrepreneur. 'But if, in fact, as a result of the economic ascendancy of the new relations of production, this resistance was unsuccessful, the workers turned toward fighting for their wages and working conditions within the framework of the new form of industrial organisation. And strikes assumed a prominent place in the new struggle.' In other words, as the independent petty-commodity producers lost their independence and were turned into the wage-labourers of merchant manufacturers, the goals and forms of their organisations no longer followed the examples set by the guilds, but slowly and with many interruptions approached those of the later labour movement.[25]

By the eighteenth century, mechanisms of differentiation had led to social polarisation in many parts of England. In the cloth-producing areas in Yorkshire and Lancashire, for example, at one pole a group of poor and dependent craft workers was to be found, while, at the other pole, a group of master craft workers and of well-to-do independent producers existed, with many of the members of the second group being the employers of others and acting as middlepersons between the marginalised craft workers and the more prosperous merchants in the principal market towns.[26]

The development of proto-industry, in conjunction with processes that concentrated landed property into fewer hands and undermined small property in land on which the independence of domestic craft workers largely depended, contributed, in other words, to the formal subsumption of labour under capital, that is to a transformation of the social position of the agents participating in production without a revolutionary change in the process of production. The labourer was being separated from the means of production often through the action of merchant capital, labour-power was being turned into a commodity, and the objective and subjective conditions of labour were beginning to assume the forms of constant and variable capital; but capital was taking over existing processes of production, developed under different and more archaic modes of production, and was producing additional surplus-value mainly by increasing absolute surplus-value.[27]

In addition the development of proto-industry was accompanied by an accumulation of monetary wealth, in the hands of merchants and merchant entrepreneurs, agents and middle-persons in the putting-out system, and some producers, who had also acquired in different degrees market connections, entrepreneurial skills, and knowledge of the techniques of production. At the same time, wealth was accumulated by commercial farmers whose sales expanded, and by landowners who received high rents from the small and fragmented farms on which rural artisans lived. In the right circumstances wealth accumulated in this way could be and was used to set up workshops and to introduce new methods of production.

So far we have outlined a number of ways in which the process of proto-industrialisation prepared the ground for the development of modern industry, we have indicated how the control of production by merchant capital acted as a stepping-stone in the transition to large-scale industry, and we have pointed to the rise of a new class of entrepreneurs. In the course of the argument we have pointed out that the emergence and growth of manufacturing and eventually of industrial capital presupposed a relaxation of guild restrictions and of the economic influence of urban governments. But it was also to depend upon the emancipation of industrial interests from the constraints associated with the granting of monopolies in the spheres of industry and trade, and with the activities of privileged trading companies on which some sections of merchant capital with close connections with absolutism depended. To these elements should be added the need for conditions that favour rather than obstruct the modernisation and transformation of the agricultural sector. It was partly for reasons of this kind that the political struggles in seventeenth-century England were of such moment, especially in view of the fact that the economic and social mechanisms and practices outlined above were mediated and profoundly influenced by political decisions and actions.

At the same time, the extended reproduction of the new relations of production that were emerging, and the continuous development of the production and exchange of commodities, entailed the establishment of a new system of political domination and a new set of relationships between state and society. Of particular importance was the establishment and the maintenance and reproduction, ultimately by means of the state's near monopoly of legitimate physical violence and coercion but also via the exercise of political hegemony, of a legal and institutional framework capable of guaranteeing formal bourgeois freedom and equality, a variety of rights with respect to the ownership and transfer of private property, and the unimpeded circulation of commodities, including labour-power, and money.

As soon as the capitalist mode of production had been firmly established, the process of reproduction of capital normally resulted in the production and reproduction of most of its material and social preconditions. But in the early phases of capitalism, the laws and institutions on which it was ultimately dependent were to play an active role in removing the restrictions on, and in establishing the general conditions for, its development, and during this period when a new legal order was being created, violence was more clearly visible both in the interior of countries and in their relations with other states than during the later period when the new system functioned regularly.[28]

It is not possible to trace the development of the state and the history of state action in any detail, but some reference must be made to the political events in mid-seventeenth-century England that were of particular importance in laying the foundations for capitalist development and, indeed, to some aspects of subsequent state policy.

In the English Revolution social and political alignments were both complex and changeable, in part because the movements against royal grants of economic privilege and monopoly, which were increasingly unwarranted from an economic point of view, were for many people not so much a struggle for a general principle as a struggle against the specific privileges enjoyed by other groups of individuals and against barriers to their own ambitions. At the same time, alignments were shaped by a complex combination not only of economic but also of political and religious issues, while many ties, including a shared fear of the lower orders, held together what Barrington Moore has called the modernisers and the traditionalists. But on the whole, monopolistic and chartered merchants and royal patentees, and the merchants who formed the traditional municipal patriciates, sought to defend the trading restrictions upon which the commercial profits they obtained largely depended; and so they allied themselves with the money-dealing capitalists, the feudal landed aristocracy, the rentier and leisured classes, which had invested in land and titles and accordingly had an interest in the stability of the existing social order, the gentry in agricultural districts in the economically less developed north and west of the country who usually succeeded in carrying their tenants with them, and the absolute monarchy in the Civil War. On the other hand, some of the members of the greater London companies played an important part on the conservative wing of the Parliamentary camp, while 'sections of the bourgeoisie that had any roots in industry, whether they were provincial clothiers or merchants of a London Livery Company who had used their capital to organise the country industry, were whole-hearted supporters of the Parliamentary cause'. But the real driving force behind the English Revolution was the new Cromwellian army and the Independents whose social base lay in provincial manufacturing interests and in sections of the squirearchy, and the small and middling yeoman farmers who preponderated in the economically more advanced south and east of the country. In other words, it was composed of strata in which free and independent peasants, small and medium industrialists, and other commercially minded elements in the agricultural and industrial sectors, who were rising according to way one, were strongly represented. Strong support for the anti-Royalist side also came from many of the common people who had been dispossesed or owned little property and who, with their levelling tendencies and opposition to large-scale property, were the most radical components of the movement. But as soon as the more limited aims of the gentry had been realised groups like the Levellers and the Diggers were isolated and defeated.[29]

In its economic and social policy, the Commonwealth introduced a number of changes which lasted into the period following the Restoration, and which were of considerable importance in clearing the path and in laying some of the foundations for the development of capitalism. The industrial monopolies were abolished, while employers and enterprises were freed from various types of government regulation and control, and the old apprenticeship laws ceased to be enforced, although they were not repealed. A series of steps were taken which were eventually to lead to the ascendancy of the improving landlord and the enclosing squire and to the disappearance of the small owner—cultivator. In the words of Hill, 'the rich inherited the earth'. A number of advances occurred in the field of communications, and the system of taxation was modified in order to fulfil the dual role of financing the legal, administrative, repressive, and military apparatuses, and of enhancing the development of the national economy. In addition, successive governments paid more attention to the interests of trade and colonial development, and to the use of sea-power, in the pursuit of aggressive, commercially oriented foreign policies in line with the views of the big company merchants and the City of London, while the right of merchants to form privileged trading companies to which access was restricted was altered but not ended. In the field of politics a divinely supported authority was replaced by a restricted system of parliamentary democracy, while at both national and local levels power was to lie in the hands of a coalition of commercially minded landowners who lived mainly by leasing out modernised farms to capitalist tenants, and of merchants and financiers who adopted a permissive attitude to capitalist industrialisation. As a result, in the fifty years following England's albeit partial and incomplete bourgeois revolution, the growth of industrial capitalism was accelerated enormously, and the stage was set for the industrial revolution of the century that was to come.[30]

In the context of an expanding world market the existing pre-capitalist relations of production, which corresponded to the acquired productive forces and to the social conditions that had previously existed and out of which they had arisen, and which were having an impact of their own on the evolution of the forces of production, were inhibiting the development and use of more modern methods of production.[31] The existence of a small peasantry was an obstacle to the introduction of improved methods of cultivation and large-scale animal-raising. At the same time, pre-capitalist relations were shackling industrial productivity, in part because they rested on labour as an activity of individual artisans which involved the use of specific craft skills and presupposed ownership of the instrument of production by the individual worker. In addition, restrictions were placed on the mobility of labour and on the concentration of a large number of workers under a single capitalist employer.

Some of the resulting tensions were eventually resolved by changes in the relations of production which permitted some of the constraints on the development of the forces of production and on the expansion of human needs to be lifted. One way in which they were slackened or lifted was through the development of domestic industry and the putting-out system. A second and related one was through the emergence of a new class of entrepreneurs. A third was through the success in the English Revolution of those classes most suited, most able, and most disposed to develop new forces of production.

The struggles between merchants, employers, and craft workers, by which this process was accompanied and conditioned, continued into the late eighteenth and early nineteenth century, when the opposing factions were more clearly defined. At this stage, an extremely important industrial and political movement emerged, when workers of craft or artisan status, who were rapidly losing what job control they enjoyed, and when small producers and small masters, whose independence was being seriously undermined and threatened by capitalist competition, organised themselves in an attempt to secure the enforcement of earlier legislation dating back to the guilds, which related to the use of apprentice labour, to customary prices and wages, to the maximum number of looms or machines that an individual employer could hold, and to the use of new machinery. The central focus of discontent lay in the ranks of those producers who were most affected by new working practices and new techniques that undermined craft standards. But widespread support was gained from the artisan class as a whole, from small masters, and from many other members of the community who had moral or political objections to the undermining of small producers, to the factory system, and, more abstractly, to the elevation of the principles of *laissez-faire* over and above questions of social welfare.

At first the protests of the workers assumed constitutional forms. But this type of action was made difficult by the use of the legal system to prevent artisans and industrial workers from organising themselves. As Thompson has pointed out:

> it was here that the flagrant class oppression of the Combination Acts bore down upon them at every point. At a time when the common law of conspiracy or 5 Elizabeth C.4 was being employed to defeat trade union action, every attempt to enforce statute law favourable to the workers' interests ended in failure or financial loss.[32]

But after the repeal or permanent suspension of much of the old legislation in the first decade of the nineteenth century, increasing resort was had to violent forms of protest. The period of greatest violence was in 1811 and 1812 when no fewer than 12,000 troops were deployed in the disturbed counties.[33] It occurred partly because of the inability of the workers to secure change constitutionally. But it was also a product of conditions of intense hardship, brought about by the interruption of trade and soaring food prices caused by the extended war with France, which itself was a source of discontent, and of the attempts by individual employers to secure as much trade as they could by cutting costs and introducing new machinery, especially in the export sectors.[34]

The struggles of these years are referred to as Luddism. But what was at stake was much more than the question of the introduction of machinery. Instead of being seen as some kind of antediluvian opposition to the use of machinery, it must, as Thompson has pointed out, 'be seen as arising at the crisis point in the abrogation of paternalist legislation and in the imposition of the political economy of *laissez-faire* upon, and against the will and conscience of, the working people'.[35] Indeed, in the framework-knitting industry in Nottingham, where specifically Luddite struggles were to break out first of all, the introduction of new machinery was not even an issue. But in the context of a widely dispersed domestic system, machine-breaking was one of the best ways of effectively stopping production, while the destruction of property was a very effective weapon against comparatively small and local employers.[36] In the second place, the technique of wrecking was not associated with unqualified opposition to the introduction of machinery, nor was it used merely in order to defend the interests of workers with relatively privileged positions in the occupational hierarchy. In cases in which the introduction of machinery was a relevant consideration, what was at stake were the terms on which it was to be introduced, and, in the view of Thompson, what lay behind it was a different morality from that embodied in the newly emerging capitalist society, with the result that it was in fact 'a quasi-insurrectionary movement, which continually trembled on the edge of ulterior revolutionary objectives'.[37]

The three main sectors and areas affected by Luddism were the framework-knitting district centred on Nottingham, the West Riding woollen industry and the croppers, and cotton industry in South Lancashire where it was led by the weavers.[38] The actual nature of the struggle and its outcome differed in each case, but in all three, the introduction of cheaper methods of production, which undermined the economic and social status of the workers concerned, was particularly important.

In the case of the framework-knitters, the outworkers who had a long-established artisan tradition were experiencing a deterioration in their status, partly as a result of a fall in the demand for fancy hose, which can be linked with the 'sombre tone of anti-Jacobin society', and, more specifically, as a result of the growing practices of 'cut ups' and 'colting'. The term 'cut ups' was used to refer to the practice of making stockings by cutting up a piece of woven cloth and seaming it. As a result, colting, or the replacement of framework-knitters by younger, unskilled workers, could occur, and the preconditions for sweating were created. In the end some concessions were made to the workers, but, as in the case of the other groups involved, the movement itself failed largely because of the way in which it was repressed.[39]

In the case of the West Riding, the immediate issue was the combined use of the gig-mill, which had been prohibited by statute, and the shear-frame, which was a more recent invention, which enabled the skills of the croppers to be dispensed with and removed the material conditions on which the croppers' status had been based. At first, the strategy they adopted was successful in preventing the machines from being used.

But, in spite of the fact that they received wide support from other workers and from small masters who lacked the resources necessary to install the machines, the struggle ultimately proved unsuccessful, and the croppers disappeared as an identifiable group of workers in the first half of the nineteenth century.[40]

8.3 The transition from the domestic and the putting-out to the factory system

By the seventeenth century a number of centralised production units, employing large numbers of workers on a wage basis, had been built, usually by aristocratic patentees. In addition, some manufacturing workshops in which production had been concentrated without any significant change in the technical process of production, had been established, as when large numbers of handlooms had been set up in a single building by cloth-manufacturers. However, the most typical forms of production were not the workshop or the factory but the domestic and putting-out systems.[41] Of course, a corollary of the growth of these new types of industrial organisation was the decline of guild-organised production, which was more expensive and had become an obstacle to increases in industrial output, and the collapse of old centres of guild-based industry. Indeed, by the early eighteenth century, large rural districts in Britain and Ireland, including the West Riding of Yorkshire, the Cotswolds, East Anglia, and Ulster, along with others on the continent, in which a large part of the peasantry had switched to industrial occupations, overshadowed in industrial importance the old industrial cities in Italy, the Southern Netherlands, and the Rhineland.[42]

The advantages for merchant manufacturers of the domestic and putting-out systems lay in part in the availability of cheap labour, and in the ability of merchant employers to impose arduous conditions on labouring families, especially when they were dependent upon them for work. The costs of labour were reduced not only because rural industrial households were capable of supplying some of their own subsistence requirements, but also because of the willingness of such households to fall back on self-exploitation in the production of craft goods if such a course of action were necessary to ensure the customary level of family subsistence.[43] At the same time this type of industrial development was associated with the appearance of social and economic conditions that fostered new marriage and family-formation patterns, population expansion, the subdivision of holdings, and the slow growth of a large group of landless or semi-landless labourers, who were almost entirely dependent upon rural industry, who were willing to work for very low wages, and whose expansion increased competition for work in the countryside.[44] The second major advantage of this type of system lay in the facts that merchant manufacturers had to advance very little in the way of fixed capital to construct or purchase buildings and equipment, and that investment in items of urban infrastructure and in the built environment was minimised. In the third place, output could within certain limits be adjusted relatively easily to fluctuations in demand, by reducing purchases of materials and goods and by varying the amount of work given out.

But with the growth of rural industry, the process of expansion increasingly came up against limits associated with the laws of functioning of the family economy. The profitability of the putting-out system, in particular, depended in part on the turnover time of circulating capital and on the success of merchant entrepreneurs in economising on the use of raw materials, while the expansion of the system could, by and large, only occur extensively. In both respects, limits were posed by the inability of merchant capitalists to supervise and control the activities of industrial families employed in their own homes and by the needs and aims of the producers themselves. In particular, the intensity of work and the amount of work undertaken were subject in part to the preferences, incomes, and agricultural commitments of rural industrial households. The employers of craft workers could do little about delays in the completion of work or to persuade rural households to take on more work than they wanted. In seasons of peak agricultural activity, members of the rural industrial labour-force who were partially engaged in farming would not normally be available for industrial employment, while the pattern of industrial work which was often based on relatively unmediated natural conditions and on natural sources of energy was in many cases itself strongly dependent on the seasons. In addition, rural industrial households were not usually ruled by the goal of maximising the family's money income. The object of labour was to provide the basic necessities for the economic and social reproduction of the household as a unit of production, consumption, and reproduction. If, as a consequence of fortuitous economic circumstances, the income of a rural industrial family rose above the level necessary for reproduction, most of them would choose additional free time rather than extra income. A result of this type of behaviour was that the individual family's labour-supply curve was backward sloping.[45] The way in which entrepreneurs tried to cope with what was for them a problem of labour supply was by mobilising additional workers and by putting work out to new producers or to producers who had formerly been employed in the workshops of others.

In addition, merchant capitalists were unable to do much about the embezzlement of stock, and fraud, or about the uneven quality of production without concentrating it in a single place and supervising the process of production. A number of laws against embezzlement were introduced, and particularly harsh punishments were inflicted, but as in the case of legislation aimed at speeding up the completion of work and increasing its intensity, they did not prove to be very successful.[46]

The limits on the pace and amount of work undertaken by individual households meant that an increase in output under the domestic and putting-out systems could only be achieved extensively by widening the operational zone. The difficulty with the strategy of this kind was that it reinforced the problems associated with the already slow turnover of circulating capital, delays in the completion of work and the difficulty in meeting production deadlines, and the lack of quality control. In addition, the costs of circulation increased sharply, but in inverse proportion to the density of the rural industrial population, giving areas with more abundant and less expensive labour a competitive advantage.

As a result of the costs associated with extensive growth, industrialists had an interest in changes that would make it necessary for rural industrial households to spend much more time on industrial work in order to satisfy their basic needs, including a more complete separation of labourers from the land, the extinction of common rights, and increased prices for necessary consumption goods. Yet changes of this kind were themselves a source of upward pressure on costs. A more important but related remedy for the problems of time and cost associated with the extension of the domestic and putting-out systems that was necessary if output was to be increased, and a way of increasing output itself, was simply to concentrate production geographically in workshops and factories without any change in the technical process of production. In centralised workshops the producers could be subjected to new and more rigorous types of industrial discipline, the traditional irregular rhythms of work could be combated, and the intensity of work could be increased. The process of production could be supervised, and the quality of the product could be controlled. In addition, capital could be saved by reductions in its turnover time and in the costs of circulation, although in other ways the commitment of capital increased.[47]

With the transition to workshop or factory production the advantages of manufacturing, that is of co-operation and division of labour upon the basis of existing craft techniques instead of upon new mechanised methods of production, could be fully realised. In fact, co-operation within and between extended household units had been developed to a considerable degree under the domestic and putting-out systems, but the organisational gains from social co-operation could be developed more effectively within a single workshop, where greater control and a more effective co-ordination of tasks could be obtained. At the same time, the development of manufacturing laid the bases for mechanisation and for the real subsumption of labour under capital, that is for a phase of development characterised by a complete and continuous alteration in the nature of the labour process and by the establishment of a specifically capitalist form of production.[48]

In other words, the decline in the relative importance of

the domestic and putting-out systems, and the development of the factory system, were not simply a result of the invention of new mechanised methods of production. In the first place, workshops and small factories in which handicraft techniques were used were frequently established, suggesting that greater co-ordination, supervision, and control of workers were primary considerations, and that organisational efficiency was in some cases of more significance than technical change. Second, the invention and even the installation of new equipment did not guarantee the success of factory-based production: for example, a water-powered spinning-mill incorporating the Wyatt—Paul spinning-machine, which in all major technical respects anticipated the first mill established by Arkwright at Cromford in 1771, was set up with the help of previously accumulated wealth in Northampton in the early 1740s, but as in the cases of several similar ventures in other locations it proved to be unsuccessful.

One of the main problems faced by the owners of the mill in Northampton was the difficulty of recruiting a sufficient number of workers on a regular basis to justify the relatively large investment in fixed capital. Indeed, with reference to the evidence provided by some comments made by Ure in *The Philosophy of Manufactures*, it has been argued by Marglin that the contribution of Arkwright lay not so much in the technical innovation for which he was responsible, as in his ability to supervise effectively and to discipline a factory labour-force, and to train human beings to renounce desultory habits of work and to adjust to the unvarying regularity of movement of complex machinery.[49]

Of course, with the passage of time this task became easier, in part because the producers were increasingly separated from the land, because alternative sources of income slowly disappeared, and because their capacity to withstand pressures towards the establishment of factory-based production were accordingly reduced, and in part because individuals were increasingly socialised into new patterns of living and working. But in the early days of factory production, labour recruitment continued to be a serious problem. Owners of water-powered mills, which were located for technical reasons and for reasons of security beside fast-flowing streams in remote rural areas in the Upper Pennines, often had to employ pauper children and itinerant workers. But a recruitment strategy of this kind did not fully solve their labour-supply problems, since some tasks required a substantial degree of skill and strength, particularly in the period preceding the introduction of self-acting machinery in the second quarter of the nineteenth century. In order to recruit and retain a labour-force with the necessary skills and qualities, early mill-owners were consequently obliged to offer relatively high wages, to keep on most of their workers even when trade was bad, and to provide housing and other services including shops, schools, and churches.[50] In addition to facilities necessary for the reproduction of their labour-force, they had in many cases to provide items of industrial infrastructure. As a result, many of the early factory entrepreneurs acted as the town-planners, architects, engineers, agents in charge of production, and the leading citizens of new communities.[51]

But with the subsequent replacement of water by steam as a source of energy, and the generalisation of factory production, the situation changed markedly. Increasingly, factories were located in urban areas with large reserves of labour in relation to the requirements of an individual firm, while the workers crowded into existing tenements or into insubstantial housing, which had been constructed speculatively with bad-quality materials by building contractors and which were let at exorbitant rents by housing capitalists.[52]

The introduction of methods of centralised production often involved an increase in expenditure on wages and on fixed capital, as we have intimated at several points. In centralised units in which a full-time proletariat lacking supplementary sources of income was employed, wages had to be higher than in many parts of the domestic and putting-out systems, even though they sometimes fell below a subsistence minimum. Only where relatively small amounts of fixed capital had been invested did intermittent operation, with the help of workers who continued to work in farming, usually make economic sense. In the second place centralised production was associated with relatively high fixed overhead costs, which would have to be paid even in periods of depression when enterprises were likely to be operating at less than full capacity.

With the exception of some preparatory and finishing processes, and of some processes in which the raw materials were particularly expensive, the increases in productivity and the savings achieved by centralising production would usually have been more than offset by increased labour and capital costs. As a result, the main phase of expansion of the factory system had to wait until the mechanisation of production and the setting in motion of the real subsumption of labour under capital, which coincided with the opening of the phase of machinofacture, gave rise to radical increases in the productivity of labour, as occurred first of all in the English cotton textile industry from the 1760s onwards. It was for this reason that the adaptability of processes of production to mechanisation and the development of the forces of production was a second and probably the major influence in the transition to the factory system.[53]

In many cases the old crafts were adapted, and survived, by shifting to areas and specialisms that had not yet been mechanised, or even by adopting new tools and sources of power such as electricity, which were compatible with more decentralised forms of production. The development of modern industry itself gave an impetus to domestic production in branches such as handloom weaving, while new crafts were created to cater for the new demands of the rising factory system and to service its products. In addition, the rural and domestic segments of an industry were often able to survive for a while as a result of a fall in wages which compensated for the lower levels of labour productivity with which they were associated, but only by worsening the conditions of the direct producers and by turning them into 'mere wage workers and proletarians under conditions worse than those under the immediate control of capital'.[54]

As in the case of other forms of industrial organisation and the geographical structures associated with them, factory production accordingly developed at different speeds in different sectors and regions, and it co-existed and was articulated with domestic industry and with manufacturing workshops over a long period of time. Until well into the nineteenth century in England and *a fortiori* on the European mainland, more value was created and more people were employed in small workshops than in centralised and mechanised production units. But, once it constituted a mode of industrial organisation existing alongside the capitalist factory, domestic industry was converted into what Marx called 'modern domestic industry', which he characterised as 'an external department of the factory, the manufacturing workshop, or the warehouse' and as an additional 'sphere in which capital conducts its exploitation against the background of large-scale industry'.[55] In many cases, what was involved was the development of sweating, in predominantly urban areas.

But in the branches in which mechanised factory production had been introduced, the steadily increasing economic superiority of factory products, which was reflected in rising levels of labour productivity and falling prices of production, undermined and eventually destroyed units of production that had not been mechanised and whose owners lacked access to the increasingly large amounts of capital necessary to establish large-scale mechanised enterprises of the kind necessary for competitiveness.[56]

At the same time, the very dynamism of industrial capitalism led to a profound reshaping of the geography of Britain. In the late fifteenth and early sixteenth century the most prosperous parts of England were heavily concentrated south of a line joining the Severn to the Wash, with marked concentrations of wealth in London and the counties surrounding it and in the West Country counties of Gloucestershire, Wiltshire, and Somerset. In the late seventeenth and early eighteenth century the great growth in midland and northern wealth began, with the expansion of the textile industry in Yorkshire and Lancashire, the North Sea trade of Hull, the Irish, African, and American commerce of Bristol and Liverpool, the iron industry in the Lower Severn Valley and in the West Midlands, the pottery industry in Staffordshire, and the coal metropolis of Newcastle.[57] The growth of some of these new centres of economic activity, and in particular of centres of the cotton industry in Lancashire and of the woollen and worsted industries in the West Riding, was enormously reinforced by the subsequent industrial revolution.

It was also at this stage that a specialisation in industrial rather than in agricultural production in accordance with the principle of absolute advantage,[58] and the rapidly increasing returns with which it was associated, had important dynamic effects, laying some of the foundations for processes of circular and cumulative growth.[59] The distance between regions whose industrial systems were revolutionised and those whose economies were not modernised increased sharply. On the European mainland industrialisation occurred later and primarily in response to the English challenge. By virtue of being late industrialisation, it lagged behind but was not completely left behind by English industrialisation, and it assumed a number of special characteristics. But between the core metropolitan regions in Europe, and the formally and informally dependent regions of the periphery, an extremely wide and widening gap was opened up.[60]

In the next part we shall go on to look at the effects of the industrial revolution on the geography of Britain and on the process of uneven development. But first of all we intend to discuss in more detail the development of three branches of production in the medieval and early modern periods, in order to illustrate and illuminate different aspects and dimensions of what we have said in general about the process of industrialisation.

8.4 The wool textile industry: changing patterns of regional specialisation

So far we have outlined some of the major changes that occurred in the organisation of industry in pre-industrial Europe, and we have indicated how they were connected with changing relations between town and country. In this section we shall look briefly at some of the main changes in the international and interregional division of labour. In order to do so, we shall focus upon the rapid and almost continuous redrawing of the map of textile production in medieval and early modern Europe, which can be attributed in part to the fact that no technological revolution occurred to lay the basis for a cumulative spiral of growth in a particular locality, and in part to the fact that the merchant capitalists who came to dominate the industry usually only advanced circulating capital and, as a result, could easily and quickly switch investment from one area to another.

In the Middle Ages the cloth industry was by far the most important industry, and the most important product was woollen cloth. Initially, cloth production was a part-time activity aimed at meeting local needs and was pursued for the most part in the countryside. But from the eleventh century onwards, a cloth industry supplying external markets, and which was located along with other craft industries in the towns, expanded spectacularly.

In medieval Europe the major cloth-making centres were the Flemish cities, in which an industry producing high-quality woollen cloth grew rapidly in the eleventh and twelfth centuries and reached its peak of prosperity in the thirteenth century, and the industrial towns of Central and Northern Italy, which, after concentrating on the finishing of cloth imported from North-West Europe, developed as centres of a domestic cloth industry in the fourteenth century and in the fifteenth.

In the twelfth century the English cloth industry was concentrated in a dozen or so towns mainly in the east and south of the country. But, until the striking growth of the industry in the 1330's and 1340s, England was a net importer of cloth and a net exporter of wool. In the thirteenth century a gradual switch towards the production of cheaper textiles was set in motion. At the same time, the distribution of the industry began to be changed, as production was diverted away from old-established centres of urban cloth production, and towards hilly regions in the west and north of the country in which water-powered fulling-mills were being built, towards a much larger number of small towns and villages which were free from urban taxes and guild controls, and towards predominantly pastoral areas where time was available for peasants to engage in what were at first supplementary occupations.[61] In the course of the subsequent expansion of the industry, the Southern Cotswolds and the West Country, East Anglia, and the West Riding of Yorkshire emerged as the three main centres of cloth production in England.

After the urban revolution in Flanders in the 1320s, and with the development in the fourteenth century of rival centres of production not only in England but also in Brabant and North Holland, the Flemish industry entered a phase of decline. At first it switched almost wholly to the production of high-priced luxury cloth, although in the end this type of product proved to have only a limited potential as a basis for long-term expansion. The reasons for its eventual decline included changes in the distribution of income and in the structure of demand. But of more importance were the rising costs of labour and transport and increases in the export price of English wool. By contrast, the availability of cheap rural labour and the large gap between the international price of English wool and its price on the home market played a central role in the rapid growth of the English cloth industry in this period.[62]

In the fifteenth century the urban industry in Flanders continued to decline, and was joined by the Florentine cloth industry. By contrast, cloth production continued to expand in Brabant and North Holland, and, after 1450 or so, the production of the new draperies expanded rapidly around Hondschoote in South-Western Flanders. In the case of England the export of cloth declined and the expansion of the domestic industry slackened in the middle of the fifteenth century. In subsequent decades England's foreign trade was predominantly with the Low Countries and involved the export of mainly unfinished cloth. It was not until the sixteenth century and, in particular, until the development of an industry producing the new draperies in England, that the English industry entered a new phase of rapid expansion.

In the early seventeenth century urban production collapsed dramatically in Italy. In addition, the rural as well as the urban industry in Flanders had entered a phase of long-run decline. With the subsequent acquisition of competitive advantages over the Dutch industry centred on Leiden, which had dominated the new draperies market in the early part of the century, England emerged as the major cloth-producing centre in Europe.

The main products of the early English woollen industry were heavy broadcloths made from carded, fine, short-staple wool. In the first half of the sixteenth century, exports, mostly of unfinished white or grey cloth, to the Low Countries, expanded rapidly. The finest cloths were produced in the West Country, which was the foremost centre of woollen broadcloth production and the most important industrial region in sixteenth-century England, and in Suffolk. The industries in these areas dominated the export trade, although important industries producing coarser fabrics existed in Devon, Yorkshire, and Northern England, while traditional worsteds were produced around Norwich (Figure 8.1).

In the second half of the sixteenth century the old broadcloth industry entered a prolonged phase of crisis and stagnation, although, by switching to the production of lighter, coloured cloths for domestic, Mediterranean, and South European markets, the industry was eventually revived in parts of Wiltshire, Somerset, and Gloucestershire. By contrast, the output of the new draperies – of lighter and cheaper fabrics made from the increasingly abundant long-staple wool, of which worsteds, which do not require fulling, bays and says, and serges were examples – expanded rapidly, particularly around Norwich in Norfolk, Colchester in Essex, and in Devon.[63] After the export slump in the early 1620s these manufactures came to supersede the products of the old draperies in the export trade.

The restructuring of the wool textile industry was aided by the continuation of government restrictions upon the export of raw wool. In addition, the export of cattle and of woollen cloth from Ireland was prohibited, virtually compelling the Irish to export raw wool to England to the benefit of the English cloth industry. Consequently, the price of wool on the domestic market fell well below international price levels, giving the English industry an important competitive advantage over rival centres of production. With the added advantages of low labour costs and of an increasingly efficient and energetic marketing network in the Mediterranean and in colonial territories, the English industry was able to force down prices to levels at which the Dutch and most other continental producers were unable to produce. As a result, by the last part of the seventeenth century, the English cloth industry had captured the rapidly expanding market for the new draperies.[64]

The assumption by the English wool textile industry of a

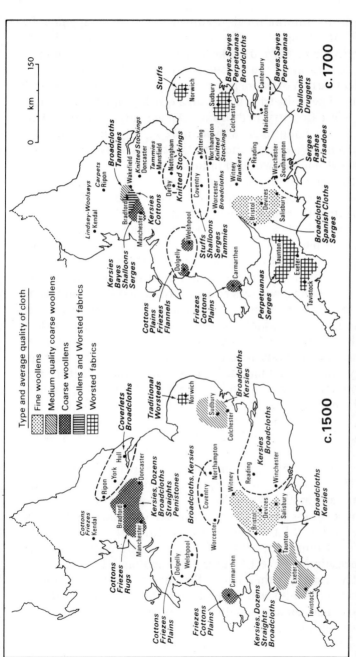

FIGURE 8.1   *The main centres and principal products of the wool textile industry in England and Wales in circa 1500 and circa 1700*

Source: based on P. J. Bowden, *The Wool Trade in Tudor and Stuart England* (London: Macmillan, 1962) pp. 46 and 49.

position of international dominance was accompanied by significant changes in the interregional division of labour within England. Of particular importance was the extremely rapid expansion of the woollen and worsted industries in the West Riding of Yorkshire from the beginning of the eighteenth century. The industries in this area quickly outstripped those in the West Country and in East Anglia, although the cotton industry was soon to grow even more rapidly and, by the end of the century, was on the point of surpassing in importance the once dominant woollen industry.

In the case of the woollen industry, the output of areas outside of Yorkshire tended to stagnate or to decline during the eighteenth century, while that of Yorkshire increased about eight-fold and must have accounted for the entire increase in national production.[65] Its share of the industry's output and exports increased from about 25 to some 60 per cent.[66] In the West Country and in East Anglia spinning stagnated or declined, whereas weaving continued to be important until the introduction and extension of machinofacture in Yorkshire in the middle of the nineteenth century made it virtually impossible for regions whose industries were based upon other methods to compete outside of the small, high-quality end of the market. In 1850, in so far as factory production was concerned, 87 per cent of the worsted spindles and 95 per cent of the worsted looms were to be found in West Yorkshire. The corresponding figures for Norfolk were 2.3 and 1.3 per cent respectively. In the same year, 87.4 per cent of the woollen spindles in England and 94.8 per cent of the woollen looms were in Yorkshire and Lancashire, while only 10.2 per cent of the spindles and 4.7 per cent of the looms were in the West Country.[67] Out of 138,000 people employed in the production of woollen cloth in Great Britain in the middle of the nineteenth century 81,000 worked in the West Riding, but substantial numbers were still employed in Lancashire, the West Country and Scotland. In the worsted industry, on the other hand, the share of national employment in Yorkshire was much larger. By 1851 the Yorkshire industry had almost totally destroyed the once-flourishing Norfolk industry, and employed 97,000 of the 104,000 persons working in this sector in Great Britain.[68]

A specialisation in the production of lower-quality fabrics, together with the low costs of wool and of labour, played an important part in the success of the Yorkshire woollen industry in the period preceding the mechanisation of processes other than dyeing and finishing; for the production of cheap coarse-quality products, in conjunction with improvements in the sphere of transport, played an important part in changing the pattern of consumption and the structure of demand in colonial and domestic markets. But the main reason for the success of the Yorkshire industry and for the competitiveness of its output of medium-quality cloth, for which markets were accordingly expanding, lay in the organisation of production and circulation.

In the West Country and in East Anglia large-scale mercantile capitalist organisation was more developed than in the West Riding. The organisation of the West Country woollen industry was mainly in the hands of a class of large and usually wealthy factors or clothiers. This group was composed for the most part of merchants or of manufacturers with fulling-mills and dyeing- and finishing-works of their own. Each of these clothiers usually put out materials to substantial numbers of spinners and weavers dispersed throughout the countryside, co-ordinated the work they undertook, and collected yarn and cloth from them. Often they managed to lock domestic workers into private clientele structures. The remaining manufacturing processes were completed by the clothiers, and most of the finished or semi-finished cloth was then sold to London-based wholesale merchants for resale either at home or abroad. Most of these clothiers only supervised a division of labour which they had established, but a minority were more directly involved in production. The members of this minority established workshops for spinning and weaving, in many cases alongside existing domestic workers, and in which similar techniques of production were used. In addition an attempt was made to modernise processes such as those involved in finishing which had been centralised at an earlier stage.

As we pointed out in Section 8.1, the Yorkshire woollen industry was dominated by small independent masters with a few acres of land. In most cases they purchased the raw materials they needed, often from merchant clothiers with little direct involvement in production outside of the finishing branches, and carried out most stages of manufacturing in small domestic workshops with the help of the members of their families and of one or two journeymen and apprentices, although some of these workshops were linked with independent domestic workers to whom some work was put out. Once water- and then steam-power could be applied to the preparatory processes of scribbling and carding, mills in which these processes were developed alongside the fulling of woven cloth were financed or rented by groups of clothiers without significantly disrupting the traditional organisation of the industry. The fulled but unfinished cloth would typically be sold to a merchant, perhaps at one of the cloth-halls in towns such as Leeds and Wakefield. As a result the merchant clothiers remained largely within the trading sphere. In other words they tended to confine their activities to the supplying of raw materials, the purchasing of undressed cloth, finishing, and the developing of direct trading links with domestic and foreign markets. Of course some merchants ultimately succeeded in subordinating groups of clothiers and in organising production on a factory basis. However, most of the merchant manufacturers of the factory system emerged from the ranks of the larger clothiers as and when they decided to bypass the cloth-halls and the existing mercantile group, and to do their own dressing, finishing, and marketing.[69]

By contrast, the West Riding worsted industry was dominated by large capitalist clothiers who organised production on an outwork basis and sold the woven cloth to merchants for resale, as occurred in the cases of the wool textile industries of East Anglia and the West Country. In addition the switch to factory production occurred much earlier because the organisational advantages of the factory system were of more importance, and because the processes of spinning and weaving were more easily mechanised, while capitalists who had had some experience of running putting-out concerns played a significant role in the construction of the first worsted factories in Yorkshire.[70]

In an account of the differential growth of the wool textile industry in England, Wilson argued that the single-mindedness and the more aggressive nature of the merchants in Yorkshire, in conjunction with the more detailed knowledge of the industry that they acquired through direct contacts with manufacturers in the local cloth-halls, gave them significant advantages over the West Country clothiers whose sales were controlled by London merchants. In addition, he maintained that they differed from clothiers in the West Country and also in Norfolk in that they responded more rapidly to changing market opportunities and were more successful in opening up new markets.[71]

But these differences in the structure of marketing were closely bound up with differences either of degree or of kind in the organisation of production itself in the various regions, with differences in the flexibility and costs of production and in the types of product, and with differences in the conditions in which production took place. In the woollen branch, the domestic system in its sweated form, when combined with the use of public or company scribbling- and fulling-mills, proved to be very flexible and very cost-effective until the spread of mechanised methods of spinning and weaving and of factory production in the 1840s.[72] In addition, the distinctive role of merchant clothiers in the West Riding meant that many masters were cut off from the market to a lesser extent than producers in areas where the market had been monopolised by powerful putting-out merchants, and that the road by which some masters were rising as merchants and capitalists was not so completely blocked. As a result, the clothiers were more able to act independently, and some of them succeeded in becoming significant employers, in enlarging the workshops they owned, in extending the scope for social co-operation and the division of labour, and in establishing some of the necessary preconditions for mechanisation. In time, some of the larger clothiers moved over to factory production. Indeed most of the early woollen-mills in the West Riding were set up and operated by individuals who had accumulated some capital in traditional manufacturing, who were able to borrow capital from merchant interests because of the competitiveness of their output and to obtain finance by mortgaging freehold and copyhold land and property, and who were helped by the relatively slow progress of technology and by the fact that the size and cost of a competitive mill remained small until well into the nineteenth century.[73]

In other words, differences in the structure of production and marketing, along with differences in the costs of labour and materials, seem to have played an important role in determining the pattern of regional specialisation and competitiveness which led to differential regional growth in the woollen industry and in the wool textile sector in the period preceding the widespread mechanisation of the industry. The process of mechanisation in the late eighteenth century and in the first half of the nineteenth was itself associated with a rapid expansion of the wool textile industry in the West Riding, but what it did was to widen a gap that had already appeared and to reinforce the region's role as the pre-eminent centre of woollen-cloth production in England and indeed in the world.

8.5 The hosiery industry: the organisational and geographical structure of a putting-out system

The knitting-frame was invented by William Lee of Calverton, near Nottingham, in 1589. At first its use was prohibited, owing to its potentially destabilising effects upon the employment of handwork knitters. Only in the early seventeenth century did the new machine begin to be introduced on any scale in England. Initially it was used mainly for the production of luxury silk goods, and the industry that emerged was centred on London. In 1664, between 400 and 500 of the country's 650 frames were located in the capital.[74] In 1657 and again in 1664 the London Company of Framework Knitters obtained charters by which it was made into a corporation. The company sought to control the prices received by stockingers for their work by regulating entry into the industry and by controlling the distribution of knitting-frames.

But with the replacement of silk by wool, worsted, and cotton, and with the switch towards the production of goods for the lower end of the market, the potential for expansion increased. Some elements within and outside of the company pressed for a relaxation of some of the company's regulations, and, when such changes were not conceded and the existing regulations continued to be enforced, avoided them by establishing production in the countryside in the East Midlands, outside of the area coming under the company's jurisdiction. The company attempted to assert its authority in the Midlands, but, after various efforts, the question was settled against it in 1753 by the decision of a committee of the House of Commons that its regulations were 'injurious, vexatious, hurtful to the trade, and contrary to the liberty of the subject'.[75]

With the extension of the use of the knitting-frame, hand-knitting declined in Norfolk, where it had been particularly important, but it continued on a small scale in many parts of the country throughout the eighteenth century, and in some isolated districts survived into the nineteenth century. But, by the eighteenth century, the issue between the hand- and framework-knitters had already been settled in favour of the latter.[76]

By 1727 there were 8,000 frames in England. Of these, 2,500 were in London, and 4,650 were in the East Midland counties. Individuals living in the East Midlands had retained a foothold in the industry over a long period of time, with the result that the necessary materials and skills were to be found locally, but the most important reason for the movement of the hosiery industry to the region from London was the existence of a cheap and abundant supply of marginal agricultural workers in a pastoral farming region lacking competing industrial pursuits. By the end of the eighteenth century this movement had been completed, and Nottingham had emerged as the centre for the production of cotton, Leicester for woollen, and Derby for silk hose.[77]

In the following century the concentration of the industry in this region was reinforced. One reason for this was the availability of low-cost labour. A second was the low cost of materials which were supplied, for example, by the cotton-spinning mills of Nottinghamshire and Derbyshire. In fact, the capital for Arkwright's early ventures in Derbyshire was provided by local merchant hosiers. So, by 1844, by which date, however, the character of the industry had changed significantly, as we shall show when we go on to discuss the delayed transition to factory production, out of 48,482 stocking-frames in Great Britain 43,890 were to be found in Leicestershire, Derbyshire and Nottinghsmshire.[78]

Within the East Midland counties the industry was organised on a putting-out basis, and was widely dispersed throughout the countryside (Figure 8.2). In 1844, stocking-frames were to be found in more than 250 towns and villages, with the largest number of frames per inhabitant not in large centres like Leicester and Nottingham, where other industries existed, but in secondary centres and in some of the villages in which production took place.

One of the main reasons for this geographical pattern lay in the organisation of the industry as a *Verlagsystem*. In the East Midland hosiery sector, work was put out by merchant hosiers and master stockingers from the warehouses they owned in the towns and larger villages to stockingers who worked in their own homes in the towns and in the surrounding countryside. The main putting-out centres were Belper and Nottingham in the north, Leicester in the south, and Loughborough in the centre of the region, while the towns of Derby, Ruddington, Shepshed, and Hinckley, which lay within the spheres of influence of the main centres, acted as secondary centres of the putting-out system (Figure 8.2). In Leicestershire it was common for the domestic stockingers to complete only a single process, producing parts of the finished product. The finished work would normally be returned to the warehouse, where it would be inspected, and where payment would be made. Often a master hosier would keep a room in the warehouse in which women would be employed to carry out finishing operations, although in some cases this work was also put out.

In the early part of the seventeenth century not only were master hosiers advancing materials to domestic producers, but they were also beginning to put out frames and to charge frame rents, and by the end of the eighteenth century it was rare for a stockinger to own the frame he or she used, even though the cost of producing frames was falling and second-hand frames were widely available. The growth of frame-renting was in part a consequence of the increasing poverty of many stockingers, but it was also stimulated by the fact that it provided master hosiers with a source of income that

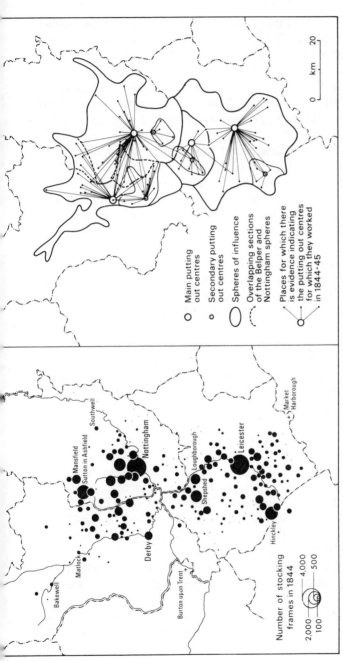

FIGURE 8.2 *The distribution of stocking-frames and the spatial organisation of the putting-out system in the East Midlands hosiery industry in 1844*

Source: D. Smith, 'The British Hosiery Industry at the Middle of the Nineteenth Century: an Historical Study in Economic Geography', *Transactions and Papers of the Institute of British Geographers*, no. 32 (June 1963) 125–42, pp. 130 and 134.

was to some extent independent of fluctuations in the demand for their products. In fact, many hosiers eventually distributed frames up to the point at which each producer was able to earn little more than the frame rent. In addition, they were able to use their monopoly position to exact ever-increasing rents by the simple expedient of boycotting or penalising individuals who bought new or second-hand frames of their own.

In the smaller villages and in the more remote rural areas the hosiery industry was organised by bagmen. Originally the bagmen were independent journeymen. But, instead of continuing to practice the craft, they became middlepersons between other stockingers living some distance away from the putting-out centres, on the one hand, and the town-based master hosiers, on the other. The bagmen made a living by paying lower prices for the work carried out by rural stockingers than those paid by merchant hosiers to producers who collected materials and delivered the work they had completed themselves, and by making profits from the sub-letting of frames to villagers. One of the reasons why bagmen were able to pay less was that many of those to whom they gave out work could meet a relatively high proportion of their own subsistence needs from small plots of land, the exercise of common rights, and a significant part-time interest in farming. However, the bagmen also exploited the isolation, and ignorance of town-rates, of the people they employed, and reduced their living conditions well below those of their urban counterparts. Moreover, when the bagmen were hard-pressed for cash in the depressed conditions that prevailed in the first half of the nineteenth century and had to go into debt to the merchant hosiers, they increased the degree to which they exploited the stockingers they employed by paying them in truck, that is in kind, usually with low-quality products valued at inflated prices.[79]

This type of industrial organisation, and the related locational requirements of the industry, resulted in its being found in all those towns and villages within reach of the centres of distribution where alternative sources of employment in agriculture or in alternative industrial pursuits were limited or provided less than full-time employment, where land was available for building and settlement, and where landowners had not been led, by the harshness and precariousness of the existence of framework-knitters and the inevitable increase in the Poor Rates that followed when work was withheld in periods of recession, to prevent or to place restrictions on settlement by those working in the industry. In particular, the actual boundaries of the hosiery-manufacturing area were defined in part by the distribution of other activities with which it could not easily be combined or which had the effect of excluding it, of which coal-mining in Eastern Derbyshire, the silk industry in Derby, the machine-lace industry in some villages to the west of Nottingham, the domestic silk-weaving industry centred on Coventry, and the prosperous farming activities in Eastern Nottinghamshire and Leicestershire and in South Western Derbyshire, are examples.[80]

In addition, the villages in which the industry was located provided large reserves of labour. Many of them grew very rapidly due both to the relatively high rate of natural increase among industrial households, and to the immigration of those displaced by enclosure and agricultural change. In turn, the availability of labour and the operation of a reserve-army mechanism played an important part in frustrating attempts by the producers to organise themselves effectively and to improve their standards of living.

The producers themselves had, in fact, enjoyed a relatively high standard of living until the early years of the nineteenth century, when depressed trade conditions encouraged the merchant entrepreneurs to abandon customary regulations and prices and to introduce the cost-cutting practices to which we referred in Section 8.2. The actions of the organisers of the industry met with considerable resistance, especially in the towns and larger villages of which Nottingham and Arnold, which were two of the major centres of Luddite activity, were examples. But the functional and geographical fragmentation of the industry, together with the existence of large reserves of labour, meant that it was difficult for the framework-knitters to achieve sufficient unity, while increasing state repression, including the deployment of troops and the introduction of the death-penalty for frame-breaking, reduced the strength of the opposition from the workers and helped to channel it into constitutional forms. The framework-knitters managed to obtain some minor improvements in their conditions, but by 1819 or so, the practice of sweating was well established. As a result, the domestic industry and the putting-out system was able to survive until well into the second half of the nineteenth century, but only as an instance of 'modern domestic industry' in which the industry acquired the status of a sweated instead of an honourable trade or occupation.[81]

Factory production was a technical possibility from 1840, but it was not until the 1860s and 1870s that factories were built on any significant scale. The framework-knitters themselves resisted the movement towards a factory system. In fact, many of them were prepared to accept very low returns as long as they could remain in their villages where they could retain some control over the division of the working day and the method of work. At the same time, many hosiers preferred the steady returns obtainable from frame-renting to the riskiness of large capital investments in factory production. However, the main reason for the persistence of the domestic system lay in labour-market conditions and in the existence of abundant supplies of cheap labour. In the words of Wittfogel, 'a famishing Lilliputian cottage industry choked off large-scale industry'.[82]

In the 1860s quite a large number of workshops were set up, often as a means of increasing labour productivity through a more effective supervision of the labour process. In the 1870s, on the other hand, provisions for compulsory education which restricted the use of child labour and undermined the domestic system with its dependence upon work by the entire family, and a growing shortage of cheap adult labour caused by the expansion of the hosiery industry itself and by competition for labour from the boot-and-shoe industry in Leicester and the lace industry in Nottingham, led to a rapid expansion of factory production.[83] As a result, the hosiery industry was transformed in a short period of time from a domestic craft into a factory industry, although as late as 1907 25,000 out-workers were still employed in this sector.[84]

8.6 Coal-mining and metal-manufacturing: early instances of large-scale capitalist organisation

In early modern Europe, industry was organised for the most part on a domestic or putting-out basis. But by the late sixteenth century and the early seventeenth there were also a few striking instances of significant technological change, and a few industries in which large plants requiring large investments in fixed and circulating capital and employing relatively large numbers of wage-labourers had been established. The sectors in which large production-units were introduced included coal-mining and metal-manufacturing, which were to play a particularly important role in the industrial revolution that was to follow.

The development of large enterprises was not simply the product of a technological imperative. In most cases it also depended upon state encouragement and upon the granting of royal patents of monopoly. The main reason for this was the riskiness of large investments in fixed capital. At the same time, the fact that many of the industries involved were important for the national economy and the country's security meant that the state was anxious to protect them, while the prospect of new sources of income in the form of royalties was an added incentive for the state to grant monopoly rights to wealthy capitalists.

In England, at the end of the fifteenth century, coal production was negligible. But from the middle of the sixteenth century it expanded rapidly. Nef's estimates suggest that annual coal output in Great Britain increased from just over 200,000 tons in the 1550s, to nearly 3 million tons in the 1680s, to over 10 million tons in the 1780s, and to more than 240 million tons in the early 1900s.[85] At first the most pronounced expansion of production occurred in the Northumberland and Durham coalfield, especially around Newcastle and Sunderland in the lower reaches of the Tyne and Wear valleys. By the 1680s this coalfield accounted for more than 40 per cent of national output.

The predominance of the Northumberland and Durham

field lay in the accessibility of its coal and in the possibility of using cheap river and sea transport, while its expansion was closely bound up with the development of the coastal trade to the rapidly growing London market and to other markets in Eastern and South-Eastern England. However, other coastal and semi-coastal coalfields in South-West Lancashire, North Wales, South Wales, Cumberland, and Scotland were also being developed at this time, as were inland fields that were accessible by river such as those in Shropshire, the Forest of Dean, and Nottinghamshire.[86] Nevertheless, the expansion of many coalfields was severely limited by the uneven development of the transport and mining sectors and by the high cost of inland transport. Indeed, in the second half of the eighteenth century, the problems posed by high transport costs acted as an important stimulus to canal construction.[87]

By 1700 coal production in Britain vastly surpassed that of Europe as a whole. Nef attributed this remarkable expansion of the British coal industry to at least three causes.[88] One was the substitution of coal or coke for wood and charcoal in many furnace-using industries, and the replacement of timber by coal as a source of domestic fuel. The process of substitution can in its turn be explained by shortages and by increases in the cost of timber, which had been used for a long time not only as a source of fuel but also as a construction material. By the middle of the sixteenth century the pressure of demand and growing competition for the use of land was making it very difficult for the growth of supply to be kept in line with that of demand.

At the same time, a more extensive exploitation of coal resources was facilitated by the dissolution of the monasteries, the confiscation and sale of church lands, and the replacement of ecclesiastical landowners by new lay owners who were keen to exploit coal reserves lying under the ground. In addition, enclosure was leading to the decline of small copyholders and freeholders, and to the growth of large estates whose owners were more interested in the exploitation of mineral resources, and were not so seriously affected by the problems associated with the fragmentation of landownership.

In the third place, increases in coal production were facilitated by technological improvements in the method of sinking shafts and by the use of drainage channels and pumping-engines, new winding equipment, improved methods of ventilation, and improved forms of underground transport. But, partly by making larger and deeper pits a possibility, these developments were often associated with the investment of large amounts of capital, and led in the direction of large-scale organisation. In some cases the necessary funds were advanced by landowners who chose to increase their incomes by directly exploiting, with the help of an agent, the mineral resources they owned. Otherwise relatively favourable leases were granted to merchant capitalists or to co-partnerships or companies of mining adventurers who employed managers and forepersons to supervise the working colliers. In many areas work was subcontracted to gangs or partnerships of colliers.

In the years preceding 1700, significant technical progress also occurred in activities connected with the extraction and primary processing of metals. In this case the industrialisation process was given particularly strong encouragement by the state, because of the great strategic importance of metallurgical industries and the role of metals in the production of armaments. Once again the introduction of innovations necessitated high levels of capital investment and was associated with the appearance of some early examples of large-scale capitalist organisation.[89] In the mining of tin, copper, lead, and iron-ores, for example, large sums of money were invested in the sinking of deeper shafts, in the cutting of adits, in the installation of drainage pumps, and in the provision of winding-engines to lift minerals to the surface. In addition, water-wheels were often installed to help with the preparation of ores for smelting, to operate the bellows of blast-furnaces and refineries, to work tilt-hammers in forges, and to operate rolling- and slitting-mills. However, it was not until the late seventeenth and early eighteenth century that the important step of smelting metallic ores with coke rather than charcoal was successfully accomplished.

Some of the most important developments occurred in the iron industry, and so we shall focus on this sector. At the end of the fifteenth century the blast-furnace, whose smelting capacity was greater than that of the medieval bloomeries that it replaced, was introduced into England from France. The output of a blast-furnace could be used to make cast-iron goods. But to convert it into bar-iron or wrought-iron the product of a blast-furnace had to be refined in a forge equipped with hearths and water-driven tilt-hammers. In the late sixteenth century water-powered rolling- and slitting-mills began to be introduced to make bars, rods, and sheets of iron for metal-using industries. In the same century, the making of steel mainly from high-quality Swedish bar-iron was developed in the Weald and Forest of Dean with the aid of skilled German workers. Subsequently this industry was concentrated around Sheffield and Newcastle upon Tyne.

With these technical developments, iron-smelting and forging became increasingly capitalist in organisation. But in the sixteenth and early seventeenth century, 'on account of its requirements of ore, charcoal, limestone, and water power . . . the industry was closely associated with the land: the land-owning aristocracy and gentry . . . either directly exploited their own mineral and timber resources or granted leases, often of furnaces and forges as well as of mines, etc., to capitalist ironmasters and merchants', who in many cases were originally of yeoman stock.[90]

The technical and social changes in the mining and metal-manufacturing sectors to which we have referred also unleashed forces that promoted processes of economic differentiation which affected groups of free miners and caused many of them to lose their independence, in spite of the existence of legal and customary rights which had been devised in order to give maximum stability to such communities.[91] Customary rights to free mining, which were usually conferred by royal charter, existed in the Forest of Dean, in the tin-mining areas of Cornwall and Devon known as The Stanneries, and in lead-mining areas in Derbyshire, the Mendip Hills, and Cumberland. In these areas it was common for any inhabitant to have the right to stake out a claim, and on payment of a fee, to the crown in the case of royal land, and otherwise to a lay lord or a religious house, to be entitled to start mining and to use local resources, such as timber for pit-props, and so on. At the same time, various regulations prevented the monopolisation and concentration of mining into the hands of a small number of people. In the Forest of Dean the free miners set minimum prices for ore delivered to furnaces in and around the Forest, restricted entry into the industry, prevented the concentration of economic power into a few hands by limiting the number of horses that any one owner was allowed to own and by prohibiting the ownership of wagons and forges, and resisted the penetration of middlepersons by confining the carriage of coal and iron-ore to the miners themselves. However, in the late seventeenth century, the free miners found themselves quite unable to enforce these regulations, to prevent the system from breaking down, and to stop large-scale exploitation by capitalists from outside of the Forest. In this case, the main reasons for the break-down of the system included the development of a monopoly in the smelting of ore, after the granting by the crown of licences to erect blast-furnaces in the Forest of Dean to capitalist adventurers in the late sixteenth century, and royal grants and sales of land in the seventeenth century. Similar fates befell other free-mining communities. In other words, technical changes were leading to changes in the legal and social relations within which production was taking place, and, as a result, the ability of independent petty-commodity producers to survive was being undermined, even when they were protected by long-standing legal and customary rights.

The early iron industry was concentrated in the Weald of Sussex, Kent, and Surrey, where ore and charcoal resources were available. In later years it developed in other areas such as Monmouthshire and South Wales, the Forest of Dean, the West Midlands, Cheshire and North Wales, the Lakeland counties, Yorkshire, and Derbyshire, where ore, charcoal, and water-power were also available, but which were generally in closer proximity to the metal-using industries in which coal fuel could be used and which were developing on the coalfields. In most cases forges and slitting-mills were located away from the furnaces in the iron-working areas of Birmingham, the Black Country, and Sheffield.[92]

In 1600, 49 blast-furnaces were to be found in the Weald, compared with 11 in the West Midlands, 8 in Yorkshire and Derbyshire, and a few others scattered elsewhere.[93] In the

216

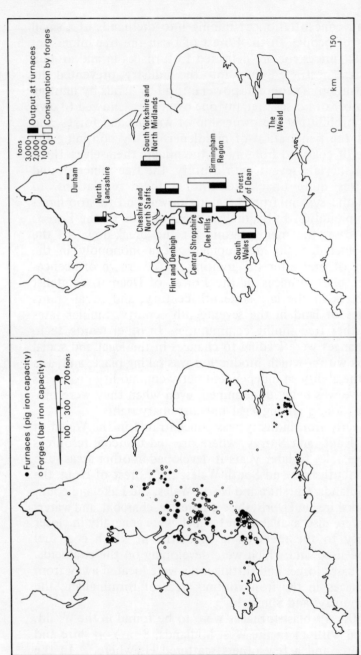

FIGURE 8.3   *The distribution of iron-furnaces and forges and the output and consumption of pig-iron in England and Wales in 1717*

Source: based on work by E. W. Hulme and B. L. C. Johnson, and on maps in H. C. Darby, 'The Age of the Improver: 1600–1800', in H. C. Darby (ed.), *A New Historical Geography of England* (Cambridge: Cambridge University Press, 1973) pp. 364–5.

seventeenth and eighteenth centuries the Wealden industry at first stagnated and then declined. One reason that has often been given is dwindling iron resources and, in particular, shortages of charcoal. However, most ironmasters were able to obtain sufficient charcoal either by importing timber, or by systematically planting new coppices. In fact, of much more importance were the unreliability of its product owing to the insufficiency of stream-flow in the region, and inadequate communications, which led to the loss of government contracts for cannon, etc., as well as the industry's isolation from many of the main finishing-centres.

By 1717 the Weald accounted for nearly 11 per cent of national pig-iron production, but over one-half came from the West Midlands and the lower Severn Valley (Figure 8.3).[94] At the same time, significant differences in the output and consumption of pig-iron had appeared in the North West, the Forest of Dean, and the West Midlands (Figure 8.3). In the Forest of Dean area, for example, the Foley family and its partners controlled two-thirds of the furnaces. In 1692 this family had entered into partnerships that linked it with the West Midland's iron industry. As a result, the economy of the Forest was reoriented away from the Bristol region, with more than one-half of the output of its furnaces being sent out of the district in the form of pig-iron, mostly to the Midlands.[95]

One of the reasons for the emergence of these differences in the location of pig-iron production on the one hand, and of forging and the manufacturing of metal goods on the other, was that coal could be used without any problems in the final manufacturing processes. As a result, the small metal trades tended to be concentrated on the coalfields, although metal-working was also practised on a significant scale in London. By 1700, increasing numbers of such workers were to be found in the Birmingham and Black Country areas, in and around Sheffield, Rotherham, and Barnsley in South Yorkshire, around Newcastle upon Tyne and in North-East Durham, and around Warrington and on the South-West Lancashire coalfield.

The most important area was the one centred on Birmingham. Its development as a major centre started with the spread

of wire-drawing machines and slitting-mills, which were used
to convert bar-iron into sheets and rods for the nail-making
industry, from Germany and Liège to England in the seventeenth century. At this time, large numbers of slitting-mills
were established along the banks of the River Stow and River
Wear in the vicinity of Birmingham. Of course the industry
also expanded on coalfields in other areas. However, its
growth was more pronounced in the West Midlands, where a
tradition of metal-working existed, and where other industries
with which it would have had to compete for labour were not
particularly important. In Lancashire, for example, the expansion of metal-manufacturing was eventually restricted by the
growth of the textile industry. As a result, the area around
Birmingham began to emerge as one of the most important
manufacturing centres in England.

The metal trades that involved the production of finished
metal goods differed very markedly from the primary and
smelting processes in the way in which they were organised.
In almost all cases the small metal trades were organised as a
Kaufsystem or as a *Verlagsystem*, with work being distributed
by merchant capitalists to families working with simple tools
in small shops or sheds attached to their own homes in the
countryside. As a result, in its early days, the Black Country,
for example, was

> a countryside in the course of becoming industrialised,
> more and more a strung-out web of iron working villages,
> market towns next door to collieries, heaths and wastes
> gradually and very slowly being covered by the cottages of
> nailers and other persons carrying on industrial occupations
> in rural surroundings.[96]

Of course some early examples of factory organisation
existed, including, in the late seventeenth and early eighteenth
century, Ambrose Crowley's nail- and file-making works in
County Durham, in the eighteenth century, button-making
factories in the vicinity of Birmingham, of which Matthew
Bolton's Soho Manufactory was a famous example, and, in
the late eighteenth and early nineteenth century, the pin-

making factory noted by Adam Smith and the file-making factory of Peter Stubs of Warrington.

> But in all these cases workers were brought together in factories not generally to operate power-driven machines, but for subdivision and specialisation of handicraft processes, for better control and regularity of output, to stop embezzlement of raw materials, and to save time and labour in putting out materials and collecting finished articles.[97]

However, these examples were somewhat atypical. In terms of output and employment most of the metal-using industries were almost entirely dominated by handicraft techniques and forms of domestic organisation until the last decades of the nineteenth century. Indeed, the availability of cheap labour and the possibility of a subdivision of tasks and specialisation within the framework of a domestic or putting-out system led, at the time of the industrial revolution, to a vast multiplication of petty-commodity producers working on bars, rods, and sheets of metal from the rolling- and slitting-mills. In addition, total employment in all the small metal-working trades was considerably greater than in the primary smelting and forging of metals, in which large-scale capitalist enterprises were established at an early stage. What is more, this multiplication in the number and density of small enterprises played an important role in forming the nuclei of some industrial cities, whose real character is often thought to have been acquired only with the extension of mechanisation and the development of the factory system.

But in qualitative terms, the advances made in the period preceding the industrial revolution in mining and metal-manufacturing, and the progress made in the industrial use of coal or coke, played an important role in the development of power-driven machinery and in the establishment of the factory system in the cotton industry, which launched the industrial revolution. In addition, they were of critical importance in the rapid increase in the rate of capital accumulation and the transformation of the industrial system that followed, and to which we shall turn our attention in the next part.

Part III

The Development of Industrial Capitalism and the Transformation of the Space-Economy

Introduction: the Rise of Industrial Capitalism in Britain

The aim of the chapters in this part of the book is to examine the way in which the geography of Britain, as it was inherited from an epoch in which feudalism had collapsed and had given way to new forms of economic and social organisation, was transformed by the establishment and by the extended reproduction of the forces and relations of capitalist production. In particular, we shall attempt to show how the industrialisation process was associated with a succession of new patterns of regional and urban development and of regional prosperity.

Innumerable accounts exist of the industrial revolution and of the initial development of industrial capitalism which occurred in a period that is variously dated, extending in some cases from 1750 to 1850, and in others from 1780 to 1820. However, many of them confine themselves to the identification and description of easily observed and measurable changes, paying little attention to the underlying dynamics of the economic and social system. It is often pointed out, for example, that before the middle of the eighteenth century Britain was still a small and largely rural country, with a predominantly agricultural economy, a low level of industrial development, and a relatively limited degree of regional specialisation, and in which production occurred for the most part in small enterprises on the basis of craft techniques and was intended in many cases for local markets. Yet within a relatively short period of time all of these characteristics had been reversed. The population had expanded considerably, and the size of the urban population had come to exceed that of the rural population, as industry expanded in rapidly growing urban areas and came to dominate the agricultural sector. In industry, the output of domestically-based craft production had given way to the machine-made product of a factory-based system. In agriculture, enterprises operated by large capitalist owner-occupiers or tenant farmers had come to assume a more important role than those of small-scale commodity producers. And in both of these sectors marked patterns of regional specialisation had emerged, as national and international markets superseded local ones, and as Britain assumed a position of military and economic superiority in the world.

The problem with many of these accounts is that they are often either purely descriptive, or else they attribute a largely autonomous role to a variety of technical innovations or to other simple factors such as population growth, the protestant ethic, and so on. In fact, neither individually nor collectively do factors of this kind form a set of sufficient conditions for, or provide an adequate explanation of, the changes that took place, either because they can be shown to have existed in other areas in which similar developments failed to occur, or because they themselves require explanation. In particular, many explanations of this kind overlook a crucial feature of the new era, which lay in the growing dominance of new social classes whose emergence was associated with the development of more advanced forces of production, and pay too little attention to changes in the mode of functioning of the economic system as a whole.

In the early modern epoch wealth had been accumulated, as a result of the extended reproduction of agricultural and industrial enterprises, and as a result of the realisation of wealth acquired in the sphere of circulation from colonial trading and so on, and had been concentrated in the hands of a relatively small number of people who were, in many cases, willing and able to exploit new market opportunities by investing capital in the production process and by introducing new cost-reducing methods of production. In addition, a class of labourers had begun to be separated from the land and from the other means of production and consumption, and was being reproduced on an expanded scale. As a result, the means of production and consumption were beginning to appear as alienable goods and as the private property of those with the wherewithal to purchase them. It was to this group that the majority of workers would have to sell their labour-power in order to exist.

In the new era the conflict between the new forces of production and traditional relations of production was intensified. As a result, the links between individual workers and the means of production were weakened, as were non-commercial relations between masters and those working for them. Similarly, those customs and practices of organisations of working people that impeded the introduction of new methods of production were replaced by new work practices.

At the same time, the establishment and growth of a class of wage-labourers and of a class of prosperous capitalists purchasing subsistence goods, means of production, and luxury products, widened the domestic market for the products of agriculture and industry. Indeed, the expansion of the domestic market which accompanied the accumulation of capital played a more important role than the growth of export demand in stimulating market-oriented production.

The state also played an important part in this process by establishing and maintaining economic, political, and legal conditions within which the process of capitalist economic and social reproduction could proceed, and by assuming certain planning and management functions. In particular, in the early years of the industrial revolution it allowed guild regulations to fall into disuse, it facilitated the transformation of agriculture and the establishment of new forms of land-tenure, and it subordinated all foreign policy to economic ends and to the demands of domestic industrial producers rather than to those of purely trading elements.[1]

The adoption of measures of this kind might be thought to imply that the British state was already modern and bourgeois in character. In fact the political system with its hierarchy, deference, civil-based elitism, secrecy in government, and amateur administration differed sharply from the more typical capitalist state systems that were subsequently established in other countries.[2] In addition it continued to be dominated by aristocratic and landowning elements. However, their control over mineral rights and of land and the fact that royalties and rents were increased by the development of capitalist economic activity, as well as the role they assumed in the provision of a new transport system, meant that their interests were in some respects in harmony with those of the emerging capitalist classes of that time.[3]

The subsequent process of capitalist growth was uneven sectorally, temporally, and geographically. Unevenness occurred within industry, and between industrial expansion and the development of the means of transport, leading at first, for example, to highly localised forms of industrial development. The factory system was not introduced immediately in every branch of production. Indeed, in some sectors the domestic system not only survived on a significant scale until late in the nineteenth century, but also accounted at first for increased levels of employment in stages in the production of commodities that were not mechanised from the outset. Nevertheless the new methods and forms of organisation of production had a profound impact upon the whole of the economy, including sectors that were not directly affected.

Unevenness also occurred over time. The rise of industrial capitalism was associated with an historically unprecedented process of economic expansion. But the growth process was itself extremely uneven, with phases of expansion alternating with phases of slackening growth, of stagnation, or of contraction. The cycles that resulted included not only the industrial cycles of some seven to ten years' duration but also long waves of development lasting about fifty years.[4]

In addition, the process of growth was geographically uneven. In phases of growth, a rapid expansion of economic activity and of urban areas in some regions usually co-existed with economic decline, depopulation, and emigration from others, while in periods of contraction, regions and cities were once again affected unequally. The regional and urban inequalities associated with different phases of capitalist development are superimposed upon one another, and upon inequalities inherited from the past and formed in part by previous modes of production, and so the structure of the space-economy at any moment in time is a complex combination or synthesis of the effects of many different phases of development and of the conditions in which they themselves unfolded.

As in the case of other forms of unevenness, geographical inequalities are not only associated with social and economic inequalities between individuals, but also often involve a misallocation and underutilisation of resources. But at the moment our aim is to explain this unevenness. In order to do this it is necessary to identify the central determinations lying behind the mode of functioning of a capitalist social formation. An understanding of the dynamics of the process of capital accumulation can then be used to help reconstruct the development of the economic and social system and its expression in the continuous transformation of the structure of the British space-economy.

9 The Accumulation of Capital and the Regulation of the Capitalist Mode of Production

9.1 Phases of accumulation and the process of spatial development

The historical development of the capitalist mode of production has been associated with the establishment of a succession of broad phases or regimes of accumulation characterised by the conditions of production, the pattern of technical change, and the nature of the labour process in the main areas of economic activity, by the leading sectors of the economy, by the ways of life and the mode of consumption of the wage-earning class, by a whole set of institutional forms and procedures and by patterns of behaviour that enable the economic and social system to function, by a pattern of territorial development, and by a system of international relations.

In this chapter, four regimes of accumulation corresponding to the long waves of growth which were originally discovered by Kondratieff are identified. They are the ones distinguished by Mandel.[1] The first one started in the late 1780s and early 1790s, reached a peak in the second decade of the nineteenth century, and ended in the late 1840s and beginning of the 1850s. The second wave peaked in the first half of the 1870s and came to an end in the first half of the 1890s. It was followed by a wave that peaked on the eve of the First World War and ended on the eve of the Second World War. The fourth long wave started in the first half of the 1940s and entered its downswing immediately after the middle of the 1960s. In this book we shall only consider the events occurring in the first three of these four cycles.

In the view of Mandel, long waves are closely associated

with movements in the rate of profit and related changes in the costs of raw materials, the size of the world market, the scope for new investment, and the rate of surplus-value, as well as with the incidence of wars and revolutions. But of particular importance in his account of the renewal of capitalist expansion at the beginning of each new wave of growth is the introduction of a revolutionary or qualitatively new form of technology. Similarly, the slowing down of growth and the onset of a crisis which brings each long wave to an end is attributed to a large extent to the generalisation of this technology and to the ending of the opportunities for reaping surplus profits with which it is associated.

In our account, the emphasis upon technology will be replaced by an emphasis upon the labour process as a central facet of any regime of accumulation. One reason for this is that it is in the capitalist labour process that surplus-value is created. The other is that the material side of the labour process is of necessity and more obviously constituted in space, and is of considerable importance in explaining the geographical location of the kinds of economic activity with which we shall be concerned. As a result, spatial form can be integrated into the analysis from the outset, while the periodisation is based upon a dynamic that is internal to the capitalist mode of accumulation, but that is at the same time an integral part of the development of geographical space, with the result that the process of spatial development is interpreted in terms of the dynamics of the dominant mode of accumulation. But in order to do this it is necessary to begin by developing a sequence of concepts whose role is to identify the whole set of relations constituting 'the invariant kernel of the capitalist mode of production'.[2] In subsequent chapters these concepts will be used as a set of tools for analysing certain aspects of the process of capitalist development in space.

9.2 Spatial forms and the laws of motion of capitalism

In the first chapter we pointed out that the spatial or territorial structure of any social formation is, on the one hand, the context or framework within which the social process of reproduction unfolds, and by which it is conditioned. As a framework for the development of society, space is both a use-value, in the sense that it refers to a set of natural and social conditions that are used in the material and social activities and processes of which reproduction is composed, and something that is subject to a set of rules of property and possession which regulate the ownership and transfer of property, which have a large influence over access to and over the control and use of land and its resources, and which give rise to certain forms of distribution of the product of human activity. In most capitalist societies, for example, the use of space is regulated in part by a system of property rights which confer upon a class of landowners a monopoly over access to many of the useful effects of land.

On the other hand, space is also in part a product, outcome, or result of the activities and processes forming part of the social division of labour and of the process of social reproduction. In other words, the spatial structure of an economy and society is produced through the action and effect of human beings in and upon an inherited spatial framework. In capitalist societies a central role is played by the processes of movement and growth or decline in space of capital. As a result, one of the central questions in any geographical analysis of the structure of the space-economy in capitalist societies concerns the way in which space is used and produced in the course of the historical process of capitalist development, and the way in which the configuration of the space-economy is governed by the relations of production and the laws of functioning and development of a capitalist mode of production and by the processes of production and circulation of capital.

9.3 The production of commodities

'The wealth of societies in which the capitalist mode of production prevails appears as an "immense collection of commodities".'[3] One of the central characteristics of a society of this kind is that the interconnection of different types of social labour is established through the private exchange of the products of labour on the market, and that the metabolism between human beings and nature, and the allocation of the total labour of society to the production of goods and services corresponding to its different needs, are not regulated by a conscious social plan, but by the exchange-value, expressed in money, of its various products.[4]

The products of labour assume the form of commodities when they are produced for exchange. In conditions of commodity production, individual producers at first pursue their private and autonomous types of labour independently of one another, deciding by themselves what and how much to produce. But each producer lives within a society and, as a result, within the framework of a social division of labour, in which his or her individual labour depends upon that of others, and vice versa, and in which the products of his or her labour are destined for others, just as the products of other producers' different kinds of labour go to him or her. The underlying social character of these determinate types of private labour is only revealed and is only validated as social labour in the exchange of the products of labour on the market.

An operation of exchange establishes 'an equivalence in which private labour appears simply as a fraction of the overall labour of society', that is as abstract labour, to which a measure known as value can be applied.[5] The reason why a value measure can be applied is that, when individual producers exchange the products they have produced, they must equalise them. In order to equalise them they must abstract from the physico-natural aspects or the characteristics of commodities as use-values, which differentiate one product from another. But in doing so they must also abstract from that which serves to differentiate their various subjective types of labour from one another, by reducing the different forms of useful labour they have performed to qualitatively equal, abstract human labour expressed in money as units of socially necessary labour time. As a result the products of their different kinds of labour are equated as values.[6]

So, in a commodity-producing economy social labour appears in the form of equal or abstract labour, and as such it acquires a distinct and independent existence. In fact, abstract labour is alienated labour. In other words, labour-power

> which is a property, a determinant or an attribute of [a human being], becomes an independent subject, by representing itself as the 'value' of 'things'. The human individuals, on the other hand, who are the real subjects become determinations of their determination, i.e. articulations or appendages of their common, reified labour-power.[7]

In addition, the necessity of particular branches of production is established by the fact that the labour time embodied in its product is exchanged for the product and symbol of labour time in general, that is for money.[8] In other words, the assignment or distribution of labour between different kinds of activity only occurs *ex post* and not *ex ante*, as would be the case with a social system in which the distribution of the members of society to different kinds of work is consciously planned. The high degree of uncertainty associated with an *ex post* form of social regulation is one of the reasons for the anarchy and unevenness of the process of capitalist reproduction, and for the value losses with which it is associated.

In a capitalist society the production of use-values takes place 'only because and in so far as they form the material substratum of exchange-value'. However, the capitalist producer of a commodity also wishes to produce a commodity whose value is greater than that of the elements purchased to produce it. It follows that 'just as the commodity itself is a unity formed of use-value and value, so the process of production must be a unity, composed of the labour process and the process of creating value', that is the valorisation process.[9] Indeed, the dual character of the social process of production as a labour process and as a valorisation process will provide us with a decisive methodological starting-point for the analysis of the spatial dimension of the social process of capitalist reproduction.

9.4   The circuit of industrial capital and the production of surplus-value

The capitalist mode of production is not simply a system of commodity production. In Marx's view, capitalism or capitalist commodity production involves a generalisation of exchange in which not only all the products of labour but also labour-power, or the capacity to work, are bought and sold as commodities. In other words, new relations of production are created in which the means of production are concentrated in the hands of one section of society, and the other section of society is transformed into a wage-earning class composed of juridically free individuals who are nevertheless obliged by their lack of property to sell their capacity to work in order to survive. The wage relation is in fact the most fundamental relation defining the capitalist mode of production, and the key to the production of surplus-value, or to the economic form in which the surplus labour of a society of this kind is appropriated.

The general formula for capital in the form in which it appears in the sphere of circulation is represented by the schema $M-C-M'$, in which a sum of money, M, is advanced to purchase commodities, C, which are subsequently exchanged for a larger sum of money, M', and where money is acting as capital since the value originally advanced is increased in size or valorised.[10]

The fundamental form of capital in general is industrial capital, since its circuit includes the direct capitalist process of production in which the value of the capital advanced is increased, or profit is made, by transforming and increasing the value of the commodities available, and in which surplus-value is accordingly created. This form of capital is also the most important determinant of the structure of the space-economy, both because of its direct and indirect impact upon the spatial structure of society, and because its movement ultimately governs the development of the capitalist economy as a whole. Industrial capital is advanced in five spheres of material production, namely in the extractive industries, agriculture, manufacturing industry, energy production, and transport, and so an analysis of the historical development of industrial capital plays a central role, for example, in accounts of the formation of agricultural and industrial space.[11]

In the circuit of industrial capital a sum of money, M, is advanced to purchase commodity inputs, C, comprising means of production, MP, and labour-power, LP, bought respectively on the commodity and labour markets with the constant and variable parts of capital. It is initially assumed that these commodity inputs are bought at their values, that is for an amount equal to the abstract labour time socially necessary for their production under existing conditions. In other words, labour-power, for example, is purchased with an amount of money equal to the value of the consumption goods that under the prevailing social and historical conditions are necessary for the reproduction of the labourer and his or her dependents.

In the next stage these commodity inputs leave the sphere of circulation and enter the sphere of production as elements of productive capital, P. They are then used in the capitalist process of production to produce new commodities, C'. The value of these new commodities exceeds the value of the commodity inputs. In the process of production the value of the means of production used up is passed on to the new commodities. By contrast, the value of labour-power is normally less than the value added by labour in production. In other words, the use-value of labour-power, or the quantity of labour supplied in return for the wage, usually exceeds the sum advanced to purchase the capacity to work of the industrial labour-force. It is this difference between the value of labour-power and the value added by labour in the capitalist labour process that gives rise to the increment in value.

At the end of the production process the commodities, C', which have been produced enter the sphere of circulation and are converted into money form, $M' = M + \Delta M$, by their sale on the commodity market, that is by the realisation of the value contained in them.

As a result, the capitalist class normally receives back the original sum advanced plus an increment or an amount that has been added to the initial outlay. At the outset an amount of value, c, was advanced in the form of constant capital to purchase means of production. In a sufficiently long period of time the entire value of the means of production would, under conditions of full realisation, be transferred to the product. In the same period the capitalist class will have had to have advanced an amount of variable capital, v, equal in value to that of the labour-power needed to transform the other material inputs into new commodities. However, the value of the labour-power employed in this period is replaced by the value added to c by the workers in the process of production, which we shall denote by the symbol l. So, while the value of the initial commodity inputs is $c + v$, the value of the final product is $c + l$, and the increase in value, which is produced because labourers work for a longer period or at a higher level of intensity than is necessary to replace the money advanced in the form of variable capital or to earn enough to

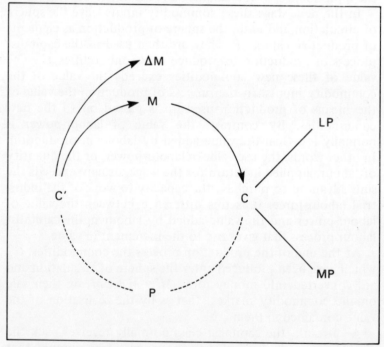

FIGURE 9.1   *The circuit of industrial capital*

Source: based on the representation of Marx's circuit in B. Fine, 'The Circulation of Capital, Ideology and Crisis', *Bulletin of the Conference of Socialist Economists*, vol. 4, no. 3 (October 1975) BF 1–14, p. BF3.

purchase the goods and services necessary for their reproduction, is $s = (c + l) - (c + v) = l - v$. This increment in value is called surplus-value.

The circuit of industrial capital can be represented by a circular flow-diagram as in Figure 9.1. The process whereby industrial capital increases its own value through the addition of surplus-value is called the valorisation of capital.

The rate of surplus-value, that is the ratio of surplus-value and the value of variable capital advanced, s/v, or the ratio of surplus and necessary labour time, can be increased in two ways when real wages are held constant. One is by increasing absolute surplus-value: that is, by increasing the amount of surplus labour time by extending the length of the working day, or by intensifying the labour process in order to reduce the amount of time during which the worker is 'idle'. The second way is by increasing relative surplus-value: that is, by reducing the labour time necessary to reproduce the value of labour-power by increasing the productivity of labour in the wage-goods sector of production.

9.5 The accumulation of capital

As the circuit of industrial capital is repeated, the production and realisation of surplus-value is continually renewed. If the increment in value is consumed unproductively, a process of simple reproduction of commodities, of surplus-value, and of the social relations of capitalist production occurs. But, if the value of the capital advanced is increased through the transformation of part of ΔM into additional capital, the circuit grows in an outward spiral movement in a process of extended reproduction or accumulation of capital. The employment of surplus-value as capital is what Marx meant when he referred to the accumulation of capital.

One consequence of the accumulation of capital is that individual capitals frequently expand in size. An increase in the size of individual capitals stemming from an increase in the amount of capital it advances is referred to as industrial concentration. But an expansion of individual capitals may also occur as a result of the merger of formerly separate capitals, in which case it is called industrial centralisation.

In *Capital*, Marx also points out that the extended reproduction or accumulation of capital on the basis of a stable ratio of constant and variable capital will come up against finite limits as more and more people are drawn into the production process, and as a relative shortage of labour develops. However, a process of extensive accumulation or of capital-widening of this kind is to some extent self-correcting because, if the workers take advantage of the situation and push up the value of labour-power, the rate of surplus-value and the stimulus to invest will fall. A subsequent decline in the amount of capital advanced will lead to a fall in the level of employment, with the result that labour will become relatively abundant, and the rate of surplus-value can be restored to a higher level. In other words, 'the mechanism of the accumulation process itself removes the very obstacle it temporarily creates'.[12]

In conditions of this kind, the ability of capital to increase the production of absolute surplus-value by lengthening the working day or by increasing the intensity of work, will of course be strengthened by pressure from the reserve army of labour whose size is increased by any slackening in the rate of accumulation.

A more effective way of attempting to maintain the rate of surplus-value and of sustaining the accumulation process is by pursuing a strategy of intensive accumulation or capital-deepening, in which the proportion of constant to variable capital and the rate of relative surplus-value are increased. In this case, total employment increases less rapidly than aggregate social capital, and shortages of labour are less likely to occur.

9.6 The labour process and the production of surplus-value

Both of these ways of increasing the rate of surplus-value can be observed in strategies adopted by capital in the sphere of production, where it continually seeks to raise the productivity of labour, by increasing social co-operation and extending the division of labour, by introducing new methods of production and new work practices, by supervising the process

of production and disciplining the labour-force, by transferring control over the work performed from the labourers to
capital, and by countering the attempts by labour to resist
these strategies. The reason for choosing a course of action of
this kind lies ultimately in the fact that the labour process is
a unity of the processes of production and valorisation and
the site at which surplus-value is produced.

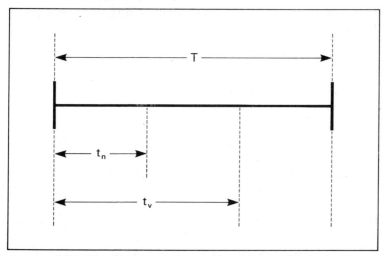

FIGURE 9.2   *The division of the working day and the production of
surplus value*

Source: C. Palloix, 'The Labour Process: from Fordism to Neo-Fordism',
in The Conference of Socialist Economists, *The Labour Process and Class
Strategies* (London: Stage I, 1976) 46–67, p. 49.

The logic underlying the development of the labour process
and an alternative formulation of the rate of surplus-value are
illustrated in Figure 9.2, where T denotes the apparent duration of the working day in which the total mass of value
produced by society is created, t_n is the time socially necessary for the production of those commodities whose consumption reconstitutes the labour-power used up in production,
and t_v denotes the uniform time in which value is actually
produced, where $t_n < t_v < T$. The difference between t_v and
t_n is equal to the amount of surplus labour time. The rate of
surplus-value can therefore be written as $s/v = (t_v - t_n)/t_n$.[13]

The object of the capitalist class is to increase the difference between t_v and t_n, and to raise s/v which can be interpreted as the rate of return on the employment of social labour-power. An increase in s/v can be achieved in three analytically distinct ways. Method 1 involves operating on the difference between T and t_v or on the 'porosity' of the production process, and results in increases in the production of absolute surplus-value. The gap between T and t_v includes the time that passes between the execution of different operations, the time involved in the setting up of tasks, 'idling' on the part of the workers, and time lost as a result of the inability of workers to sustain without interruption a certain pace of work. Increased co-operation, which occurred at first when a collective work rhythm was established by the workers themselves, but which was subsequently imposed by the continuous and uniform movement of the machine system and its speed of operation, enabled capital to reduce this margin. But it can also be reduced by means of a fragmentation of tasks, as a result of which each worker is likely to spend more time performing a single task in a prescribed way, and as a result of which the loss of time involved in changing between tasks, in setting up a task, and in deciding how to execute it are avoided.

Method 2 leaves the ratio of t_v to T unchanged but increases s/v by extending T. This type of strategy was frequently pursued with some success in the phases of manufacture and of machinofacture in the nineteenth century. But since then, this method of increasing absolute surplus-value has become more and more difficult to apply, owing to the existence of finite limits to what human beings can endure, to social resistance, and to the immense growth in the forces of production. However, a similar effect can be achieved by introducing shift-work.

In the present century the main ways of raising s/v have been instances of method 1 or of method 3. Method 3 involves increases in the difference between t_v and t_n, obtained by reducing t_n and, therefore, by increasing the production of relative surplus-value. The most important of the set of procedures by means of which t_n can be lowered are changes in the methods of production which increase the productivity of labour in the wage-goods sector of the economy, though the discovery of new and less expensive sources of supply of necessary consumption goods will have the same effect. However, an increase in the production of relative surplus-value can also be accomplished by lowering the value of labour-power employed in production as a result of an increase in the fragmentation of the labour process, which leads to a parallel differentiation of the labour-force and to a reduction in the overall level of skill required. In such a case all skilled operations tend to be concentrated in the hands of a small group of specialised workers, while the majority are reduced to agents required only to perform routine operations, producing, in the words of Maignien, 'the maximum dequalification of the maximum proportion of manual workers' and 'the maximum skill in the smallest possible proportion of mental labourers'.[14]

These three methods of increasing the production of surplus-value were combined in different ways in each of the main phases in the historical development of the labour process.

(1) In the phase of manufacture, the concentration of workers into workshops made it possible for more control to be exercised over the amount of time devoted to useful production and over the length of the working day (methods 1 and 2). The intensity of production could also be raised by fragmenting the work process and by establishing a new rhythm of work (method 1). At the same time, the amount of skill required for the completion of any partial task was reduced (method 3), although in the early stages of the introduction of new systems of production which require new forms of socialisation of the labour-force, the workers involved often acquire a relatively privileged status. In addition, the separation of tasks that occurred at this time was based on craft techniques, with the result that labour was only formally subsumed under capital.

(2) In the phase of machinofacture, capital seized hold of the labour process as a whole and reconstituted it with the help of mechanical power and of scientific as opposed to empirical reasoning. As a result, human beings were largely reduced to 'hands', and capital was able to make consider-

able progress in overcoming many of the links with, and many of the constraints imposed by, craft traditions and human capabilities, including the ability to synchronise thought, the expenditure of energy, and the use of limbs. In effect, a fine division of tasks and the use of machinery made it possible for workers with little, if any, formal training to be used in the production process. At this stage surplus-value could be increased by each of the three methods outlined above.

(3) The principles of scientific management and Fordism built on the principle of mechanisation, by introducing new forms of work organisation, by simplifying jobs to such an extent that they frequently involved little more than the repetition of a few elementary movements, and by intensifying work. Of particular importance in enabling the fragmentation of tasks to be pushed to an extreme limit was the development of the conveyor-belt or flow-line principle as a method of integrating and recombining tasks in a more efficient way. In addition, the subdivision of tasks involved among other things a conscious attempt to separate all conceptual and mental activities from those of execution. One result of the consequent separation of mental and manual labour was a more pronounced differentiation of the labour-force into technical and office workers on the one hand and production workers on the other. With the introduction of these principles surplus-value was raised predominantly by methods 1 and 3.

The development and application of these principles were in most cases aimed at resolving some of the contradictions associated with earlier forms of organisation of work, involved conflicts between labour and capital and between different fractions of capital, and gave rise at least initially to higher profits for innovating capitals. But new techniques were not equally applicable to all sectors of the economy. In addition, each stage was superimposed upon the ones that preceded it, entailing the introduction of new methods of production in new and in some existing branches, and altering the way in which old-established techniques were employed. However, the role of the leading sectors of a capitalist economy, and of the most dynamic agents in any particular sector, exceeded in importance the share of economic activity for which they accounted by virtue of the roles they played in creating the framework and establishing the conditions in which accumulation proceeded. In the second half of the nineteenth century, for example, the development of machinofacture in the north of England led to an intensification of manufacture in London.

9.7 Regimes of accumulation and the regulation of the capitalist mode of production

In the reproduction of a commodity-producing system a set of crucially important links exist between the production and circulation of commodities, consumption, and the distribution of income to those participating in production and exchange. One reason for this is that what is produced must be sold if the value contained in goods and services produced for exchange is to be realised, and if the circuit of industrial capital and of capital in general is to be repeated. A second but related reason is that demand, on which realisation depends, is to some extent structured in advance by the way in which money is advanced to purchase means of production, and by the way in which incomes are distributed in the form of wages, rent, interest, distributed profits, and so on. Of course the distribution of income is itself influenced by the way in which production is organised. In other words, the possibility of the accumulation process proceeding depends not only upon the existence of opportunities for investing capital profitably, but also upon a sufficient amount of income being distributed in such a way in the course of the accumulation process as to enable what is produced to be sold.

In addition, the level of activity and the reproduction of the system and of those whose livelihoods are connected with it, depend in part upon individuals being able to translate the needs they have into demands that are backed by adequate purchasing-power, and that are, therefore, effective. Of course the existence of an ability to buy depends in its turn upon the receipt of money incomes and, therefore, in most cases, upon the employment of the resources owned by the individuals concerned or the realisation of the commodities in which they are embodied. In the course of time the importance of this dimension of the process of social reproduction has tended to increase. The reason for this is that the formation of a wage-earning class and the generalisation of capitalist commodity production has broken down many aspects of traditional modes of consumption, and has led to the development of a mode of consumption that is specific to capitalism, and that must be integrated with the reproduction of capital if accumulation is to proceed.

The integration of production, consumption, distribution, and exchange is complicated by the fact that the methods of production and circulation are revised as technical change occurs and is embodied in new investments. As a result, the structure in value and volume terms of supply and demand depend upon changes in the labour process and its conditions and in the norms of production, on the one hand, and upon changes in the distribution of income and in the norms of consumption, on the other.

The different ways in which these elements of the process of capitalist reproduction have been integrated with one another historically form the basis for a reconstruction of the waves of growth outlined above.

A pattern of economic and social reproduction in which changes in the conditions of production, in the conditions of consumption, and in the conditions of existence of the wage-earning class occur in such a way as to ensure that they are kept approximately in alignment with one another and that outlets exist for what is produced, and in such a way as to maintain the general rate of profit over a relatively long period of time, will be called a regime of accumulation.

The main characteristics of any regime can be summarised by a reproduction schema indicating the way in which production is divided between different departments of production. The simplest division is into two departments, with department 1 being composed of those production processes whose products are means of production and, therefore, commodities that are purchased as elements of constant capital, and with department 2 being the combination of production processes that result in the creation of means of consumption.

Of course a regime of accumulation cannot be reduced to a

schema of reproduction. In particular, for any given schema to be established and to be reproduced for some period of time, it is necessary that institutional forms and procedures and social practices be developed such that individuals and social groups act in a way that is consistent with the functioning of the system. This collection of what Aglietta calls structural forms, which include forms of wage determination, corporate structures, and a monetary system, is called a mode of regulation.[15]

So far we have outlined briefly some concepts that can be used to analyse some of the fundamental characteristics of the accumulation process and of the evolution of society in long waves of capitalist economic development. However, the process of capitalist development is punctuated by crises. Of these the most significant tend to divide one epoch or one long wave from another. In this book, the major crises and turning points in the development of capitalism will be interpreted as products not simply of the operation of the law of value and of the laws of motion of the capitalist mode of production, but also of the inappropriateness of a mode of regulation to a regime of accumulation or of the exhaustion of the possibilities of growth within the context of a particular regime of accumulation.

In the last section we outlined a sequence of stages in the development of the capitalist division of labour, and suggested that they are of fundamental importance in characterising different phases in the development of capitalism. One of the main implications of the ideas introduced in this section is that the resulting changes in the conditions of production can be linked with changes in the sectoral structure of the economy, with changes in the mode of consumption and in the methods of wage determination, with changes in the monetary system, and with changes in international economic relations.[16]

Similarly, switches in the regime of accumulation are associated with a quantitative and qualitative transformation of certain branches of production and with forms of sectoral redeployment. In the nineteenth century, for example, accumulation was centred upon industries producing food, clothing, textiles, and leather goods, or upon heavy industries

producing iron and steel, railway equipment, and other commodities produced by industries belonging to department 1.
By contrast, in the twentieth century, the establishment and
extended reproduction of a regime of intensive accumulation
based on the introduction and use of the principles of scientific
management and Fordism, involved the development of
sectors producing items of industrial equipment and durable
consumption goods such as housing, motor-vehicles, and
electrical household appliances. As a result the mechanism of
growth was modified, with an increase in the outlets for the
products of department 2 leading the growth process and
providing outlets for the products of department 1. In turn
these changes were associated with changes in the pattern of
regional inequality.

These events were connected with changes in the way in
which wages were determined and in the practices of consumption.[17] Until the 1840s or so, the real wage tended to
vary with changes in the supply of and in the demand for
labour, and fell sharply in periods of rising agricultural prices.
In the second half of the nineteenth century a social norm of
working-class consumption, which included some capitalistically produced commodities, began to be formed. In the first
half of the twentieth century the wage was often linked with
the cost of living. But with the subsequent development and
more general application of a working-class consumption
norm, which included individual ownership of standardised
housing and of a variety of mass-produced commodities, a
minimum guaranteed wage was introduced in some developed
capitalist countries, and real wages were linked with productivity growth, ensuring that aggregate demand increased
broadly in line with industrial production. At the same time,
indirect wages were to assume considerable importance as a
means of guaranteeing the continuity of the maintenance
cycle of labour-power. In the case of Britain, changes of this
kind were beginning to occur in the 1930s and were often
translated into concrete proposals for reform at the time of
the Second World War.

In addition, capital has been internationalised, and the
international division of labour has been transformed. In very
general terms, an internationalisation of commodity exchange

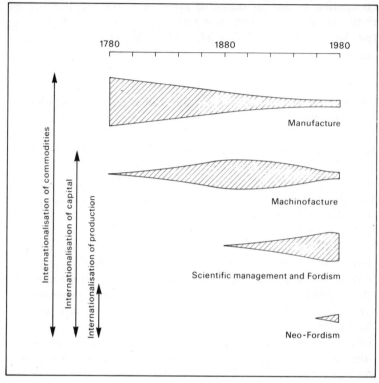

FIGURE 9.3 *A schematic representation of the development of the labour process and of international economic relations*

has been supplemented and modified by the export of capital or an internationalisation of capital, and by an internationalisation of the production process itself as the technical division of labour within the firm is extended across national boundaries (Figure 9.3).[18] As a result, the economic space in which a coherent regime of accumulation unfolds has been extended to include the whole of the capitalist world, with each national economy including a qualitatively different part of this world system, and occupying a position in a hierarchy of nation states and economic blocs largely according to the extent to which it is specialised in the production of those department 1 goods conferring control over the norms of international competition. But in order to appreciate the significance of these more recent developments one needs to look beyond the Second World War with which this study nevertheless ends.

9.8 Economic and social reproduction as a process of class struggle

So far we have introduced some theoretical tools for the analysis of the way in which the structure of the space-economy is conditioned by the processes of reproduction and accumulation of capital, and by the historical process of capitalist development. However, it is important to realise that the perspective we are adopting amounts to more than an economic analysis of spatial structures, since our conception of the economy is fundamentally different from the one that is most often employed. The processes of production and reproduction of capital are not simply processes of material production and of valorisation. They also involve the production and reproduction of the relations of production and of the social classes of which society is composed. In other words, the analysis of these processes is simultaneously the basis for an analysis of the class structure of capitalist societies.

In addition, the processes of production and reproduction of capital are processes of class conflict and of class struggle. Struggles of this kind are always based upon specific objective conditions, such as specific forms of development of the processes of concentration and centralisation of capital, specific changes in the organisation and composition of the labour-force, and specific changes in the organisation of work, but they are not monocausally determined by these conditions, since they also involve moments of class consciousness and class organisation that cannot be reduced to the conditions in which the process of social reproduction unfolds. The process of accumulation and the laws of this process are, in other words, the result of a constant struggle between capital and labour, and between competing capitals and capital groups, while the results of these conflicts as mediated by the law of value give rise to new conditions for the subsequent development of class struggles.

It is possible to draw more distinctions between this and other conceptions of the economy. But it is enough to point out that the differences in scope stem from the fact that Marx conceived production or labour as both the production of things and the production or objectification of ideas, as production and intersubjective communication, and as material production and the production of social relations.[19]

Of course a more comprehensive account of the development of the space-economy would include a discussion of those activities that play an important role in the processes of consumption and reproduction that occur outside of the immediate control of capital, and of the role of the institutional structure and actions of the state, as well as of the way in which the structure of space itself conditions the process of social reproduction. Some of the concepts relating to these questions will be introduced as and when they are required.

10 The Transition from Manufacture to Machinofacture 1780-1850

10.1 Introduction

In the transition from manufacture to machinofacture, major disparities emerged between a small number of rapidly growing industrial areas and rural areas which were slowly deindustrialised and in the end were largely reduced to a sphere of agricultural activity. The most pronounced division was between the central-core area of England stretching from London to the North West and peripheral areas in Britain and Ireland.

. In the period between the 1760s and 1790s the most important innovatory changes occurred in about ten 'small islands of industrialisation'. In some cases, development was based on localised resource deposits in otherwise under-developed regions. In others, nuclei of modern industry were located in and surrounded by zones of traditional industry itself.[1] Of these, four declined soon after the major advances with which they were associated had occurred. They were Cornwall, which was an important centre of tin- and copper-mining and smelting until the 1840s, Shropshire, which was a centre of coal-mining, of iron-making and iron-using industries and of several other industries until 1815, North Wales, whose industrial base was more diversified but which declined as an industrial region in the early nineteenth century, and the uplands of Derbyshire, which acted as a major centre of the cotton industry for about fifteen years.

The Tyneside region and the Clyde Valley were developed but only survived as centres of modern industry as a result of subsequent changes in their industrial structures. The industrial region around the Tyne and Wear was based on coal-mining. In addition, salt-works, glass, soap, and chemical industries, shipbuilding, iron-works, and some steel-making were developed, but its expansion as a region producing anything other than coal was comparatively limited until the rise of iron- and steel-shipbuilding and of armaments manufacture in the second half of the nineteenth century. In the Clyde Valley the linen industry had been important in the eighteenth century, while Glasgow came to play an extremely important role in the tobacco trade. In the late eighteenth century the nearby coalfield was opened up, and the region became the second most important centre of the cotton industry. But in the 1820s it was to experience a second switch with the decline of cotton production and the growth of iron-working, and subsequently it was to be developed as an important centre of shipbuilding, engineering, and the manufacture of armaments.

The area of South Staffordshire referred to as the Black Country, whose inhabitants had a long tradition of skilled metal-working, was developed as a centre of coal-mining, and of glass-, chemical-, engineering-, and armaments-works, and, in a period beginning in 1810 to 1830 and ending in the 1880s, acted as the most important iron-making region in the country.

But the two most clear-cut cases were the West Riding of Yorkshire and, in particular, the south of Lancashire and adjacent parts of Cheshire and Derbyshire. The West Riding was of course the area in which the factory-based worsted industry developed from the 1790s and in which the woollen industry was concentrated. The south of Lancashire was the classic industrial region. Its main role was as the centre of the cotton industry, but a tradition of metal-working existed in the Warrington area, and a chemical industry based on coal and salt was soon to develop in the vicinity of St Helens.

In the period between the 1790s and the 1820s North Wales, Shropshire, and Upland Derbyshire declined markedly, but one and perhaps two major new industrial regions emerged. With the full opening-out of the iron-and-coal field as a result of canal-building in the 1790s, and with the growth of copper-smelting and of the making of tin-plate, South Wales was

TABLE 10.1 *Industrialisation and population growth in England and Wales, 1701–1831*

	Estimated population (in thousands)				Average decennial rate of population growth (in percentages)		
	1701	1751	1801	1831	1701–1751	1751–1801	1801–1831
Agricultural counties including Wales	1,949.0	1,960.0	2,605.0	3,691.0	0.11	5.85	12.32
Mixed counties	1,922.0	1,930.0	2,786.0	4,043.0	0.08	7.62	13.22
Industrial and commercial counties	1,955.0	2,251.0	3,765.0	6,318.0	2.85	10.84	18.83
Of these the counties of Durham, Lancashire, Staffordshire, Warwickshire and the West Riding	811.8	1,016.3	1,904.6	3,360.1	4.60	13.39	20.83
Total	5,826.0	6,141.0	9,156.0	14,052.0	1.06	8.32	15.35

1760–1830 (Oxford: Oxford University Press, 1991) p. 25

established as an important industrial area, while, in Ireland, linen-spinning was concentrated around Belfast, although the area did not really become a major industrial centre until late in the nineteenth century. At the same time, the rest of Ireland was deindustrialised as handloom-weavers moved to the vicinity of the spinning-factories in the north of the country, and as the woollen industry in the south collapsed in the face of English competition.

In the northern and midland counties the sustained growth of modern industry was associated with rapid demographic growth and a rapid expansion of factory villages, single-industry towns, and mixed industrial cities (Table 10.1 and Figure 10.1). By contrast, most parts of the periphery were marginalised and, in the nineteenth century, were depopulated mainly under the impact of changing agricultural practices and of a switch from arable to pasture farming.[2] As a result, the roles in the developing British economy of peripheral and dependent countries like Ireland and of peripheral regions like the Scottish Highlands were transformed. But it is important to remember that the inhabitants of rural areas in Southern England also experienced severe distress, especially during the agricultural depression in the years following the Napoleonic Wars, as did individuals living in some of the rural districts in the North when at first spinners and then weavers working in the domestic system were reduced to a peripheral status within the textile industry before being displaced altogether.

In 1750 most industrial activity took place in the countryside. By 1850, however, it was overwhelmingly concentrated in urban districts. This switch in the location of economic activity was accompanied by a radical change in the distribution of population not only by region but also by the type of settlement in which people lived. In 1801 about five people lived in the countryside for every person that lived in a town, but, by 1851, when the total population had nearly doubled, increasing from 11 million to 21 million persons, the distribution between town and country was approximately equal, and in the second half of the nineteenth century most rural districts in England and Wales were deindustrialised and

252

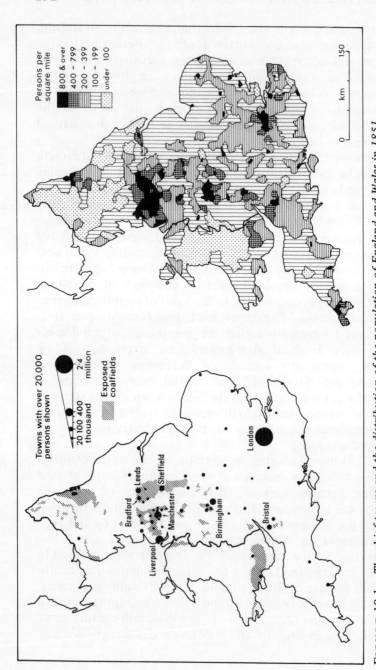

FIGURE 10.1 *The chief towns and the distribution of the population of England and Wales in 1851*

Source: J. B. Harley, 'England Circa 1850', in H. C. Darby (ed.), *A New Historical Geography of England*, pp. 579 and 530.

started to record population losses as a process of rural depopulation was set in motion.

The pattern of urban growth was very uneven, and the pre-existing urban hierarchy was overturned, reflecting the change in the determinants of urban growth. London continued to be the largest city in the country. But of the others in the top six in the 1720s only Bristol still belonged to this group in 1801. The towns of Norwich, Newcastle, Exeter, and York, which had been among the largest towns in the country for several centuries, were overtaken and came to occupy much lower positions in the urban hierarchy, while the positions they had held in the top six came to be occupied by Manchester–Salford, Liverpool, Birmingham, and Leeds, whose expansion in the second half of the eighteenth and in the first half of the nineteenth century was associated primarily with the growth of the cotton, metal-manufacturing, and wool textile industries, and of related commercial activities.[3]

The new pattern of urbanisation was of course not simply a product of a quantitative expansion of these activities. It also stemmed from a qualitative and revolutionary change in the manner of production as well as in the location of economic activity. The new manner or mode of production contained within itself a capacity for self-expansion because of the direct involvement of capital in the process of production, and it was this enlarged role for capital that provided the constant stimulus to innovation and expansion of the economic base and to the emergence and growth of new urban centres.

The adoption of specifically capitalist techniques of production, and the development of large-scale, machine-based industry or of machinofacture, occurred first of all in the cotton industry whose main centre was in Lancashire, and so it was to this region and in particular to the city of Manchester that contemporary observers referred when they spoke of an industrial revolution, rather than to Birmingham, which also expanded at this time because of the growth of its industrial base and of related activities, but which did so essentially on the basis of an expansion and intensification of manufacture.[4]

10.2 The transition from manufacture to machinofacture

The development of a capitalist mode of industrial production occurred as a result either of an emergence of capitalist relations of production within existing spheres of activity or of a penetration of existing activities by capital.[5] In either case the methods of production were not changed in a revolutionary way at first, but the ownership by capital of the means of production, and the corresponding increase in the dependence of labour on capital as well as the growing involvement of capital in the sphere of production itself, enabled it to assume greater control over the way in which production was organised, while in newly established centralised workshops and mills the supervision of the handicraft-person's work was important as a means of controlling quality, of preventing embezzlement, of lowering distribution costs, and of increasing the intensity of work and the amount of time during which workers were actually engaged in productive activity.

At the same time, the growing control of production by capital and its transfer to centralised production-units made it possible for further increases in the social productivity of labour to be achieved, since independent handicrafts were brought together under one roof, the skills of craft workers were split up into detail operations, social co-operation and the division of labour were extended, and many of the problems posed for capital by the isolation of workers under the domestic system were overcome. In particular, it permitted a differentiation of tasks on the basis of the different levels of skill required for different detail operations, and led to a corresponding hierarchisation of the labour-force into skilled and less-skilled categories according to the types of craft skill required and to the natural, acquired, or socially determined capabilities of different groups of workers.[6]

In many cases less-skilled jobs were performed by women, for, although in practice they often possessed equivalent skills to male workers, most of them had not obtained formal qualifications, largely as a result of the subordinate social position they occupied and of the way in which they were excluded from membership of the guilds and organisations of craft workers, but also as a result of the fact that they were given primary responsibility for household tasks.[7]

By leading to an extension of the social division of labour, not only did early forms of capitalist control of production make it possible for increases in the social productivity of labour to be realised, but also the ground was prepared for the development of machines.[8]

In the view of Marx the introduction of machinery represented a decisive break with the past. But in speaking of a machine he was not simply referring to the development of more sophisticated tools or to the application of mechanical power in the sphere of production. What he wished in particular to denote was the construction of mechanical means of working on the object of labour which eliminated the need for almost all human intervention except for that involved in the task of supervision. The importance of machinery seen from this point of view lay in the fact that it enabled many of the limitations associated with the use of manual tools and with largely unaided human labour to be overcome, because it made it possible to have many parts acting simultaneously, since a mechanical apparatus was not subject to the constraints posed by the number of human limbs and by the ability of a human subject to co-ordinate them.

The development of a motor mechanism and of a source of power which could be regulated by human beings but which escaped the limitations of strength that applied to the power supplied by animals or by human beings themselves, which was unaffected by the vagaries of the weather, and which was capable of producing a regular and uniform motion of sufficient force for indefinite periods of time, was also of considerable significance, in part because it facilitated the further development of machinery. At the time of the industrial revolution it was Watt's double-acting steam-engine that performed this function, but it must be remembered that it was 'the invention of machines that made a revolution in the form of steam engines necessary'.[9]

The use of steam-engines was also important for another reason. In contrast to some of the natural sources of energy by which it was preceded, the steam-engine provided large concentrations of power that were in some ways independent of location, and that could be used wherever sufficient quantities of coal and water, with which it was fuelled, could be obtained. As a result industry could be concentrated relatively easily in urban areas.[10] But owing initially to the prohibitively high costs of transport by land and even by water, the centres of modern industry and the towns and cities which increased substantially in size were located for the most part on or near to coalfields.

The introduction and use of machines made a further increase in the productivity of labour possible, and, as the machine systems were developed, the co-operative character of the labour process assumed increasing importance, and the skills and the value of the output of ever more specialised individual workers increasingly had meaning only in the context of the enterprises in which they worked, with the result that the control of labour by capital was further increased. At the same time, of course, the extension of the division of labour was associated with a tendency for the size of individual capitals to increase and for a self-sustaining process of industrial concentration to occur.

Unlike the manual tools they replaced, the machine systems were controlled by capital rather than by the workers who used or operated them, and so, in a second way, control of the rhythm and speed of work was transferred from the labourers to capital, and, in so far as the machine systems were efficient, much of the porosity of the working day was eliminated. It was at this stage that the real subsumption of labour under capital occurred.[11]

At the same time, the task of manipulating the object of labour was transferred to the machine, and the skills of the workers were incorporated in the machinery itself, with the result that the nature of the work involved was changed, and it became possible for each worker to mind several machines simultaneously. The nature and complexity of the work involved in minding machines varied between different activities, both between and within sectors. But in many cases the necessary skills could be acquired without long apprenticeships. As a result, categories of workers that had been deemed to be unskilled as well as those with little industrial experience could be employed. In particular, women and children were at first to play an extremely important role as a source of the type of unskilled labour required by modern industry, and formed a very significant proportion of the early factory-workers, although highly skilled workers, who in the vast majority of cases were men, were needed for the maintenance of the machinery itself and, indeed, for its construction.[12] On the other hand, in the case of cotton-spinning, the development of the large jenny and then of the mule resulted in the displacement of women by adult men, who came to form a skilled minority of operatives in the cotton-spinning factories, reversing a long-tradition of female domination of employment in this stage of cotton production.[13] The male mule-spinners succeeded almost immediately in achieving a form of craft control and in forming a new category of craft workers. But with the successful invention of a self-acting mule in the 1820s and the application of mechanical power the technical conditions on which their superior status was based disappeared.

In the cotton industry in virtually every other European country the cotton spinner was displaced by a poorly paid female operative. Yet in England the cotton spinners managed to retain a special social and industrial status for themselves in spite of the breach in craft control, in part because they continued to perform an important supervisory role in a situation in which direct managerial control was still relatively weak.[14]

In the next section we shall focus in more detail on the development of machinofacture in the English cotton industry. But it must be remembered that the speed and extent of the introduction of machine-based and productivity-increasing methods of production varied sharply between sectors and varied geographically. Until 1848 only in the cotton and woollen textile industries was significant technological change the basis of economic growth. In many spheres of activity manufacture survived until well into the nineteenth century or even into the twentieth. In the cotton industry, which increasingly acted as a leading sector and prompted changes in a wide range of related activities, manufacture started to give way to machinofacture in the last third of the eighteenth century. Yet even in the leading sectors of the economy progress was uneven, with spinning being mechanised well ahead of weaving, and the transition of capital to real control over the process of production had only partially been completed by the middle of the following century.

A number of important geographical contrasts also appeared. In this phase of development it was, in fact, only in Britain that much modern industrial growth occurred, and the British economy acquired an unprecedented lead. At the end of this period there were 21 million cotton spindles in Britain compared with 6 million in the rest of Europe, and in 1851 about one-half of the population lived in towns compared with about 25 per cent in France and Germany. Only one-quarter of the British male working population was engaged in the agricultural sector. In Germany more people worked in agricultural than in industrial production as late as 1895, while in France the industrial sector was outnumbered until after the Second World War. Yet even in mid-nineteenth-century Britain the two most important occupations were agriculture and domestic service followed by textiles and by housebuilding, which was a traditional sector.[15]

The transformation of the British and, subsequently, of other economies by the introduction of the techniques and forms of organisation of industrial capitalism was part of a worldwide movement. The fact that mid-eighteenth-century Britain was already a major country with access to foreign markets, obtained by conquest as in the case of India, or by a careful imposition of superior force as in the case of Portugal, was of considerable importance for its early industrial development. And very quickly the needs of an industrialising economy for supplies of raw materials and for markets brought into being a new international division of labour, at first between the British economy and a large number of mainly agrarian regions, and subsequently between Britain and other industrialising countries. In addition it led to the emergence of sharp inequalities between those countries in which economic development was occurring and the areas of the world with traditional agrarian economies and laid the foundations for the subjugation of the latter by the former. The areas inhabited by Europeans in which modern industry first developed were accordingly to acquire a dominant role in international economics and politics which they were to retain for a whole historical epoch.

In considering the events occurring in a particular sector in a particular country it is particularly important to keep in mind this international context and the way it has changed.

10.3 The development of machinofacture in the cotton industry

Most of the major technical innovations on which the transition from manufacture to machinofacture was originally based occurred in the cotton industry, where the technical problems involved were more easily overcome, and where opposition from the workers to technical change was less pronounced and less effective. One reason for the lack of opposition was that the workers concerned were more dependent on manufacturing than those in other sectors for whom supplementary sources of income existed. A second reason lay in the relatively recent origins of the industry which meant that divisions between different kinds of work and customary practices were less firmly established. Nevertheless the introduction of similar innovations was not long delayed in the Yorkshire worsted industry.

In the cotton industry itself technical change played an important role in its development and, in particular, in the extremely rapid increase in its output, which accounted for some 1 per cent of the national product of Britain in 1781–3, for between 4 and 7 per cent in 1800, and for a maximum of between 7 and 8 per cent in 1811–13.[16] It is also important to recall, however, that the successful introduction and use of new methods of production entailed and depended upon organisational changes within the industry, a more widespread development of a proletariat, the development of slave plantations for the exclusive production of cotton in the West Indies and the Southern USA, and the collapse of the Indian cotton industry which was initiated by the adoption by the British government of protectionist measures.

The transition from manufacture to machinofacture in the cotton industry was associated with four major innovations. The first was Kay's flying shuttle which was introduced in the 1750s and 1760s, which increased the productivity of weaving, and which subsequently led to the development of more advanced forms of spinning. The second was the spinning-jenny which was developed by Hargreaves of Blackburn in 1774. The spinning-jenny had the effect of increasing the spindleage capacity of a single wheel, at first by a moderate amount such that the jenny could be accommodated within the domestic system, but subsequently to such an extent that its use in the producers' homes was no longer a practical possibility. The third innovation was the water frame which was developed by Arkwright of Preston in 1769, and which was factory-based from the outset. The fourth was the mule which was developed by Crompton of Bolton in the late 1770s, and which made it possible for pure cotton to be produced with the help of a single machine. As in the case of the spinning-jenny the mule was initially hand-operated, but was subsequently enlarged and powered by steam.[17] Indeed the greater levels of productivity obtained by using these innovations came at first primarily from the changes in the method of working on the object of labour with which they were associated. Only subsequently was productivity increased by the application of mechanical power.

The three important advances that occurred in spinning led to a dramatic increase in the productivity of labour and, despite the increase in the amount of capital per worker, to an important fall in costs. In fact, the number of operative hours necessary per 100 pounds of cotton fell from more than 50,000 in the case of eighteenth-century Indian hand-spinners, to 2,000 in 1780 with the use of Crompton's mule, to between 250 and 370 in the 1780s and 1790s with the introduction of Arkwright's rollers, to 300 in about 1795 with the use of a power-assisted mule, and to 135 by about 1825 with the introduction of Robert's automatic mule.[18]

The advances in spinning and the increases in output with which they were associated led to pressures for improvements in productivity in the preparatory processes and in weaving. The processes of carding and scribbling were mechanised, and many workers were displaced, but in weaving the absence of significant technical change led at first to an enormous increase in the number of handloom weavers. In the cotton industry the number of handloom weavers and of other auxiliary domestic workers rose from an estimated 90,000 in 1795 to 270,000 in 1811 and to 300,000 in 1833.[19]

In the second half of the nineteenth century, when weaving was mechanised and was transferred into factories, a similar mechanism led to a proliferation of employment in the clothing industry. Indeed the whole history of the discovery and introduction of different inventions in the textile industry demonstrates the way in which the gains from an innovation in one sphere could only be fully realised when corresponding changes were made elsewhere, and the way in which changes and a momentum built up in the forces of production increasingly required and gave rise to changes in the organisation of production. In practice, the strength of social resistance and conditions in the labour market, on the one hand, or characteristics of the industry's structure which reduced the competitive advantages that could be derived as a result of the technical superiority of new methods of production, on the other hand, could slow down the introduction of productivity-increasing techniques or of new forms of industrial organisation. But in the end the process of competition usually ensured that methods and organisational forms that reduced costs and increased rate of profit were generalised.

The development of the cotton industry has been emphasised because of its role as a leading sector in the transition to machinofacture, and because of its effects on other branches of production. But even in Lancashire, where it was centred, and in Yorkshire, in which the wool textile industry was concentrated, and in which some processes of production were transferred to centralised installations at an early stage, the factory system did not become dominant in terms of employment until the second quarter of the nineteenth century. In the case of the handloom weavers, the expansion of outworking stemmed in part from delays in the perfection of the power-loom. In addition, the size of the reserve army of labour in textile-producing regions was increased by changes in the structure of the local economy;

by relatively high demographic growth-rates; by the immigration of workers from other rural areas, and, especially, from Ireland, in which domestic crafts were declining and agriculture was being transformed; by returnees from the Napoleonic Wars; and by changes in the Poor Laws which reduced the scope of outdoor relief. As a result, the costs of handloom weaving by domestic workers were kept down. A third reason was that considerable resistance to the externally imposed discipline of the factory system existed. In particular, regulated time-keeping, the loss of individual control over the process of production, of variety in work, and the associated loss of status, the general unpleasantness of factory environments, and the fact that factories had traditionally been regarded as workhouses for pauper children and itinerant workers, made factory work very unpopular.[20] At the same time, the flexibility of the domestic and putting-out systems meant that they had certain advantages over factory production in situations in which demand was fluctuating sharply.

But the survival of domestic industry was in most cases a transitional situation. In time, the mechanisation of weaving and the growing competitive superiority of machinofacture led to an increase in industrial concentration, and the very small firms in the industry, the small masters, and the independent outworkers tended to disappear. In the 1830s, for example, some 100,000 handloom weavers were displaced in the cotton industry alone.[21]

The extent of the process of concentration was limited, however, by the fact that the different branches of the industry tended to evolve separately and to remain under the control of different capitals. So firms that introduced advanced forms of spinning often did not become involved in weaving or in the finishing-branches of the industry. As a result, individual units of production remained comparatively small by the standards of the middle of the twentieth century, with an average of about 100 workers or, where spinning and weaving were combined, of about 350 workers, although some firms employed more than 1,000 people. It has been pointed out by Hobsbawm, however, that an industrial structure of this kind had the advantage of flexibility that was essential in the early stages of an industry's expansion.

But in the second half of the nineteenth century it made it more difficult to adopt the more integrated forms of production that evolved, and consequently contributed to the comparative backwardness of the British industry.[22]

In the early nineteenth century the British cotton industry was the most efficient in the world. But the structure of the industry and the fluctuating nature of demand with which it was associated 'deprived capitalists in the industry of the possibility of developing, either individually or collectively, a strategy to reshape the technical structure of production'.[23] As a result, 'it ended as it had begun by relying not on its competitive superiority but on a monopoly of the colonial and underdeveloped markets which the British Empire, the British Navy, and British commercial supremacy gave it', and eventually it lost its leading position on the world market.[24]

Even though the switch to machinofacture was accompanied by an increase in the productivity of labour, it was associated at first with a lengthening of the working day, or at least with an increase in the amount of time spent working at a sustained pace. In the early years of development of large-scale industry in the last third of the eighteenth century the length of the working day was increased, in fact, to between twelve and sixteen hours or even more, especially in the case of women whose working day was extended by the performance of domestic in addition to paid work.

An increase in the length of the working day, or in its intensity, or in both, was technically possible because the new processes typically involved less physical exertion. As a result, the purely physical limits of human strength were not likely to be exceeded.[25] The apparently paradoxical conjunction of higher levels of productivity and longer working hours can only be explained, however, by reference to the social relations of capitalist production and to the fact that the labour process was in part a process of valorisation of capital.[26]

One of the reasons for the lengthening of the working day lay in the fact that individual capitals were anxious to take advantage of the excess profits that could be made prior to the more widespread adoption of a machine, and to realise the value embodied in new instruments of production as quickly as possible and at any rate before they were devalued by the introduction of newer and more productive methods and processes.[27] Second, capital savings could be made by employing a smaller work-force over a longer period of time rather than a larger one over a shorter period. At the same time, of course, the control over labour exercised by the reserve-army mechanism was correspondingly increased.[28] In the third place, the introduction of new machine-based processes of production was associated with a change in the composition of capital. A part of the capital that had been advanced in the form of variable capital, that is had been turned into living labour, was converted into machinery, that is into constant capital, and, other things being equal, the organic composition of capital increased. At the same time as the rate of surplus-value was being raised by the application of machinery, the number of workers simultaneously employed by a given amount of capital was accordingly lowered, exerting downward pressure on the mass of surplus-value. In this situation each capitalist was led to prolong the working day and to increase the production of absolute surplus-value in order to compensate for the relative fall in the number of workers exploited.[29]

The long hours of work that resulted from pressures of this kind, the squalid conditions in which people lived and worked, the increased involvement of women and children in work outside of the home, and the loss of independence and status of male workers, eventually generated forceful working-class resistance and a certain amount of philanthropic concern.[30] One of the issues that was widely discussed throughout the nineteenth century was the question of female factory employment. The arguments put forward were underpinned by a large set of diverse and conflicting motives and attitudes, and often indicated a considerable degree of ignorance about the nature of female work in the period preceding the factory age. However, the case against the employment of women rested on two main groups of arguments. One of these reflected a resentment of the reversal of traditional roles within the family, and of the fact that women and children were both employed at much lower rates of pay than had been customary for male workers. The second group of arguments stemmed from a humanitarian concern about the health of pregnant women and the care of newly born children, as well as from a concern about the social and moral implications of the neglect of household 'duties' by married women. These two sets of arguments led to demands for a reduction in the length of the working day for women and children and, ultimately, for all factory workers, and for the payment to male workers of a family wage that would remove the need for married women to work.

In time, some of these demands were conceded, in part because of a growing concern on the part of the capitalist class as a whole about the ability of the working class to reproduce itself qualitatively as well as quantitatively. In particular, with the development of machinofacture and the growing technical sophistication of the process of production, certain operations required a more reliable and well-disciplined labour-force, whose reproduction could not be guaranteed in the living and working conditions prevailing in the early part of the factory era. A family wage was accordingly conceded to more skilled workers. Indeed, it subsequently became an integral part of the pay differential between skilled and unskilled workers, and the possession of a wife not working outside of the home became a status symbol in line with the cult of female domesticity adopted by the Victorian bourgeoisie.[31]

In most cases a family wage barely provided the subsistence needs of a family. Nevertheless the selectivity with which it was paid suggests that a humanitarian concern for the welfare of women and children was not the primary reason for its introduction. Indeed, in areas in which it was widely introduced, such as Wigan where mining was important, or Oldham where textile machinery was produced, its overall effect was to depress female wages in the textile industry, since work by women came to be regarded as a subordinate activity. As a result, conditions for single women were particularly harsh. By contrast, in areas in which the textile industry was the most important activity, and female employment was more marked, wages for women were in general higher. In areas where weaving predominated, for example, and where men and women were both employed, wages were nominally equal, although men were typically given the higher-paid work.[32]

The changes in the structure of wages and in the role of female employment that occurred in the second half of the nineteenth century, were only two of many interrelated facets of the reconstruction of the way of life and of the conditions in which people lived and worked in different parts of the country that occurred in response to the economic and political conflicts and to the economic crisis of the 1830s and early 1840s.

In the period between the last years of the Napoleonic Wars and the middle of the 1840s, successive gusts of social discontent blew across Britain:

> Luddite and Radical, trade unionist and utopian socialist, Democratic and Chartist. At no other period in modern British history have the common people been so persistently, profoundly, and often desperately dissatisfied. At no other period since the 17th century can we speak of large masses of them as revolutionary, or discern at least one moment of political crisis (between 1830 and the Reform Act of 1832) when something like a revolutionary situation might actually have developed.[33]

The discontent itself arose in part out of the hopelessness and hunger of the masses, out of the difficulties of adapting to a new type of society and the hostility it engendered amongst workers whose estimation of their own social worth and position differed from that accorded to them by the newly developing production relations of industrial capitalism, and out of the prospects of a breakdown of the underlying model of economic and social development. It was most acute in the 1830s and early 1840s when both the middle classes and the working classes pressed for what they regarded as fundamental changes in the social and political order of Britain, at first in conjunction with one another in the Parliamentary Reform Movement, but, subsequently, separately and in opposition to one another 'under the banner of the Anti-

Corn-Law League' and in 'the giant movement for the People's Charter'.[34]

But after the 1840s the rate of profit increased again, and the rate of expansion of markets was sufficiently rapid to absorb much of what could be produced at the relatively high rates of growth which the industrial system was capable of achieving. The working-class movements of the 1830s and 1840s failed in spite of the gains they achieved, but not without playing an important role in changing the structure and trajectory of the social and economic system.

After 1850 many employers switched from extensive to intensive methods of exploitation, and the length of the working day was reduced. The mechanised factory and a modern factory proletariat were consolidated at the expense of artisan workers, who had enjoyed various degrees of craft autonomy, and around whose interests Chartism had been constructed. A new phrase of industrialisation involving an accelerated development of producer-goods sectors, including the railway, coal, iron and steel, and engineering industries, was set in motion, and the imbalances between the modern industrial sector and the rest of the economy were lessened. In addition, some small improvements in working-class living conditions and standards of consumption occurred, and patriarchy was reimposed. In these new economic and social conditions the process of development was accompanied by class harmony and social stability rather than by open class conflict. Indeed, it is to these years, and to the subsequent Victorian boom, that working-class reformism, with its nationalistic component and the self-consciousness of the working class as an estate with particular interests to defend and to advance within the framework of the prevailing social and economic system, which was to play such an important role in the subsequent history of England, can be traced.[35]

10.4 Urban growth and the development of the cotton industry

In the first half of the nineteenth century, outworking survived in the cotton and in the wool textile industry, but, in both of them, factory production came to play an increasingly important role. But, whereas the early factories had been located in upland valleys, with mechanisation and the increasing use of steam-power the mills were concentrated in rapidly growing urban areas, producing the industrial landscapes and industrial cities that have been described so vividly.[36] Of these, it was Manchester, which acted as the centre of the cotton industry, that experienced the greatest and most striking growth.

In the early eighteenth century, Manchester was a small market town with about 10,000 inhabitants. It lacked corporate status. In addition, there were no craft guilds and few restrictions on industrial development. It was also located in a region with a high density of population, limited agricultural potential, and a lack of industrial employment, but a material environment supplying pure water and coal fuel which were essential for the bleaching, dyeing, and printing of cotton, and which could be used for industrial power. As a result, the region was ideally suited as a base for the development of the cotton industry, while Manchester was well placed to act as a commercial centre from which a putting-out system could be organised.

In 1700, legislation forbidding the import of printed calicoes was passed, owing to the potentially destablising effects of cotton goods on the woollen industry, and in 1721, the buying and selling and even the wearing of printed-cotton goods was prohibited. On the other hand, the production of fustians, which were mixtures of a linen warp and cotton weft, was allowed by the Manchester Act of 1736. This type of cloth was already being produced in the region, but was made mainly for local consumption. But, in 1774, when the manufacture of cotton goods had been developed in this country, the 1721 prohibition was repealed.[37]

By the first decade of the nineteenth century the cotton industry had become the most important manufacturing industry in Britain, and cotton had overtaken woollen cloth as the most important export. Indeed, in years between 1820 and 1850, cotton goods accounted for about one-half of the total value of all British exports.

Because of the role of Manchester as the centre of the

cotton industry, the population of the city doubled between the beginning of the eighteenth century and 1770, and increased more than eight-fold by the turn of the century, reaching 84,000 inhabitants in 1801. By 1851 its population had reached 400,000 inhabitants, as a result of a high rate of natural increase, immigration from the surrounding area, and immigration from Ireland and elsewhere. Yet towns also grew in the surrounding area forming concentric arcs around Manchester itself. Indeed, while there had been only 6 places with over 2,000 inhabitants within a 26-mile radius of Manchester in 1750, by 1780 there were 12, and by 1821 there were 16. The rate of growth of these towns was also rapid, but in terms of size and function Manchester dominated all of them.[38]

The growth of Manchester occurred largely as a result of its role as a commercial centre from which the putting-out system and handloom weaving in particular were organised, as a centre of steam-powered spinning and eventually of mechanised weaving, which occurred in 'hundreds of five- and six-storied factories, each with a towering chimney by its side which exhaled black coal vapour',[39] and as the centre of a region in which the industry came to be particularly heavily concentrated. In fact, by 1830, some 90 mills had been built in the vicinity of Manchester itself, and the area around the city accounted for about one-quarter of all cotton-spinning and contained over one-half of the power-looms in the country, while by 1851 more than two-thirds of the factories, factory workers, spindles, and power-looms were located in Lancashire as a whole, with most of the remainder being found in the neighbouring areas of Cheshire, the West Riding, and Derbyshire.[40]

At first, the development of the cotton industry did little to stimulate the development of other industries. The production of coal was mainly for domestic consumption, and most of the early machines were made of wood and were produced to individual specifications in the cotton-mills themselves. Moreover, the industry's main raw material was imported, and few downstream activities were developed as most of its output was exported, especially to colonial markets and to less-developed countries.[41] In time, however, the cotton industry's growth stimulated the development of the chemical industry, of engineering and the production of textile machinery, and of coal-mining, and helped to diversify the industrial structure of Manchester and its region. In addition, Manchester acquired important functions because of its role as a commercial centre for the industry and as a shopping and administrative centre for the surrounding area.

Nevertheless most of the small- and medium-sized towns in the region continued to be heavily dependent not simply upon the cotton industry, but upon the particular branches of the industry in which they were specialised. Spinning, for example, was concentrated in the southern part of Lancashire in towns such as Oldham, Bolton, Bury, and Stockport, while weaving was the main activity to the north in towns like Preston, Burnley, and Blackburn and in the surrounding villages of Nelson and Colne. The separation of spinning and weaving was not a hard and fast one, but it increased during the course of the century, so that, by the 1880s, three-quarters of the spindles were to be found in the south and three-fifths of the looms were to be found in the north of the county's cotton-producing zone.[42] In addition, each town within one of these sub-regions tended to specialise in a particular branch of spinning or weaving. In Bolton, for example, a specialisation in fine spinning emerged, while in Oldham coarser yarn was produced.

As a result, when other countries manufactured and exported their own cotton goods and could no longer be prevented from doing so by British political interference, the cotton towns were faced with a severe and long-lasting depression, whose causes lay in a high degree of specialisation in cotton production as well as in a failure to remain internationally competitive; whereas Manchester itself was protected for a while by the relative diversification of its economy and, in particular, by the development of an industry producing textile machinery for whose output demand increased as other countries pursued their own industrialisation programmes.

10.5 The internal structure of the cotton towns

In the nineteenth century the cotton towns of Lancashire were often 'as tightly knit and socially compact as many mining communities', but expressed in their internal physical and social structure a division of society into two broad social classes 'separated in work, areas of residence, and in politics'. In Manchester, for example, one of the most striking contrasts lay in the juxtaposition of the Stock Exchange which acted as a symbol of bourgeois prosperity, and the slum housing in which the vast majority of the working class lived. Among some of the more enlightened sections of the bourgeoisie the conditions in the slums were a matter of some concern, for it was feared that they would give rise to moral turpitude, radical politics, and health hazards, or to the three evils of crime, Chartism, and cholera.[43]

The origins of the slums lay essentially in the combination of circumstances that forced the costs of reproduction of labour-power down to the barest minimum. Of particular importance in this respect was the competition for jobs and housing in conditions of an excess supply of labour and in the absence of an established norm of working-class consumption. The conditions in the early industrial cities were in fact very different from those obtaining in the early industrial villages, largely because the relations of paternalism between employer and employee had been removed and replaced by the discipline of the market. In particular, the relations of capitalist production were more fully developed, employers were able to hire and fire workers according to the state of trade, and the labour-force of an individual factory merged into a general labour-force whose members competed with one another for work, pushing wages down sometimes below a subsistence minimum. At this time most employers showed little concern about the inability of workers to maintain themselves adequately on the wages provided, or about the fact that the average life expectancy of a person born in Manchester in 1843, for example, was only 24.2 years compared with a national average of 40.2 years.[44] In addition, employers did not need to provide housing or other items of collective consumption. Instead they left the workers they employed 'to crowd into the garrets and cellars of existing tenements', and relied 'on private building contractors to adjust the supply of housing accommodation to the demand for it by running up jerry-built houses to be let out at exorbitant rents'.[45]

In the cotton towns the situation was exacerbated by the rapidity with which the urban areas grew, and by the role of speculative building subject to virtually no legislation or planning controls in constructing the urban environment. Yet, from the point of view of the agents involved in the provision of housing, investments of this kind carried a substantial degree of risk and uncertainty, not only because of the low wages received by the tenants of such housing, but also because of fluctuations in the cotton industry and the way in which many of the costs of the business cycle were passed on to the workers themselves.[46] One of the main ways of meeting what were high rent payments in a situation in which incomes were not only low but also varied markedly was by increasing the overcrowding of dwellings that were already grossly inadequate.

So in the early nineteenth century the living conditions of the urban proletariat were giving rise to serious problems of public health and social order. In addition hardly any segregation existed between different categories of workers, with the result that the more skilled sections of the working class were affected in much the same way as less-skilled and marginal workers. Yet by the middle of the century the expansion of machinofacture was creating a need for a more efficient central proletariat 'that had . . . internalised the needs and imperatives of the production system, and that was accordingly capable of self-discipline and moral restraint, of taking modest initiatives in the performance of labour tasks, and of enduring the psychological costs of an intensified rhythm of factory work'.[47] In addition, a norm of working-class consumption was beginning to be established under the impact of working-class pressure.

Some new factory villages and workers' settlements were founded by individual capitalists in the quest for profit, but in large settlements, in which employers did not have a captive labour-force, any attempt by individual capitalists to improve the living conditions of the working class or to create a more pronounced differentiation within it in the field of consumption would have been irrational, because they would have ended up by creating externalities from which other capitalists, who chose to bear none of the costs, would have benefited.

As a result, it was left to the state to intervene in the interests of capital in general.[48]

In the second half of the nineteenth century a succession of urban reforms was accordingly introduced. However, the way in which they were implemented varied markedly between localities and was strongly affected by local conditions.

10.6 Conclusion

In this phase of development, machinofacture was limited for the most part to the textile industry in which it was nevertheless complemented by outworking. Of course innovations occurred and output expanded in other sectors. The output of the coal industry in Britain increased from 16 million tons in 1816 to 49 million tons in 1850, and iron output expanded in England and Wales from 220,000 tons in 1806 to nearly 1.5 million tons in 1847, but in both cases expansion occurred by means of a proliferation of non-mechanised undertakings. Similarly, the metal-using industries and the making of machinery expanded on the basis of techniques requiring the employment of highly skilled craft workers, while many of the machines and products were custom-built.

In fact the lack of technical progress and the dependence on skilled workers in the capital-goods sector were important constraints on the development of the economy as a whole. They were also one of the reasons why the development of the technologically advanced cotton industry was almost continually threatened by falling levels of profitability, and was characterised by a succession of violent booms and slumps in the 1830s and 1840s; for, while the introduction and generalisation of innovations raised labour productivity and lowered the costs of production, the costs of machinery increased relative to the exchange-value of cotton goods, as did the price of food and unit wage-costs.[49] At the same time the situation was exacerbated by fluctuations in foreign demand and by trade speculation.

In the next era some of the resulting limits on the expansion of the industrial economy were lifted not simply by the cheapening of food products associated with improvements in transport, but also by the extension of machinofacture to the capital-goods sector. The major breakthrough came with the design of machines to build machines and with the development of the machine-tool industry at the beginning of the 1840s. The hold of the artisan over the method and pace of work along with other aspects of craft control were diminished significantly, even though the earliest machines were relatively unsophisticated, and in spite of the fact that considerable skill was involved in making and in using them. But the resulting increase in the productivity of labour in the machine-making and engineering sectors, and the fall in the costs of capital goods, lowered some of the obstacles to the extended reproduction of capital.

11 The Golden Age of British Capitalism, 1845-1890s

11.1 Introduction

In this phase of development the growth process was led not by the textile industry but by the expansion of coal-mining, iron- and steel-making, railway construction, shipbuilding, and other branches of mechanical engineering, such as the manufacture of steam-engines, textile machinery, and machine tools.

In Britain, the railway-building boom occurred between 1830 and 1850. At that time it stimulated the growth and modernisation of the capital- and intermediate-goods sectors, and played an important role in increasing the speed of transport and in lowering the turnover time of fixed and circulating capital. In addition it provided an outlet for vast accumulations of surplus capital for which profitable investment opportunities were limited, and a solution to the crisis of the first phase of British capitalism. But the stimulus was not exhausted with the completion in 1850 of much of the English railway network. In the world as a whole the construction of railways continued on an increasingly massive scale at least until the 1880s. To a large extent these railways were built 'with British capital, British materials and equipment, and often by British contractors'.[1]

The expansion of the world railway system reflected a twin process of industrialisation of the more developed metropolitan economies and an economic opening-up of relatively undeveloped areas that created a new world-economy and consigned one part of the globe to a specialisation in the production of food and raw materials for the more developed countries, of which the most advanced was Britain. In these decades, areas like the North American prairies, the South

American pampas, and the Russian steppes were turned over to an export agriculture, the resistance of China and Japan to foreign trade was broken down with flotillas of warships, and the foundations of tropical and subtropical economies based on the export of minerals and agrarian products were laid.[2]

At the same time, industrialisation and economic development in the rest of the world 'provided a rapidly increasing market for the kind of capital goods which could not be imported in any quantity except from the "workshop of the world", and which could not yet be produced in sufficient quantity at home'.[3]

In Britain itself, employment in agriculture fell from a peak of 2.1 million persons in 1851 to 1.6 million in 1891, or from 21.7 per cent to 10.5 per cent of the total labour-force,[4] and in the 1870s and 1880s the import of cheap grain, in particular, initiated a major contraction of agriculture, and especially of tillage. In the mid-Victorian era rural crafts declined along with agricultural employment, and so large numbers of people left the countryside. Several million workers, equal in fact to one-half of the total population in 1801, were forced to leave the country altogether.[5] Others found work in domestic service, in the industrial and commercial sectors of the London economy, and in the booming industrial areas that had for the most part already been established. In some cases the coming of the railways helped to extend the workable parts of a coalfield, as in South-West Durham, the East Midlands, and the Scottish Lowlands, and played a part in the development of mineral areas such as Teeside and the Furness district of Cumberland. In addition they were instrumental in locating spas and seaside resorts frequented by an expanding class of rentiers. But the main outlines of the economic geography of nineteenth-century Britain had already been established.[6]

At the same time, the area that was to become Germany in 1871, and the USA, were turned into major industrial economies. Indeed, as growth slackened in the 1870s, the economies of these countries were as, if not more, competitive than the British economy in many sectors, while less-developed countries such as Russia and Japan were developing textile and other industries of their own, and were beginning to succeed in capturing some of the markets on which British goods had been sold.

11.2 The coal and the iron and steel industries and the development of the industrial regions

Introduction

The uneven sectoral composition of the growth process led to uneven regional development and to a progressive widening of the disparities between existing and new industrialised areas and the rest of the country. The areas experiencing the most rapid development were areas in which the capital- and intermediate-goods sectors were located, while 'every traveller in Britain noticed the extraordinary way in which industry and population were being concentrated on or near the coal measures'.[7]

Yet, while the existence of some towns and villages depended solely upon the local availability of coal or iron-ore, and while their growth was more or less closely correlated with the size of the known reserves and the rate of extraction of the mineral, in other cases the pattern and pace of development depended on other pre-existing or new industries whose implantation and expansion were governed by more than the degree of access to raw materials in different parts of the country.

In the shipbuilding industry, for example, a major switch occurred in the course of the nineteenth century, from a widely dispersed pattern, in which almost every port around the coast of Britain and Ireland was represented, but with its centre of gravity in the south and along the banks of the Thames in particular, to a highly concentrated one, in which production was dominated by yards in the North East, on the Clyde, and to a lesser extent in Belfast in the north of Ireland. The suggestion that this change in the geographical distribution of the industry can be attributed to changes in technology from wood to iron and from sail to steam, and to a decision to locate production at sites close to the materials required to build the new kind of vessels, has to be qualified in several ways. In the first place the shift to the north predated the change in technology. Indeed, by the 1830s, one-third of the ships built in the country were being launched from the River Wear. Second, the shipbuilding industry on the Thames was the first to experiment with the new technology, having been encouraged to do so by the Admiralty.[8]

The explanation of the change in the industry's location seems to lie in part in the fact that its growth in the north of the country was at first stimulated by the general industrial expansion occurring in the region; for shipping, which expanded with the growth of industry, and shipbuilding were closely related. More important, with the introduction of the new technology the industry underwent a profound change, and came to draw more upon the skills of the boilermaking and metal trades than upon those of the traditional shipwright. As a result, proximity to engineering industries and to workers with engineering skills became important. In itself this would not have been a problem in the London region. Instead, the major obstacle seems to have been the existence of a highly organised work-force, versed in the traditional skills of the shipwright and unwilling to modify existing practices and to allow the introduction of the new skills into the shipyards. At the same time the wage-costs of shipyard workers were generally higher in London, rents were higher, and congestion on the Thames was growing. Of course the disposition of raw materials was an important consideration. But all of these other factors also played an important role in the decline of shipbuilding on the Thames, and in the conversion of most of the shipyards that remained to repair work and to some forms of marine engineering.[9] In many other sectors the same point about the absence of a simple relationship between the availability of coal and the implantation and growth of an industry can be made.

The new age was, however, the age of coal and of iron and steel. In the case of the coal industry, output increased from 10 million tons per annum in 1800, to over 50 million by 1850, and to 287 million in 1913. The production of pig-iron rose from 2 or 3 million tons per annum in the early 1850s to 6 or 7 million in the early 1870s, while steel production, which only took place on a relatively small scale in the 1850s, expanded rapidly in subsequent decades. As a result, by 1870 British producers accounted for over one-half of the world's production of pig-iron and nearly the same proportion of its steel. On the other hand, by 1913 the relative importance of the British iron and steel industry had declined significantly. In that year only 14 per cent of the world output of pig-iron and 10 per cent of world steel production came from Britain.[10]

Within the country the growth of these industries was associated with significant changes in the relative importance of different production centres and in the map of regional growth.

The coal industry and the regions

In the case of coal, all of the coalfields, with the exception of the one in South Staffordshire, experienced an absolute increase in output, with especially rapid growth occurring in the Yorkshire, Derbyshire and Nottinghamshire, the South Wales, and the Northumberland and Durham fields. In the first of these, expansion was such that by the turn of the century its output exceeded that of the Northumberland and Durham field, which had previously dominated coal production, as did the output of the South Wales field, which expanded rapidly from the first half of the nineteenth century until the early 1920s.

Because of the extreme variability in the types of coal found in different fields and in different seams within the same field, and because of the high degree of variation in the demand for coal associated with fluctuations in the need for domestic heating and with the industrial cycle, the development of the industry was highly uneven both temporally and geographically. Indeed it would be to some extent correct to argue that each coalfield had, as a result, a unique history.[11] Nevertheless some general characteristics of the development of the industry can be identified.

In particular, the exhaustion of some of the shallower reserves together with improvements in the methods of drainage and ventilation led to the development of deeper and larger pits on the concealed parts of the coalfields, and gave rise to geographical changes in the pattern of mining. In Yorkshire, for example, events of this kind were associated with a shift in the focus of the industry from the area around Bradford and Halifax in the west of the county, where mining was carried out for the most part by small family enterprises, most of whose output went to the textile industry, to South Yorkshire whose coal was for the most part exported from the county. A movement from west to east also occurred on the Derbyshire and Nottinghsmshire parts of this coalfield, while similar movements towards the concealed parts of coalfields occurred in other areas.[12]

The development of deeper pits in conditions of expanding demand was associated with a process of concentration in the industry, with the formation of limited-liability companies, and in some cases with the penetration of the industry by capital from outside of the region. The degree of concentration varied between regions, and in numerical terms the industry as a whole continued to be dominated by large numbers of relatively small firms. As late as 1913 there were 3,289 collieries operated by 1,589 separate undertakings. However, one-quarter of the companies accounted for four-fifths of the total output of the industry, and 'the characteristic miner would be working in relatively large groups for companies which owned more than one mine'.[13]

The methods of working at the coal-face made little progress and remained under the control of the miners themselves. In the 1860s mechanical coal-cutters began to be patented, and 'in times of strike high hopes were entertained by employers of the "revolution" they might effect'.[14] But in 1901 only 1.5 per cent of total output was produced with the aid of mechanical cutting equipment. By 1913 this figure had increased to 8.5 per cent compared with over 40 per cent in the USA.[15] The reasons for this lay in part in differences in the structure of the coal industry in the two countries. In Britain, the existence of a multiplicity of pits of varying sizes militated against industrial reorganisation and technological change. In addition the existence of a plentiful supply of relatively inexpensive labour, geological difficulties, and a distribution and form of surface-land-ownership that acted as an obstacle to efficient underground working, delayed mechanisation at the point of production. Similarly, only a small proportion of the coal was conveyed to the surface mechanically. Instead, the number of hauliers was increased, and the number of pit-ponies used for underground haulage increased from 11,000 in 1851, to 25,000 in 1881, and to 70,000 in 1911.[16]

Nevertheless the industry continued to expand and continued to be competitively efficient until the First World War. In addition, the gradually increasing scale of production prepared the ground for a finer division of labour and a differentiation of the labour-force by skill category and by form of payment. The aim of this strategy was to increase the intensity of work, to increase output, and to discipline the workers in a situation in which the work itself was not normally directly supervised by management.[17] However, capital was quite unable to break down the solidarity generated by the need for co-operation between workers in what were extremely dangerous working conditions and by the structure of the communities in which the miners lived. It was this solidarity, of course, that conferred enormous political significance on this category of workers.[18]

Until the early 1880s, productivity continued to increase, rising from an annual output per person employed of 220 tons in 1851 to 326 tons in 1881. But it then fell gradually to 260 tons in 1913, in part because of diminishing returns. As a result, the expansion of coal output was associated with a vast increase in the number of coal-miners, from around 255,000 in 1851, to about half a million in 1880, and to more than 1.1 million in 1913. In fact, over the century as a whole, a twenty-eight-fold increase in coal output was associated with a twenty-five-fold increase in employment in the coal industry.[19]

The iron industry and the development of the steel industry

In the case of the mining and smelting of iron there were also important changes in location following on from the changes outlined in Chapter 8. In the 1850s, over 95 per cent of the iron-ore mined in the country came from the Coal Measures.

The production of pig-iron was concentrated on some of the coalfields where ore and fuel could be obtained, sometimes from the same pit. At that time, about 85 per cent of output in Britain was produced in the West Midlands and by the more rapidly advancing industries of South Wales and Monmouthshire and of Scotland.[20] In South Wales, the Dowlais works was probably the largest iron-works in the world, employing over 7,000 people to work its mines, its 18 blast-furnaces, its puddling-ovens, and its rolling-mills, while a further 11 blast-furnaces were installed in the nearby Cyfarthfa works.[21] By contrast, only about 5 per cent of British output was produced in the North-East of England, which was soon to emerge as the most important iron-smelting region in the country. Some steel was also made, mainly in the vicinity of Sheffield.

Until the 1850s, steel could only be produced in much smaller quantities and at a much higher cost than cast- or wrought-iron. But in the next few decades the production of steel was revolutionised by the invention of the Bessemer converter in the early 1850s, of the open-hearth furnace in the early 1860s, and of the basic process in the late 1870s. The development of the Bessemer and open-hearth processes made it possible for steel, which is a much more durable and a stronger material, to be produced on a sufficiently large scale, with a sufficiently even quality, and at a sufficiently low cost to challenge wrought-iron as the predominant construction material and, eventually, to replace it for most uses.

The development of new methods of steel-making, and technical progress in other stages in the production of iron and steel, rendered puddling and other wrought-iron-making craft occupations, which required substantial strength, skill, and metallurgical judgement, obsolete, and made new steel-making skills important. Many of the skills associated with the experience of the old craft workers were replaced by instrumentation and by more precise forms of chemical control. At the same time, the mechanisation of furnace-charging and -tapping, and the introduction of more efficient methods of transferring the materials between the different stages of production and of manipulating the metal in the rolling process, reduced the number of unskilled labouring jobs, but created new semi-skilled machine-minding occupations. In addition the number of craft workers employed to carry out maintenance work increased. As these changes occurred, the contracting system and the relationship between skilled and unskilled workers with which it was associated declined, and managerial control of production increased. Yet, while some types of skill and knowledge were transferred from the workers to capital, the responsibility of the work of semi-skilled machine-minders, for example, increased markedly in comparison with that of the workers they replaced, as the volume of throughput was so much greater that minor mistakes would have been extremely costly.[22]

The revolution in the production of iron and steel that occurred in the second half of the nineteenth century was also a revolution in the location of iron-mining and of metal-manufacturing. In the mining sector the production of the Coal Measure ores declined, so that in 1913 they contributed only 10 per cent or so of a much higher level of domestic ore production.[23] One reason for this was that the new steel-making processes required a much higher quality of iron-ore than was found in areas like the northern part of the Welsh coalfield or the West Midlands. In any case, the ore deposits in these areas were on the verge of being worked out, and iron-making was expanding in other regions.

In the years between 1850 and 1870 the output of the rich haematite of Cumberland and North Lancashire expanded sharply with the growth in demand for non-phosphoric ores for the production of Bessemer steel, and, by the early 1870s, imports of haematite from Spain and of other foreign ores were beginning to rise sharply, reaching nearly a million tons in 1873.[24] In addition, the low-grade bedded ores in the Jurassic rocks between Oxfordshire and the North Riding began to be worked fairly extensively in the 1850s, at first for the production of pig-iron. In particular, ores in the Cleveland hills were mined to supply the Teeside region until they were replaced by imported ores. The orefields in the East Midland counties of Lincolnshire and Northamptonshire were rediscovered and came to account for a rising proportion of home production, but were less fully and less rapidly exploited than similar deposits in other parts of Europe, and did not lead to a major shift in the location of iron- and steel-making. By the turn of the century, between 6 and 7 per cent of the total make of pig-iron was produced on the new Jurassic orefields. In Scunthorpe the production of steel started only in 1890, and in Northamptonshire the making of basic steel did not begin until 1927.[25]

In the second half of the nineteenth century the old centres of pig-iron production in the coalfield areas marked time for a while and eventually stagnated or declined, while new centres of production were developed on the orefields or on the coast, in part because of the switch to new sources of iron-ore and the albeit limited economies achieved in the use of coal. In areas like Shropshire and Staffordshire output declined as their iron-ore resources were exhausted and iron-ore had to be imported from other regions. Often, pig-iron was imported for further processing, or steel was imported for rerolling. At Dowlais, a Bessemer converter was installed. But the works was dependent upon imported ore, its output was destined for markets outside of the region, and the transport facilities linking it with other areas were not very good. So, while iron- and steel-making continued until 1920, the works declined in importance, and, in the 1890s, the Dowlais Iron Company built a coastal works at Cardiff.[26] The Scottish industry, which had risen to second place in Britain in two decades on the strength of its Blackband ores and the application of Neilson's hot-blast technique, continued to gain slightly and occupied the first position for a while in the late 1850s and in the 1860s. But, in time, contraction set in.[27]

The most successful of the new areas was the one centred on the grimy boom-town of Middlesbrough in north-east Cleveland. The town itself was established as a planned settlement in the early part of the century for the purpose of transferring coal from the terminus of the Stockton-to-Darlington railway line to ships engaged in the coastal trade,[28] but the area's prosperity was based on the proximity of easily worked ores and coking-coal, its estuarine site, and the relatively large size and greater efficiency of its plant and equipment which lay behind the expansion of iron-making. Its production increased from 145,000 tons in 1852 to something over 1.6 million tons in 1869, and by 1875 it accounted for about one-third of British pig-iron production.

In the late 1850s and, in particular, in the 1860s, output also increased sharply in the vicinity of Barrow-in-Furness in Cumberland, and in North Lancashire, when the region's deposits of haematite iron proved to be the only major source of ore suitable for the acid Bessemer process in Britain and Ireland. In 1855, output was equal to some 16,570 tons, but it reached 169,200 tons in 1860, 678,000 in 1869, and 1,045,000 in 1875. The growth in output in these two areas accounted for two-thirds of the entire increase in the national production of pig-iron in the 1850s and 1860s.[29]

Until 1879, Sheffield was the main centre of Bessemer and open-hearth steel production and of the manufacture of rails. The city had a long history as a centre of small-scale, handicraft-based metal trades. In the 1860s and 1870s some of these crafts were beginning to be mechanised and to be moved over to factory production, partly as a result of the effects of German competition.[30] However, with the revolution in steel-making, the most dramatic increases in industrial employment occurred to the east of the city in the Don Valley, where metal-manufacturing and heavy engineering, including boiler-making and the production of armaments and railway equipment, expanded rapidly. But because of the somewhat unfavourable geographical position of the city, the survival of the steel sector in the area depended upon a specialisation in the production and use of special steels for which demand was increasing rapidly, especially when steel production developed in the north-east of the country in the 1870s.[31]

In the late 1850s, the suitability of local ores led to a rapid expansion of steel-making in the north-west, and to the development of the largest steel-works in the country at that time, at Barrow-in-Furness. Its production of pig-iron reached a peak of nearly 1.6 million tons, or 18 per cent of British output, around 1900. In the same year, its output of steel was equal to about 13 per cent of the national total, but by 1913 it had fallen to 5 per cent. One reason for its decline in importance as a steel-making region lay in the gradual introduction of processes that allowed basic ores to be used. The others included the high cost of mining its ore, its remoteness from a source of coking-coal, and the lack of major local markets for its steel or for engineering products.[32] In 1869 shipbuilding started, and in the present century Barrow-in-Furness was in effect a single-industry and a single-company town, sustained by government contracts for war-related products to the Vickers' shipyards and their associated marine-engineering works, until some diversification occurred in the 1960s.[33]

In Britain, the steel industry as a whole was slow to adopt the Gilchrist—Thomas process, in spite of the abundance of ores with a high phosphorus content to be found in the country. But, eventually, the area around Middlesbrough emerged as a major centre for the production of Bessemer steel, and established an early lead at a national level in the making of Thomas or basic Bessemer steel. With the introduction of the Siemens—Martin or the open-hearth process, and the use of steel plates in the shipbuilding industry, the North East became the major centre of steel production in the country. In the early twentieth century it accounted not only for some 35 per cent of British pig-iron production, but also for more than 2 million tons of steel per year or about 27 per cent of British output.[34] As a result of this growth of the iron and steel sector, and of the expansion of the shipbuilding, chemical, and heavy-engineering industries, the structure of the regional economy was transformed. In particular a landscape composed of dispersed mining settlements in an otherwise rural interior, and of ports from which coal was exported, was replaced by an industrial landscape of interrelated industrial activities on each of the three main estuaries with scattered but booming mining towns and villages in between and in the hinterland.

The way in which the steel industry developed in Britain was, however, very different from the way in which it developed in Germany and in the USA. As a result, in the late nineteenth and early twentieth century, the industries of these two countries, in which the rate of growth of output and the level of investment were substantially higher, rapidly caught up with and then overtook the British iron and steel industry.[35]

With the introduction of the Bessemer process the minimum efficient scale of production increased enormously, and backward and forward linkages were stimulated as a means of securing the requisite quantity and quality of pig-iron and of handling the large quantities of steel produced. In turn, up-stream and downstream integration, together with the large amounts of capital required to install and operate a Bessemer converter, acted as a stimulus to, and to some extent presup-posed, the concentration and centralisation of capital in the industry. At a local level, of course, these trends were associ-ated with a decline in the role of the local iron-masters and of local family-based firms, and with an increase in the role of external capital in the development of the industry. By con-trast, open-hearth steel-making provided less impetus to vertical integration and to an increased scale of production, and was more suited to small-scale production. In addition, the slow rate of conversion and the lower nitrogen content of open-hearth steel gave this method advantages in the produc-tion of high-quality grades of steel.

In the USA, the production of Bessemer steel increased rapidly until the end of the nineteenth century, due to the soaring demand for steel, mainly for railway construction. As a result, large-scale production was established. In addition, rolling-mill technology, in which British producers had a lead until the 1870s, was transformed. In Britain, on the other hand, not only was the rate of growth of demand slower, but also an early switch to open-hearth production occurred, in part because the demand for rails grew more slowly, and began to decline in the 1880s with the virtual completion of the home railway network and with the exclusion of the steel industry from the market in the USA and in some other countries by tariffs and by its lack of competitiveness. Instead, the demand for ship plates, for which Bessemer steel was too unreliable in quality and for which its use was opposed, and for other high-quality flat products, was the most dynamic element shaping the structure of the British steel industry. In addition more emphasis was placed upon the production of custom-made as opposed to standardised products. As a result, the impetus to mechanisation and to large-scale production associated with the Bessemer process was weakened, a policy of piecemeal investment and of patching-up existing installa-tions was adopted, and the small-scale and geographically dispersed structure of the industry and the functional and geographical separation of different stages in the production of steel, inherited from the era in which the main product had been wrought-iron, survived.

By contrast, when the more concentrated steel industry in the USA increased its proportion of open-hearth production, the process was incorporated in plants characterised by vertical integration and large-scale production. As the new method of production was adopted, the process itself was transformed by the introduction of mechanised methods of hot-metal-charging and of continuous processes, while more emphasis was placed on the production of standardised products more suited to the needs of mechanised metal-using industries.

So in the late nineteenth and early twentieth century the iron and steel industry in Britain preserved its traditional structure and entered a long period of falling competitiveness and of relative economic decline, as the industries in the USA and also in Germany were expanded and modernised.[36] In Britain, the structure of the industry and the structure of demand and of costs, including, for example, the abundance of relatively inexpensive skilled workers, made the strategy adopted by British entrepreneurs a rational one from the point of view of the individual capitals involved. But in many cases what is rational in a market economy is, in practice, quite different from what is necessary for the long-term economic survival of an industry, or of the economy of a region in which it is concentrated, and whose inhabitants are dependent on it for their livelihood.

Conclusion

The growth of the staple industries in nineteenth-century Britain was associated with the appearance of very marked forms of regional sectoral specialisation. In some cases settlements and regions depended almost entirely upon the extraction and primary processing of raw materials, and upon the growth of a few related service and administrative activities, with the pattern of spatial development typically assuming the form of relatively small communities densely packed around mines and processing plants, and usually scattered throughout the region in which the minerals were found. In other areas the staple industries were integrated with existing or new capital- and consumption-good industries. As a result the pattern of spatial development was more complex, and the economies of the towns and regions concerned were more stable and diversified and were more able to withstand the subsequent collapse of the staple industries.

11.3 Industrial London

Introduction

The city of London was not merely a centre of commercial, financial, and governmental activities. It was also a major port and a very important industrial centre. But it differed from the areas of modern industry, and yet was in a sense more typical than they were of the industrial structure of the country as a whole in the first two-thirds of the nineteenth century, in that its industrial base was composed of an extremely large range of industries carried on for the most part in small workshops and dwellings in which production was organised on manufacturing lines. In fact,

> 19th century London was a city of clerks and shopkeepers, of small masters and skilled artisans, of a growing number of semi-skilled and sweated outworkers, of soldiers and servants, of casual labourers, streetsellers, and beggars. But with the exception of some isolated communities on its periphery it was a city virtually without a factory proletariat.[37]

The structure and development of its industry were however profoundly affected by the process of capitalist industrialisation. Indeed, 'the industrial history of London indicates the strength of Marx's dictum that the capitalist mode of production revolutionises the character of every manufacturing industry whether or not modern industry is introduced'.[38]

In 1861 the bulk of London's industrial population, with the exception of those employed in the building and transport sectors, were employed in the clothing and boot-and-shoe trades, the making of wood products and furniture, metal-manufacturing and engineering, printing and paper-making, and the manufacture of precision instruments.[39] In the century as a whole, the city's industrial activity was predominantly located in old-established industrial quarters, where there was economic advantage 'in grouping around the main processes of an industry those allied and subsidiary trades and processes, which, combined with adequate means of distribution, go to secure the maximum of aggregative efficiency'.[40] It was to be found in the City of London and more especially in an industrial zone running around its northern, eastern, and southern edges where medieval guild regulations did not apply, and where settlement by foreign immigrants was allowed, although some of the honourable trades were located in the West End near to the elite market they supplied. The zone of industrial activity was closely associated with areas of working-class housing, since proximity to sources of employment was vital in view of the predominantly casual nature of much of the work and the absence of effective means of public transport. In the industrial area itself different activities tended to be located in different districts, with

> printing, book-binding, and precision work in Holborn and Clerkenwell, furniture, silk weaving, and toy making in Shoreditch and Bethnal Green, metal work, slop clothing, and dealing in Whitechapel and Mile End, co-opering, food processing, lightering, and other port work in St George's-in-the-East and Stepney, timber, docking, wharf work, leather dressing, brush making, and hat manufacture in Southwark and Bermondsey.[41]

But the evolution of the economy of London can be understood more clearly by dividing its industrial activities into four main types.

The growth of the port

The earliest parts of the dock system were constructed at the time of the Napoleonic Wars to reduce the congestion caused by the lack of capacity of the legal quays. At the same time, attempts were made to minimise the use of casual labour and to recruit a more responsible labour-force with a view to reducing the petty theft and embezzlement that had been rife in the port. By the 1830s these attempts were abandoned, and the workers were employed for the most part on a casual basis. One reason for this was the fall in profitability of the dock companies that followed from the sweeping-away in the 1820s of the monopoly privileges over foreign trade which they had enjoyed. The others were the seasonal nature of the work and the existence of a large reserve army of labour.

In the second half of the nineteenth century the dock companies found themselves facing much more serious difficulties, while the problems they faced led to a significant deterioration in the conditions of employment in most branches of riverside work, especially in the original areas of dock development. The completion of the Royal Victoria Dock in 1855 and of the Millwall Dock in 1868 coincided with a fall in the demand for warehouse space and led to a large excess supply of warehousing. In addition, the substitution of steamships for sailing vessels, and the construction of larger ships that were less dependent on the weather but required deep-water channels and more rapid turn-round times, led to a ruinous competitive process of dock construction by the two major dock companies operating on the north of the river. After the London and St Katherine's Dock Company's takeover of the Victoria Dock Company in 1864, the East and West India Dock Company responded by building the South-West India Dock in 1870. In 1880 the former opened the Royal Albert Dock, and in 1886 the latter retaliated by building the Tilbury Docks at a site twenty-six miles downstream from the Pool of London. As a result, supply far outstripped the immediately foreseeable demand for deep-water dock facilities. In short, the ending of monopoly privileges in the movement towards free trade in the 1820s led to an intensification of competition whose result was a poorly co-ordinated and unplanned dock system and massive overcapacity.

One of the outcomes of these events and of related changes in the demand for dock facilities was a marked fall in the demand for unskilled and casual labour in the East End. At the same time, a series of changes in the fortunes and location of the city's industries that were related to the extension of machinofacture in the industrial regions in particular expanded the number of people seeking work in London.[42]

The large-scale industries of nineteenth-century London

In the first quarter of the nineteenth century the staple industries of London were shipbuilding, engineering, and silk-weaving. In the forty years after 1830 these industries either collapsed or moved away, and by the 1870s industries producing raw materials, semi-finished goods, and heavy capital goods in which factory or large-scale production had been established, and which were not amenable to sweating and were not concerned with final finishing for a luxury or specialised market, were under-represented in London. The high costs of fuel, the distance from necessary raw materials, the fierce competition for metropolitan land, and the composition of the labour-force left firms in London unable to compete effectively with enterprises in other centres of production, outside of certain specialised high-quality branches in which craftspersonship rather than cost was the relevant criterion.[43]

After a speculative boom in the 1860s, employment in shipbuilding and in related engineering activities fell sharply from 27,000 jobs in 1865 to 9,000 in 1871, and a number of ancillary trades such as sail-making, rigging, and rope-making, which were closely connected with the building, equipping, and repairing of wooden sailing-ships, disappeared, swelling the ranks of the marginalised proletariat. What remained was repair work, work connected with large but infrequent government orders, and the manufacture of small marine engines.[44]

In the first quarter of the nineteenth century, engineering works specialising in the production of anchors and pumps, in cable-making, and in railway-signal-making had been set up on the newly reclaimed marshlands of Pimlico and Lambeth. But after the 1850s there was an exodus of heavy-engineering firms to industrial areas in the north of the country. By the 1880s the bulk of the engineering and metal-working in London was concerned with repair work or with specialised work such as the making of torpedoes, gas-meters, and specialised printing machinery.[45] At the turn of the century, however, firms engaged in electrical engineering and in motor-manufacturing were developing and were beginning to move to, or to set up in, new suburban industrial areas to the west of London in particular.[46]

Some other industries in which production was at least in part factory-based, and which relied on London as a source of raw materials or as a market, were moved out of inner London. In the case of the 'noxious trades', such as the making of soap, chemicals, rubber, paint, glue, tarpaulins, matches, and gas, the impact of London overheads and the enforcement in London of building regulations, of factory legislation, and, towards the end of the century, of London County Council regulations led to the location of works along the river to the east of the city and, in the 1880s, east of the River Lea. Similarly, processing industries like the refining of sugar were moved eastwards to larger sites with the movement downstream of the port and as the scale of production increased. By the 1890s, in industries for which market factors had more or less dictated a central location, and in which mechanisation and factory production were the only ways of reducing costs, such as printing and bookbinding, new methods of production had sometimes been successfully introduced *in situ*, but wherever possible industries of this kind had also been moved out of inner London.[47]

Nineteenth-century London was essentially a centre of small-scale production. In 1851 the results of the census indicated that 86 per cent of London's employers employed less than 10 people each, and only 12 factories were recorded as employing more than 300 people.[48]

The honourable trades

The other major industry of nineteenth-century London was silk-weaving. In the middle of the eighteenth century the chief centre of the industry in the country was in Spitalfields, but in the forty years after 1830 the industry declined in this area, swelling the size of the industrial reserve army in the capital. In the 1850s the weaving branch was mechanised, and the industry expanded at a national level, but from the 1860s and 1870s onwards it declined steadily, mainly because of growing foreign competition.

In 1773 legislation protecting the wages of silk-weavers in Spitalfields and other parts of Central London was passed, following serious unrest and rioting in the 1760s. As a result, silk-weaving began to be transferred and to grow more rapidly in the eastern counties where it replaced the worsted industry, and in towns such as Coventry, Derby, Leek, Congleton, Macclesfield, and Manchester where weaving was already practised. In all of these areas costs were lower, not only because the weavers were extremely poorly paid, but also because more efficient looms were sometimes used.

Yet in 1824 silk-weaving was estimated as employing 50,000 people in East London. In the same year, the Spitalfields Act was repealed following the replacement of a total prohibition on imported silk by a 30 per cent import duty. But in the 1830s the movement away from London continued, and the industry declined rapidly. By 1860, when the Cobden Treaty abolished all duties on imported silk goods, employment had fallen to 9,500 persons. In the next twenty years the industry practically disappeared from London, with employment in the capital falling to 3,300 jobs. Only some of the older workers remained in the trade. Most of the 'young workers and the weavers' children either emigrated or more usually swelled the casual labour market in the East End'.[49]

In the nineteenth century the capital continued to be viable as a finishing-centre for a group of luxury trades, meeting the needs of an elite market for individually designed clothes, shoes, riding gear, carriages, jewellery, and precision instruments. The main reason for this was the overriding importance of proximity to the market. At the same time, the trades involved produced commodities of high value and required relatively little in the way of space and fixed capital.

In these sectors, organisations of highly skilled craft workers who, outside of certain trades such as millinery and dressmaking, were almost exclusively male, and who generally received high wages, were able to control entry into the trade. But in the second half of the nineteenth century the relative importance of this market declined, and a mass market developed in which they were unable to compete except by establishing mechanised production and moving away from Central London, or by subdividing skilled work within the shell of a system of small-scale production and drawing upon unskilled and sweated labour. As a result the luxury trades underwent a gentle decline, and, by the end of the century, the only important difference between some of them and the dishonourable trades was the market for which they produced and not the methods of production.[50]

The sweated trades

In finished-consumption-good sectors, in which a mass demand for ready-made goods was established by rising working-class prosperity, and in which mechanised methods of production were beginning to be introduced in the provinces, the position of many firms in London was open to challenge. In certain cases, like those of mat-making and felt-hatting, enterprises located in the capital were crushed by provincial competition. But in many other activities, related to the making of clothing, footwear, and furniture in particular, existing and new employers resorted to sweating as an effective way of responding to competitive pressures to cheapen commodity production.[51] Sweating was a means of reducing the costs of labour, rent payments, and other overheads to a minimum in a situation in which a switch to factory production was not a viable option, and of adapting the conditions prevailing in London to the advantage of individuals employing workers. In particular it involved an exploitation of the enormous and growing pool of unskilled female and immigrant workers who were forced to work for sub-subsistence wages, and, in the 1880s in particular, of un- or under-employed male workers.

This strategy rested on a splitting-up of the production process into a series of unskilled tasks and an allocation of different tasks to different workers, such that individual workers would be engaged in the production of parts of commodities for an unknown market. The previously skilled craft of making a dress was, for example, subdivided into a sequence of operations such as the making of sleeves and of collars, pleating, button-holing, and so on, each of which would be executed by different workers in different homes or workshops clustered in a single area.

In addition, sweating involved the application of comparatively inexpensive hand-driven machinery which increased the ability of employers to dispense with the services of skilled workers. Of particular importance was the invention of the sewing-machine and of the band-saw in 1846 and in 1858 respectively. Nevertheless, sweating was a strategy in which employers, instead of investing in capital equipment to reduce the costs of production, relied primarily on the use of very large numbers of unskilled and poorly paid workers who were required to work for long hours in bad conditions. A strategy of this kind was particularly applicable to finishing-processes in which machinofacture was at this stage less fully developed. In other words, it was applicable to precisely the kind of work that was most strongly represented in London.

The alternative to factory production that was made possible by these conditions was a reduction of factory work to an absolute minimum and a rapid expansion of homework and of production in tiny workshops. In the food-processing sector the production of sugar in large processing plants existed alongside sweet-making 'in the back street courts and kitchens of the East End'. In furniture-making, the development of saw-mills in which steam-power was applied from the late 1840s was associated with an expansion of sweating, and of outwork or of work in small workshops in cabinet-making in which many former shipwrights were employed.[52] On the other hand, in button-holing, factory work was preferred because it was feared that workers might otherwise pawn the almost finished garments.[53]

A system of this kind was particularly well suited to the needs of wholesalers, who often operated on a large scale, and of the middlepersons and small masters, who proliferated with its growth and transmitted the pressures they experienced to those working for them, in that its flexibility enabled them to expand or contract production according to the state of the market, to adjust quickly to changes in fashion, and to impose many of the costs of lighting, heating, and so on onto those they intermittently employed.

But, for those at the bottom of this pyramid, outwork or occasional work in tiny workshops was combined, if possible, with work in other trades, such as street-selling or various types of paid domestic work in the case of women, or dock · work in the case of men. In the 1880s, in particular, many inhabitants of the East End were unemployed or underemployed for much of the time. What is more, even those in work were badly paid and lived in intense poverty. The organisations of workers which lent some kind of social stability to the situation in the industrial regions were absent. In addition, the casual poor were herded together into a diminishing stock of increasingly overcrowded housing in the areas near to what employment existed.

The existence of a seething mass of marginalised people in the East End was a cause of immense alarm in the ranks of the middle classes, and led to the advocacy of a variety of extreme solutions. A number of groups proposed the establishment of labour colonies for the 'depraved and criminal classes' who lay at the foot of the social ladder, but who were thought to have been indiscriminately mixed with, and to be bringing down, the 'respectable working class'. Another proposal was for the segregation of men and women with a view to reducing the fertility rate of the casual poor. Yet with the reappearance of conditions of comparatively full employment in the late 1890s, which was associated at first with the development of new engineering industries in the suburbs of London, this class and the threat it posed suddenly disappeared, revealing the inadequacy of explanations of this phenomenon other than those which related it to the reserve-army mechanism.[54]

Conclusion

'By the 1880s the inner industrial perimeter, once the focal point of London manufacture, was fast becoming an industrial vacuum.'[55] The staple industries of nineteenth-century London had declined, and some consumption-good industries had been converted to factory production and moved to the periphery, where modern engineering firms were subsequently to develop. In the old industrial areas the 'pre-industrial' characteristics of small-scale production in homes and small workshops were accentuated, yet the work that remained for a while was in declining sectors. One reason for this was com- petition from the products of the factory system that had developed in the provinces and, with the opening up of the national economy, the operation of the law of international value. Another was the way in which, in the period after 1870 in particular, the unparalleled growth of specialised services of banking, insurance, and marketing and their con- centration in London, which lay at the centre of the world market, increased the pressure on central urban land and 'cut into the complex of housing and small workshops in the inner industrial perimeter'. As a result, 'the City was transformed from a residential–industrial area into a depopulated con- glomeration of banks, offices, warehouses, and railway stations. Its poorer inhabitants were unceremoniously evicted to make way for this glittering symbol of late Victorian capit- alism'.[56]

11.4 Industrial development in the Midlands

A wide variety of industries which for the most part were not characterised by large-scale forms of industrial organisation were also to be found in the East and West Midlands. In these two areas the eventual development of mechanised workshops, and of factory production in existing and in new industries transferred to the area from the capital, often occurred some- what earlier than in London; yet the pressures were once again the low costs of factory products and foreign competition, while the effects on the supply of cheap labour of the intro- duction of compulsory education for children between the ages of five and fourteen years also played a part in the tran- sition to factory production. Of particular importance in the emergence of modern industry in this part of the country, however, was the development of new lines of economic activity based in many cases upon the existing industrial traditions of the Midlands.

In the 1870s and 1880s the old industries on which the growth of Midland towns had been based in the first three-quarters of the nineteenth century declined, and some of them virtually ceased to exist, but at the same time new branches of production characterised by new products and by new forms of organisation were beginning to be developed, and existing enterprises whose productive capacity could be adapted to meet the needs of new industries were starting to be switched to new lines of production.[57]

In Coventry the most important nineteenth-century industry was the silk-ribbon-weaving trade. In the 1840s and 1850s employers started to build increasingly large factories in which steam-powered looms were used, but in general the units of production remained small in size compared with those in other areas. Yet by 1859 a total of 1,250 power-looms had been installed in 15 large factories, and another 1,000 had been set up in 300 cottage factories, each of which was in fact a weaving family's dwelling that shared with similar adjacent dwellings a common source of power. However, in the years after 1860, production was concentrated into larger units, and employment declined. Indeed, in the 1860s the population of Coventry as a whole declined, and in the next twenty years or so it stagnated along with the economy of the town. But in the 1880s the bicycle industry expanded rapidly in Coventry, while its growth was followed by that of the motor-cycle and car industries. As a result, the town was subsequently to become one of the fastest growing and richest of the large towns in the country.[58]

In the vicinity of Birmingham, conditions conducive to the development of the same industries were created by the existence and transformation of the small metal trades. In the nineteenth century the West Midlands was a major centre of metal-manufacturing and metal-using industries. The area of South Staffordshire had been an important centre for coal- and iron-mining, for the production of pig-iron and of malleable iron, and for the making of railway and construction equipment. In addition it was the home of industries manufacturing nails, chains, bolts, locks, and keys, in which production was carried out for the most part by sweated home-workers. By contrast the area around Birmingham was a centre of industries producing finished goods such as guns, jewellery, and buttons, and a multitude of small products of the foundry, stamp, and press. In many cases the finished goods manufactured by its small metal trades were composite products in which a very detailed division of labour had been established, and whose production involved a large number of distinct processes and the work of many different highly skilled craft workers. The units of production were small in size, and were often concentrated in specialised industrial districts in the inner city.[59]

By the time of the Great Depression the iron industry of the Black Country had been declining for some time, while the traditional metal-using industries were suffering from acute competition. The small metal trades of Birmingham were similarly facing growing international competition. In addition they were confronted by a movement of demand away from individually designed products and items of luxury consumption. As a result, the industries of inner Birmingham and its vicinity were declining, stagnant, or expanding only very slowly.

But in the years after 1886 in particular, new factory-based industries were established on the edge of the growing city, aided by improvements in transport. In the place of the old industries, the cycle, electrical-engineering, machine-tool, and food-processing industries were developed, and in the early twentieth century the production of motor-vehicles and of artificial silk became important local industries. At the same time, some of the existing industries for whose products demand was falling switched to the production of standardised components and semi-finished goods for the motor-vehicle and electrical-engineering industries and adopted new cost-reducing methods of production. By the 1890s the city of Birmingham 'was poised between the town of a thousand workshops and the home of the great industries of the 20th century',[60] while in the years between 1880 and 1914 the West Midlands was to become 'one of the most important engineering areas in Britain, and a disproportionate part of the new effort was to be concentrated in Birmingham'.[61]

12 The Geography of the Transition from Machinofacture to Scientific Management and Fordism, 1890s-1945

12.1 Introduction: the second industrial revolution and the process of national economic development

In the middle of the 1870s the wave of unprecedented economic expansion of the mid-Victorian era came to an end and gave way to the Great Depression which lasted, with only a brief period of prosperity in 1880–82, until the middle of the 1890s. One response of the dominant classes in countries affected by the crisis was to engage in a competitive process of empire-building with a view to securing new guaranteed markets and new supplies of cheap raw materials. As a result, in the years between 1876 and 1914 over 11 million square miles of territory were annexed by the colonial powers in the search for land and spheres of influence that has been referred to as the new imperialism.[1]

A second response was to seek ways of regaining or expanding markets and of restoring profitability, by increasing the rates of relative and absolute surplus-value and by reducing the costs of commodity production, especially in sectors of the economy that still relied heavily on craft skills such as the metal trades and engineering. As a result, what is sometimes called the second industrial revolution was set in motion in the last few decades of the nineteenth century. Yet its impact was most marked not on the economy of Britain, which remained wedded to an earlier and increasingly archaic pattern of industrial development, but on the newer industrial economies of Germany and the USA.

One of the elements of the second industrial revolution was a series of changes in technology that occurred mainly in the second half of the nineteenth century, including the development of electrical energy and electric motors and of the internal-combustion engine, advances in chemistry, the development of the oil and rubber processing industries, progress in the machine-tools sector resulting from the invention of the turret lathe in about 1845, the universal milling machine in 1861, and the automatic lathe in about 1870, and the development of steel alloys.[2] As a result, the electricity, electrical-engineering, chemical, and motor-manufacturing industries were beginning to appear as new growth sectors, while the production of armaments in which technical progress had also occurred expanded rapidly in the phase of growth leading up to the First World War.

These changes in technology were associated with significant changes in the way in which production was organised. A series of revolutionary developments in the labour process based on the principles of scientific management and Fordism led to a major increase in the productivity of labour and laid the foundations for a marked increase in the rates of relative and absolute surplus-value. The term 'scientific management' was introduced by Taylor who, from his own experience of working on the shop floor, recognised that the amount of work actually performed by a worker in a given period of time fell far short of the amount that could potentially be obtained. In particular a considerable amount of porosity existed in the working day. Taylor attributed this porosity to what he called 'soldiering' on the part of the workers. But he maintained that it was perfectly rational for workers to behave in this way given the prevailing methods of wage determination which, in his view, involved setting wages equal to some socially accepted norm, and not to an amount of money related to the level of productivity. In addition, soldiering was possible because the workers possessed a greater knowledge of the labour process and more control over it than management. As a result management had no very clear idea of the potential level of output.

In order to raise output, and in order to obtain from each worker a 'fair day's work' or, in the words of Taylor, 'all the work a worker could do without injury to health at a pace that could be sustained throughout a working lifetime', three principles of scientific management were devised.[3] It has been suggested by Braverman that Taylor's principles were built upon and gave coherence to the arguments of Smith and Babbage, and yet added a new dimension to them.[4] In his account of these ideas he pointed out that the first principle of scientific management can be defined as the 'dissociation of the labour process from the skills of the workers' with a view to concentrating into the hands of management all of the craft skills and the skills of improvisation which had been acquired by workers through extended practice, but had been withheld from management in order to prevent increases in the expected level of work from occurring. As a result, new ways of fragmenting the labour process aimed at reducing the value of labour-power through a more effective differentiation of the labour-force could be developed and introduced.[5]

The second principle required that 'all possible brainwork be removed from the shop and centred in the planning or laying out department'.[6] In other words, it required the introduction of a rigid division between conception, which was to be one of management's roles, and execution, which was to be the only activity with which workers were to be entrusted.

The last of the principles of scientific management was essentially an extension of the second one. It introduced the concepts of a task and of advance planning according to which the workers were to be given detailed instructions which at first were set out on daily task cards, specifying 'not only what is to be done but how it is to be done and the amount of time allowed for doing it'.[7] In the engineering industry the same process has recently been carried much further by the introduction of computer tapes, which are fed without examination by the workers into numerically controlled machine tools.

In short, the role of scientific management was 'to render conscious and systematic the formerly unconscious tendency of capitalist production'.[8] One of its aims was to increase capital's control over the production process at the very moment at which scientific knowledge was being applied to it. A second was to increase the intensity of work and the productivity of labour by ensuring that workers spent less time thinking about the way in which a job ought to be performed, and spent as much time as possible mechanically carrying out predefined tasks whose manner and speed of execution were determined and controlled by capital. Indeed one of its effects was to reduce many types of human labour to the repetition of unthinking movements. As a result, the distinction between the work performed by human beings and that performed by members of the animal kingdom, which, in the view of Marx, lies in the fact that human production involves the realisation of the subjective ideas and projects with which human beings enter the process of production, was narrowed.[9] Indeed it was precisely to this tendency of capitalist production that Marx was referring when he spoke of the immiserisation of the working class.[10]

Of course, workers tend in general to contest and to resist this type of strategy, and, even when scientifically timed and controlled tasks are defined, they usually manage to find ways of carrying them out more effectively, with the result that gains in the form of unauthorised breaks and so on can be obtained. Yet, at the same time, capital is continually searching for and seeking to introduce new practices with a view to economising on time and enhancing the process of valorisation.

The other main aim of scientific management was to reduce the significance of craft skills and to make it possible for less-skilled and less-experienced workers to be used. But as with its other aims, changes were not introduced without creating new contradictions. On the one hand, not only was the use of more complex and more expensive machine systems associated in many cases with running-in problems and with delays in the realisation of expected technical economies that offset some of the potential benefits of economising on craft labour, but also success in using them was heavily dependent upon the conscientiousness of the operators employed by capital.[11] On the other hand, a fall in the number of craft workers was usually accompanied by an increase in the number of hyperqualified technical workers, and of clerical workers employed to carry out tasks such as record-keeping. But in most cases what was happening was that new tasks associated with high-productivity methods of production or tasks that had been done informally and perhaps inefficiently on the shop floor were being assigned to specialised workers. The development of a new category of workers did not in fact mean that a duplication of work had occurred, and other things being equal the overall effect of the resulting changes in the division of labour was a fall in the value of the labour-power employed by the capitals concerned.[12]

The increases in productivity made possible by scientific management were enhanced by the introduction of Fordism, at first in vehicle-manufacturing plants in the first half of the twentieth century and subsequently in other branches of production. The development of the flow-line principle and of assembly-line work dramatically increased the potential for raising labour productivity. One way in which it did this was by ensuring a more efficient recombination of tasks, which in turn made it possible of course for the subdivision of production into detail operations to be carried even further. The other way was by making it possible for time to be saved and for the intensity of work to be increased for, by establishing a straightforward linear flow of the material under transformation, and by rooting the workers to fixed positions, the losses of time associated with the movement of workers around the workshop or with the assembly of the materials required for the completion of a partial task could be avoided. In addition, the introduction of the conveyor-belt whose speed was ultimately determined by capital meant that the ability of the workers to control the collective rhythm of work was reduced.[13]

As in the case of the transition to machinofacture, the advances that occurred at this time in the organisation of production were associated with a sharp increase in the minimum scale of plant and in the amount of fixed capital required to start production. As a result, they presupposed and were associated with a concentration and centralisation of capital and an increase in the scale of economic enterprises in most branches of production. Indeed, as early as the 1880s, in Germany and in the USA in particular, the rise of an economy dominated by a handful of great trusts, monopolies, and oligopolies was under way.[14] In the USA, in the wave of growth that lasted from 1893 or so, until 1914, the family firm gave way to the national corporation, and, in the years following the First World War, the first multidivisional corporations were appearing, while 'the first wave of US direct foreign capital investment occurred around the turn of the century'.[15]

The introduction of scientific management and Fordism in large-scale enterprises and the development of new branches of production were associated with significant changes in the location of economic activity. In particular, the broad division between mental and manual tasks and the establishment of specialised departments in large firms, in conjunction with improvements in the means of communication and transport, laid the foundations for a geographical separation of the tasks involved in the production of commodities from the other activities of manufacturing firms. As early as 1926 Haig was able to point to 'a territorial subdivision of functions which were formerly united in the same place', as a result of which Fourth Avenue in New York '[was] full of establishments having the names of manufacturing plants, but no fabrication [was] in evidence', and, while the city itself '[was] the centre of the silk industry, not a loom [was] to be found'.[16]

In addition the introduction of the flow-line system, which required a horizontal rather than a vertical layout, was associated with a sharp increase in the amount of space required by manufacturing establishments, and with a movement of industry away from congested central areas to the edges of existing industrial cities or to new centres of modern industry in areas that were equipped with adequate supplies of electricity, that had suitable industrial structures, where plenty of workers were available for employment or could be recruited, and where conflicts with organised groups of workers were less likely to occur. In the case of England much of the new development occurred in the Midlands and in the South East.

The success of the economies of the Midlands and of the South East in adapting to new markets and new methods of production and in pioneering new branches of industry contrasted sharply with what happened elsewhere in the country. In fact, in the period extending from the 1860s until the 1890s or the turn of the century, the economy of Britain as a whole lost its position as the most important and most dynamic in the world and was turned into one of the most sluggish and conservative of the industrial economies,[17] while the leading role passed to Germany and, in particular, to the USA where new methods of production were adopted and new industries were developed more quickly and on a more extensive scale than in Britain. In the case of the USA, the shortage of skilled workers and the relatively abundant supply of unskilled immigrant workers arriving from the rural parts of Europe and from the southern states, in conjunction with the extent of the domestic market, played an important role in fostering the growth of modern industry,[18] while in Germany the recruitment of workers without a tradition of working in industry, the role of the state in promoting scientific and technical education and in supporting and protecting national capitals, and the role of the investment banks were important in shaping the process of industrialisation.[19]

In spite of substantial advances in production, the growth of industry in Britain was, in other words, soon far surpassed by that of the newly emerging industrial nations. In the years leading up to the First World War the deficiencies of the British economy were disguised by a massive growth in foreign demand for the products of the old staple industries and by the expansion of the shipbuilding industry in particular, but subsequently the slow growth, under-representation, or lack of competitiveness of the steel industry, of the machine-tools sector, and of new science-based industries, proved to be an immense source of weakness, while economic backwardness was closely correlated with an archaic and reactionary social system which reinforced the weaknesses of the economy.

Of course the industries of Britain were bound to lose ground relatively as other countries were industrialised, but a process of catching-up by newly industrialising countries need not have been accompanied by a loss of impetus and efficiency and an inability to initiate changes in the structure and organisation of industry, especially in a country which was better supplied with capital than other countries that were ahead of it in the introduction of capital-intensive techniques of production. In many cases the loss of impetus has been attributed to the complacency of the leaders of British industry. In reply it has been argued by some writers that, while it may be true that British industrialists were slow in the introduction of new methods of production, the country's factor endowments were such as to justify the methods of production and the pattern of specialisation they chose to retain or to adopt. The problem with this objection is that it ignores the dynamic character of the accumulation process. The continuing growth of an economy and material prosperity do not simply depend upon a passive adjustment to changes in the methods of production, in resource endowments, and in the pattern of demand. In a capitalist economy they depend to an even greater degree upon the capacity of individual capitalists to initiate and promote change and to modify the data with which they are presented by creating new combinations of resources.[20] The fact that adjustment did not occur is an index of the inability of the market mechanism to promote the kind of redeployment of capital, the development of new skills, and the reshaping of the mode of consumption that would have been necessary if the country were to have maintained its position as a leading industrial nation.

In fact the best explanation of the loss of dynamism of British industry is that it was a result 'ultimately of the early and long-sustained start as an industrial power',[21] and of the inability of the market mechanism on its own to promote change from an old and obsolete pattern to a new one, whose establishment involved a scrapping of large amounts of capital, a major reorganisation of the ownership of capital, a major programme of investment, and profound changes in the sphere of consumption.[22] One reason for this was that firms in traditional branches of production, such as cotton and steel-making, were able to survive by retreating into as yet unexploited parts of Britain's satellite world of formal and informal colonies.[23]

On the other hand the British economy as a whole retreated into international lending and the provision of financial, insurance, and trading services from which very satisfactory profits could be made. According to Imlah's estimates, overseas investments or capital exports rose from a mere £10 million in 1815, to a total of about £250 million by 1850, and to a staggering £4,000 million by 1913. Of this total most was in railways and in foreign or colonial government bonds, but some was in industrial enterprises, mines, and plantations. Around 1870, annual investments abroad began to exceed net capital formation in the domestic economy, and in the great boom that immediately preceded the First World War at least twice as much was invested abroad as at home.[24] In the words of Hobsbawm, the economy of Britain 'was becoming a parasitic rather than a competitive economy, living off the remains of world monopoly, the underdeveloped world, her past accumulations of wealth, and the advance of her rivals'. As a result it was symbolised 'by the country house in the stockbrokers' belt of Surrey and Sussex and no longer by hard-faced men in smoke-filled provincial towns'.[25] In his treatise on imperialism Hobson made a similar comment when he referred critically to 'the economic and social condition today of districts in Southern England', whose character and appearance were largely determined by the presence of a few members of a wealthy financial aristocracy drawing dividends and pensions from abroad, and of 'a somewhat larger group of professional retainers and tradesmen and a large body of personal servants and workers in the transport trade and in the final stages of production of the more perishable goods' who in almost every case were largely dependent upon them.[26]

After a fall in the level of industrial production in the industrialised countries of about 20 per cent in the war years, a brief economic upswing, in which productivity increased sharply but was not matched by an increase in outlets for the products of the new consumption-good industries, occurred in the period 1924–9. Yet in Britain a brief boom in 1919–20 was followed by slump conditions in the early 1920s, caused in part by the difficulties of the old staple industries whose competitiveness had declined and which were damaged by falling demand, by growing foreign production, and by protectionism, and in part by the adoption of deflationary policies with a view to returning to the gold standard at the pre-war parity, which, when it occurred in 1925, resulted in a 10 per cent over-valuation of sterling and further damaged the competitiveness of export sectors.

In 1929 the imbalance between the norms of production and the norms of consumption, associated with the changes in the process of production that had been occurring since the end of the preceding century, suddenly led to a crisis of overproduction in all the major industrial countries except Japan and the USSR, and to the opening of the slump of 1929–32 in which output was reduced temporarily by about one-third and world trade in manufactured goods and in primary products collapsed.[27] In the developed countries the effects of the collapse of international trade were counter-balanced by improvements in the terms of trade which occurred at the expense of the producers of primary products in the colonial and semi-colonial world. Yet the crisis in the form of articulation of underdeveloped economies with the economies of mutually competing metropolitan countries reinforced the depth of the slump, as did the fact that the international financial system was centred on the City of London and on sterling, in spite of the fact that England was no longer the workshop of the world and no longer possessed a sufficiently strong currency to assume a role of this kind.[28]

It was at this time that the Victorian economy of Britain crashed in ruins.

> At the very moment when Britain emerged on the victorious side in the first major war since Napoleon, when her chief continental rival Germany was on her knees, when the British Empire . . . covered a greater extent of the world map than ever before, the traditional economy of Britain not only ceased to grow, but contracted . . . At all times between 1921 and 1938 at least one out of every ten citizens of working age was out of a job. In seven out of these eighteen years at least three out of every twenty were unemployed, in the worst years one out of five.[29]

As a result, the lives of millions of men and women in towns dependent upon single industries in the depressed regions were ruined.

In 1932 the adoption of a general policy of protection and the agreement on a system of imperial preference gave some protection to the traditional sectors of the economy. But at the same time, new sectors producing for the home market continued to expand mainly in the Midlands and in the South East, and in the inter-war period as a whole contributed to an overall growth of industrial production. The establishment and growth of new consumption-good sectors, producing vehicles and electrical goods in particular, enabled some of the constraints on the modernisation of the economic system and on the establishment of a regime of intensive accumulation to be lifted.[30] In some cases important investments occurred with the help of US capital. The degree of concentration of capital was increased, working-class consumption norms started to be transformed, the system of marketing was reorganised to manage the mass circulation of commodities, and the involvement of the state in the management of the economy and in the process of economic reproduction increased. Yet the economy remained comparatively backward, with much of its capital tied to sectors that had played a dominant role in earlier phases of growth, and the size of the market was relatively limited compared with those of the countries that now headed the hierarchy of nation states.[31]

12.2 The restructuring and redeployment of the industrial sector

The old and declining industries

In the early years of the long wave of *circa* 1895–1945, the old cotton and wool textile, coal, iron and steel, and shipbuilding industries, the relatively small pottery industry, and the older branches of the mechanical-engineering sector such as steam-engine-making and the building of textile machinery, continued to expand. But after a brief period of renewed expansion in the years immediately following the First World War, in all of these old-established sectors except the steel industry, output fell, stagnated, or increased only very slowly in comparison with its level in 1913, employment declined sharply, and unemployment reached extraordinarily high levels, as it did in the regions whose inhabitants depended on these industries, and where very little alternative employment was available.

The cotton industry

The industry that collapsed most dramatically was that of cotton. The industry was very much geared to the export market and reached its peak in the years before 1914, when over 80 per cent of its output was shipped overseas, when cotton goods accounted for 25 per cent of Britain's exports by value, and when some 65 per cent of the cotton yarn and piece goods traded internationally were made in Britain. In the war, production was curtailed, but, after a boom in which very high profits were made, but in which nothing of any significance was done to replace obsolete capacity or to improve techniques, exports collapsed, and the industry contracted, with output standing only at one-half of its pre-war level at the end of the 1930s.

The reasons for this lay in the rise of newly established competitors abroad, the lack of investment in plant and machinery, and the inability of capital to reorganise the industry and to increase productivity in such a way as to make it competitive with the industries that had been established in other developed countries or in countries where cheap labour was being used. In turn, the industry's loss of competitiveness can be attributed to the lack of integration of the spinning, weaving, and finishing stages and to the existence of a large number of small and independent firms in each branch.[32]

Up to 1930 some attempts were made to increase efficiency in the industry, but after the world depression the emphasis switched to cuts in capacity, in spinning in particular, at first through voluntary schemes, and from 1936 through government intervention. Nevertheless the average firm continued to be small in size, much excess capacity remained in existence, and the industry continued to be outdated and inefficient compared with its main competitors.[33]

Between 1913 and 1932 employment in the cotton industry

fell by more than one-third, and in 1931—2, 43.2 per cent of cotton operatives were unemployed. 80 to 90 per cent of employment was concentrated in the North West, with the result that very high levels of unemployment were recorded in this part of the country. However there were considerable intraregional variations in unemployment, with below-average figures in areas in which some diversification into other sectors, or into the production of finer or mixed products such as cotton and rayon combinations, had occurred, and with exceptionally high figures in towns like Blackburn and Burnley and in smaller centres such as Nelson and Colne where the industry had specialised in the production of basic cotton goods for export markets.[34]

The wool textile industry

Structurally the woollen and worsted industry was similar to the cotton industry in that it consisted of a very large number of small firms, although in the woollen section vertical integration was common and most firms engaged in both spinning and weaving. But, since it had always relied less on the external market and more on the home market than the cotton industry, it suffered less from the general decline in the volume of world trade, and it benefited from the buoyancy of the home market in the 1930s and from the imposition of protective tariffs in 1932 which led to a sharp drop in imports. In addition its share of world trade did not fall, in part because of the relative importance of the production of high-quality goods, but productivity was low, and yet 'pleas for an enabling act to permit reorganisation to take place on the model of the cotton industry were not widely supported and were dropped when sales increased in 1935—37 in the home market'. But even in this sector employment fell steadily, and in 1931, 36.4 per cent of the industry's workers were unemployed.[35]

The coal industry

In the coal industry output had fallen and coal had been in short supply in the war years, while in 1917—19 vigorous attempts had been made to increase the output produced by a depleted number of workers. But in 1925 demand fell sharply as domestic demand stagnated and exports fell. The reasons for the collapse of export demand included the growth of coal production in other countries, the substitution of other fuels for coal and economies in its use, the depressed state of industry, and the relatively slow growth of productivity, which, in conjunction with the overvaluation of sterling, reduced the competitiveness of the British coal industry.

Yet the fact that the industry was dominated by a large number of small, independent and competing concerns made it virtually impossible for the industry to be reorganised through the market mechanism or through agreements between voluntary associations of producers. As a result, and because of the central role of the coal industry in the economy and the militancy of the miners in the face of attempts by the coal-owners to solve the industry's problems by cutting wages, several limited attempts were made by the state to disorganise the miners and to reorganise the industry.[36]

A set of proposals for the reorganisation of the coal industry had been put forward in the 1890s. In 1919 the Sankey Commission narrowly recommended nationalisation, while almost all of its members supported the view that the nationalisation of the coal royalties was a precondition for the modernisation of the industry. However, its proposals were largely ignored by the government, and little was done until the middle of the 1920s, when demand collapsed, and an agreement introduced to settle a strike that had occurred in the early 1920s was broken, with the coal-owners attempting to cut wages, to increase the length of the working day, and to replace national by regional wage agreements. The result was a seven-month strike, which was supported at first by the TUC, which called a General Strike in 1926, but which in the end failed.

In 1926 an attempt was made to implement the recommendations of the Samuel Commission of 1925 that neighbouring collieries be amalgamated, but the results of the legislation were insignificant, with the amalgamations that did occur resulting from initiatives taken by some coal-owners. In the late 1920s some cartel schemes were introduced, and in 1930 the Coal Mines Act set up a compulsory cartel in order to allocate sales and quotas between districts and collieries, with a view to reducing output, to keeping up prices, and to removing some of the less efficient pits from production. But the cartel was to be operated by the coal-owners themselves, and so 'in reality the law became a device by which the available business was spread among all concerns regardless of their relative efficiency and all enjoyed the benefits of fixed prices and restricted output'.[37] The length of the working day was reduced, and an unsuccessful attempt was made to institute national wage-bargaining. In addition, a Coal Mines Reorganisation Commission charged with the task of promoting amalgamations and concentrating production was set up. However, determined opposition from the coal-owners prevented the Commission from carrying out its task, and its powers were transferred to the Coal Commission by the Coal Act of 1938 which also authorised the nationalisation of the coal royalties. This step was completed in 1942 at a cost of £66.5 million.[38]

Of course some modernisation occurred, especially in the larger coalfields on the eastern side of the country and in the Yorkshire, Nottinghamshire, and Derbyshire field in particular, where geological conditions facilitated the mechanisation of the mining process, and where high levels of productivity were achieved. As a result the problems of regions like South Wales, where the structure of the pits made mechanisation more difficult, were aggravated. But even in this region the fortunes of different subregions varied considerably according to the type of coal produced and the nature of the market. The areas to suffer most were those like the Rhondda and Aberdare valleys whose pits were producing steam coal for export. The problems that resulted were compounded by closures and job losses in the iron and steel industry, and by the problems of the engineering industry in the region, which was geared to the production of heavy capital goods such as mining equipment. As a result, in Merthyr Tydfil and Dowlais unemployment reached 80 and 60 per cent respectively.[39]

Overall output fell from an annual average of 268 million tons in 1907–14, to 232 million tons in 1927–33, and to 228 million tons in 1934–8. But, since output per person–

shift increased by about 10 per cent between 1913 and 1936, employment fell even more sharply than output, changing from 1.1 million persons in 1913 to a peak of 1.226 million in 1920, and declining to 0.97 million in 1929 and to 0.702 million in 1938. After 1925, seldom were fewer than 25 per cent of miners unemployed, and often the figure was much higher. Yet by European standards the increases in productivity were low. In the Netherlands it increased by 117 per cent, in the Ruhr by 81 per cent, in Poland by 73 per cent, in Belgium by between 50 and 51 per cent, and in France by between 22 and 25 per cent.[40]

The iron and steel industry

The steel industry was not, strictly speaking, a declining industry, but the demand for steel switched from the old to new industries, output fluctuated and was well below capacity until 1937, productivity increased, employment fell, and unemployment among steelworkers was high, reaching 47.9 per cent in 1931–2, while among pig-iron workers it reached 43.8 per cent.[41] In the iron and steel sector the production of pig-iron declined from 10.26 million tons in 1913 and was only 8.5 million tons as late as 1937, in part because of its replacement by scrap in the steel-making process and because of the substitution of steel for cast- and wrought-iron, but the production of steel increased from just under 8 million tons in 1913 to well over 9.5 million tons in 1917 and, after falling sharply in the early 1920s and by 45 per cent in the slump of 1929–32, soared to nearly 13 million tons in 1937 with the growth of demand from new sectors such as the vehicle- and aircraft-manufacturing and the electrical-engineering industries and as a result of rearmament. Only then was the industry operating anywhere near full capacity, which had stood at 12 million tons for both pig-iron and steel since the First World War. The industry's share of world pig-iron production fell from 13.2 to 8.3 per cent between 1913 and 1937, while its share of steel production fell from 10.2 per cent in 1913 to 8.1 per cent in 1929, due to the effects of tariffs abroad and of foreign cartels and, in particular, to the high costs of production and the relative inefficiency of the British industry, but in the 1930s it increased, reaching 9.7 per cent in 1937.[42]

In the 1920s the steel industry moved in the direction of increased scale and improved techniques, but it was structurally very weak and technically inefficient compared with the industries of other countries. The trend towards a concentration of ownership and management was slow, small units using old methods of production survived, an emphasis was placed on piecemeal investments, and it has been argued that new works such as the reconstructed plant at Consett were badly located.[43] But the industry was switching from the production of acid to the production of basic steel, and from the Bessemer to the open-hearth process, and its centre of gravity was shifted towards the Lincolnshire and East Midland ore-fields where the production of pig-iron increased from 18.7 per cent of the national total in 1920 to 37.4 per cent in 1932. In the steel sector a similar shift occurred but was much less pronounced.[44]

As a result of the collapse of output in the slump of 1929–32, a new wave of mergers occurred, and many works were closed, including the iron- and steel-making units at Ebbw Vale in 1929 and the Dowlais works in 1930. All in all, 135 blast-furnaces were dismantled between 1932 and 1939. At this time the government stepped in to promote amalgamations and concentration, rationalisation, and modernising investments, as did the leading London banks, although in the view of Aldcroft the banks' main concern was to protect the money they were owed, and so primary attention was 'given to reorganising capital structures rather than to bringing about a more efficient structure, as, for example, by eliminating excess capacity or reallocating plants to ensure that blast furnaces and steel works were placed in close proximity to each other'.[45]

But of more significance was a third change in the institutional context. At the end of 1930 the industry was only working at 30 per cent of capacity and imports were exceeding exports for the first time, with the exception of 1927, since the eighteenth century. As a result, the opposition of the government to protection was lessened, and in 1932 a

$33\frac{1}{3}$ per cent tariff was imposed. Until then there had been considerable conflict between the owners of the industry and the government as to whether modernisation should precede protection or vice versa. The government was reluctant to introduce protection without some guarantee that modernisation would follow, lest the producers of steel simply charged monopoly prices, while the companies were reluctant to invest in the absence of guaranteed markets. In an attempt to ensure that protection had the desired effect and that steel-users were protected the Import Duties Advisory Board was to supervise the conduct of the industry, and in 1934 an organisation of producers called the British Iron and Steel Federation was established to foster schemes of reorganisation.[46]

In the 1930s a substantial amount of new investment occurred, including the construction by Stewart and Lloyd's of an integrated plant at Corby to produce steel from local ores by the long-abandoned basic Bessemer process and to shape it in continuous and semi-continuous tube-, strip-, and pipe-mills, and the building of new works at Cardiff, Shotton, and Ebbw Vale. The works at Ebbw Vale included the first continuous wide-strip-mill to be installed in this country. Its output was of a sufficiently high quality to be shaped immediately by automated presses and to be used in the production of cars and durable household goods, and the plant was one of the most modern in the world. The original intention had been for it to be located in Lincolnshire. Its inland location in a Welsh valley was a result of a carrot-and-stick policy pursued by the government because of the high unemployment among iron and steel workers in the region, and the fact that many of the area's tin-plate mills were expected to be closed as soon as the new plant came on stream. But as a result of design problems the capacity of the plant that was actually built was greater than had been intended originally, with the result that the site at Ebbw Vale proved to be less than ideal, costs increased, and the company soon ran into financial difficulties. Only the intervention of the Bank of England enabled the company to survive, but the Governor of the Bank would only act on the advice of the British Iron and Steel Federation, which recommended that assistance be given on the condition that the mill accept production quotas whose purpose was to protect the interests of other less competitive producers. As a result the potential competitive advantage of the new plant could not be fully exploited.[47] What is more, the building of a modern plant at Jarrow was also blocked by the Federation for similar reasons.

So, while the profitability of the industry was increased, and while its structure and the methods of production were modernised in the 1930s in such a way as to enable it to catch up with the relatively backward French industry which had actually overtaken it in the 1920s, it remained 'retarded',[48] and, by international standards, continued to be a relatively inefficient and high-cost producer. The reasons for this lay in part in the lack of dynamism of the economy and in the structure of the industry itself. Indeed in the words of one contemporary observer, 'the lamentable history of the attempt to reorganise the iron and steel industry on its present basis, in return for protection, seems to indicate that a very wide measure of public control will be necessary if the badly needed work of rationalisation is ever to make any real progress'.[49]

The shipbuilding industry

The shipbuilding industry was something of an exception among the staple industries in that its share of world output continued to be very high into the twentieth century, accounting for an average of 78.6 per cent of the gross tonnage launched in 1892–6 and of 60 per cent in 1910–14. The main reasons for this lay in the competitive superiority of the British industry at a time when the advantages of technique, skill, and organisation acquired at the time of the steamship revolution of the 1870s outweighed the gains from new technology, and in the country's shipping and naval supremacy. But at the same time, new capacity was being installed in other countries, and in the years between 1913 and 1921 the growth of the shipbuilding sector was accelerated, both abroad as other nations sought to become self-sufficient and in Britain where capacity increased by 30 or 40 per cent to reach some 3 or 4 million tons gross per year. As a result the capacity of the world's shipyards was more than doubled.

TABLE 12.1 *United Kingdom and world shipbuilding output, 1913–38 (gross tonnage launched in thousand tons)*

Year	United Kingdom	World	United Kingdom as a percentage of world total
1909–13*	1,522	2,589	58.7
1920	2,056	5,862	35.1
1923	646	1,643	39.4
1924	1,440	2,248	64.0
1926	640	1,675	38.3
1929	1,523	2,793	54.5
1933	133	489	27.2
1938	1,030	3,034	34.0

* Average value.

Source: L. Jones, cited in A. Musson, *The Growth of British Industry* (London: Batsford, 1978) p. 308.

However, after the war and the immediate post-war boom the demand for ships increased more slowly due to the stagnation of world trade which resulted in a large amount of shipping being redundant, laid up, or scrapped, and to an increase in the average speed and carrying capacity of vessels. In addition demand fluctuated sharply (Table 12.1). At the same time, naval construction slackened until rearmament started in the late 1930s. As a result the orders placed for new ships were far less than the capacity of the shipyards. In Britain even in the busiest years the industry was barely using one-half of its capacity, and in the seven years between 1923 and 1929 about one-third of its capacity would have been sufficient to meet all requirements.

At the same time as demand fell, the share of the British industry in world production declined, in part because of the competitive climate created by the excessive amount of world shipbuilding capacity and the assistance given by foreign governments to their shipping and shipbuilding industries, and because of the relative weakness of home demand which stemmed from the decline of the British merchant fleet, the low rate of replacement, and, in the 1930s, from the fact that an increasing number of orders were being placed abroad.[50]

But of more importance was the growing uncompetitiveness of the industry in Britain, whose main cause lay in the fact that British yards were becoming obsolete and were not keeping abreast of technical advances and new working practices. The industry failed to maintain a sufficiently high rate of technical innovation, was slow to introduce new forms of shipyard layout, organisation, and management, and was slow in responding to changes in ship design, to the use of oil-fired engines, and to the replacement of riveting by electric welding.[51]

At first few firms were forced out of the industry, but some had to merge in order to survive, and substantial amounts of capital were written off. In 1930 a formal rationalisation scheme was introduced with the establishment of the National Shipbuilders' Security Limited to remove excess capacity by buying up, renovating, and reselling obsolete and redundant shipyards for any purpose other than shipbuilding with the help of loan funds. The loan was to be paid off by means of a 1 per cent levy on the sales of new ships by participating firms. By 1937, yards belonging to 28 firms with an aggregate capacity of more than 1 million tons had been closed down in this way, reducing the industry's total capacity to about 2.5 million tons gross per year. In addition a few other firms had been forced into liquidation.[52] But little was done to increase the specialisation and concentration of production on particular types of ships with a view to achieving scale economies or to improve the technical efficiency of the industry, while the cuts in existing types of capacity did not have to go further because of the increase in demand generated by the approaching war. As a result, in the 1950s the share of the British shipyards in world production was to decline further, while that of the modernised Japanese industry and of other producers who had switched into the production of new types of commercial shipping increased.[53]

In the inter-war period the number of insured workers in the industry was halved from about 350,000 at the height of the post-war boom to 175,000 in 1938, while unemployment was very high and reached 62 per cent in 1931–2.[54] Since the industry was very heavily concentrated in the North East and on Clydeside, the existence of idle or only partially active yards, and yard closures, led to incredibly high levels of localised unemployment, reaching 80 per cent at Jarrow after the closure of Palmer's shipyard.

Conclusion

So, in the 1920s and 1930s, the staple industries declined or stagnated for roughly similar reasons. One was the development of new industries abroad and the loss of foreign markets that followed from the adoption of policies of protection. Second, the staple industries of Britain had become uncompetitive. In the words of Pollard, they 'appeared antiquated, badly sited for expansion or in relation to raw materials, operating often under increasing costs, and in a period of low profits unable to modernise their equipment, preferring instead restrictive and monopolistic schemes'. In the third place 'the staple export industries on which Britain had concentrated in the past were no longer the growth sectors in world demand' (Figure 12.1). In addition, 'after 1925 the relative loss of markets was aggravated by the over-valuation of the pound'[55] and its causes, which lay in part in the hegemony of the financial sector and in the role of international finance capital in the British economy.

Of course very significant changes occurred in these sectors of production, yet by international standards they were limited in the sense that the gap between the practices of British and foreign producers was not closed. What this indicates is not only the way in which the structure of the industries involved and the fall in profitability impeded reorganisation, but also the inability of the market mechanism to effect it. In addition, what state intervention did occur, in spite of a dominant ideology that was extremely hostile to direct intervention in industry or to measures aimed at relieving unemployment, was largely determined by the interests of dominant groups wedded to the existing pattern of development, while the establishment of protected markets and of exclusive spheres of influence abroad in which monopoly prices could

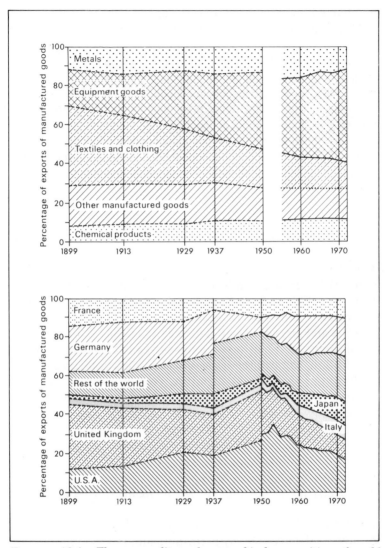

FIGURE 12.1 *The commodity and geographical composition of world trade in manufactured goods, 1899–1973*

Source: based on Maizels's estimates of the value of the exports of manufactured goods from industrial and other countries as reworked and extended in J. Mistral, 'Compétitivité et Formation du Capital en Longue Période', *Economie et Statistique*, no. 97 (February 1978) 3–23, pp. 4 and 6.

be charged enabled much excess capacity to be retained and reduced the need to invest in new plant and equipment, as did rearmament.

At the same time, new and potential growth industries which had made only slow progress before the war expanded more rapidly, recruiting some of the workers released by the collapse of the traditional export sectors. But they grew comparatively slowly, in part because of the weakness of the domestic market, and were located for the most part outside of the depressed regions. What is more, as the switch occurred 'without planning and with scarcely any understanding of its direction it was done hesitantly, clumsily, and expensively'.[56]

The new and expanding sectors and the building industry

The industries in which output expanded at a rate near or above the average for industry as a whole in the years between 1913 or 1920, and 1938, included a group of new industries, composed of the electricity-supply and electrical-engineering, vehicle- and aircraft-manufacturing, precision-instrument, and rayon industries, and new branches of the chemical industry. In addition, some of the traditional consumption-good sectors, such as the timber and furniture, food-processing, clothing, and paper and printing industries, recorded moderate rates of output growth, while the building industry was one of the fastest-growing sectors of the inter-war economy and had strong multiplier effects on related activities.[57]

The electricity-supply and electrical-engineering industries

Until the middle of the 1920s the use of electricity as a source of power advanced slowly in Britain, and, in the period before the war in particular, in some branches of the electrical-goods industry, such as the manufacturing of electrical machinery and electric lamps, a high proportion of the needs of the home market were met by imports or by the output of German and American branch plants.

But after 1926 the haphazard and scattered structure of

the electricity-supply system was transformed as a result of the establishment of the Central Electricity Board, with the task of purchasing bulk supplies from existing generating authorities, controlling its transmission, and reselling it to authorised distributors. Its actions led the way to a concentration of production on a relatively small number of efficient stations, and to the erection of high-tension transmission lines to interconnect these stations and to link existing regional systems into a National Grid. As a result of this step, and of an improvement in the efficiency of generating equipment, electricity was made available in almost every part of the country, although distribution continued to be chaotic until nationalisation. In addition its costs fell, and its use was pro-progressively extended to less and less affluent sections of the community.[58] As these events occurred, the demand for electricity from households and from industry expanded rapidly, while the dependence of industry on coalfield locations was reduced, and footloose enterprises found themselves free to set up in the Midlands and in the South East.

The growth in the production and consumption of electricity was closely associated with a rapid expansion of the electrical-engineering industry, as large-scale production was established by a comparatively small number of firms producing cables, heavy machinery and generating equipment, on the one hand, and a host of consumption goods such as cookers, irons, vacuum-cleaners, water-heaters, washing-machines, refrigerators, and radios on the other hand. In the 1920s the British industry was relatively weak in the consumption-good sectors in which mass-production techniques were being used abroad, but in the 1930s, in the context of tariff protection and of a more rapid expansion of the home market, the industry grew more quickly. Yet by 1938, while 65 per cent of homes were wired for electricity, only 27 per cent had vacuum-cleaners, only 18 per cent had electric cookers, and a mere 3 per cent had refrigerators and washing-machines. Only radios and electric irons were widely owned, and so 'despite falling prices and the extension of hire-purchase facilities the purchase of consumer durables was still confined largely to the wealthier classes', in contrast to what was happening in the USA.[59]

Yet between 1924 and 1938 the output of the electrical-engineering industry more than doubled, and employment increased from 156,000 persons to 325,500, of which a large part was concentrated in the Greater London region, because of the adaptability of the existing industrial structure of the region and the availability of a large pool of semi-skilled workers in the new industrial suburbs or in nearby towns.[60]

The motor-manufacturing industry

At first the development of the car industry, which was the most important part of this sector, was constrained in Britain by the enforcement of highly restrictive speed-limits, and most of the early vehicles were imported from the USA, France, and Germany. In 1896 the rule that all vehicles had to be preceded by a person carrying a red flag was replaced by a 14-miles-per-hour speed-limit, and the development of the British industry was set in motion with the establishment of the Daimler plant to work on continental patents in an old cotton-mill in Coventry.[61] In the years between 1896 and 1914 the number of firms and of models proliferated. The industry was in effect in an experimental stage with few standard designs, frequent innovations, and a high rate of turnover of firms. The typical firm was small in size, producing no more than a few hundred custom-built cars per year individually or in small batches with the help of skilled and semi-skilled workers, for a luxury market, and by 1914 only a few were producing more than 1,000 cars per annum. Indeed in 1896–1914 some 393 firms were founded, of which 280 had been wound up by 1914, and nearly 200 different models were designed and produced.[62] The most important works was the Ford assembly plant at Trafford Park near Manchester, but the industry was largely concentrated in Coventry, Birmingham, and Wolverhampton in the West Midlands, because of its tradition of metal-working and of employment in sectors like bicycle manufacturing out of which it often grew, the existence of many firms capable of producing the range of products that were needed in the early stages of the industry's development, and the existence of a large pool of unorganised workers who were unlikely to oppose the use of new kinds of machinery.[63] In the war the advantages of the region were reinforced by the establishment of some large firms in the machine-tools sector, such as Alfred Herbert. In fact the growth of the engineering sector in the region created a market for the products of related industries and laid the foundations for a cumulative spiral of growth.

After the war, the McKenna duty of 1915 of 33⅓ per cent *ad valorem* on cars and components imported from abroad was maintained and, with a single break in 1924–5, was retained until the 1950s. In the first few years scores of new firms entered the industry to meet the demand that had been built up. But in the 1920s, assembly-line methods were adopted for the production of cheap saloon cars by Austin, Morris, and other leading British makers, as well as by General Motors, which gained entry to the British motor industry by taking over Vauxhall in 1928, and by Ford, which established a production plant at Dagenham in 1929. As a result of the expansion of these firms which benefited from the economies of scale and technical progress associated with the introduction of elementary mass-production techniques, and of the elimination of many small firms under the impact of competition from the more rapidly growing firms and the subsidiaries of American companies, the number of firms fell from 88 in 1922, to 31 in 1929, and to 22 in 1938.[64] At the same time the number of firms producing commercial vehicles and motor-cycles fell. In 1929 about three-quarters of the industry's total output was produced by three firms: Morris with 35 per cent of output, Austin with 25 per cent, and Singer with 15 per cent. But in the 1930s these three firms failed to maintain their leading position. In 1938 over 90 per cent of car production was in the hands of 6 companies: Morris with 24 per cent of the market, Austin with 20 per cent, Ford with 17 per cent, Vauxhall with 11 per cent, and Rootes and Standard with 10 per cent each.[65]

With the introduction of mass-production techniques the average factory price of a private car fell from £308 in 1912, to £259 in 1924, and to £130 in 1935–6.[66] As prices fell, the market was widened, and output increased from about 25,000 cars in 1913, to 35,000 in 1920, to 182,000 in 1929, and to 341,000 in 1938. A large part of the industry's output was sold on the home market, but exports increased, mainly to countries which formed part of the British Empire and in which British industry enjoyed tariff preferences. In the late 1930s exports reached about one-fifth of the industry's output.[67]

In the 1930s, the competitiveness of the industry was enhanced by the modernisation of the process of production, and by the relatively low levels of capacity utilisation in countries with whose industries it competed for export markets in less-developed countries. But concentration had not gone nearly as far as in the USA, where the 3 leading companies accounted for nearly 90 per cent of total output in the late 1930s, and, in spite of the fact that in 1937, for example, the 6 leading British producers turned out roughly 350,000 private cars in comparison with some 3.5 million produced by the top 3 American firms, the range of models was wider and production runs were shorter, while significantly less use was made of standardised parts and components than in the USA. As a result, the full economies of scale offered by flow-line production were not being realised by the British vehicle-manufacturing industry. At the same time, parts and components were in most cases being produced at less than optimal scales, in spite of the fact that many of them could be used interchangeably in different models. One of the main reasons for the existence of production-runs that were too short to reap the economies of scale that were being achieved by other producers, was the fact that firms like Austin and Morris were consciously adopting a strategy of putting more and more models with different sizes and types of engine and body onto the market, instead of one of developing more concentrated and standardised methods of production. Indeed it was estimated that a doubling of the output of a model produced in 1939 at a rate of 20,000 cars per annum would have resulted in a reduction of 20 per cent in manufacturing costs. But instead of choosing to widen the market by cutting the costs of production, the strategy of firms such as Austin and Morris was one of attempting to increase their shares of the replacement market. At the same time, it was because firms like Ford, Vauxhall, Rootes, and Standard were establishing mass production in Britain that they were able to increase their market shares at the expense of the leaders of 1929. In addition they were quicker in adjusting to a switch in demand towards small cars.[68]

In the 1930s the industry tended to become increasingly concentrated in the West Midlands, and in the South East, whose importance as a centre of production was increased by the growing role of American firms in the British industry. The early Scottish firms were quickly eliminated, while the area around Manchester lost Ford to Dagenham and Rolls Royce to Derby. The area around Coventry, Birmingham, and Wolverhampton with its great variety of metal-working and components firms continued to be the hub of the industry. But areas near to the metropolitan market where land and large numbers of semi-skilled workers could be found, such as Dagenham, Luton, and Oxford, had come to form a second major centre of large-scale production. On the other hand, the manufacture of heavy commercial vehicles with its greater reliance on heavy engineering was concentrated in Lancashire and North Cheshire, with a few firms being found in London and in the Home Counties.[69]

By 1938 more than half-a-million workers were engaged in the construction of motor and other vehicles.[70] A high proportion of them were employed in large plants located at some distance from the existing industrial zones of the regions in which they were located, where land was cheap and space for expansion was available. It was to these areas that large numbers of semi-skilled workers were drawn not only from other activities in the region but also from declining industries in other parts of the country.

At the same time, the development of the motor-manufacturing industry was a major stimulus to other parts of the economy. In some cases, firms in other sectors supplying the industry with its needs and some of the closely associated specialist suppliers of components also established large-scale production, although quite a lot of work was subcontracted to small firms in the older parts of the industrial region in order to spread some of the risks and capital commitments.

As a result, the industry's growth played a major role in the modernisation of the economy and in reshaping the geography of the country and of the regions in which it was implanted.

The building industry

In the years between 1920 and 1938 the output of the building and contracting sector increased, according to the Lomax index, at an average annual rate of 5.4 per cent or at double the rate for all industry. Its rate of growth was surpassed only by that of the vehicle-manufacturing industry. At the same time the output of building materials doubled. Investment in building as a proportion of total fixed investment increased from 32.0 per cent in 1900–9, to 44.2 per cent in the 1920s, and to nearly 50.0 per cent in the 1930s. But the rate of growth of productivity was low, and so employment in building and allied trades increased substantially from 924,400 in 1920, when the industry was beginning to recover after the war, to 1,344,100 in 1938, or from 10.4 to 15.2 per cent of total industrial employment.[71]

In the early 1920s, non-residential construction predominated, as it had in the pre-war period, but from 1925 and especially in the recovery in the 1930s the construction of housing assumed a leading role, with investment in dwellings running on average at more than double the investment in non-residential building. In the years between March 1920 and March 1939, 4.36 million houses were constructed, of which nearly 3 million were built in the 1930s.[72]

At the end of the war an acute shortage of housing existed. The number of dwellings had failed to keep pace with the growth of the population and the rate of family formation, due to the low level of housebuilding activity before and during the war. In addition, urban slum dwellings were in urgent need of replacement. In order to prevent rents from rising and to keep down the cost of living, the rent controls, imposed as a result of the protests by Glasgow munitions workers in 1915, were retained and extended; and, in part because private investment in housing built for letting had been made unprofitable and was unlikely to occur, the state, in a series of acts passed in 1919, 1923, and 1924, sought to stimulate the construction of housing by advancing subsidies both to local authorities to help them to build council-housing and to private builders. The policy of a general subsidisation of housebuilding was continued until the early 1930s, at which time the state's attention was switched to the problems of slum-clearance and overcrowding.

In the 1930s, a predominantly private-enterprise building boom occurred, in which nearly 3 million new houses were provided, overwhelmingly for letting to middle-class tenants, or for sale to owner-occupiers belonging to the middle classes and to the top group of artisans. In the late 1920s and in the 1930s in particular, the costs of construction fell, in part because of improvements in the productivity of labour in the production of building materials, although the resulting savings were not always passed on by the increasingly concentrated firms in this sector,[73] and in part because of the downward pressure on wages and on building costs exerted by the high levels of unemployment among building workers and the need felt by small building firms to sell quickly. As a result the average capital cost of new houses fell from £422 in 1928, to £361 in 1934, according to Bowley's estimates.[74] In addition, purchasers were assisted by a fall in interest rates, and by an expansion of the building societies and a liberalisation of the terms on which they were prepared to lend money. But of most importance was the increase in real incomes associated with the improvements in the terms of trade and with the fall in the costs of living, and the growth in the numbers of white-collar workers with the expansion of the 'salariat' in industry and of salaried occupations in the service sector.[75]

12.3 The transformation of the conditions of existence of the wage-earning class and the mode of consumption of Fordism

The growth of the building industry, and of new high-productivity sectors in which consumption goods were produced for the home market by a few large firms, were in fact two of the characteristics of a transition from a regime of predominantly extensive accumulation to one of predominantly intensive accumulation, in which the conditions of existence and the way of life of the wage-earning class were transformed and new methods of relative surplus-value production were generalised throughout much of department 2. But a transition of this kind posed several sets of problems of which some were only solved in and through a protracted and extremely wasteful crisis.[76]

On the one hand, the development of new branches of industry producing consumption goods for individual households depended in part upon a transformation of the housing situation and upon the provision of a variety of items of urban infrastructure. But of more importance was the problem posed by the fact that the incorporation of a new commodity into a working-class consumption norm could only occur when its unit exchange-value was, on the one hand, sufficiently low for it to be afforded, and was, on the other hand, declining, so that the market could be extended progressively to include ever-wider sections of the population. In most cases what this meant was that the market for a commodity could only be widened when it was being produced with the help of the standardised processes of mass production. But for such methods to be in use, a sufficiently large and rising demand had to exist already.

According to Aglietta, the process by which this circle was squared and by which this problem was overcome was the following. At first, a social division of labour was established in department 2, as a result of a differentiation of this department into a sub-department producing luxury goods purchased in exchange for a part of surplus-value consumed as revenue, and a sub-department producing commodities bought with the monetary equivalent of the value of the labour-power purchased by capital. In time, a process of centralisation of capital, and the adoption of new methods of management and circulation, led to an increase in the size of salaried social categories in industry itself, and in the autonomous activities of the service, commercial, and financial sectors, who were paid in part out of centralised surplus-value, while the expansion of these new strata gave rise to a growing demand for the products that previously were considered to be luxuries. At this stage the commodities concerned began to be produced on a growing scale by capital, and an impetus was given to the production of housing, household consumption goods, motor vehicles, and related products.

However, the adoption in department 2 of the advances made in department 1, which were radically changing the process of production, led at first to a reduction, initially in department 2 itself, in employment per unit of output, increasing the inequality in the distribution of income, and reducing the demand for the products of department 2. As a result, the disproportion between the development of department 2 and accumulation in department 1 increased rapidly, and the demand for the products of department 1 also declined. In short, the installation of mass-production methods ran counter to the need to expand the markets for department 2 products.

By 1926, the expansion of new sectors in the countries whose economies were leading the growth process had come up against limits of social demand of this kind, and only after a deep and protracted crisis, at the end of which the market began to be widened by the inclusion of working-class households, could the foundations of a new wave of expansion be laid. In turn, this step required far-reaching changes in the mechanisms of wage formation and in the methods of work organisation, a socialisation of some of the expenses and risks associated with exceptional consumption expenditures and with the insecurity of employment, an extension of credit to new sections of the population, an extension and diversification of state economic intervention, and an acceleration of transformations in the conditions of production.

But, once new structural forms had been established, the norm of working-class consumption evolved dynamically. On the one hand, advances in productivity, developed in department 1, were incorporated into production processes in department 2, and helped to lower the value of the means of consumption, and the production of relative surplus-value increased sufficiently to make it possible for real wages to be increased without harming the rate of profit. On the other hand, with expanding markets, capacity and output increased and partially offset the effects on employment of rising productivity. As a result, the conditions of existence of the working class were produced on an increasing scale by capital, a link was established between mass production and mass consumption, and accumulation could proceed rapidly in both departments. However, it was not until after the Second World War that a wave of growth of this kind was to occur.

The sphere of consumption was radically changed, not simply in order to supply outlets for new types of consumption good and to harmonise the expansion of the two departments of production; it also had to be transformed in such a way as to enable workers suited to the new kinds of production to reconstitute the energies expended in performing the new kinds of work, and to preserve and reproduce the abilities and attitudes that they required. As Gramsci pointed out, the development of Fordism was connected with attempts to transform the structure of society and to select and develop new types of worker with 'new, more complex and rigid norms and habits of order, exactitude, and precision' adapted to the new kinds of work, by means of coercion and persuasion. Among other things it was associated with prohibition, with the implantation of a new sexual ethic and new family arrangements, with the growth of puritan ideologies 'which give an external form of persuasion and consent to the intrinsic use of force', and with high wages which were necessary to restore the strength and energy worn down by forms of work that were more wearying and exhausting and that demanded new levels of expenditure of muscular and nervous energy. At the same time, individuals who were weak or nonconforming were gradually forced 'into the limbo of the lumpen-classes'.[77]

The development of Fordism was associated with the creation of a norm of consumption in which individual ownership of capitalistically produced commodities governed the concrete practices of consumption, while various modes of traditional consumption and the environment moulded by pre-capitalist forms of production were destroyed, or, as in the case of Britain, the urban and industrial environment shaped by earlier waves of accumulation was transformed, albeit slowly. As Aglietta has pointed out, the development of Taylorism and Fordism sharply increased the intensity of work and systematically reduced the amount of wasted time. As a result, time for recuperation at the work-place itself disappeared, and the increased exhaustion of labour-power in the labour process had to be repaired in its entirety at home. At the same time, the separation of work-place and residence, and increases in the distance between them, lengthened journey-to-work times, with the result that the time taken up by work-related activities did not fall by as much as the length of the working day was reduced. In the view of Aglietta, 'individual commodity consumption is the form of consumption that permits the most effective recuperation from physical and nervous fatigue in a compact space of time within the day, and at a single place, the home'.

The structure of the consumption norm was governed by two commodities: 'standardised housing that is the privileged site of individual consumption; and the automobile as the means of transport compatible with the separation of home and work place'. In addition, the use of the motor car was closely related to the relatively low density of many residential developments. The production of standardised housing was associated with the implementation of minimum housing standards and rising space-consumption, and it permitted the installation of a variety of household appliances that to some extent reduced the burden of domestic work. The subsequent generalisation of the new mode of consumption was connected with a breaking-down of ties of family and neighbourhood and with the generation in the working class of the small family and household as the unit of expenditure and consumption. Women were encouraged to move back into the home to perform a variety of domestic tasks at least until the outbreak of war and until the new regime of accumulation itself came up against new constraints on the growth of demand on the one hand and limits of labour discipline and of labour supply on the other hand.

At the same time, the process of production of these and of other commodities became central processes in the development of the mode of consumption. In particular, the consumption of use-values adapted to capitalist mass production involved the creation of a 'functional aesthetic', which in the view of Aglietta, had three major characteristics. In the first place, the process of design had to respect the constraints of engineering and cost and was based on a conception of use-values as 'an assembly of standardised components capable of long production runs'. Second, it was connected with the introduction of planned obsolescence and the establishment of 'a functional link between use values to create the need for their complementarity'. In the third place, the real relationship of an individual with an object was duplicated by an imaginary relationship created through advertising techniques whose aim was to objectify status by linking it with specific patterns of consumption.[78]

The development of new sectors of production and of a new mode of consumption also had extremely significant spatial implications. One of the most important was the sub-urbanisation of industry and a shift of population from town centres towards the suburbs. The suburbanisation of population was not an entirely new phenomenon. It had occurred in the second half of the nineteenth century, but at this time movement to the suburbs was largely confined to the wealthier sections of the middle classes. In the late nineteenth and early twentieth century this shift was accelerated, and in the inter-war years it became the most important trend in the distribution of population. 'Of the 131 districts in England and Wales which increased their population by 30 per cent or more between 1921–31 no less than 116 were suburban areas, the remainder being seaside resorts.' All of the major urban areas had rapidly growing suburban areas, while the population of the central areas remained constant, or declined.[79]

In the case of London, the beginnings of middle-class migration to new suburbs can be dated back to the middle of the eighteenth century, but only a minority of prosperous merchants and government employees were involved. In the last two-thirds of the nineteenth century the residential population of the central area was drastically reduced by redevelopment and the building of warehouses, workshops, railway yards, offices, and new streets, while overcrowding in adjacent districts increased markedly.[80] At the same time, the advent of suburban trains and of a system of tramways, in conjunction with waves of speculative building, were associated with a growing outward movement of wider sections of the middle classes to suburbs located on radial routes emanating from the city centre. Yet in the 1880s a serious housing crisis emerged, because 'the demolition of dwellings had not been accompanied by a sufficient extension of cheap transport and [by a] . . . significant decentralisation of industry'.[81]

In the 1890s the underground system began to be developed, and in the new century the railway network began to be electrified and the electric tram slowly gave way to the bus. It was at this stage that members of the lower middle classes and of the respectable working classes joined the exodus from the central area. In the years between 1919 and 1939 the population of Greater London increased from 6 to 8 million persons, and its area expanded about five-fold, with suburban housing being built more freely and more extensively at a generally uniform standard of about 12 two-storey dwellings to the net residential acre on land that was relatively inexpensive. The fall in the real costs of transport and housing enabled substantial numbers of people to move out to the suburbs. At the same time many people were migrating to the capital from the provinces, but the growth associated with this influx was more than offset by the effects of the process of surbanisation. In fact, between 1921 and 1937 the population of outer London rose by nearly 1.4 million persons, while the number living in central London fell by almost 400,000.[82]

The advent of the motor-car gave an additional impetus to the process of suburbanisation. In addition, the tendency for industry to be located and to expand more rapidly in suburban districts, which can be dated from the 1890s, continued to play an important role by creating new foci around which low-density housing could be constructed. But the way in which sprawling urban areas were devouring the countryside was in its turn to be one of the impulses behind the setting-up of a sequence of committees, and behind the introduction of a system of town and country planning, in the years following the Second World War, whose aims were urban containment, the preservation of the countryside, and the development of new communities.[83]

12.4 The regional problem and the origins of regional policy

The restructuring of metropolitan areas that occurred as industry and population were relocated in suburban zones and as urban centres were redeveloped, was not the only spatial consequence of the redeployment of capital and of the switch in the sources of economic growth that were under way in the inter-war years. At the same time, the collapse of the old staple industries, and the growth of new and old sectors supplying the domestic market, were associated with a decisive shift in the location of industry and population from the old industrial regions in the north and west of the country to the Midlands and South East.[84] In the short interval between the

TABLE 12.2 *The distribution of net industrial output by Census of Production regions, 1924–35 (in percentages)*

	Year		
Region	1924	1930	1935
Lancashire, Cheshire, and parts of Derbyshire	20.8	17.8	15.5
West Riding	12.6	10.6	10.1
Northumberland, Durham, and North Riding	5.9	5.3	4.3
South Wales and Monmouthshire	5.3	3.8	3.2
West Central Scotland	5.0	4.9	4.5
Old industrial regions	49.6	42.4	37.6
Greater London	17.1	21.2	24.8
Warwickshire, Worcestershire, and Staffordshire	11.6	12.2	12.3
New industrial regions	28.7	33.4	37.1
Rest of Great Britain	21.7	24.2	25.3
Total Great Britain	100.0	100.0	100.0

Sources: Political and Economic Planning, *Report on the Location of Industry* (London: PEP, March 1939) p. 44; and S. Pollard, *The Development of the British Economy, 1914–1967*, 2nd edn (London: Edward Arnold, 1969) p. 126.

Census of Production of 1924 and that of 1935, the share of the northern industrial regions and of Scotland and Wales in net industrial output declined from 55.4 per cent to 43.7 per cent, while that of Greater London and of the rest of England rose from 44.6 per cent to 57.3 per cent (Table 12.2). A similar shift occurred in the distribution of the working and of the total population (Table 12.3), and in the distribution of employment (Table 12.4).

The shift was to a large extent the result of differences in the industrial structure of the two parts of the country, and of the fact that at the beginning of the period the south

TABLE 12.3 *The regional distribution of the insured and of the total population of Great Britain, 1921–37 (in percentages)*

Region	Insured population		Total population	
	1923	1937	1921	1937
Lancashire	15.7	13.8	11.6	10.9
West Riding, Nottinghamshire, and Derbyshire	13.0	12.2	10.9	10.8
Northumberland and Durham	5.7	4.9	5.2	4.8
Mid Scotland	7.3	6.6	6.2	6.0
Glamorgan and Monmouthshire	4.2	3.3	4.0	3.4
Old industrial regions	45.9	40.8	37.9	35.9
London and the Home Counties	22.4	26.0	23.5	25.7
Staffordshire, Warwickshire, Worcestershire, Leicestershire, and Northamptonshire	11.2	11.7	9.5	9.7
New industrial regions	33.6	37.7	33.0	35.4
Rest of Great Britain	20.5	21.5	29.1	28.7
Total Great Britain	100.0	100.0	100.0	100.0

Sources: Great Britain. The Royal Commission on the Distribution of the Industrial Population, *Report*, Cmnd 6153 (London: HMSO, 1939) pp. 22–4; and S. Pollard, *The Development of the British Economy, 1914–1967*, p. 127.

TABLE 12.4 *The distribution of the number of insured persons aged 16—24 in employment by Ministry of Labour divisions, 1923—37 (index numbers)*

Region	June 1923	June 1929	June 1932	June 1936	June 1937
North West	100	109	96	105	112
North East	100	105	92	106	114
North	100	99	77	94	102
Scotland	100	105	91	106	112
Wales	100	85	69	75	86
London	100	120	118	139	145
South East	100	127	127	153	159
South West	100	117	114	132	140
Midlands	100	111	101	124	132
Great Britain	100	110	100	117	124

Source: M. P. Fogarty, *Prospects of the Industrial Areas of Great Britain* (London: Methuen, 1945) p. 15.

already contained many of the industries that were to expand, while the main industries of the north and west were declining (Table 12.5).[85] Some of the industries in which employment was declining, such as the railway and shipping sectors of the transport industry, were widely scattered, but mostly, as in the cases of the coal, iron and steel, shipbuilding, and textile industries, they were highly concentrated in small and clearly defined areas in South Wales, West Central Scotland, the North East, the North West, and the West Riding. Some of these areas were almost totally dependent on one or more of the staple industries and on the multiplier effects of the spending with which they were associated, and most of them had little success in attracting firms in the growing sectors. At the regional level the most extreme case was Wales, in which 70 per cent of the workers enumerated in the Census of Production of 1930 were employed in the making of iron and steel and of tinplate, and in coal- and slate-mining and quarrying. In 1935 the proportion was still 65 per cent.

With the exception of the heavy chemicals industry the expanding sectors were located in old industrial areas with a different kind of industrial tradition, in the Midlands and in parts of London, or in newly industrialised areas in the Midlands, and in the South East, which had been one of the most depressed parts of the country in the years following the agricultural depression of the late nineteenth century. With a reduction in the dependence of industry on bulky fuels and raw materials, an improved transport network, a need for new kinds of industrial skills and for unskilled and often female workers, and sales oriented to the home market, many firms were set up in the South East in particular, and at this time some of the new industrial suburbs to the north and west of London were turned into some of the fastest-growing areas in the country. In the six years between 1932 and 1937 nearly five-sixths of the net increase in the number of factories employing twenty-five or more persons, some two-fifths of employment in new factories, and nearly one-third of all factory extensions were located in Greater London, even though it had only one-fifth of the population. But to some extent every industry grew more rapidly in the expanding than in the contracting areas because of the multiplier effects of local growth, which were most pronounced in the case of the industries serving the local market, and in the building sector in particular.

In the inter-war years the fall in employment in the depressed industries more than offset the increase in the numbers employed in the growing industries and in the service sector, and so total employment fell. It declined from 20.3 million jobs in 1920 to less than 18 million in 1922 and only regained its 1920 level in 1936, after which it increased to 21.4 million in 1938.[86] At the same time the size of the potential labour-force increased. Between 1921 and 1939 the national unemployment rate averaged about 14 per cent of all insured workers. It never fell much below 10 per cent, and in the worst year of 1932 it nearly reached 23 per cent. In absolute terms at least 1 million, and in 1932 3 million, persons were out of work.

But very pronounced differences existed between industries and between and within regions. In particular there was a marked contrast between the relatively low levels of unemployment in the southern part of the country and the very

TABLE 12.5 *Changes in the number of workers insured against unemployment by industry divisions and by region, 1923–37 (in percentages)*

	London and Home Counties	Midland Counties	West Riding, Notts and Derby	Mid Scotland	Lancs	Northumberland Durham	Glamorgan and Monmouthshire	Great Britain
I Insured workers in 1923 in:								
7 'local' industries[1]	35	16	14	25	19	16	13	24
16 rapidly expanding 'basic' industries[2]	21	26	9	10	9	6	4	14
5 rapidly declining 'basic' industries[3]	1	12	43	24	36	49	59	23
18 other industries[4]	43	46	33	40	36	28	24	39
All industries[4]	100	100	100	100	100	100	100	100
II Increase (+) or decrease (−) in 1923–37 in:								
7 'local' industries	+54	+67	+69	+43	+47	+63	+59	+57
16 rapidly expanding 'basic' industries	+69	+51	+75	+46	+86	+63	+49	+66
5 rapidly declining 'basic' industries	−4	−28	−15	−31	−28	−29	−34	−25
18 other industries	+21	+17	+15	+5	+2	+18[6]	+26[6]	+14
All industries	+43	+28	+15	+10	+8	+5	—	+22

III 'Hypothetical' increase in 1923–37:[5]	+40	+29	+ 9	+18	+11	+ 4	+ 1	+22
IV Insured workers in 1937 in:								
7 'local' industries	38	20	21	33	26	25	22	30
16 rapidly expanding 'basic' industries	25	30	14	13	16	9	6	19
5 rapidly declining 'basic' industries	1	7	32	15	24	33	41	14
18 other industries	36	42	33	39	35	32	31	37
All industries	100	100	100	100	100	100	100	100

1 The distributive trades, the building, gas, water, and electricity supply, road transport, tramway and omnibus service, laundry, job-dyeing, and dry-cleaning, bread, biscuit, and cake-making sectors.

2 The 16 non-local industries which expanded more rapidly than all industry in Great Britain, excluding public-works contracting.

3 The coal-mining, cotton, wool textile, iron and steel, and shipbuilding and ship-repairing sectors.

4 This group includes (a) all those separately distinguished basic industries other than the '5 rapidly declining basic industries', that declined, or expanded at less than the national rate (+22.3 per cent), in Great Britain; (b) public-works contracting; (c) a large group of industries which were included in the Ministry of Labour evidence, under the heading 'all other industries and services' and which included both 'basic' industries (some rapidly expanding) and also some industries, such as 'local government service', which should probably be called 'local'.

5 The rate at which the number of insured persons in an area would have increased if each industry had expanded (or contracted) in the area at the same rate as in Great Britain.

6 The high rates of increase in the '18 other industries' in Northumberland and Durham and in Glamorgan and Monmouth may be accounted for by high rates of increase in those areas in 'public-works contracting' (+377 per cent and +333 per cent as compared with +142 per cent in Great Britain). If this industry is excluded, the expansion in the remaining seventeen is seen to have been considerably lower in the two areas than in Great Britain.

Source: Great Britain. Royal Commission on the Distribution of the Industrial Population, *Report*, Cmnd 6153 (1939) p. 276.

TABLE 12.6   *The regional distribution of unemployment,
1912–36 (in percentages)*

Region	1912–13	July 1929	July 1932	July 1936	1929–36[1]
London	8.7	4.7	13.1	6.5	8.8
South East	4.7	3.8	13.1	5.6	7.8
South West	4.6	6.8	16.4	7.8	11.1
Midlands	3.1/2.5[2]	9.5	21.6	9.4	15.2
North East	2.5	12.6	30.6	16.6	22.7
North West	2.7	12.7	26.3	16.2	21.6
Scotland	1.8	11.2	29.0	18.0	21.8
Wales	3.1	18.8	38.1	28.5	30.1
South Britain		6.4	16.2	7.4	11.0
North Britain and Wales		12.9	29.5	18.0	22.8
Great Britain	3.9	9.7	22.9	12.6	16.9

(Column header group: **Year** spanning July 1929, July 1932, July 1936)

[1] Average values
[2] West and East Midlands

Source: W. H. Beveridge, cited in D. H. Aldcroft, *The Inter-War Economy, 1919–1939* (London: Batsford, 1970) p. 80.

high levels in the northern and western part (Table 12.6). In the depressed areas the major cities were exempted from the worst effects of the crisis. Indeed the areas centred on Manchester and Liverpool were not included in the original list of special areas, and the boundaries of the areas that were designated were drawn so as to exclude the main population centres of Cardiff, Newcastle upon Tyne, and Glasgow. But in smaller towns in the depressed areas with economies that were highly specialised in one of the declining sectors, astronomical rates of unemployment were recorded. In January 1933, 91 per cent of the labour-force were out of work in the Yorkshire town of Saltburn, 77 per cent at Jarrow, 70 per cent at Stornoway in Scotland, and in Wales 82 per cent were unemployed at Taff Wells, 72 per cent at Pontycymmer, 68 per cent at Merthyr, and 66 per cent at Abertillery.[87] The rate of unemployment was lower among non-insured workers, but the official figures understate the magnitude of the problem in that they do not indicate the extent of short-time working in the depressed areas or the fact that markedly lower proportions of the population in active age groups were seeking employment.

A substantial number of people moved from the depressed areas to the more prosperous parts of the country (Table 12.7). Between 1923 and 1936 London and the Home Counties, the South East, and the South West attracted over 1.1 million net immigrants, while Wales, Scotland, and the North East lost over 1.2 million persons through migration. At the same time there was a considerable movement of population within the more prosperous regions.

In the years after 1928 the movement of population was facilitated by the financial assistance provided under an industrial transfer scheme by the Ministry of Labour. The scheme

TABLE 12.7 *Net migration by Ministry of Labour division,*
1923–36

Regions	1923–31	1931–36
North West	−19,275	− 6,942
North East	−30,516	−24,180
Scotland	−37,559	+ 1,299
Wales	−31,350	−22,092
London and the Home Counties	+62,205	+71,623
South East	+ 8,733	+18,334
South West	+10,582	+11,445
Midlands	− 4,964	+ 5,521
Net inward (+) or outward (−) overseas migration	−42,144	+55,008

Source: H. Makower, J. Marschak, and H. W. Robinson, cited in M. P. Fogarty, *Prospects of the Industrial Areas of Great Britain*, p. 4.

TABLE 12.8 *Industrial development in the Special Areas, in Greater London, and in Great Britain,*
1932–8

	1932	1933	1934	1935	1936	1937	1938	Total 1932–8
Number of factories employing								
25 or more persons opened in								
the Special Areas	15	11	13	4	12	23	61	139
of which								
South Wales	1	1	0	0	0	5	19	26
West Cumberland	0	1	2	0	1	0	2	6
Northumberland and Durham	7	6	5	2	5	14	26	65
Scotland	7	3	6	2	6	4	14	42
Number of factories extended in								
the Special Areas	6	2	3	8	5	4	6	34
Number of factories closed in								
the Special Areas	12	10	22	5	10	6	13	78

Number of factories opened in Greater London	261	218	235	215	256	204	168	1557
Number of factories extended in Greater London	44	29	50	54	61	58	44	340
Number of factories closed in Greater London	94	107	164	185	164	152	191	1057
Number of factories opened in Great Britain	636	467	520	514	542	522	414	3615
of which percentage located in the Special Areas	2.4	2.4	2.7	0.8	2.2	4.3	14.7	3.8
percentage located in Greater London	41.0	46.7	45.2	41.8	47.2	39.7	40.6	43.1
Number of factories extended in Great Britain	174	109	151	201	185	178	145	1143
Number of factories closed in Great Britain	418	416	502	485	394	362	432	3009

Source: based on Great Britain. Board of Trade, *Survey of Industrial Development*, Annually 1932–8 (London: HMSO, 1933–9).

also involved the setting up of industrial training and rehabil-
itation centres. Between 1928 and the middle of 1937, nearly
190,000 men and women were assisted in moving from areas
in which they had little prospect of finding employment,
yet 56,000 of this very small number actually returned after
transfer.[88]

In years characterised by persistently high rates of unemployment in every region, migration was no answer to the
general problem and had hardly any effect upon inequalities
in the regional distribution of unemployment. In any case,
migration itself was selective, and contributed to a cumulative
process of decline in the depressed areas in which a group of
older and less skilled workers and of workers whose skills
were unsuited to the needs of newer industries was concentrated. It was this group that constituted the core of the long-
term unemployment problem.

In the end the government was forced to intervene in order
to be seen to be attempting to bring some work to the depressed areas. A series of five industrial surveys was sponsored by
the Board of Trade, and another was carried out privately.
The government followed them up with investigations of its
own, and in 1934 four 'special areas' were designated. In all,
three acts were passed, as a result of which two commissioners
were appointed to promote the economic and social development of areas in Central Scotland, on the one hand, and in
South Wales, West Cumberland, and the North East on the
other; aid was given to firms setting up in the Special Areas,
and industrial estates were developed at North Hillington
near Glasgow, Treforest near Pontypridd, and in the Team
Valley near Gateshead, and at a few other sites, on the model
of the ones established at Trafford Park in 1894 and at
Slough, and in Welwyn and Letchworth garden cities near
London, and of the ones planned for Wythenshawe near
Manchester, and Speke near Liverpool.[89]

By the late 1930s some 12,000 jobs had been provided in
government-owned factories, and, according to Aldcroft, up
to 50,000 jobs had been created in activities aided in one way
or another by the Special Areas legislation. But hardly any
impression was made on a surplus population in the Special
Areas, whose size has been variously estimated at between

200,000 and 400,000 insured workers and their families, and by 1938 the inequalities in unemployment showed no signs of narrowing and were, if anything, wider than in 1934. A very high proportion of new factories continued to be located in the more prosperous regions, and only in 1938 did the proportion located in the Special Areas exceed the figure of about 10 per cent that would have been expected on the basis of their share of the country's population (Table 12.8).[90]

The majority of the authors of the Barlow Report, which was completed in August 1939, were in favour of the setting-up of a national authority to regulate the establishment of additional industrial undertakings in London and the Home Counties, as part of a strategy for redeveloping congested urban areas, decentralising industry and population, and promoting a more balanced pattern of regional development, while the authors of its Minority Report and of a study by Political and Economic Planning demanded the setting-up of bodies with more drastic powers to curb development in any part of the country.[91]

But with the onset of the Second World War these proposals were set on one side. In any case the rearmament boom of 1938–9 and economic recovery in the late 1930s were leading to a recovery of the staple industries, while the threat of war was acting as a stimulus to a dispersal of industry and of government munitions factories and firms with government orders for war-related products in particular. As a result, the problems of adjustment, which could be solved neither by the market nor by the forms of economic management envisaged and implemented by the state in the 1930s, were put off until the 1950s, and the old industrial regions were left with economies that were heavily dependent upon industries which, through a lack of investment, had suffered from a fall in competitiveness, and with industrial structures whose origins lay in a model of externally orientated capitalist development which had been a source of some prosperity but was now well on the way to being bypassed.

Part IV

Further Outlook and Some Conclusions

Conclusion: Space and Society

In the 1930s and again at the end of the Second World War one of the most striking characteristics of the geography of Britain was the dichotomy between the more prosperous metropolitan areas in the Midlands and South-East and the old industrial regions situated in the north and west of the country whose economies were dependent on a narrow range of secularly declining industries. In addition, an important gap existed between the densely populated areas of modern industry and services which were concentrated along an axis extending from the capital to the North-West and the West Riding and the marginal rural areas of Scotland and Wales. But in Britain the significance of the problem of marginal rural districts had been reduced by the extent of rural depopulation and by the existence of the more obvious problems of declining industrial regions. By contrast, in the case of many other European countries in which the transition towards a system of capitalist farming assumed a different form, and in which industrialisation occurred later and was led by more modern branches of production using more recently developed and more efficient methods, the problem of declining rural regions was to be a much more central aspect of the regional problem in the period following the Second World War.

The gaps themselves are, of course, a product of what we have described as a process of uneven development. A graphic example of unequal development has been presented in the following way by Raymond Williams:

To stand on the Brecon Beacons and look south and then north is to see, on the ground and then very readily in the history, the reality of this apparent abstraction. To the south, now, are the dwindling remains of that explosive development of the iron and coal trade. To the north are the depopulated but marginally surviving pastoral hills. It can be seen as simultaneous overdevelopment and under-development, within a turn of the head. But the reality now is that both are old and both marginal.[1]

The pattern of regional specialisation at the end of the Second World War, and the inequalities with which it was associated, are a good index of the way in which the spatial distribution of social production and of the population of a capitalist country is stamped by its history. In each country the arena of capital is in fact a palimpsest, in which each new layer of human social activity and each new structure is shaped by those with whose erasing they are associated, while an examination of space also reveals elements of continuity whose roots lie in the modification, reproduction, or preserva-tion of historically given conditions, as a result, it must be emphasised, of a new logic of development.

But at the same time we have also given considerable em-phasis to the way in which historically determined conditions are transformed. In capitalist societies, in particular, a rapid and profound redrawing of the map of human activity has occurred.

In examining the way in which space has been used and transformed, we have paid particular attention to the changing functional and spatial differentiation of the process of social reproduction. The process of reproduction is an expression used to refer to the totality of processes involved in the pro-duction and reproduction of the means of human existence and of human life itself. It is composed of four interdependent moments: production, distribution, circulation, and consump-tion, where each of these moments is simultaneously material and ideal, and material and social. As a consequence, the process as a whole results in the production and reproduction not only of the material basis of society and of its individual members, but also, and simultaneously, of the social relations and social classes of which the society is composed, and of the ideas and meanings through the medium of which human experience and the processes of material and social reproduc-tion are lived and understood. In other words, it is simultane-ously a process of economic, political, cultural, and ideological reproduction. In this book we have admittedly focused mainly on the economic and social dimensions of the processes involved.

But it is also important to remember that the processes of reproduction and the demographic movements aimed at reproducing society as a whole are at the same time new production. As a result, the subjective and objective conditions on which the society concerned is based are gradually modified and eventually suspended, instead of being reproduced, and accordingly the ground is slowly prepared for the transition to a new type of society and new levels of material development.

An emphasis upon the functional and spatial differentiation of social reproduction is, in our view, of the utmost importance.[2] In looking at what is happening in particular areas one is often struck more by the differences with other districts than by what it has in common. At one stage in human history specific local economies and societies were relatively self-contained. The natural and social conditions of existence differed from one area to another, as did the modes of production, ways of living, and the products of different communities. But, when these communities came into contact, these differences called forth a mutual exchange of products and a gradual conversion of more and more products into commodities. With the generalisation of commodity production and, in particular, of capitalist commodity production, the inhabitants of a particular area were integrated much more completely into a national and international economy, and were assigned increasingly specialised and often new roles in a wider and more developed division of labour.[3] At the same time, each region was integrated politically, culturally, and ideologically into a nation state of which it was merely a constituent and subordinate part. The reason why these considerations are important is that as soon as one sees the events occurring in a particular region as a product of a splitting-up into interdependent parts of a single mechanism, what appear to be differences turn out to be to a significant extent a product of an internal division of a common history, and of a pattern of development which itself, in our view, has to be changed.

In Britain in the 1930s, what was emerging was a new mode

of development or regime of accumulation characterised by (i) mass production of durable consumer goods, (ii) mass consumption, (iii) state management of the economy and state provision of a wide range of collective means of consumption and general conditions of production, and (iv) major transfers of workers from peripheral areas and countries, of agricultural workers, and subsequently of women into the modern industrial and service sector. In the sphere of industrial production the leading role was played by new equipment-good industries, but they could only expand if they were supplied with intermediate goods such as steel and chemicals. These different types of activity were the outcome of a splitting-up of the collective labour of society, and were often located in different types of area. In Britain, at least until the end of the 1950s, increases in manufacturing employment in the growth sectors continued to be concentrated in the Midlands and South East, but with some dispersion of industry within the core regions to new and overspill towns, while the intermediate-goods sector tended to be located in some of the old industrial regions, as did many firms producing traditional consumption goods. It was this particular assignment of functions to areas, along with the overall dynamics of different activities, that lay behind the reinforcing of a pattern of a concentration of employment in central areas and of decline in peripheral areas.

The different roles or functions played by the inhabitants of different areas are, in turn, a source of inequality. Often, activities that generate high levels of income per capita are located in core regions, while those generating smaller amounts of income, and activities that are declining, are found in the periphery. In the preceding chapters we have indicated how existing patterns of inequality are accordingly reinforced and how regions that fall behind tend to stay behind. We have also noticed that under capitalism, in particular, a pattern of inequality is continually reproduced. In fact, it was with the rise of industrial capitalism that wide disparities in the value of marketed output per capita arose. But we have also shown how the pattern of inequality has itself been changed with changes in the overall trajectory of society.

In discussing the process of social reproduction, with which

different types of spatial differentiation and of spatial inequality are connected, we have placed considerable emphasis
on the labour processes of which its analytically distinguishable parts were composed. In Part I we emphasised that human
labour involves both (i) the action and effect of human beings
on the natural and social world in which they live and work,
that is finalism or ideal casuality, and (ii) the action and effect
of socially mediated natural and technical conditions and of
socially determined conditions on human activity, as well as
the way in which such conditions function as means and
instruments for the realisation of human aims and projects,
that is efficient or material causality. A corollary of the interaction of these two types of causality is, of course, that the
conditions with which human beings are confronted are
increasingly the result of previous human activity.

Yet, while conscious goal-determined human activity plays
a crucial role in the conception of human praxis advanced in
Part I, in the studies in Parts II and III we have not given
much explicit attention to questions of human agency. One
of the reasons for this is that we have tended to focus on the
consequences of human action, instead of discussing in detail
all of the competing human projects existing at each moment
in time, and of explaining how they interacted and were
modified in determining the actual course of events. As a
result, we have not had to take on the difficult question of
the relative weight of human agency *vis-à-vis* structural factors
in determining the course of history. But it should perhaps be
emphasised that much human activity is of a routine kind. In
an overwhelming majority of cases human agency has not
been directed at transforming the relations of production
under which people lived or at radically changing the collective
conditions of human life. At those moments when significant
changes were occurring, the groups who were most successful
in bending the course of events in the direction they desired
were generally not simply the powerful, but also those who
were capable of developing the forces of production. In the
case of pre-industrial history we would also, in general, tend
to stress the 'overpowering weight of structural necessity' in
determining which projects had the greatest impact on the
overall trajectory of an economy and society.[4] But as the

years have passed, the moment of subjective human intervention has asserted itself in increasing measure over the material provided by nature and the conditions resulting from previous human labour. Yet at the same time a new set of constraints, in the form of the relations of capitalist production and the patterns of socially and politically determined behaviour with which they are associated, have been and continue to be imposed and to act as limits to human freedom.

The account of the overall evolution of space and society has been organised around the identification of a series of long waves, that is, cycles of a duration of about fifty years in which phases of expansion alternated with phases of slackening growth, of stagnation, or of contraction. We have also pointed out that each long wave, at least under capitalism, has been connected with important developments in technology and in the forces of production. In the 1780s the industrial revolution was under way, and in the 1890s a second industrial revolution is said to have been occurring. Indeed, the upturn of each long wave was preceded by a cluster of often interrelated inventions and innovations, and by a downswing in which the seeds of the subsequent upswing were laid. The foundations of the post-1945 boom were laid, for example, in the 1930s and 1940s, as we pointed out in the last chapter.

But in explaining Kondratieff cycles, we have ascribed an important role to social factors and to the dynamics of the social and economic systems with which we were concerned, and we have placed an emphasis on the labour process, instead of upon technology, which is merely a component of it. In the cases of long swings in the medieval and early modern epochs, we have contested demographic explanations that have often been advanced by historians, and we have tried to link long-term economic and demographic movements with mechanisms of surplus appropriation and with the laws of motion of feudal and early modern societies, while the crises that have punctuated the history of capitalist development have, in turn, been attributed largely to the centrality of profitability as a variable influencing the behaviour of the system, to the anarchy of capitalist competition, and to the difficulty experienced in market economies of adapting to change without a deep crisis.

The argument developed in this book could, in our view, be extended to analyse and explain what has happened since the Second World War. In that period, an almost unprecedented boom occurred in the context of a regime of intensive accumulation, characterised mainly by a generalisation of the methods of scientific management and Fordism and by the expansion of new equipment-good sectors. The wave of intensive accumulation was accompanied at first by a concentration of employment in the growth sectors in core regions, and only after 1960 or so by an attempt to modernise and diversify the structure of the old industrial regions.

But in the late 1960s and early 1970s, growth gave way to a world crisis of Fordism. In the 1970s, the strategy of some of the leading fractions of industrial capital was consequently to alter in the direction of an experimentation with neo-Fordist techniques. The aim behind the resulting changes in the organisation of the labour process is to overcome some of the obstacles to increases in the productivity of labour and in the rate of surplus-value which have arisen on the semi-automatic assembly line. Of particular importance is the way in which advances in the development of electronic information systems and in computer technology, and the development of new methods of measurement and control, have made it possible to construct machines that control their own operations. The introduction of automatic production control or automation, and the new principles of work organisation now in embryo, hold out the possibility of a substantial increase in the rate of surplus-value, and of a reduction in the value of constant capital capable of counteracting the rise in the organic composition of capital. In addition, 'a far more advanced centralisation of production becomes compatible with a geographical decentralisation of the operative units' and with a new geographical division of labour,[5] yet, as in the past, new trends in the location of industry do not in any sense represent an end of regional inequality: only the form, and to some extent the pattern, of inequality is changing.

As in the cases of earlier crises to which we have referred, a solution for capital to the crisis of Fordism does not simply depend upon the development of new methods of surplus-value production and upon a sectoral and geographical redeployment of capital. It also presupposes among other things a major transformation in the methods of production and in the mode of use of the means of collective consumption, as well as a reorganisation of the sphere of consumption and a reconstruction of the relations between department I and department 2. Any change in the methods of production and in the modes of provision and use of collective services, or indeed in other aspects of the regulation of capitalism, would of course lead to a profound reshaping of the geographical environment. But whether a transformation of the foundations of the regime of intensive accumulation which safeguards the reproduction of the wage relation and which respects the law of accumulation is possible is, at the moment, an open question.[6]

Notes and References

Part I Historical Materialism and Geography

Introduction: Towards a Materialist Conception of Geography

1. Its object of study is similar to that of studies like W. Smith, *An Historical Introduction to the Economic Geography of Great Britain* (London: G. Bell, 1968); H. C. Darby (ed.), *A New Historical Geography of England* (Cambridge: Cambridge University Press, 1973); and R. A. Dodgshon and R. A. Butlin (eds), *An Historical Geography of England and Wales* (London: Academic Press, 1978).
2. In addition to the work of Marx and Engels we are thinking of studies like M. Dobb, *Studies in the Development of Capitalism*, rev. edn (London: Routledge & Kegan Paul, 1963); R. Hilton (ed.), *The Transition from Feudalism to Capitalism* (London: New Left Books, 1976); F. Braudel, *Civilization and Capitalism, 15th–18th Century: Vol. I. The Structures of Everyday Life. The Limits of the Possible* (London: Collins, 1981); and E. Hobsbawm, *Industry and Empire* (Harmondsworth: Penguin, 1976).
3. The concepts we shall be using are developed in particular in M. Aglietta, *A Theory of Capitalist Regulation* (London: New Left Books, 1979).
4. A. J. Fielding, 'What Geographers Ought to Do: the Relation between Thought and Action on the Life and Work of P. A. Kropotkin', *University of Sussex Research Papers in Geography*, no. 1 (1980); M. M. Breitbart, 'Peter Kropotkin, the Anarchist Geographer', in D. R. Stoddart (ed.), *Geography, Ideology and Social Concern* (Oxford: Basil Blackwell, 1981) pp. 134–53; and G. S. Dunbar, 'Elisee Reclus, an Anarchist in Geography', in Stoddart (ed.), *Geography, Ideology and Social Concern*, pp. 154–64.

1. The Object of Geographical Analysis

1. J. A. May, *Kant's Concept of Geography and its Relation to Recent Geographical Thought* (Toronto: University of Toronto Press, 1970) pp. 21–2 and 52–3.

2. B. Russell, *History of Western Philosophy*, 2nd edn (London: George Allen & Unwin, 1961) p. 525.
3. D. H. Ruben, *Marxism and Materialism: A Study in Marxist Theory of Knowledge* (Brighton: Harvester Press, 1977).
4. J. M. Blaut, 'Space and Process', *Professional Geographer*, vol. XIII, no. 4 (July 1961) pp. 1–7.
5. Cited in May, *Kant's Concept of Geography*, pp. 256, 261 and 259.
6. E. A. Wrigley, 'Changes in the Philosophy of Geography', in R. J. Chorley and P. Haggett (eds), *Frontiers in Geographical Teaching*, 2nd edn (London: Methuen, 1970) pp. 3–20.
7. P. Q. Hirst, *Social Evolution and Sociological Categories* (London: George Allen & Unwin, 1976).
8. D. R. Stoddart, 'Darwin's Impact on Geography', *Annals of the Association of American Geographers*, vol. 56, no. 3 (December 1966) pp. 683–98.
9. Ibid.
10. V. Gerratana, 'Marx and Darwin', *New Left Review*, no. 82 (November–December 1973) pp. 60–82; and R. Williams, *Problems in Materialism and Culture* (London: New Left Books, 1980) pp. 86–102.
11. R. Hartshorne, 'The Nature of Geography. A Critical Survey of Current Thought in the Light of the Past', *Annals of the Association of American Geographers*, vol. XXIX, no. 3 (September 1939) pp. 171–412 and vol. XXIX, no. 4 (December 1939) pp. 413–658, pp. 239–40.
12. K. A. Wittfogel, 'Geopolitik, Geographischer Materialismus und Marxismus', *Unter dem Banner des Marxismus*, vol. III, no. 3 (1929) pp. 17–51 and vol. III, no. 4 (1929) pp. 485–500.
13. J. M. Blaut, 'Object and Relationship', *Professional Geographer*, vol. XIV, no. 6 (November 1962) pp. 1–7.
14. P. Vidal de la Blache, 'Les Genres de Vie dans la Géographie Humaine', *Annales de Géographie*, vol. 20 (1911) pp. 193–212; and *Principles of Human Geography*, ed. E. de Martonne, trans. M. Todd Bingham (London: Constable, 1926).
15. R. E. Dickenson, cited in Wrigley, 'Changes in the Philosophy of Geography', p. 120.
16. Hartshorne, 'The Nature of Geography', p. 4
17. Ibid, p. 372.
18. R. Hartshorne, *Perspective on the Nature of Geography* (Chicago: Rand McNally, for the Association of American Geographers, 1959) pp. 19–53.
19. A. Hettner, cited in Hartshorne, *Perspective on the Nature of Geography*, p. 13.
20. A. Cholley, cited in Hartshorne, ibid. p. 18.

21. Hartshorne, ibid, p. 21.
22. Ibid, p. 182.
23. Ibid, p. 182.
24. Blaut, 'Object and Relationship', p. 4.
25. D. Gregory, *Ideology, Science and Human Geography* (London: Hutchinson, 1978) pp. 29–32; and R. A. Sayer, 'Epistemology and Conceptions of People and Nature in Geography', *Geoforum*, vol. 10, no. 1 (1979) pp. 19–44.
26. F. K. Schaefer, 'Exceptionalism in Geography: A Methodological Examination', *Annals of the Association of American Geographers*, vol. XLIII, no. 3 (September 1953) pp. 226–49; and R. J. Johnston, *Geography and Geographers: Anglo-American Human Geography Since 1945* (London: Edward Arnold, 1979).
27. M. Ball, 'A Critique of Urban Economics', *International Journal of Urban and Regional Research*, vol. 3, no. 3 (September 1979) pp. 309–32.
28. Hartshorne, *Perspective on the Nature of Geography*, pp. 30–2 and p. 4.
29. B. Ohlin, *Interregional and International Trade*, rev. edn (Cambridge, Mass.: Harvard University Press, 1967).
30. K. Marx, *Grundrisse, Foundations of the Critique of Political Economy* (Harmondsworth: Penguin, 1973) p. 83.
31. It should be emphasised that the possibility of levelling this criticism at contemporary location theory as a whole stems from the fact that some important early developments have been reconceptualised along neo-classical lines. The original contribution of von Thünen dates from the second quarter of the nineteenth century and must accordingly be situated in the context of classical political economy, while the work of Weber was embedded in a historical conception of the overall process of economic reproduction. The ideas of Weber are situated in their social and intellectual context in D. Gregory, 'Alfred Weber and Location Theory', in D. R. Stoddart (ed.), *Geography, Ideology and Social Concern* (Oxford: Basil Blackwell, 1981) pp. 165–85.
32. K. Bassett and J. Short, *Housing and Residential Structure, Alternative Approaches* (London: Routledge & Kegan Paul, 1980) pp. 9–13; and M. Castells, *The Urban Question: A Marxist Approach* (London: Edward Arnold, 1977) pp. 75–85, 96–112 and 115–24.
33. C. Pickvance, 'On a Materialist Critique of Urban Sociology', *Sociological Review*, vol. 22, no. 2, new series (May 1974) pp. 203–20.
34. Blaut, 'Space and Process', p. 4.
35. L. Althusser and E. Balibar, *Reading 'Capital'* (London: New Left Books, 1970) pp. 91–118.

36. F. Lamarche, 'Property Development and the Economic Foundations of the Urban Question' in C. Pickvance (ed.), *Urban Sociology, Critical Essays* (London: Tavistock Publications, 1976) pp. 85–118, pp. 101–3.
37. Cited in Blaut, 'Space and Process', pp. 2–3.
38. J. Brunhes, *La Géographie Humaine*, 3rd edn, 2 vols (Paris: Alian, 1925); and J. Brunhes, *Human Geography*, abridged edn by M. Jean-Brunhes Delamarre and P. Deffontaines (London: Harrap, 1952.
39. R. Williams, *The Country and the City* (St Albans: Paladin, 1975) pp. 12–13.
40. Blaut, 'Space and Process', pp. 2–3.

2.   The Question of Method

1. In our account of empiricism we have drawn in particular upon materials presented in a course of lectures given by R. Edgley at the University of Sussex in 1974, entitled Concepts, Methods and Values in the Social Sciences.
2. K Popper, *The Logic of Scientific Discovery* (London: Hutchinson, 1959; K. Popper, *Conjectures and Refutations: The Growth of Scientific Knowledge* (London: Routledge & Kegan Paul, 1963); and K. Popper, *Objective Knowledge* (Oxford: Clarendon, 1972).
3. T. S. Kuhn, *The Structure of Scientific Revolutions*, 2nd edn (Chicago: University of Chicago Press, 1970) and 'Logic of Discovery or Psychology of Research', in I. Lakatos and A. Musgrave (eds), *Criticism and the Growth of Knowledge* (London: Cambridge University Press, 1970) pp. 1–23, p. 22.
4. P. Feyerabend, *Against Method* (London: New Left Books, 1975).
5. K. Popper, *The Poverty of Historicism*, 2nd edn (London: Routledge & Kegan Paul, 1961) pp. 143–7.
6. H. Marcuse, *Studies in Critical Philosophy* (London: New Left Books, 1972) pp. 191–208.
7. P. Anderson, *Considerations on Western Marxism* (London: New Left Books, 1976).
8. L. Colletti, *Marxism and Hegel* (London: New Left Books, 1973) p. 119.
9. Ibid, p. 119.
10. Ibid, p. 204.
11. G. Myrdal, cited in L. Colletti, *From Rousseau to Lenin: Studies in Ideology and Society* (London: New Left Books, 1972) p. 75.
12. Colletti, ibid, pp. 75–6; and Colletti, *Marxism and Hegel*, pp. 204–5.
13. L. Colletti, 'Introduction', in K. Marx, *Early Writings* (Harmondsworth: Penguin Books, 1978) pp. 7–56, pp. 18–22.

14. Ibid, pp. 28–46.
15. Ibid, pp. 27–8.
16. Dobb, cited in ibid, pp. 25–6.
17. M. Dobb, *Political Economy and Capitalism: Some Essays in Economic Tradition*, 2nd rev. edn (London: Routledge & Kegan Paul, 1940) pp. 127–33; and M. Dobb, *Theories of Value and Distribution since Adam Smith* (London: Cambridge University Press, 1973) pp. 25–8.
18. M. Aglietta, *A Theory of Capitalist Regulation* (London: New Left Books, 1979) pp. 9–17.
19. K. Marx, *Grundrisse: Foundations of the Critique of Political Economy* (Harmondsworth: Penguin, 1973) pp. 100–02.
20. Colletti, *Marxism and Hegel*, pp. 126–8.
21. Ibid, pp. 128–30.
22. A. J. Ayer, *Language, Truth and Logic*, 2nd edn (London: Gollancz, 1946); and D. Hume, *Enquiries Concerning the Human Understanding and Concerning the Principles of Morals*, ed. L. A. Selby-Bigge, 2nd edn (Oxford: Oxford University Press, 1962).
23. K. Marx, cited in G. della Volpe, *Rousseau and Marx and Other Writings* (London: Lawrence & Wishart, 1978) p. 199.
24. Colletti, *From Rousseau to Lenin*, pp. 72–6.

3. The Concept of Nature

1. S. Timpanaro, *On Materialism* (London: New Left Books, 1975) pp. 13–18 and 29–54.
2. Ibid, pp. 13–18 and 29–54.
3. K. Marx and F. Engels, 'The German Ideology', in K. Marx and F. Engels, *Collected Works*, vol. 5 (London: Lawrence & Wishart, 1976) p. 31.
4. P. Anderson, *Lineages of the Absolutist State* (London: New Left Books, 1974).
5. K. Marx, *Grundrisse: Foundations of the Critique of Political Economy* (Harmondsworth: Penguin, 1973) p. 389.
6. A. Schmidt, *The Concept of Nature in Marx* (London: New Left Books, 1971) p. 29.
7. Ibid, p. 63.
8. V. Gerratana, 'Marx and Darwin', *New Left Review*, no. 82 (November–December 1973) pp. 60–82, p. 64.
9. L. Colletti, *Marxism and Hegel* (London: New Left Books, 1963) p. 204.
10. K. Marx, *Capital, A Critique of Political Economy*, vol. I (Harmondsworth: Penguin, 1976) p. 275.

11. Marx and Engels, 'The German Ideology', pp. 41–3.
12. Marx, *Capital*, vol. I, p. 283.
13. Marx, *Grundrisse*, pp. 87, 83, and 85.
14. L. Colletti, *From Rousseau to Lenin. Studies in Ideology and Society* (London: New Left Books, 1972) pp. 66–7.
15. Colletti, *Marxism and Hegel*, pp. 227–30; and Colletti, *From Rousseau to Lenin*, pp. 67–8.
16. Marx, *Capital*, vol. I, p. 283.
17. Ibid, p. 284.
18. Ibid, p. 285.
19. Ibid, pp. 285–7.
20. Ibid, p. 270.
21. K. Marx, *The First International and After* (Harmondsworth: Penguin, 1974) p. 341.
22. Marx, *Capital*, vol. I, p. 282
23. Ibid, pp. 133–4.
24. Ibid, pp. 646–51; and Schmidt, *The Concept of Nature in Marx*, pp. 90–1.
25. Schmidt, *The Concept of Nature in Marx*, p. 66.
26. Ibid.
27. Ibid, pp. 80 and 76–93.
28. Marx, *Capital*, vol. I, p. 290.
29. Colletti, *Marxism and Hegel*, pp. 229–30.
30. Marx and Engels, 'The German Ideology', p. 32 and pp. 41–3.
31. Marx, *Capital*, vol. I, p. 283.
32. Colletti, *Marxism and Hegel*, pp. 226–8.
33. L. Colletti, 'A Political and Philosophical Interview', *New Left Review*, no. 86 (July–August 1974) pp. 3–28, p. 12.
34. K Marx, *Wage Labour and Capital* (Moscow: Progress Publishers, 1952) p. 28
35. Marx, *Grundrisse*, p. 87.
36. G. A. Cohen, *Karl Marx's Theory of History: A Defence* (Oxford: Clarendon Press, 1978) pp. 88–90.
37. Schmidt, *The Concept of Nature in Marx*, p. 98.
38. R. L. Meek, *Marx and Engels on Malthus* (London: Lawrence & Wishart, 1953) pp. 23–7.
39. Ibid, p. 23.
40. Marx, *Capital*, vol. I, pp. 762–94.
41. Ibid, pp. 854–70; and T. E. Cliffe Leslie, 'Political Economy and Emigration', reprinted in O. MacDonagh (ed.), *Emigration in the Victorian Age. Debates on the Issue from 19th Century Critical Journals* (Westmead: Gregg International, 1973).
42. H. M. Enzensburger, 'A Critique of Political Ecology', *New Left Review*, no. 84 (March–April 1974) pp. 3–31, pp 3–4.
43. Ibid.

4. The Concept of Space

1. P. Haggett, *Locational Analysis in Human Geography* (London: Edward Arnold, 1965); and P. Haggett, A. Cliff and A. Frey, *Locational Analysis in Human Geography*, 2nd edn (London: Edward Arnold, 1977).
2. M. Castells, *The Urban Question: A Marxist Approach* (London: Edward Arnold, 1977) pp. 115 and 142.
3. M. Godelier, 'Infrastructures, Societies and History', *New Left Review*, no. 112 (November–December 1978) pp. 84–96, pp. 90–3.
4. Ibid, pp. 85–7 and 92.
5. M. Godelier, 'L'Appropriation de la Nature. Territoire et Propriété dans quelques Sociétés Précapitalistes', *La Pensée*, no. 198 (March–April 1978) pp. 7–50, p. 16.
6. J. Lojkine, 'Stratégies des Grandes Entreprises, Politiques Urbains et Mouvements Sociaux Urbains', *Sociologie du Travail*, vol. 17, no. 1 (January–March 1975) pp. 18–40, p. 21.
7. K. Marx, *Capital: A Critique of Political Economy*, vol. III (London: Lawrence & Wishart, 1974) p. 781.
8. J. Lojkine, 'Contribution to a Marxist Theory of Capitalist Urbanisation', in C. G. Pickvance (ed.), *Urban Sociology, Critical Essays* (London: Tavistock Publications, 1976) pp. 99–146, p. 139; and Lojkine, 'Stratégies', p. 21.
9. Godelier, 'L'Appropriation de la Nature', pp. 11–19.
10. K. Marx, *Grundrisse. Foundations of the Critique of Political Economy* (Harmondsworth: Penguin, 1973) pp. 88–100.
11. A. Whitehead, ' "I'm hungry mum": the Politics of Family Budgeting', in K. Young, C. Wolkowitz and R. McCullagh (eds), *Of Marriage and the Market. Women's Subordination in International Perspective* (London: CSE Books, 1981) pp. 88–111.
12. D. Läpple and P. van Hoogstraten, 'Remarks on the Spatial Structure of Capitalist Development: the Case of the Netherlands', in J. Carney, R. Hudson and J. Lewis (eds), *Regions in Crisis. New Perspectives in European Regional Theory* (London: Croom Helm, 1980) pp 117–66.
13. Castells, *The Urban Question*, pp. 125–7.
14. The question of the relative weight of human action and of 'structural necessity' in determining the course of history is discussed in L. Althusser and E. Balibar, *Reading 'Capital'* (London: New Left Books, 1970); L. Althusser, *Politics and History. Montesquieu, Rousseau, Hegel and Marx* (London: New Left Books, 1972); E. P. Thompson, *The Poverty of Theory and Other Essays* (London: Merlin Press, 1978); and P. Anderson, *Arguments within English Marxism* (London: New Left Books, 1980) pp. 16–58. See also D.

Gregory, 'Human Agency and Human Geography', *Transactions and Papers of the Institute of British Geographers*, vol. 6 (1981) pp. 1–18.

5.   Modes of Production and the Structure of the Space-Economy

1. P. Dockès, *L'Espace dans la Pensée Economique du XVIème au XVIIème Siècle* (Paris: Flammarion, 1969) pp. 427–8.
2. A. J. Scott, *Land and Land Rent: An Interpretive Review of the French Literature* (Louvain–la Neuve: SPUR, Université Catholique de Louvain, 1975) p. 6.
3. J. Scheibling, 'Débates et Combats sur la Crise de la Géographie', *La Pensée*, no. 194 (July–August 1977) pp. 41–56, p. 56.
4. D. Harvey, *Social Justice and the City* (London: Edward Arnold, 1973). But see his subsequent comments in D. Harvey, *The Limits to Capital* (Oxford: Basil Blackwell, 1982).
5. K. Marx and F. Engels, 'The German Ideology', in K. Marx and F. Engels, *Collected Works*, vol. 5 (London: Lawrence & Wishart, 1976) pp. 32–5 and 64–74.
6. K. Marx, *Grundrisse. Foundations of the Critique of Political Economy* (Harmondsworth: Penguin, 1973) pp. 417–514.
7. Marx and Engels, 'The German Ideology', p. 33.
8. Marx, *Grundrisse*, p. 479.
9. Marx and Engels, 'The German Ideology', pp. 33–45 and 64–74.

Part II   The Geography of the Transition from Feudalism to Capitalism

Introduction: Modes of Production and Spatial Development

1. G. Bois, *Crise du Féodalisme. Economie Rurale et Démographie en Normandie Orientale du Début du 14ème Siècle au Milieu du 16ème Siècle* (Paris: Presses de la Fondation des Sciences Politiques, 1976) pp. 18–19.
2. In the case of sociology, which has a similar theoretical goal, it was pointed out by Weber that 'sociological analysis both abstracts from reality and at the same time helps us to understand it' and, consequently, that 'the abstract character of sociology is responsible for the fact that compared with actual historical reality they

[i.e. sociological concepts] are relatively lacking in fullness of concrete content': M. Weber, *The Theory of Social and Economic Organisation* (New York: Free Press, 1964) pp. 109–12.

6. The Restructuring of Agricultural Space in the Transition from Feudalism to Capitalism

1. K. Marx and F. Engels, 'The German Ideology', in K. Marx and F. Engels, *Collected Works*, vol. 5 (London: Lawrence & Wishart, 1976) p. 85; and P. Anderson, *Passages from Antiquity to Feudalism* (London: New Left Books, 1974) pp. 18–19 and 108–9.
2. Anderson, *Passages from Antiquity to Feudalism*, pp. 154–72.
3. W. Kula, *An Economic Theory of the Feudal System. Towards a Model of the Polish Economy, 1500–1800* (London: New Left Books, 1976) p. 9.
4. R. H. Hilton, *Bond Men Made Free. Medieval Peasant Movements and the Rising of 1381* (London: Methuen, 1977) pp. 44–6.
5. In this chapter, the word 'peasant' is used to refer to a rural cultivator or agricultural producer who holds or owns land that is worked predominantly by family labour, and whose output is to a significant extent destined for autoconsumption. In communities in which a peasantry exists, a part of what is produced is transferred to dominant groups in the form of *corvée*, rent, interest, unfavourable terms of trade, and so on. In most cases a landless or nearly landless element, which finds work on larger holdings, is also found especially in areas where non-partible inheritance is practised or where economic processes of social differentiation have been operating for some time. We shall attempt to avoid the term 'landless peasant' by referring to individuals relying predominantly on wage-labour as agricultural labourers.
6. Hilton, *Bond Men Made Free*, pp. 55–61; and R. H. Hilton, *The Decline of Serfdom in Medieval England* (London: Macmillan, 1969) pp. 12–17.
7. J. Banaji, 'Modes of Production in a Materialist Conception of History', *Capital and Class*, no. 3 (Autumn 1977) pp. 1–44, p. 19.
8. Ibid, pp. 18–19.
9. Bois, *Crise du Féodalisme*, pp. 352–6.
10. Kula, *An Economic Theory of the Feudal System*, p. 9.
11. G. Duby, *Rural Economy and Country Life in the Medieval West* (London: Edward Arnold, 1968) pp. 31–6.
12. P. Sweezy, 'A Critique' and 'A Rejoinder' in R. Hilton (ed.), *The Transition from Feudalism to Capitalism* (London: New Left Books, 1976) pp. 33–56, 102–8; and H. Pirenne, *Economic and Social*

History of Medieval Europe, trans. I. E. Clegg (London: Routledge & Kegan Paul, 1936), and *Medieval Cities: Their Origins and the Revival of Trade*, trans. F. D. Halsey (Princeton, N.J.: Princeton University Press, 1925).

13. Banaji, 'Modes of Production'; Kula, *An Economic Theory of the Feudal System*; Bois, *Crise du Féodalisme*; G. Bois, 'Against the Neo-Malthusian Orthodoxy', *Past and Present*, no. 79 (May 1978) pp. 60—9; and R. Hilton 'A Crisis of Feudalism', *Past and Present*, no. 80 (August 1978) pp. 3—19.

14. G. Duby, *The Early Growth of the European Economy. Warriors and Peasants from the Seventh to the Twelfth Century* (London: Weidenfeld & Nicolson, 1974).

15. Banaji, 'Modes of Production', p. 20.

16. Bois, *Crise du Féodalisme*, pp. 354—5 and 364—5; and Bois, 'Against the Neo-Malthusian Orthodoxy', pp. 63—4.

17. Bois, *Crise du Féodalisme*, pp. 356—60; and J. Robinson and J. Eatwell, *An Introduction to Modern Economics* (London: McGraw-Hill, 1973) pp. 61—88.

18. Bois, *Crise du Féodalisme*, pp. 343—6; and Bois, 'Against the Neo-Malthusian Orthodoxy', p. 64.

19. Duby, *Rural Economy and Country Life in the Medieval West*, pp. 103—4.

20. Ibid, pp. 71—93.

21. Ibid, pp. 93—9 and 157—63.

22. Ibid, pp. 120—2; and R. A. Dodgshon, 'The Early Middle Ages 1066—1350', in R. A. Dodgshon and R. A. Butlin (eds), *An Historical Geography of England and Wales* (London: Academic Press, 1978) ch. 4, pp. 87—8 and 83—4.

23. Hilton, *The Decline of Serfdom in Medieval England*, pp. 12—17 and 24.

24. Hilton, 'A Crisis of Feudalism', pp. 3—19.

25. M. M. Postan, *The Medieval Economy and Society. An Economic History of Britain in the Middle Ages* (Harmondsworth: Penguin, 1975) pp. 33—5 and 40—4.

26. Duby, *Rural Economy and Country Life in the Medieval West*, pp. 301—2.

27. A. R. H. Baker, 'Changes in the Later Middle Ages', in H. C. Darby (ed.), *A New Historical Geography of England Before 1600* (Cambridge: Cambridge University Press, 1976) ch. 5, pp. 207—13.

28. Hilton, *The Decline of Serfdom in Medieval England*, pp. 44—51.

29. Ibid, pp. 29—32.

30. Hilton, 'A Crisis of Feudalism', pp. 15—16.

31. Bois, *Crise du Féodalisme*, pp. 346—7.

32. Bois, 'Against the Neo-Malthusian Orthodoxy', pp. 63—7.

33. R. Brenner, 'Agrarian Class Structure and Economic Development in Pre-Industrial Europe', *Past and Present*, no. 70 (February 1976) pp. 30–75, pp. 68–73 and 63.

34. P.- P. Rey, *Les Alliances de Classes* (Paris: François Maspero, 1973) pp. 69–70 and 156–65; M. Gervais, C. Servolin and J. Weil, *Une France sans Paysans* (Paris: Editions du Seuil, 1965); A. Lipietz, *Le Capital et Son Espace* (Paris: François Maspero, 1977) pp. 28–53; and M. Dunford, 'Capital Accumulation and Regional Development in France', *Geoforum*, vol. 10, no. 1 (1979) pp. 81–108, pp. 87–91.

35. Bois, 'Against the Neo-Malthusian Orthodoxy', pp. 65–6.

36. Hilton, 'A Crisis of Feudalism', pp. 17–18.

37. Bois, 'Against the Neo-Malthusian Orthodoxy', pp. 64–7.

38. Brenner, 'Agrarian Class Structure and Economic Development in Pre-Industrial Europe', p. 63.

39. J. Saville, 'Primitive Accumulation and Early Industrialisation in Britain', in R. Miliband and J. Saville (eds), *The Socialist Register 1969* (London: Merlin Press, 1969) pp. 247–71, pp. 250–6.

40. Ibid, p. 261.

41. C. Hill, *Reformation to Industrial Revolution* (Harmondsworth: Penguin, 1969) p. 147.

42. Saville, 'Primitive Accumulation', pp. 261–4.

43. Ibid, pp. 256–8.

44. Baker, 'Changes in the Later Middle Ages', pp. 210–13.

45. Brenner, 'Agrarian Class Structure and Economic Development in Pre-Industrial Europe', pp. 61–5.

46. Ibid, pp. 65–6. For a discussion of the distinguishing characteristics, and of the causes, of the crises of shortage characteristic of the agrarian societies of medieval and early modern Europe see P. Kriedte, H. Medick and J. Schlumbohm, *Industrialisation before Industrialisation. Rural Industry and the Genesis of Capitalism* (Cambridge: Cambridge University Press, and Paris: Editions de la Maison des Sciences de l'Homme, 1981) pp. 31–2 and 117–25.

47. W. G. Hoskins, *The Making of the English Landscape* (Harmondsworth: Penguin, 1970) pp. 177–210.

48. K. Marx, *Capital. A Critique of Political Economy*, vol. I (Harmondsworth: Penguin, 1976) pp. 873–940.

49. H. Medick, 'The Proto-Industrial Family Economy: the Structural Functions of Household and Family during the Transition from Peasant Society to Industrial Capitalism', *Social History*, no. 3 (October 1976) pp. 291–315, pp. 304–6; and Kriedte, Medick and Schlumbohm, *Industrialisation before Industrialisation*, in which Medick's arguments are developed at greater length.

50. A. Thun, cited in Medick, 'The Proto-Industrial Family Economy', p. 306.
51. For a discussion of the effect of the English agricultural revolution on the demand for agricultural labour see P. J. Timmer, 'The Turnip, the New Husbandry, and the English Agricultural Revolution', *Quarterly Journal of Economics*, vol. LXXXIII, no. 3 (August 1969) pp. 375–95.
52. I. Pinchbeck, *Women Workers and the Industrial Revolution, 1750–1850* (London: Frank Cass, 1977) pp. 86–7.
53. Saville, 'Primitive Accumulation', pp. 261–2.
54. Brenner, 'Agrarian Class Structure and Economic Development in Pre-Industrial Europe', pp. 66–8.

7. Town and Country in the Transition from Feudalism to Capitalism

1. J. Merrington, 'Town and Country in the Transition to Capitalism', in R. Hilton (ed.), *The Transition from Feudalism to Capitalism* (London: New Left Books, 1976) pp. 170–95, p. 171.
2. R. Hilton, 'Introduction', in Hilton (ed.), *The Transition from Feudalism to Capitalism*, pp. 9–30, p. 20.
3. F. Braudel, *Capitalism and Material Life* (London: Fontana/Collins, 1974) p. 5.
4. Hilton, 'Introduction', pp. 20–1.
5. J. C. Russell, 'Population in Europe, 500–1500', in C. M. Cipolla (ed.), *The Fontana Economic History of Europe. The Middle Ages* (Glasgow: Fontana, 1972) ch. 1, pp. 34–5.
6. P. Anderson, *Passages from Antiquity to Feudalism* (London: New Left Books, 1974) pp. 165–7.
7. Braudel, *Capitalism and Material Life*, p. 93.
8. R. A. Dodgshon, 'The Early Middle Ages, 1066–1350', in R. A. Dodgshon and R. A. Butlin (eds), *An Historical Geography of England and Wales* (London: Academic Press, 1978) ch. 4, pp. 105–10.
9. R. Hilton, 'Towns in English Feudal Society', *Review*, vol. III, no. I (Summer 1979) pp. 3–20.
10. Merrington, 'Town and Country', p. 171 and pp. 175–95.
11. K. Marx, *Grundrisse. Foundations of the Critique of Political Economy* (Harmondsworth: Penguin, 1973) pp. 498–500, 502 and 512.
12. R. Hilton, *The Decline of Serfdom in Medieval England*, (London: Macmillan, 1969) p. 13.
13. Marx, cited in Merrington, 'Town and Country', p. 117.

14. Merrington, 'Town and Country', pp. 176–7.
15. Hilton, 'Towns in English Feudal Society', pp. 12–13.
16. Merrington, 'Town and Country', pp. 183–5.
17. M. M. Postan, *The Medieval Economy and Society. An Economic History of Britain in the Middle Ages* (Harmondsworth: Penguin, 1979) pp. 239.
18. A. B. Hibbert, 'The Economic Policies of Towns', in M. M. Postan, E. E. Rich, and E. Miller (eds), *The Cambridge Economic History of Europe, Vol. III Economic Organisations and Policies in the Middle Ages* (London: Cambridge University Press, 1965) pp. 157–229, pp. 162–71.
19. Merrington, 'Town and Country', p. 181.
20. Postan, *The Medieval Economy and Society*, pp. 245–9.
21. Hibbert, 'The Economic Policies of the Towns', pp. 197–8.
22. Marx, cited in Merrington, 'Town and Country', p. 182.
23. J. de Vries, 'Patterns of Urbanisation in Pre-Industrial Europe, 1500–1800', in H. Schma! (ed.), *Patterns of European Urbanisation since 1500* (London: Croom Helm, 1981) pp. 79–109, p. 96.
24. de Vries, 'Patterns of Urbanisation', pp. 81–6; R. Mols, 'Population in Europe, 1500–1700', in C. M. Cipolla (ed.), *The Fontana Economic History of Europe. The Sixteenth and Seventeenth Centuries* (Glasgow: Fontana, 1974) ch. 1, pp. 38–44; and R. A. Butlin, 'The Late Middle Ages, c. 1350–1500', in R. A. Dodgshon and R. A. Butlin (eds), *An Historical Geography of England and Wales*, ch. 5, pp. 141–3.
25. F. Braudel, *The Mediterranean and the Mediterranean World in the Age of Philip II*, 2nd edn, 2 vols (Glasgow: Collins, 1972) vol. II, pp. 326–8.
26. de Vries, 'Patterns of Urbanisation', pp. 98–102.
27. Ibid, pp. 98–9.
28. Ibid, pp. 102–4.
29. P. Anderson, *Lineages of the Absolutist State* (London: New Left Books, 1974) pp. 15–24.
30. J. de Vries, *Economy of Europe in an Age of Crisis, 1600–1750* (Cambridge: Cambridge University Press, 1976) pp. 149–52.
31. E. A. Wrigley, 'A Simple Model of London's Importance in Changing English Society and Economy, 1650–1750', *Past and Present*, no. 37 (July 1967) pp. 44–70, pp. 44–9.
32. Braudel, *Capitalism and Material Life*, pp. 414 and 439.
33. R. Williams, *The Country and the City* (St Albans: Paladin, 1975) pp. 181–2.
34. F. Braudel, *Afterthoughts on Material Civilisation and Capitalism* (Baltimore and London: Johns Hopkins Press, 1977) pp. 95–9.

35. Ibid, pp. 83–5.
36. I. Wallerstein, *The Modern World System. Capitalist Agriculture and the Origins of the European World Economy in the Sixteenth Century* (New York: Academic Press, 1974) pp. 38–52.
37. Braudel, *Afterthoughts on Material Civilisation and Capitalism*, pp. 86–7 and 98–9.
38. Ibid, pp. 85–6 and 87–9.
39. F. Braudel, 'A Model for the Analysis of the Economic Decline of Italy', *Review*, vol. II, no. 4 (Spring 1979) pp. 647–62, p. 655.
40. Merrington, 'Town and Country' p. 183.
41. Braudel, *Afterthoughts on Material Civilisation and Capitalism*, pp. 98–9.
42. Ibid, pp. 89–94.
43. Ibid, pp. 99–104.
44. G. Arrighi, *The Geometry of Imperialism* (London: New Left Books, 1978).
45. de Vries, *Economy of Europe in an Age of Crisis*, p. 152.
46. F. Walker, *The Bristol Region* (London: Thomas Nelson, 1972) pp. 190–4.
47. Marx, cited in Merrington, 'Town and Country', p. 177.
48. Braudel, *Afterthoughts on Material Civilisation and Capitalism*, pp. 79–110', and Merrington, 'Town and Country', pp. 183–7.
49. M. Dobb, *Studies in the Development of Capitalism*, rev. edn (London: Routledge & Kegan Paul, 1963) pp. 217–19.
50. Merrington, 'Town and Country', p. 187.
51. Ibid, pp. 189–91.

8. Industry in the Transition to Capitalism

1. In addition to a large body of writing on rural industry, the main works, on whose basis a model of proto-industrialisation has been developed, include F. F. Mendels, 'Proto-Industrialisation: the First Phase of the Industrialisation Process', *Journal of Economic History*, vol. XXXII, no. I (March 1972) pp. 241–61; H. Medick, 'The Proto-industrial Family Economy: the Structural Functions of Household and Family during the Transition from Peasant Society to Industrial Capitalism', *Social History*, no. 3 (October 1976) pp. 291–315, pp. 304–6; and P. Kriedte, H. Medick and J. Schlumbohm, *Industrialisation before Industrialisation. Rural Industry and the Genesis of Capitalism* (Cambridge: Cambridge University Press, and Paris: Editions de la Maison des Sciences de l'Homme, 1981). The spatial dimension of 'industrialisation before

industrialisation' is discussed, mainly in relation to the Italian case, in G. Garofoli, 'Decentramento Produttivo, Mercato del Lavoro e Localizzazione Industriale', *Archivio di Studi Urbani e Regionali*, New Series, no. 4 (1978) pp. 21–64, pp. 32–40.

2. J. Thirsk, 'Roots of Industrial England', in A. R. H. Baker and J. B. Harley (eds), *Man Made the Land* (Newton Abbot: David & Charles, 1973) pp. 93–108, pp. 106–8; Mendels, 'Proto-Industrialisation', p. 242; F. F. Mendels, 'Seasons and Regions in Agriculture and Industry during the Process of Industrialisation', in S. Pollard (ed.), *Region und Industrialisierung. Studien zur Rolle der Region in der Wirtschaftsgeschichte der letzten zwei Jahrhunderte* (Göttingen: Vandenhoeck & Ruprecht, 1980) pp. 177–95, pp. 177–87; F. F. Mendels, 'Les Temps de l'Industrie et les Temps de l'Agriculture. Logique d'une Analyse Régionale de la Proto-Industrialisation', *Revue du Nord*, vol. LXIII, no. 248 (January–March 1981) pp. 21–33, pp. 21–32; and P. Kriedte, 'The Origins, the Agrarian Context, and the Conditions in the World Market', in Kriedte, Medick and Schlumbohm, *Industrialisation before Industrialisation*, pp. 12–37, pp. 13–21.

3. Thirsk, 'Roots of Industrial England', pp. 94–106; Medick, 'The Proto-Industrial Family Economy', pp. 296–7; Mendels, 'Proto-Industrialisation', pp. 249–53; Mendels, 'Seasons and Regions', pp. 181–2; and Mendels, 'Les Temps de l'Industrie', pp. 26–7.

4. Kriedte, 'The Origins', pp. 23–4.

5. Medick, 'The Proto-Industrial Family Economy', p. 28.

6. J. Schlumbohm, 'Relations of Production–Productive Forces–Crises in Proto-Industrialisation', in Kriedte, Medick and Schlumbohm, *Industrialisation before Industrialisation*, pp. 94–125, pp. 98–107.

7. P. Hudson, 'Proto-Industrialisation: the Case of the West Riding', *History Workshop. A Journal of Socialist Historians*, no. 12 (Autumn 1981) pp. 34–61, pp. 38–45.

8. K. Marx, *Capital. A Critique of Political Economy*, vol. III (London: Lawrence & Wishart, 1974) pp. 334–5; M. Dobb, *Studies in the Development of Capitalism* (London: Routledge & Kegan Paul, 1963) p. 123; and K. Takahashi, 'A Contribution to the Discussion', in R. Hilton (ed.), *The Transition from Feudalism to Capitalism* (London: New Left Books, 1976) pp. 68–97, pp. 87–97.

9. Marx, *Capital*, vol. III, p. 287.

10. Dobb, *Studies in the Development of Capitalism*, p. 123.

11. Takahashi, 'A Contribution', pp. 88–90.

12. Dobb, *Studies in the Development of Capitalism*, pp. 123–4.

13. Marx, *Capital*, vol. III, p. 335.

14. Ibid, p. 336.
15. K. Marx, *Grundrisse. Foundations of the Critique of Political Economy* (Harmondsworth: Penguin, 1973) pp. 510–12.
16. Schlumbohm, 'Relations of Production', p. 107.
17. Ibid, p. 110.
18. Dobb, *Studies in the Development of Capitalism*, pp. 129–34.
19. Ibid, p. 134–38.
20. Schlumbohm, 'Relations of Production', pp. 105–7.
21. Ibid, pp. 111–17; and Dobb, *Studies in the Development of Capitalism*, pp. 144–5.
22. P. Kriedte, 'Proto-Industrialisation between Industrialisation and Deindustrialisation', in Kriedte, Medick and Schlumbohm, *Industrialisation before Industrialisation*, pp. 135–60, p. 142.
23. H. Medick and J. de Vries, cited in Hudson, 'The Case of the West Riding', pp. 144–5.
24. Marx, *Grundrisse*, pp. 510–11.
25. Schlumbohm, 'Relations of Production', p. 106.
26. Dobb, *Studies in the Development of Capitalism*, pp. 148–81; and Hudson, 'The Case of the West Riding'.
27. K. Marx, *Capital. A Critique of Political Economy*, vol. I (Harmondsworth: Penguin, 1976) pp. 1019–23 and 1025–34.
28. A theoretical and empirical analysis of the state is beyond the scope of this study. The relation between economics and politics is analysed in an interesting and pertinent way in some of the articles in J. Holloway and S. Picciotto (eds), *State and Capital. A Marxist Debate* (London: Edward Arnold, 1978); and in J. Hirsch, 'Remarques Théoriques sur l'Etat Bourgeois et sa Crise', in N. Poulantzas (ed.), *La Crise de l'Etat* (Paris: Presses Universitaires de France, 1976) pp. 103–29; while the question of the impact of different political and institutional arrangements on the development of proto-industry is discussed briefly in J. Schlumbohm, 'Excursus: the Political and Institutional Framework of Proto-Industrialisation', in Kriedte, Medick and Schlumbohm, *Industrialisation before Industrialisation*, pp. 126–34; and the nature of the English Revolution is examined in a materialist way in Dobb, *Studies in the Development of Capitalism*, pp. 161–76, and in C. Hill, *The Century of Revolution, 1603–1714*, 2nd edn (London: Thomas Nelson, 1980), pp. 94–164.
29. Dobb, *Studies in the Development of Capitalism*, pp. 161–74.
30. Ibid, pp. 174–6; Hill, *The Century of Revolution*, pp. 124–38; and on the agrarian aspects of the Civil War, Barrington Moore, Jr, *Social Origins of Dictatorship and Democracy. Lord and Peasant in the Making of the Modern World* (Harmondsworth: Penguin University Books, 1973) pp. 14–20.

31. Marx, cited in G. A. Cohen, *Karl Marx's Theory of History. A Defence* (Oxford: Clarendon Press, 1978) p. 160.
32. E. P. Thompson, *The Making of the English Working Class*, rev. edn (Harmondsworth: Penguin, 1968) p. 575.
33. Ibid, p. 617.
34. Ibid, pp. 515—16 and 578—9.
35. Ibid, p. 594.
36. E. J. Hobsbawm, 'The Machine Breakers', in *Labouring Men. Studies in the History of Labour* (London: Weidenfeld & Nicolson, 1964) pp. 5—22, p. 8.
37. Thompson, *The Making of the English Working Class*, pp. 603—4.
38. Ibid, p. 570.
39. Ibid, pp. 579—91, 602—3, 608 and 657.
40. Ibid, pp. 570—9 and 602.
41. Dobb, *Studies in the Development of Capitalism*, pp. 138—43.
42. J. de Vries, *Economy of Europe in an Age of Crisis, 1600—1750* (Cambridge: Cambridge University Press, 1976) p. 105.
43. Medick, 'The Proto-Industrial Family Economy', pp. 298—300.
44. Ibid, pp. 301—5.
45. Ibid, p. 299.
46. S. A. Marglin, 'What Do Bosses Do? The Origins and Functions of Hierarchy in Capitalist Production', in A. Gorz (ed.), *The Division of Labour. The Labour Process and Class Struggle in Modern Capitalism* (Brighton: The Harvester Press, 1976) pp. 13—54, p. 35.
47. P. Kriedte, 'Proto-Industrialisation between Industrialisation and Deindustrialisation', in Kriedte, Medick and Schlumbohm, *Industrialisation before Industrialisation*, p. 137.
48. Marx, *Capital*, vol. I, pp. 1023—25 and 1034—38.
49. Marglin, 'What Do Bosses Do?', pp. 28—32.
50. P. Deane, *The First Industrial Revolution* (Cambridge: Cambridge University Press, 1969) pp. 147—8.
51. S. Pollard, *The Genesis of Modern Management. A Study of the Industrial Revolution in Great Britain* (London: Edward Arnold, 1965) pp. 197—8.
52. Deane, *The First Industrial Revolution*, p. 149.
53. Mendels, 'Seasons and Regions', p. 190; Schlumbohm, 'Relations of Production', pp. 107—10; and Kriedte, 'Proto-Industrialisation', pp. 137—9.
54. Marx, *Capital*, vol. III, pp. 334—5; and Mendels, 'Proto-Industrialisation', pp. 246—7.
55. Marx, *Capital*, vol. I, pp. 588—99 and 695; and Kriedte, Medick Schlumbohm, *Industrialisation before Industrialisation*, pp. 1—2.
56. In this new phase, in which capital was advanced in the sphere of production and was increasingly tied up in instruments of produc-

tion and machinery and in centralised manufacturing plants, and in which it could not respond as flexibly to economic fluctuations as in the past, an endogenous economic and specifically industrial cyclical movement and different types of crises were to appear as central characteristics of the process of economic reproduction: Mendels, 'Proto-Industrialisation', pp. 255–7; and Schlumbohm, 'Relations of Production', pp. 117–25.

57. D. C. Coleman, *The Economy of England, 1450–1750* (London: Oxford University Press, 1977) pp. 9–10.

58. A Shaikh, 'Foreign Trade and the Law of Value', part I, *Science and Society*, vol. XLIII, no. 3 (Fall 1979) pp. 281–302, and part II, *Science and Society*, vol. XLIV, no. I (Spring 1980) pp. 27–57; and A Shaikh, 'The Laws of International Exchange', in E. J. Nell (ed.), *Growth, Profits, and Property. Essays in the Revival of Political Economy* (Cambridge: Cambridge University Press, 1980) pp. 204–35.

59. G. Myrdal, *Economic Theory and Underdeveloped Regions* (London: Gerald Duckworth, 1957); and N. Kaldor, 'The Case for Regional Policies', *Scottish Journal of Political Economy*, vol. 17 (November 1970) pp. 337–48.

60. Mendels, 'Seasons and Regions', pp. 187–9; Mendels, 'Les Temps de l'Industrie', pp. 31–2; and Kriedte, 'Proto-Industrialisation', pp. 139–40 and 145–60.

61. R. A. Donkin, 'Changes in the Early Middle Ages', in H. C. Darby (ed.), *A New Historical Geography of England before 1600* (Cambridge: Cambridge University Press, 1976) ch. 3, pp. 112–14.

62. M. Postan, *The Medieval Economy and Society. An Economic History of Britain in the Middle Ages* (Harmondsworth: Penguin, 1975) pp. 213–21.

63. A. E. Musson, *The Growth of British Industry* (London: Batsford, 1978) pp. 44–5.

64. de Vries, *Economy of Europe in an Age of Crisis*, pp. 100–3.

65. R. G. Wilson, 'The Supremacy of the Yorkshire Cloth Industry in the Eighteenth Century', in N. B. Harte and K. G. Ponting (eds), *Textile History and Economic History. Essays in Honour of Miss J. de L. Mann* (Manchester: Manchester University Press, 1973) ch. 9, p. 214.

66. Musson, *The Growth of British Industry*, p. 86.

67. W. Smith, *An Historical Introduction to the Economic Geography of Great Britain* (London: G. Bell, 1968) p. 135.

68. Musson, *The Growth of the British Industry*, pp. 88–9.

69. Hudson, 'The Case of the West Riding', pp. 47–8.

70. Ibid, pp. 45–6 and 50–1.

71. Wilson, 'The Supremacy of the Yorkshire Cloth Industry', pp. 225–46.
72. D. Gregory, *Regional Transformation and Industrial Revolution: a Geography of the Yorkshire Woollen Industry* (London: Macmillan, 1982); Hudson, 'The Case of the West Riding', p. 48.
73. Hudson, ibid, p. 48.
74. D. Smith, 'The British Hosiery Industry at the Middle of the Nineteenth Century: an Historical Study in Economic Geography', in A. R. H. Baker, J. D. Hamshere and J. Langton (eds), *Geographical Interpretation of Historical Sources. Readings in Historical Geography* (Newton Abbot: David & Charles, 1970) pp. 359–76, p. 362. This study was originally published in the *Transactions and Papers of the Institute of British Geographers*, no. 32 (June 1963) pp. 125–42.
75. J. L. and B. Hammond, *The Skilled Labourer* (London: Longman, 1979) p. 187.
76. I. Pinchbeck, *Women Workers and the Industrial Revolution, 1750–1850* (London: Frank Case, 1977) pp. 226–30.
77. J. L. and B. Hammond, *The Skilled Labourer*, pp. 181–2.
78. D. Smith, 'The British Hosiery Industry', p. 363; and A. Friedman, *Industry and Labour. Class Struggle at Work and Monopoly Capitalism* (London: Macmillan, 1977) pp. 160–2.
79. Friedman, *Industry and Labour*, pp. 162–4.
80. D. Smith, 'The British Hosiery Industry', pp. 365–73.
81. Thompson, *The Making of the English Working Class*, pp. 580–8 and 602–3.
82. K. A. Wittfogel, cited in Medick, 'The Proto-Industrial Family Economy', p. 300.
83. Friedman, *Industry and Labour*, pp. 166–7.
84. J. T. Coppock, 'The Changing Face of England, 1850–circa 1900', in H. C. Darby (ed.), *A New Historical Geography of England after 1600* (Cambridge: Cambridge University Press, 1976) ch. 5, p. 343.
85. J. U. Nef, cited in Musson, *The Growth of British Industry*, pp. 31–2.
86. Musson, *The Growth of British Industry*, pp. 30–1.
87. W. Smith, *Economic Geography of Great Britain*, pp. 144–8.
88. J. U. Nef, cited in Musson, *The Growth of British Industry*, pp. 31–2.
89. Musson, *The Growth of British Industry*, pp. 36–8.
90. Ibid, pp. 38–9.
91. Dobb, *Studies in the Development of Capitalism*, pp. 242–50.
92. Musson, *The Growth of British Industry*, p. 39.
93. H. C. Darby, 'The Age of the Improver: 1600–1800', in H. C. Darby

(ed.), *A New Historical Geography of England after 1600*, ch. 1, pp. 62–3.

94. W. Smith, *Economic Geography of Great Britain*, pp. 104–8.
95. F. Walker, *The Bristol Region* (London: Thomas Nelson, 1972) pp. 176–8.
96. W. H. B. Court, cited in W. G. Hoskins, *The Making of the English Landscape* (Harmondsworth: Penguin, 1970) p. 212.
97. Musson, *The Growth of British Industry*, p. 108.

Part III   The Development of Industrial Capitalism and the Transformation of the Space-Economy

Introduction: the Rise of Industrial Capitalism in Britain

1. One example is the case of the monopoly given to the East India Company, which was undermined first by the protection given to British producers of cotton cloth in 1700, and subsequently by the opening of the Indian market to any British producer in 1813, i.e. and not just to the East India Company. E. J. Hobsbawm, *Industry and Empire* (Harmondsworth: Penguin, 1969) pp. 30–49.
2. T. Nairn, 'The House of Windsor', *New Left Review*, no. 127 (May–June, 1981) pp. 96–100, p. 99.
3. Hobsbawm, *Industry and Empire*, pp. 30–49.
4. E. Mandel, *Late Capitalism* (London: New Left Books, 1975) ch. 4.

9.   The Accumulation of Capital and the Regulation of the Capitalist Mode of Production

1. E. Mandel, *Late Capitalism* (London: New Left Books, 1975) pp. 108–46.
2. M. Aglietta, *A Theory of Capitalist Regulation. The US Experience* (London: New Left Books, 1979) p. 37.
3. K. Marx, *Capital. A Critique of Political Economy*, vol. I (Harmondsworth: Penguin, 1976) p. 125.
4. K. Marx, 'Letter to Kugelmann in Hanover, 11th July 1868', in K. Marx and F. Engels, *Selected Correspondence*, 2nd edn (Moscow: Progress Publishers, 1965) pp. 208–10.
5. Aglietta, *A Theory of Capitalist Regulation*, pp. 38–9.
6. L. Colletti, *From Rousseau to Lenin: Studies in Ideology and Society* (London: New Left Books, 1972) pp. 76–97. We do not plan to

discuss the question of the transformation of values into prices. A clear presentation of the problem can be found in A. Shaikh, 'Marx's Theory of Value and the "Transformation Problem"', in J. Schwartz (ed.), *The Subtle Anatomy of Capitalism* (Santa Monica, California: Goodyear, 1977) pp. 106—39; and in A. Shaikh, 'The Poverty of Algebra', in I. Steedman *et al.*, *The Value Controversy* (London: Verso Editions and New Left Books, 1981) pp. 266—300. The position we would want to maintain is the one held by Aglietta, *A Theory of Capitalist Regulation*, ch. 5, and elaborated in M. De Vroey, 'Value, Production, and Exchange', in Steedman *et al.*, *The Value Controversy*, pp. 173—201.

7. Colletti, *From Rousseau to Lenin*, pp. 82—6.

8. K. Marx, *Grundrisse. Foundations of the Critique of Political Economy* (Harmondsworth: Penguin, 1973) pp. 526—7.

9. Marx, *Capital*, vol. I., p. 293.

10. Ibid, pp. 257 and 252.

11. Several other forms of capital, each of which plays a distinctive and important role in the formation of the space-economy, can be identified, namely commercial and banking capital and what Lamarche has called property capital. See F. Lamarche, 'Property Development and the Economic Foundations of the Urban Question', in C. Pickvance (ed.), *Urban Sociology: Critical Essays* (London: Methuen, 1976) pp. 85—118; and K. Marx, *Capital. A Critique of Political Economy*, vol. III (London: Lawrence & Wishart, 1974) parts IV, V and VI.

12. Marx, *Capital*, vol. I, pp. 762—802.

13. C. Palloix, 'The Labour Process: from Fordism to Neo-Fordism', in Conference of Socialist Economists, *The Labour Process and Class Strategies* (London: Stage I, 1976) pp. 46—67, pp. 49—51; and Aglietta, *A Theory of Capitalist Regulation*, pp. 49—52.

14. Y. Maignien, cited in Palloix, 'The Labour Process', p. 48. Ideas about deskilling must be treated with circumspection, for a number of important countertendencies exist.

15. Aglietta, *A Theory of Capitalist Regulation*, pp. 68—72.

16. J. Laffont, D. Leborgne and A. Lipietz with the participation of R. Boyer, *Redéploiement Industriel et Espace Economique: une Etude Intersectorielle Comparative* (Paris: Centre d'Etudes Prospectives d'Economie Mathématique Appliquées à la Planification, 1980) pp. 6—16.

17. Laffont *et al.*, *Redéploiement Industriel*, pp. 12—13.

18. C. Palloix, *L'Economie Mondiale Capitaliste et les Firmes Multinationales*, 2 vols (Paris: François Maspero, 1975); C. Palloix, *L'Internationalisation du Capital. Eléments Critiques* (Paris:

François Maspero, 1975); and D. C. Perrons, 'The Role of Ireland in the New International Division of Labour. A Proposed Framework for Regional Analysis', *Regional Studies*, vol. 15, no. 2 (April 1981) pp. 81–100.
19. Colletti, *From Rousseau to Lenin*, p. 67.

10. The Transition from Manufacture to Machinofacture, 1780–1850

1. S. Pollard, *Peaceful Conquest. The Industrialisation of Europe, 1760–1970* (New York: Oxford University Press, 1981) pp. 14–26.
2. M. Geddes, 'Uneven Development and the Scottish Highlands', *University of Sussex Working Papers in Urban and Regional Studies*, no. 17 (December 1979); and H. C. Prince, 'England circa 1850', in H. C. Darby (ed.), *A New Historical Geography of England after 1600* (Cambridge: Cambridge University Press, 1976) ch. 2, p. 159.
3. H. C. Darby, 'The Age of the Improver: 1600–1800', in Darby (ed.), *A New Historical Geography*, ch. 1, pp. 81–2.
4. E. J. Hobsbawm, *Industry and Empire* (Harmondsworth: Penguin, 1969) p. 34.
5. Marx, *Capital. A Critique of Political Economy*, vol. I (Harmondsworth: Penguin, 1976) p. 1021.
6. Ibid, pp. 1021 and 469–70.
7. S. Alexander, 'Women's Work in Nineteenth Century London: a Study of the Years 1820–50', in J. Mitchell and A. Oakley (eds), *The Rights and Wrongs of Women* (Harmondsworth: Penguin, 1976) ch. 2, pp. 75–9.
8. Marx, *Capital*, vol. I, p. 461.
9. Ibid, pp. 492–508.
10. Ibid, p. 497.
11. Ibid, pp. 1025–7.
12. Ibid, p. 545.
13. I. Pinchbeck, *Women Workers and the Industrial Revolution, 1750–1850* (London: Frank Cass, 1977) p. 117.
14. G. Stedman Jones, 'Class Struggle and the Industrial Revolution', *New Left Review*, no. 90 (March–April 1975) pp. 35–69, pp. 50–3 and 63–5; and W. Lazonick, 'Industrial Relations and Technical Change: the Case of the Self Acting Mule', *Cambridge Journal of Economics*, vol. 3, no. 3 (September 1979) pp. 231–62, pp. 257–8.
15. D. Landes, *The Unbound Prometheus. Technological Change and Industrial Development in Western Europe from 1750 to the Present* (Cambridge: Cambridge University Press, 1969) pp. 187–8.

16. S. Pollard, *Peaceful Conquest*, p. 26.
17. Pinchbeck, *Women Workers*, p. 116; and P. Deane, *The First Industrial Revolution* (Cambridge: Cambridge University Press, 1969) pp. 85–7.
18. S. D. Chapman, cited in Pollard, *Peaceful Conquest*, p. 26.
19. Ibid, p. 25.
20. E. P. Thompson, *The Making of the English Working Class* (Harmondsworth: Penguin, 1974) pp. 307–9, 334 and 337–40.
21. Ibid, pp. 333–4.
22. Hobsbawm, *Industry and Empire*, p. 65.
23. Lazonick, 'The Case of the Self Acting Mule', p. 258.
24. Hobsbawm, *Industry and Empire*, p. 58.
25. Marx, *Capital*, vol. I, pp. 517 and 527.
26. Ibid, p. 532.
27. Ibid, pp. 528–9.
28. Ibid, pp. 531–2.
29. Ibid, pp. 530–1.
30. Stedman Jones, 'Class Struggle and the Industrial Revolution', p. 53.
31. J. Liddington and J. Norris, *'No Cause Can Be Won Between Dinner and Tea, and Most of Us Who Were Married Had to Work With One Hand Tied Behind Us': The Rise of the Women's Suffrage Movement* (London: Virago, 1978) p. 54.
32. Ibid, pp. 47–54, 60 and 93.
33. Hobsbawm, *Industry and Empire*, p. 73.
34. Ibid, pp. 73–8 and 122–6; and Stedman Jones, 'Class Struggle', pp. 53–4.
35. Stedman Jones, 'Class Struggle', pp. 65–8.
36. See, for example, F. Engels, *The Condition of the Working Class in England* (London: Panther, 1969); and A. Briggs, *Victorian Cities* (Harmondsworth: Penguin, 1975).
37. A. E. Musson, *The Growth of British Industry* (London: Batsford, 1978) pp. 79–80.
38. J. Anderson, 'Engels' Manchester: Industrialisation, Workers' Housing and Urban Ideologies', *Architecture Association Studies in the Political Economy of Cities and Regions*, no. 1 (1977) pp. 11–12.
39. Cited in Hobsbawn, *Industry and Empire*, p. 56.
40. Musson, *The Growth of British Industry*, pp. 82–3.
41. Hobsbawm, *Industry and Empire*, p. 58.
42. Liddington and Norris, *One Hand Tied Behind Us*, p. 57.
43. Anderson, 'Engels' Manchester', p. 19.
44. W. Farr, cited in A. Harris, 'Changes in the Early Railway Age: 1800–1850', in H. C. Darby (ed.), *A New Historical Geography*, ch. 3, p. 168.

45. Deane, *The First Industrial Revolution*, p. 148.
46. Anderson, 'Engels' Manchester', pp. 3–23.
47. A. Scott, *The Urban Land Nexus and the State* (London: Pion, 1980) p. 196.
48. Ibid, pp. 194–203.
49. J. Foster, *Class Struggle and the Industrial Revolution. Early Industrial Capitalism in Three English Towns* (London: Weidenfeld & Nicolson, 1974) pp. 19–22.

11.   The Golden Age of British Capitalism, 1845–1890s

1. E. J. Hobsbawm, *Industry and Empire* (Harmondsworth: Penguin, 1969) pp. 109–15.
2. Ibid, p. 116.
3. Ibid, p. 109.
4. P. Deane and W. A. Cole, *British Economic Growth, 1688–1959. Trends and Structure* (Cambridge: Cambridge University Press, 1969) pp. 141–4.
5. E. J. Hobsbawm, *The Age of Capital, 1848–1875* (London: Weidenfeld & Nicolson, 1975) pp. 193–207.
6. S. Pollard, *Peaceful Conquest. The Industrialisation of Europe, 1760–1970* (New York: Oxford University Press, 1981) p. 23.
7. J. H. Clapham, cited by W. Smith, *An Historical Introduction to the Economic Geography of Great Britain* (London: G. Bell, 1968) p. 117.
8. R. T. Harrison, 'Space, Time and Technology. The Case of the Shipbuilding Industry', Paper read at the Institute of British Geographers Industrial Activity and Area Development Study Group Conference, September 1979, p. 15.
9. Ibid, pp. 13–16.
10. J. Benson, *British Coalminers in the Nineteenth Century: A Social History* (Dublin: Gill & Macmillan, 1980) p. 6; and A. E. Musson, *The Growth of British Industry* (London: Batsford, 1978) pp. 95–102 and 170–7.
11. Benson, *British Coalminers*, p. 9.
12. Ibid, pp. 13–17; and J. T. Coppock, 'The Changing Face of England, 1850–circa 1900' in H. C. Darby (ed.), *A New Historical Geography*, ch. 5, pp. 328–31.
13. A. H. John, *The Industrial Development of South Wales, 1750–1850* (Cardiff: University of Wales Press, 1950) p. 166.
14. R. Samuel, 'The Workshop of the World: Steam Power and Hand Technology in mid-Victorian Britain', *History Workshop*, no. 3 (Spring 1977) pp. 6–73, p. 21.

15. W. Smith, *An Historical Introduction to the Economic Geography of Great Britain* (London: G. Bell, 1968) p. 160; and Musson, *The Growth of British Industry*, p. 171.
16. Samuel, 'The Workshop of the World', p. 21.
17. D. Douglass, 'The Durham Pitmen', in R. Samuel (ed.), *Miners, Quarrymen and Salt Workers* (London: Routledge & Kegan Paul, 1977) part 4, pp. 207–91.
18. Hobsbawm, *Industry and Empire*, p. 116.
19. Samuel 'The Workshop of the World', p. 27; Musson, *The Growth of British Industry*, pp. 170–1; and Hobsbawm, *Industry and Empire*, p. 116.
20. W. Smith, *Economic Geography of Great Britain*, pp. 138–42.
21. J. Gross, *A Brief History of Merthyr Tydfil* (Newport: Starling Press, 1980) p. 43.
22. B. Elbaum and F. Wilkinson, 'Industrial Relations and Uneven Development: A Comparative Study of the American and British Steel Industries', *Cambridge Journal of Economics*, vol. 3, no. 3 (September 1979) pp. 275–303, pp. 277–83.
23. J. T. Coppock, 'The Changing Face of England, 1850–circa 1900', in H. C. Darby (ed.), *A New Historical Geography of England after 1600* (Cambridge: Cambridge University Press, 1976) ch. 5, pp. 331–6.
24. Musson, *The Growth of British Industry*, p. 172.
25. Coppock, 'England 1850–circa 1900', pp. 331–6; and P. Hall, 'England circa 1900', in Darby (ed.), *A New Historical Geography*, ch. 6, pp. 397–400.
26. Gross, *History of Merthyr Tydfil*, p. 43.
27. D. Landes, *The Unbound Prometheus. Technological Change and Industrial Development in Western Europe from 1750 to the Present* (Cambridge: Cambridge University Press, 1969) p. 228.
28. A. Briggs, *Victorian Cities* (Harmondsworth: Penguin, 1975) ch. 6.
29. Landes, *The Unbound Prometheus*, p. 228; Musson, *The Growth of British Industry*, p. 172; and Coppock, 'England 1850–circa 1900', pp. 336–8.
30. Samuel, 'The Workshop of the World', p. 52; F. Callis, 'The Cutlery Trade of Sheffield', in M. Berg (ed.), *Technology and Toil in Nineteenth Century Britain* (London: CSE Books, and Atlantic Highlands, New Jersey: Humanities Press, 1979) pp. 137–44; and Hall, 'England circa 1900', pp. 403–5.
31. Hall, 'England circa 1900', pp. 403–5.
32. Coppock, 'England 1850–circa 1900', pp. 338–9; and Hall, 'England circa 1900', p. 400.
33. B. Rodgers, 'The North West and North Wales', in G. Manners, D. Keeble, B. Rodgers and K. Warren (eds), *Regional Development in Britain*, 2nd edn (Chichester: John Wiley, 1980) pp. 265–6.

34. Coppock, 'England 1850–circa 1900', p. 339; and Hall, 'England circa 1900', p. 400.
35. Elbaum and Wilkinson, 'Industrial Relations and Uneven Development', pp. 275–83.
36. Landes, *The Unbound Prometheus*, pp. 249–69; and Elbaum and Wilkinson, 'Industrial Relations and Uneven Development', p. 282.
37. G. Stedman Jones, *Outcast London. A Study in the Relationship Between Classes in Victorian Society* (Oxford: Clarendon Press, 1971) p. 337.
38. S. Alexander, 'Women's Work in Nineteenth Century London: a Study of the Years 1820–50', in J. Mitchell and A. Oakley (eds), *The Rights and Wrongs of Women* (Harmondsworth: Penguin, 1976) ch. 2, p. 110.
39. Stedman Jones, *Outcast London*, p. 21.
40. E. Aves cited in Hall, 'England circa 1900', p. 429.
41. Stedman Jones, *Outcast London*, pp. 140–3. See also Alexander, 'Women's Work in Nineteenth Century London', pp. 66–72.
42. Stedman Jones, *Outcast London*, pp. 111–24.
43. Ibid, pp. 19–21.
44. Ibid, pp. 102–6.
45. Ibid, p. 21.
46. Hall, 'England circa 1900', pp. 434–6.
47. Stedman Jones, *Outcast London*, p. 26.
48. Ibid, p. 27.
49. J. L. and B. Hammond, *The Skilled Labourer* (London: Longman, 1979) pp. 168–80; and Stedman Jones, *Outcast London*, pp. 100–02.
50. Alexander, 'Women's Work in Nineteenth Century London', p. 103.
51. Stedman Jones, *Outcast London*, pp. 22–3.
52. Ibid, pp. 21–50 and 99–110.
53. Alexander, 'Women's Work in Nineteenth Century London', pp. 59–111.
54. Stedman Jones, *Outcast London*, pp. 332–6.
55. Stedman Jones, *Outcast London*, pp. 152–4.
56. Ibid, pp. 151–3.
57. G. C. Allen, *British Industry and Economic Policy* (London: Macmillan, 1979) chs 2, 3 and 4.
58. A. Friedman, *Industry and Labour. Class Struggle at Work and Monopoly Capitalism* (London: Macmillan, 1977) p. 116.
59. Allen, *British Industry and Economic Policy*, pp. 4–7 and chs 2, 3 and 4.
60. P. W. Kingsford, cited in Hall, 'England circa 1900', p. 409; and Allen, *British Industry and Economic Policy*.
61. Hall, 'England circa 1900', p. 410.

12. The Geography of the Transition from Machinofacture to Scientific Management and Fordism, 1890s–1945

1. D. Landes, *The Unbound Prometheus. Technological Change and Industrial Development in Western Europe from 1750 to the Present* (Cambridge: Cambridge University Press, 1969) pp. 240–1.
2. Ibid, p. 235.
3. F. W. Taylor, cited by H. Braverman, *Labour and Monopoly Capital. The Degradation of Work in the Twentieth Century* (New York and London: Monthly Review Press, 1974) p. 97.
4. Braverman, *Labour and Monopoly Capital*, p. 89.
5. Ibid, p. 113.
6. Ibid, p. 113.
7. Ibid, p. 118.
8. Ibid, pp. 120–1.
9. Ibid, p. 113.
10. K. Marx, *Capital. A Critique of Political Economy*, vol. I. (Harmondsworth: Penguin, 1976) p. 799.
11. D. F. Noble, 'Social Choice in Machine Design: the Case of the Automatically Controlled Machine Tools', in A. Zimbalist (ed.), *Case Studies on the Labour Process* (New York and London: Monthly Review Press, 1979) pp. 18–50, pp. 41–2.
12. Braverman, *Labour and Monopoly Capital*, pp. 126–7.
13. M. Aglietta, *A Theory of Capitalist Regulation. The US Experience* (London: New Left Books, 1979) pp. 117–19.
14. E. J. Hobsbawm, *Industry and Empire* (Harmondsworth: Penguin, 1969) pp. 177–8.
15. S. Hymer, 'The Multinational Corporation and the Law of Uneven Development', in H. Radice (ed.), *International Firms and Modern Imperialism* (Harmondsworth: Penguin, 1975) ch. 2, pp. 40–8.
16. R. M. Haig, cited in S. Hymer and P. Semonin, 'The Multinational Corporation and the International Division of Labour', in R. B. Cohen *et al.*, *The Multinational Corporation. A Radical Approach. Papers by Stephen Herbert Hymer* (Cambridge: Cambridge University Press, 1979) pp. 140–64, p. 157.
17. Hobsbawm, *Industry and Empire*, p. 178.
18. Aglietta, *A Theory of Capitalist Regulation*, pp. 77–8.
19. On the role of the investment banks in Germany, see Landes, *The Unbound Prometheus*, pp. 206–10, 333–4 and 349–50.
20. G. C. Allen, *British Industry and Economic Policy* (London: Macmillan, 1979) pp. 1–8.
21. H. J. Habbakuk, cited in Hobsbawm, *Industry and Empire*, p. 187.
22. Hobsbawm, *Industry and Empire*, pp. 187–91.
23. Ibid, p. 191.

24. A. Imlah, cited in A. E. Musson, *The Growth of British Industry* (London: Batsford, 1978) pp. 160–1, and Hobsbawm, *Industry and Empire* pp. 191–2.
25. Hobsbawm, *Industry and Empire*, pp. 192–3.
26. J. A. Hobson, cited in V. Lenin, *Imperialism. The Highest Stage of Capitalism* (Peking: Foreign Languages Press, 1973) pp. 123–4. The way in which processes of this kind were worked out in a particular locality is referred to in A. J. Fielding, 'Place, Work, and Folk: a Study of the Development of Crowborough, Sussex', *University of Sussex Research Papers in Geography*, no. 5 (1981).
27. Hobsbawm, *Industry and Empire*, pp. 200–11.
28. R. Boyer, 'La Crise Actuelle: une Mise au Point en Perspective Historique. Quelques Réflexions à partir d'une Analyse du Capitalisme Français en Longue Période', *Critiques de l'Economie Politique*, new series, nos 7–8 (April–September 1979) pp. 5–113, pp. 31–42 and 66–7.
29. Hobsbawm, *Industry and Empire*, pp. 207–9.
30. Aglietta, *A Theory of Capitalist Regulation*, pp. 25–6, 116–17 and 155–61; and Hobsbawm, *Industry and Empire*, pp. 212–23.
31. M. Dunford, M. Geddes and D. Perrons, 'Regional Policy and the Crisis in the UK: a Long-Run Perspective', *International Journal of Urban and Regional Research*, vol. 5, no. 3 (1981) pp. 377–410.
32. D. H. Aldcroft, *The Inter-War Economy: Britain, 1919–1939* (London: Batsford, 1970) pp. 155–8; and S. Pollard, *The Development of the British Economy, 1914–1967*, 2nd edn (London: Edward Arnold, 1969) pp. 120–22.
33. Aldcroft, *The Inter-War Economy*, pp. 158–60; and Pollard, *The Development of the British Economy*, pp. 122–24.
34. Musson, *The Growth of British Industry*, p. 318; and Hobsbawm, *Industry and Empire*, pp. 208–9.
35. Pollard, *The Development of the British Economy*, pp. 123–4; and Musson, *The Growth of British Industry*, pp. 321–2.
36. Pollard, *The Development of the British Economy*, pp. 110–14.
37. Aldcroft, *The Inter-War Economy*, p. 155.
38. Pollard, *The Development of the British Economy*, p. 113.
39. K. Morgan, 'State Policy and Regional Development in Britain: the Case of Wales', D.Phil. thesis submitted at the University of Sussex, 1982, ch. 1, pp. 54–66.
40. Pollard, *The Development of the British Economy*, pp. 111 and 114.
41. Hobsbawm, *Industry and Empire*, pp. 208–9.
42. Pollard, *The Development of the British Economy*, pp. 114–15; Aldcroft, *The Inter-War Economy*, pp. 169–72; and Musson, *The Growth of British Industry*, pp. 301–2.

43. Landes, *The Unbound Prometheus*, pp. 467–73.
44. Pollard, *The Development of the British Economy*, p. 115.
45. Landes, *The Unbound Prometheus*, pp. 473–4; and Aldcroft, *The Inter-War Economy*, pp. 172–3.
46. D. McEachern, 'Party, Government and the Class Interests of Capital: Conflict Over the Steel Industry, 1945–1970', *Capital and Class*, no. 8 (Summer 1979) pp. 125–43, p. 128.
47. Landes, *The Unbound Prometheus*, pp. 475–7.
48. D. L. Burn, cited in Pollard, *The Development of the British Economy*, pp. 116–17.
49. A. F. Lucas, cited in Aldcroft, *The Inter-War Economy*, p. 174.
50. Aldcroft, *The Inter-War Economy*, pp. 162–7; and Musson, *The Growth of British Industry*, pp. 308–10.
51. R. T. Harrison, 'Space, Time and Technology. The Case of the Shipbuilding Industry', paper read at the Institute of British Geographers Industrial Activity and Area Development Study Group Conference, September 1979, p. 10.
52. Musson, *The Growth of British Industry*, pp. 309–10; Aldcroft, *The Inter-War Economy*, pp. 167–9; and Pollard, *The Development of the British Economy*, pp. 118–19.
53. Harrison, 'Space, Time and Technology', p. 5.
54. Musson, *The Growth of British Industry*, p. 309; and Hobsbawm, *Industry and Empire*, pp. 208–9.
55. Pollard, *The Development of the British Economy*, pp. 124–5.
56. Ibid, pp. 92–3.
57. Aldcroft, *The Inter-War Economy*, pp. 120–26.
58. Musson, *The Growth of British Industry*, pp. 354–6; and Aldcroft, *The Inter-War Economy*, pp. 191–4.
59. Musson, *The Growth of British Industry*, pp. 356–7, Aldcroft, *The Inter-War Economy*, pp. 195–8; and Hobsbawm, *Industry and Empire*, p. 220.
60. Aldcroft, *The Inter-War Economy*, p. 196.
61. A. Friedman, *Industry and Labour. Class Struggle at Work and Monopoly Capitalism* (London: Macmillan, 1977) pp. 188–9.
62. S. B. Saul, cited in Aldcroft, *The Inter-War Economy*, p. 179.
63. Friedman, *Industry and Labour*, pp. 190–5.
64. G. Maxcy, cited in Friedman, *Industry and Labour*, p. 195.
65. Friedman, *Industry and Labour*, pp. 196–200.
66. Allen, cited in Pollard, *The Development of the British Economy*, p. 102.
67. Friedman, *Industry and Labour*, pp. 190, 195 and 206.
68. Aldcroft, *The Inter-War Economy*, pp. 183–5; and Friedman, *Industry and Labour*, pp. 205–7.
69. Musson, *The Growth of British Industry*, p. 348.

70. Aldcroft, *The Inter-War Economy*, p. 187.
71. Ibid, pp. 202 and 180—1.
72. Ibid, pp. 127—9; and Pollard, *The Development of the British Economy*, pp. 254—61.
73. R. Issacharoff, 'The Building Boom of the Inter-War Years: Whose Profits and at Whose Costs', in M. Harloe (ed.), Proceedings of the Urban Change and Conflict Conference held at York University in January 1977, *Centre for Environmental Studies Conference Series*, no. 19 (April 1978) pp. 280—325.
74. M. Bowley, cited in J. R. Mellor, *Urban Sociology in an Urbanised Society* (London: Routledge & Kegan Paul, 1977) p. 41.
75. Pollard, *The Development of the British Economy*, pp. 287—9.
76. Aglietta, *A Theory of Capitalist Regulation*, pp. 79—100.
77. A. Gramsci, 'Americanism and Fordism', in Q. Hoare and G. Nowell Smith (eds), *Selections from the Prison Notebooks of Antonio Gramsci* (London: Lawrence & Wishart, 1971) pp. 279—318, pp. 294—7, 298—306 and 310—13. See also Aglietta, *A Theory of Capitalist Regulation*, pp. 157—9. In recent years a points system has been used in recruiting workers in the motor-vehicle industry in Britain, with priority being given to applicants who are married, have a few but not too many children, and are debt-encumbered. Institute of Workers' Control Motors Group, *A Workers' Inquiry into the Motor Industry* (London: CSE Books, 1978) p. 11.
78. Aglietta, *A Theory of Capitalist Regulation*, pp. 152—61.
79. Aldcroft, *The Inter-War Economy*, pp. 98—9.
80. G. Stedman Jones, *Outcast London. A Study in the Relationship Between Classes in Victorian Society* (Oxford: Clarendon Press, 1971) pp. 159—78 and 207—9.
81. Ibid, pp. 215—35.
82. Political and Economic Planning (PEP), *The Containment of Urban England* by P. Hall *et al.*, 2 vols (London: Allen & Unwin, 1973) vol. 1, pp. 76—85.
83. Ibid, pp. 106—13.
84. Pollard, *The Development of the British Economy*, pp. 125—34; and Musson, *The Growth of British Industry*, pp. 283—8.
85. Aldcroft, *The Inter-War Economy*, pp. 90—8.
86. C. H. Feinstein, cited in Musson, *The Growth of British Industry*, pp. 273—7.
87. G. McCrone, *Regional Policy in Britain* (London: George Allen & Unwin, 1969) p. 91.
88. W. H. Beveridge, cited in Aldcroft, *The Inter-War Economy*, p. 101.
89. Pollard, *The Development of the British Economy*, pp. 132—4; and

PEP, *Report on the Location of Industry* (London: PEP, 1939) pp. 90–120.
90. Aldcroft, *The Inter-War Economy*, pp. 103–4; and Pollard, *The Development of the British Economy*, pp. 133–4.
91. Royal Commission on the Distribution of the Industrial Population, *Report* (London: HMSO, 1940) pp. 204–6 and 218–32; and PEP, *Report on the Location of Industry*, pp. 233–61.

Part IV Further Outlook and Some Conclusions

Conclusion: Space and Society

1. R. Williams, 'For Britain, see Wales', *The Times Higher Educational Supplement* (15 May 1981) p. 14.
2. A similar point is made in D. Läpple and P. van Hoogstraten, 'Remarks on the Spatial Structure of Capitalist Development: the Case of the Netherlands', in J. Carney, R. Hudson and J. Lewis (eds), *Regions in Crisis. New Perspectives in European Regional Theory* (London: Croom Helm, 1980) pp. 117–66.
3. K. Marx, *Capital. A Critique of Political Economy*, vol. I (Harmondsworth: Penguin, 1976) pp. 471–2.
4. L. Althusser, cited in P. Anderson, *Arguments within English Marxism* (London: New Left Books, 1980) pp. 16–58.
5. M. Aglietta, *A Theory of Capitalist Regulation* (London: New Left Books, 1979) pp. 122–30.
6. Ibid, pp. 162–9.

Author Index

Subject Index